At the Eye of the Storm

At the Eye of the Storm
JAMES WATT
And the Environmentalists

Ron Arnold

A Project of the Free Congress
Research and Education Foundation

Regnery Gateway
Chicago

The Free Congress Research and Education Foundation is a 501(c) (3), tax-exempt, research organization engaged in a variety of educational projects in two separate areas of concentration. The Political Division of the Foundation analyzes U.S. House and Senate elections and studies current political trends which are of national significance. The Family Policy Division focuses on trends affecting the stability and well-being of American family life. The Free Congress Research and Education Foundation is located at 721 Second St., NE, Washington, DC 20002.

Published by Regnery Gateway
360 West Superior Street
Chicago, Illinois 60610

LC: 82-60660

ISBN: 0-89526-634-2

CONTENTS

To those men and women, past, present and future, who *are* the United States Department of the Interior

INTRODUCTION

Men of different habits are not enemies; they are godsends.

—Alfred North Whitehead

Secretary Watt. The controversial Mr. James Gaius Watt is the forty-third Secretary of the Interior of these United States. His tenure as Interior Secretary has been filled with dramatic incidents: Militant environmentalists shouted that his appointment was like "hiring a fox to guard the chickens." His religious beliefs came under withering attack. His policy initiatives drew heavy fire from members of the opposition party, and from some members of his own. A million-signature petition was brought to Washington demanding his ouster.

Yet Watt has held his ground. His steely response to critics reads like an inscription on a monument: "I have an accounting to the President, to the American people, and to God, and I take it seriously." The fact that he remains in office is a source of wonder and astonishment to many of his fellow citizens.

Controversy over his policies and his forthright personal style has shrouded Watt in a smokescreen of invective ranging from epithets such as "Secretary of Ecological Disaster," to barbed cartoons ridiculing his bald head and thick glasses, to word images of a religious fanatic using the Second Coming as an excuse for rape, ruin and run tactics.

There has been little effort to probe the reality behind the feisty image, to comprehend Watt's viewpoint, or to question the assumptions of his critics. As a result, the James Watt many Americans perceive is a one-sided caricature drawn for the most part by detractors of the man and opponents of his policy.

This book is a search for the "real" Jim Watt. It is the product of months of research, hours of taped interviews with key Interior Department officials and many others, and close personal observation of Watt in action, before the cameras and behind the scenes. It will take the reader inside Washington, inside the Department of the Interior, in an attempt to understand how President Ronald Reagan's embattled "chief of natural resources" has handled the challenges of high office—the huge bureaucracy, bitter partisan politics, clashes with Congress, hard policy decisions, harsh media attacks, and blistering environmentalist opposition.

As the subject is unusual, so the chapter arrangement of this book is also unusual. I have written not merely the biography of a brash Westerner in Washington who says he is "fighting to restore America's greatness," but also a clarification of the environmental policy questions at stake in order to put the man in context. The chapters alternate between straightforward story-telling of Watt's life and times, and in-depth analysis of the issues: a chapter on Watt, a chapter on issues, a chapter on Watt, and so forth, until there emerges a fully rounded, fully detailed American panorama.

The point is this: If we are to understand Watt and his convictions, we must scrutinize more than the track record of the man himself. We need to examine the problems he inherited when he took over Interior (Chap. 2). We need to devote a few chapters to his opponents, who reside for the most part in the leadership of several large environmental organizations and in the Democratic majority of the powerful House Interior and Insular Affairs Committee (chaps. 4, 6, and 8). And we need to understand the changes in our society that shaped those clashing public perceptions of this Secretary of the Interior (parts of Chap. 2 and all of chaps. 10 and 12). These three features, then—the Interior Department itself, opposition from environmentalists and certain Democrats, and the social changes of the past two decades—are part and parcel of the story of James G. Watt.

Therefore, we should prepare ourselves for a dash of history, political science and social psychology. But let me give you fair warning: this is not going to be a dry treatment full of academic pomp and fastidious language. The world of Jim Watt is the world of blood-and-guts politics, and his story has all the elements of a rip-roaring adventure: cliff-hangers, cowboys in black hats and white hats, public brawls, dramatic revelations, unlikely events and just plain fun. We will see a great deal of the irrepressible Watt humor that critics take so seriously. The Jim Watt I discovered is a politically savvy multi-dimensional human being, and to capture his essence we must track him in his native habitat, ranging through the intricate webs of Washington's nitty-gritty political ecology, where predator and prey trade places hourly, where the dominant species tend to be recycled every two, four, six, or eight years, and where certain parasites have been known to assume protective coloration at the drop of a public opinion survey. And we will try to the extent possible to get inside Jim Watt's mind; at least we will beard the lion in his own den deep within the gray marble territory of Interior headquarters at 18th and C Streets N.W., Washington, D.C. 20240.

Until Watt appeared on the scene, what goes on in the Department of the Interior was one of the best kept secrets in America—not intentionally, mind you; it was not even classified information. Some few citizens west of the 100th meridian had a pretty fair idea of Interior functions, simply because their states contain a great deal of federal land controlled by Interior or some other federal agency that deals with mining, grazing, timber, oil and other resources. To many citizens of the eastern United States, the Department of the Interior was a remote presence that probably had something to do with running the National Parks. To a large number of Americans regardless of region, the Department did not even exist. One of Watt's favorite stories highlights this lack of awareness in an ego-deflating experience he had soon after taking office. It seems that an air line stewardess was introduced to the new Secretary of the Interior. The stewardess solemnly shook hands with Watt and asked, "Interior of what?"

If nothing else good has come of the swirl of controversy surrounding Secretary Watt, it has at least centered national attention on issues of vital importance that have previously been left to all manner of special-interest groups. Those issues are frequently lost in objections to Watt's combative personality. Watt is keenly aware of this problem.

In early 1982, when we talked in his austere wood-paneled office on the sixth floor of Interior's Washington, D.C., headquarters building, Jim Watt, just turned 44, told me,

When the environmentalists send their storm troopers to the media prior to my arrival at a press conference in one city or another and drill all these press people on how I'm supposedly destroying the world, I'm pleased. The reason is that the journalists then know the right questions to ask, not just about my personality, but good questions about the issues of the day. Of course, some are just looking to trap me, but with a tough and realistic question I can come back with the hard facts to prove my good stewardship of America's natural resources, and the facts are all on the public record. The environmentalists are undercutting their own credibility and helping me to get the story of Interior out at the same time.

Today, many Americans are familiar with the basics of the Interior Department: It is responsible for administering over 500 million acres of federal land. It has trust responsibility for 50 million more, mostly Indian reservations. It has jurisdiction over disposition of the rich untapped ocean resources of the Outer Continental Shelf (OCS). It is concerned with the social and economic development of the territories of the United States and in the Trust Territory of the Pacific Islands.

Interior has long been recognized by a sizable public as the nation's principal conservation agency. In recent years, it has been less well acknowledged for its role as one of America's principal natural resource development agencies. The federal lands under the Department of the Interior's jurisdiction contain enough energy and mineral resources to meet our needs for centuries, including 85 percent of our undiscovered crude oil, 40 percent of undiscovered natural gas, 35 percent of our coal, 80 percent of our oil shale, nearly all of our tar sands, substantial portions of uranium and geothermal energy, along with huge reserves of strategic non-fuels hardrock minerals such as chromium, copper, platinum and cobalt, and over 300 dams for hydro-electric power generation and water reclamation for municipal, industrial and agricultural use.

The fame of Interior's National Park Service, its Fish and Wildlife Service and its Wilderness Area responsibilities has recently outshone the more mundane duties of its Bureau of Mines, Bureau of Land Management, U.S. Geological Survey, and Bureau of Reclamation, to name less than half of its key development-oriented agencies. Many Americans have grown highly conscious and appreciative of preservation efforts, but some tend to forget that as advanced as we are, we still need the sound economic base of orderly natural resource development in order to survive.

Much of the tension and dispute over Secretary Watt derive from his Congressionally-mandated dual role as Dr. Jekyll and Mr. Hyde, as chief preservation officer of our cherished National Parks and Wildlife Refuges and as one of our chief development officers, our head game warden, dam builder, miner, engineer, logger, oil driller, and Indian chief.

This grab-bag nature of the Department of the Interior means that the Secretary must answer to many contradictory demands from constituents, which makes it a lot easier to be outside criticizing the bureaucrats than inside making the tough decisions. Over the 133 years of its existence since it was created by Congress March 3, 1849, various functions have been added and removed so that the Department of the Interior's role has changed considerably with time. To see what the Department was like when it first came into being, I went to the Library of Congress and looked up their copy of the *United States Statutes At Large, Thirtieth Congress,* "An Act to establish the Home Department," which contradicted itself three lines down by saying this "Home Department" is to be called the Department of the Interior.

The new Department received an incredible assortment of odd jobs; to it were transferred the General Land Office (the agency that gave us the phrase "doing a Land Office business" from its land rush days later in the 1800s), the Office of Indian Affairs, the Pension Office, and the Patent Office. As if this were not sufficiently bizarre, the Department also had responsibility for supervision of the Commissioner of Public Buildings, the Board of Inspectors and the Warden of the Penitentiary of the District of Columbia, the census of the United States, and the accounts of marshalls and other officers of the United States courts, and of lead and other mines in the United States. President Taft in 1911 said, "The Interior Department is the lumber room of government into which we put everything that we don't know how to classify, and don't know what to do with." A disgusted historian a few years ago dubbed this melange "The Department of Miscellany."

Time did indeed change Interior's role. Jurisdiction over the accounts of court officers went to the Department of Justice when it was created in 1870. The Census Bureau went to the new Department of Commerce and Labor in 1903. The Bureau of Education came in 1867 and went eventually to the modern Department of Education by way of the old Department of Health, Education and Welfare. But with the turn of the century, a new responsibility came to Interior and stayed: conservation. Teddy Roosevelt didn't invent conservation, but he did put government agencies behind the idea. Interior had been given responsibility for the National Parks (both of them) when Yellowstone was established in 1872; Hot Springs National Park in Arkansas had been created in 1832, but it was nothing more than a spa. The Rough Rider decided that the government should help conservation and reclaim arid lands by means of irrigation, and the Reclamation Service was established in 1902. The Bureau of Mines came in 1910, the National Park Service in 1916, The Fish and Wildlife Service in 1940, The Bureau of Land Management in 1946, and the Office of Surface Mining Reclamation and Enforcement in 1977. Obviously, time has not done much in one respect: Interior is still "The Department of Miscellany," and being Secretary of Miscellany has given fits to more men than Jim Watt.

In fact, the office of Secretary of the Interior tends to be a lightning rod. The very first man to occupy that hot seat began the long tradition of getting hit by potshots from the press. Thomas Ewing only lasted as Secretary of the Interior from 1849 to 1850, which is not the shortest tenure on record; his successor Thomas M. T. McKennan served for only part of 1850. But Ewing began another long tradition by firing scores of employees he inherited and replacing them with his own cronies, and the opposition press nailed him with the appellation "Butcher Ewing."

In more modern times, Republican President Dwight D. Eisenhower appointed his Secretary of the Interior from the State of Oregon, a man named Douglas McKay. Secretary McKay refused to block the privately-owned Idaho Power Company's application to build a utility dam in Hell's Canyon, thus seeming to favor a private monopoly. He also recommended building a dam that would have flooded part of Dinosaur National Monument. Conservationists and Democrats had a field day with the stories and came up with the catchy nickname "Giveaway McKay," which plagued him until his resignation in 1956, thanks to editors and cartoonists of the fourth estate.

The very fact that Ronald Reagan is only the fortieth President of the United States, while his Interior Secretary is the forty-third, should tell us something. We've had Presidents since 1789, but Interior Secretaries since only 1849. Executive turnover in Interior is a definite problem. It has always been a hot spot in the President's Cabinet and most likely always will be.

The political opposition to Jim Watt is not very difficult to grasp: all you have to remember is that he is a conservative Republican as well as the Secretary of the Interior and you can see how a liberal Democrat might not be too pleased with him regardless of what he did. In fact, Watt is one of the few Reagan Administration appointees who enjoys broad support from the New Right, from people like Richard A. Viguerie, now 49 (all ages cited in this book are as of 1982), who runs his own mail-order firm helping conservative candidates and issues, and Paul Weyrich, 40, who founded the conservative think-tank, the Heritage Foundation, and went on to set up the conservative campaign organization, Committee for the Survival of a Free Congress (CSFC) and its companion operation, Free Congress Research and Education Foundation. While John Lofton, Jr., editor of the *Conservative Digest,* accuses Vice-President George Bush of turning the Reagan Administration soft, he and his spiritual kin see Jim Watt for the most part as a conservative's conservative.

And they are correct. Watt is a firm believer in the conservative philosophy, and he is devoted to his President. On several occasions Watt has told me flatly that if he ever became a political liability to President Reagan he would be honor-bound to offer his resignation. There seems little chance of that happening, however; Watt has enjoyed unwavering White House support and is second only to President Reagan in popularity as a Republican political speaker and fundraiser—so far.

Watt and Interior have two primary watchdogs in Congress: the Senate Committee on Energy and Natural Resources (it used to be called the Senate Interior and Insular Affairs Committee), and the House Committee on Interior and Insular Affairs. On the Senate side, the 1980 elections brought a Republican majority, which means that all Senate committees are constituted of more Republicans than Democrats and that a Republican chairs every committee. Thus long-time Democratic Chairman of the Energy and Natural Resources Committee Henry M. "Scoop" Jackson of my home State of Washington passed the gavel to Republican James A. McClure of Idaho. So Jim Watt has friends in high places as well as the "biggest gang" in this committee, which made a substantial impact on his confirmation.

Several Energy and Natural Resources Democrats are closely tied to environmentalist causes, including Senators Dale Bumpers of Arkansas, Howard M. Metzenbaum of Ohio, and Paul E. Tsongas of Massachusetts. Yet only 2 of the 12 votes cast against Watt' Senate confirmation as Interior Secretary came from this 20-man committee: Bumpers and Metzenbaum. Tsongas voted for Watt, saying that he did it in order to "hold him accountable for his commitment to achieve balance."

Watt's trouble starts on the House side: Democrats still controlled the House after the 1980 elections and Democrat Morris K. Udall of Arizona still chaired the House Interior and Insular Affairs Committee. Representative Udall has been around Congress for more years than he would probably like to admit and has become one of the true professionals of his trade. A Watt adviser calls Udall "the finest liberal mind in Congress," sincerely and without sarcasm. But there are some other liberal Democrats on this committee who have their own agendas and the power to make them work: Congressman Phillip Burton of California, second-ranking majority member of the full committee, is believed by many to wield as much influence as Chairman Udall. Burton has been called by his conservative foes "Congressman from the Sierra Club" and "Emperor of Land Grabs" for his unflagging advocacy of environmentalism and centralized federal power, particularly in the taking of private lands for public parks. Congressman John F. Seiberling of Ohio (the Seiberling of the tire fortune), who chairs the Subcommittee on Public Lands and National Parks, is an equally energetic advocate for environmentalist organizations and their liberal legislative programs. These two Congressmen and a few of their soul-mates on the committee such as Representatives Jim Weaver of Oregon and Pat Williams of Montana bristle at the very mention of Jim Watt's name. These Watt opponents are not namby-pamby-Bambi lovers or wild-eyed eco-freaks, but shrewd and sagacious strategists who genuinely believe in their environmental protection mission. Watt has had major clashes with the House Committee on Interior and Insular Affairs (and with the Energy and Commerce Committee chaired by Representative John D. Dingell of Michigan, which has cited him for contempt of Congress), but has also been able to work constructively with them on many issues, as we shall see.

The environmentalist opposition is not so easy to grasp—not because it is incomprehensible that an environmentalist could oppose Jim Watt's policies, but because environmentalism is a relatively new American institution and we still tend to accept its symbols at face value, to let them work on our emotions and sink roots deep in our unconscious mind. Such unexamined symbols are thus difficult to identify and analyze by those of us who live under them. We still tend to become environmentalists by a sort of "cultural osmosis," soaking up environmentalist sentiments without much critical thought. That can get us into a lot of trouble.

A scholar named Abner Cohen published a 1974 study of such belief systems—not just environmentalism, but any set of beliefs that we might accept without careful scrutiny—and he gave it an elegant title: *Two-Dimensional Man—An Essay on the Anthroplogy of Power and Symbolism in Complex Society.* We can forgive him his long-winded title because of the plain and blunt language he used to warn us against acting like moral sponges:

The symbols of society are manipulated by interest groups for their own benefits and . . . unless we understand the nature of the symbols and of the ways in which they are manipulated we shall be exploited without our knowledge.

Do we understand the nature of environmentalist symbols? Not very well, I'm afraid.

Take "wilderness" as a first example. Say the word to yourself, let it resonate for a moment through your mind—wilderness . . . wilderness. . . . It strikes deep, calls forth images and emotions of profound connection to the earth, of pristine primal peace, of nature in perfect harmony, of a time and place unmarred by the meddling hand of man. That is the environmentalist symbol. It has a wholesome ring and vast popular appeal.

Then why has there been such horrendous controversy over it? Merely because every greedy, ripping, gouging mindless developer in America wants to get out there and destroy every square inch of it in the name of filthy lucre? Don't bet on it. More likely it is because most of us do not have the foggiest idea what an officially designated wilderness really is. A 1978 public opinion survey by Opinion Research, Inc., discovered that 75 percent of Americans did not realize the difference between just any woodsy recreation spot and an official Wilderness. The difference is monumental. A Wilderness (capital *W*) is not a wilderness (small *w*).

The Wilderness Act of 1964, which created the National Wilderness ' Preservation System, mandated that Wilderness is an area of federally-owned land of at least 5,000 acres. Further, "A Wilderness, in contrast to those areas where man and his works dominate the landscape, is hereby recognized as an area where the earth and its community of life are untrammelled by man, where man himself is a visitor who does not remain." So far, so good.

But this law also forbids any roads, any visitor facilities and any motorized travel of any kind: hiking trails only. Opinion Research found that most Americans did not realize that. Most of us did realize that Wilderness consisted of federal land, and that such economic activities as logging were forbidden in Wilderness Areas, but most people were shocked to discover that in a Wilderness they could not take Granny and Gramps for a Sunday drive, they could not buy a meal, and they could not take the kids to the toilet because even a PortaPotty is illegal there. Another survey by Opinion Research, Inc., taken in 1977 found that the majority of Americans wanted recreation areas that permit more development and facilities than Wilderness.

Even these strict limitations on permitted usage in Wilderness Areas may have been all right in 1964 when the total size of the system was envisioned at about 15 million acres. That, most people agreed, was not too much to preserve in its untouched natural state, and to reserve for the use of the six or seven million people who visited them annually. But now we have 80 million acres of Wilderness with more being added all the time and it is still used by less than 5 percent of the total American population.

Many will recall that Secretary Watt caught a lot of flak because he advocates taking a mineral inventory of those lands. A number of less-than-candid environmentalist groups accused Watt of wanting to change the law to accomplish this goal, but they knew better. Howard Zahniser of the Wilderness Society drafted the Wilderness Act with the help of the Sierra Club's David Brower back in 1964, and their organizations knew perfectly well that the law contained this clause: "Such areas shall be surveyed on a planned, recurring basis consistent with the concept of wilderness preservation by the Geological Survey and the Bureau of Mines to determine the mineral values, if any, that may be present."

And this clause: "Mining locations lying within the boundaries of said wilderness areas shall be held and used solely for mining or processing operations and uses reasonably incident thereto."

Note the Congressional use of the mandatory word "shall," not the permissive "may." Even allowing for the legalese language, it is not too hard for an ordinarily intelligent person to understand what Congress was getting at, yet James. G. Watt was the first Secretary of the Interior since the law was written who has seen fit to obey the intent of Congress, and his opponents screamed at him for doing it.

Yet how many Americans know about any of this? Too few, too few. Wilderness, to the minds of many of our fellow citizens, is all symbol and no substance. Armchair advocates who do their Wilderness jaunting in magazines and coffee-table books may feel good just knowing that vast untouched areas are safe out there somewhere, but they never think that every tree put off-limits to timber harvesting and replanting drives up the price of the remaining trees available for commercial forestry. Congress has not yet managed to repeal the law of supply and demand, try as it may.

And while we're talking about trees, how many people know the difference between a National Forest and a National Park? Opinion Research,

Inc, again found that the symbol outweighs the substance. A majority did not realize that a National Forest is part of the Department of Agriculture, managed these days by Secretary of Agriculture John Block, and that providing commercial timber is a primary element of the multiple-use mandate of all the National Forests. National Parks, on the other hand, are, of course, managed by the Department of the Interior, Secretary Watt presiding, and the law clearly states that such National Parks shall permit no commercial logging of any description. Critics who claim that Watt is out to log the National Parks either do not know the difference between National Parks and National Forests, or they are deliberately doing strange things to the truth. Secretary Watt has no legal power to log the Parks, as pointed out in the June 29, 1981 issue of *Newsweek*: "It is simply false to suggest, as some of his critics have, that Watt would favor mining or timbering in the National Parks. Parks are inviolate, by decree of Congress, and he has no quarrel with that." And if Secretary Watt tried to order logging in the National Forests, where it is very legal and happens every day, I think Secretary Block would take him aside and speak to him.

When it comes to another environmentalist symbol, wildlife, we Americans are better romantics than realists. This was the general conclusion drawn from a study by Yale University's Dr. Stephen Kellert, which was conducted for Interior's U.S. Fish and Wildlife Service (no, Kellert is not a hired gun for Jim Watt—this study was commissioned and carried out under Cecil Andrus when he had Watt's spot). The study found that 75 percent of those surveyed did not know that the coyote is not an endangered species. Half of the public did not know that the statement "Spiders have 10 legs" is false. Only slightly more than half knew that veal does not come from lamb. And 75 percent said they know little about ecosystems or population dynamics of wild animals.

Fifty-eight percent of the public said they cared more about the suffering of individual animals than about species population levels. Residents of rural areas generally knew more about animals, participated in more wildlife activities, were generally more supportive of practical uses of animals, and were less concerned about "animal rights" than urban residents.

In all, most Americans do not know very much about animals or wildlife conservation issues and are more likely to see wild animals on television or in zoos than in the wild. Watt's Assistant Secretary for Fish and Wildlife and Parks, G. Ray Arnett, was concerned about these findings when he assumed office, and said, "It indicates that the public is not prepared to make informed decisions about the complex wildlife problems and controversies that we will undoubtedly face in the remainder of this century."

With such vast gaps in our factual knowledge about these environmentalist symbols of wilderness, National Parks, National Forests, and wild-life, among many others, we are inviting national tragedy. It is all too easy to tug on our heartstrings or appeal to our idealistic romanticism or to evoke our wrath against oil companies, timber firms, mining outfits, and other scoundrels who keep us alive. As Abner Cohen warned, "Unless we understand the nature of the symbols and of the ways in which they are manipulated we shall be exploited without our knowledge." The greatest tragedy could be brought about by well-meaning but uninformed citizens supporting initiatives of environmentalist leaders pushing for more and more centralized federal power and ever-increasing restrictions on our vital economic producers, resulting in the twin disasters of a changed form of government and economic collapse. We will hear James Watt elaborate on this theme time and again.

I think America's love affair with environmentalism is sufficiently mature now that we can afford to probe a bit beneath the symbols and search for the substance. We will devote several chapters to that search in the course of examining the second context of the legend of Jim Watt, his opposition.

In a way, the symbols of environmentalism blend into our third context, which is the state of our society today after two decades of rapid change. Among the many changes we will investigate in this book, one stands out: the fact that we have become an urban, service-sector, information-based society—a post-industrial society, as sociologist Daniel Bell called it. By that, Bell did not mean, as some back-to-nature enthusiasts have insisted, that industry was going to vanish, but rather that our manufacturing technology had been matched and outstripped by our intellectual technology of computers and knowledge handling, and that the industrial sector had been outnumbered by the service providers. The reason that this particular change is so important for our purposes is the impact it has on our understanding of basic natural resource issues in the Department of the Interior.

We can get some glimmer of that impact from a 1981 *Scientific American* article which pointed out that today nearly 70 percent of all jobs are in the service sector while only a little more than 30 percent are in the "total goods" sector—the producers in agriculture, mining, forestry, fisheries, construction, and manufacturing combined. It does not take even a third of us to feed, clothe, shelter, and supply goods for all of us. Well, that's efficiency for you.

But consider the implications. Industry is now a tiny minority, some might say a persecuted minority. You can win most votes with a 70 percent majority. And what of that 70 percent majority? People working in service jobs normally live and work in urban and suburban settings, comfortably buffered from and unaware of the needs and travails of the hurly-burly basic resource industries that ultimately support our richly endowed lifestyles. A sizeable majority of us today simply have no vital connection to the productive industrial sources of our economic nourishment, and we feel a false independence from them.

Just as a previous generation became enamored of urban industry and forgot its rural roots in the earth, so today our own generation has become enamored of the environment as an intellectual, recreational, aesthetic and spiritual delight, and has come to look with a certain disdain upon our productive roots in the industrial process. Marshall McLuhan saw this in a flash of insight in his *Understanding Media:* "Each new technology creates an environment that is itself regarded as corrupt and degrading. Yet the new one turns its predecessor into an art form." An easy example is the power loom and electric sewing machine, which "don't get no respect" themselves, but which have helped turn the spinning wheel into an item of family room decor. "The machine," McLuhan said, "turned Nature into an art form. For the first time men began to regard Nature as a source of aesthetic and spiritual values." There is obviously nothing wrong in taking a new delight in the earth. It is worth cautioning ourselves, however, that we still must get our living from that same earth. And a human being, as the now hackneyed *Desiderata* anonymously pointed out, is "a child of the Universe, no less than the trees and the stars; you have a right to be here."

We may feel that we can make a living selling dancing lessons or taking in each others' laundry or flying a desk in some office building. And the truth is, many of us can. About 70 percent, to be exact, if we can believe our economists. But we cannot continue to do so for long if the service 70 percent chokes the basic 30 percent to death. We cannot survive by putting fences with "Keep Out" signs around all our natural resources. We cannot survive by saddling our producers with excessive regulation that needlessly raises costs and lowers productivity. Just because industry is now a minority does not mean that we can abuse it any more than we can abuse the environment without inviting disaster.

These issues, these contexts, are closely tied up with the Department of the Interior and with the story of Jim Watt. We all have a proprietary interest in their outcome.

The greatest difficulty in searching for the real Jim Watt is plowing through the mythology, the distortions, and—let's be blunt about this—the plain lies, and there are plenty of them, that have been put forward by critics. There are several ways to deal with this problem. One way is to set the record straight, to find out what really happened, to the extent the facts can be discovered. That will be the purpose of the chapters on the life and times of Jim Watt in this book. I should warn the reader that there are likely to be some sharp rebuttals to falsehoods which have arisen.

But setting the record straight is not enough. In a controversy as stormy as that raging about Secretary Watt, it is important to explore the motives and methods of those who are doing the distorting. That is one of the functions of the chapters on issues in this book. Although these chapters are based on facts, they consist of much analysis, and that inevitably involves value judgments. I would suggest that there is a distinction between the environment and environmentalists. It may be a new idea that one can oppose environmentalists without opposing the environment, but it is a distinction worth considering. By the time you have finished reading this book, you may also have some new ideas about what environmental protection actually consists of.

To those who are unalterably opposed to James Watt, and hope to see all traces of his Secretariat quickly vanish, I can only leave the immortal words of Yogi Berra — "It ain't over till it's over."

CHAPTER 1
WHO IS JIM WATT?

One's self I sing, a simple separate person.
—Walt Whitman

"Change can't come without conflict," Jim Watt has said. "And change can't be achieved without paying a price. But if the objectives are liberty and freedom, then we will pay the price."

That is a slice of the real Jim Watt.

He stands six-foot-two, weighs in at a lanky 185 pounds, and a ghost of the raw Western land still follows him as he strides in a three-piece pin-striped suit through the gray marble eminences of Washington. Hanging above his desk is the motto of West Point: "Duty, Honor, Country." On a nearby wall is a plaque reading: "Persistence Forges Results."

When asked who the real Jim Watt is, he once answered: "He's a very blunt, simple guy who says what he means and means what he says. No hidden agenda. He makes decisions in a framework of patriotism that's not easy for some people to understand."

Who is Jim Watt? In some ways that depends on who you listen to.

If you listen to his opponents, he's "a short-sighted exploiter, double-talker and religious nut"; he's "America's most arrogant and dangerous man"; he's "a barbarian" who has "broken faith with the Republican Party."

If you listen to his supporters, he's "the best Interior Secretary of this century"; he's "a finely balanced, attentive human being"; he's "a sensitive man" who has "the perspective and understanding to restore America's greatness."

The Jim Watt I discovered in personal interviews, in travels, in policy meetings, in political rallies, in researching the record of his life, and from those who know him best, was not the person I expected him to be. He was not the goody-two-shoes adored by his friends nor the fiendish villain hissed by his enemies. He appears to be blessed and cursed with the normal blend of

1

strengths and frailties common to the human condition. I found Watt to be neither perfection personified nor evil incarnate, but I did find him above all to be interesting and interested.

I also found Watt to be much more congenial than his public image would indicate; even his enemies give him that—one Senator who voted against his confirmation called him "a charming and engaging personality." I had expected to find a pinched and peevish moralistic fuddy-duddy, but was astonished at a man bursting with energy, bubbling with laughter and beaming with intelligence.

After studying his life, I found Watt to be more complex and enigmatic than his forthright manner reveals or than he himself may be aware of. One does not have to hold some hidden agenda in order to be multi-dimensional and puzzling. There is indeed a consistency in the events of Watt's life, all seeming to drive in a single-minded direction toward greater scope and power, but there are eddies and backwaters of his thought that combine such things as a deep appreciation of nature with an admiration of technology and civilization, which baffles and puzzles people who cannot or will not reconcile those seeming opposites.

In observing Watt in action making policy decisions I found him to be much more tough and wily and politically savvy than even his environmentalist opponents fear. Before coming to a conclusion, Watt routinely counts every vote and calculates the political fallout on every issue. His well-known disgust with "paralysis by analysis," falls entirely on "paralysis" and not at all on the "analysis." I watched the Watt management team, for example, making the final decision on the Powder River Coal Leasing Project, the largest federal coal sale in history. In about two hours, nearly a year's worth of data-gathering and analysis were presented and debated around a table peopled by some of the best mineral policy minds in the country. When all the consequences had been assessed, market impact, social and economic impact, environmental impact, technical feasibility, national interest, and "good neighbor" provisions for contacting the states involved before final implementation, Watt unhesitatingly selected what he saw as the best alternative to balance all the competing demands of this decision. Contrary to critics' assertions, environmental and national interest elements were not swept under the rug, but were presented and debated with the same professional seriousness as the technical and economic elements. Watt's action in this instance was indeed decisive but could hardly be called unanalytical or a snap judgment.

One of my most interesting discoveries, however, was that many of the several hundred people in the Interior Department who must work closely with Watt said of him simply, "He's fun to work with."

No, this is not the man I expected to find. And I daresay this does not sound much like the Jim Watt you think you know.

There are some aspects of Jim Watt that supporters and critics alike agree upon. He is 44 years old. He has dated one woman in his life, his wife of 25 years, Leilani (he calls her Lani). He has two children, a daughter, Erin, 22, who is married to a theological student, and a son, Eric, 20, who is himself studying for the ministry. Religion is important in Jim Watt's life; he is a "born-again" Charismatic Christian who firmly believes that God plans his life. He neither smokes nor drinks, not even coffee. He is scrupulously moral; as *Time* writer Robert Ajemian said, "even his harshest critics consider him incorruptible." Watt describes himself as a "fundamentalist in economic, social, spiritual and political matters."

Environmentalist opponents regard Watt as the man they love to hate. Why? The most obvious answer is Watt's pro-development policy, his opening of federal lands to mineral leasing, his support for a strong economy in general, and other views that do not sit well with the environmentalist leadership. Another dimension of this feud is also obvious: Jim Watt's conservative politics clash mightily with the liberal philosophy of most environmentalists. Watt's belief in reduced and decentralized federal power and in the private enterprise system automatically sets him at odds with the large environmentalist organizations that have spent the last 20 years lobbying successfully for stronger federal power to deal with matters of ecology. Democrats have taken up the cudgels against Watt as a campaign issue; a fund-raising letter from Congressman Toby Moffett of Connecticut asserted that "With anti-conservationists like James Watt running the Interior Department, our environment's last line of defense has become the Democratic majority in the House," and Watt was described by *New York Times* columnist John Oakes as an "extremist ideologue" and a "fanatical believer in the maximum development of resources in even the most protected of public lands."

But a more subtle aspect of this political war was caught in a June 29, 1981, *Newsweek* report: "What environmentalists find so infuriating about Watt is not just that he disagrees with them, but that he challenges their most deeply held convictions. . . . He opposes them on their own terms, matching his idealism with theirs. He undercuts their basic claim to legitimacy, which is that they alone are disinterested champions of the commonweal." Environmental writer Ron Wolf said much the same thing in different words: "Although his opponents have criticized his words and deeds, the real source of their objections springs from who he is."

And this leads us back to the question, Who is Jim Watt?

Lusk, Wyoming

Jim Watt came into the world in the middle of the night during a howling blizzard on the coldest day of the winter: January 31, 1938. His father, William Gaius Watt, now 75, was then a young lawyer in the little ranching town of Lusk, Wyoming, seat of Niobrara County. His mother, Lois M. (Williams) Watt, now 71, faced a crisis when it came time to leave for the hospital to have her baby that chill January day: the car wouldn't start.

As Jim's mother tells the story, she called the family physician, Dr. Walter Reckling, and told him of her predicament. "Don't you worry, Mrs. Watt," comforted the good doctor, "I'll come to pick you up myself right away." The doctor was the only man in town with a heated garage; it was a tool of his trade.

Many have wondered where Jim Watt got his middle name. Some have wrongly guessed it came from Gaius Julius Caesar, better known as Julius Caesar. But William Gaius Watt passed the name down to his son James from a biblical source, the Third Epistle of John, which begins, "The elder unto the wellbeloved Gaius, whom I love in the truth." (The Watts use the American pronunciation "*Gay*-us" rather than the Latin "*Guy*-us.") Jim Watt in turn has passed the name to both his children: his son is Eric Gaius and his daughter Erin Gaia, the feminine form.

As a child, James Gaius Watt was indeed the "wellbeloved." He was blessed with loving parents who gave him both encouragement and firm discipline. He was evidently a bright youngster. When he grew old enough, he began spending his summers on the family ranch some 250 road miles north of Lusk in Sheridan County. There he helped with the chores, and was given the responsibility of pumping water for the cattle and, later, mending fences. There, Watt says, he also gained an abiding love for the land, and an idea of what is necessary to make it productive for the needs of people. The working summers and winter visits to the ranch taught him, he says, "to respect the West in the special way of those who have had to grapple with its sometimes hostile environment."

The family ranch was a legacy from the time of Jim's grandparents. One of these grandparents had come to Wyoming from St. Louis in a covered wagon in the 19th century as a homesteader. Watt's seven uncles and aunts continued the family's agrarian tradition, homesteading parcels of land adjacent to Jim's grandfather's. Jim's father homesteaded his own family ranch nearby after graduating from Nebraska Wesleyan University.

The Watts may or may not be related to the Scottish James Watt who developed the first commercial steam engine. With typically wry Watt humor, Watt says, "We claim to be related, but we don't develop our family tree to prove it. We just pick people we'd like to be related to."

Watt is the middle of three children. He has an older and a younger sister. The Watt family's eldest is now Judith Schneider, living in Manhattan, Kansas, where her husband is a professor at Kansas State University. Watt's younger sister is now Elizabeth Scott, who teaches school in Las Vegas, Nevada.

When Watt was in the third grade, his mother organized the family into a club called the Five Rabbits, an easy introduction to parliamentary procedure. "We'd elect officers, and the kid that got to be president held office for a month and set the club agenda," says Mrs. Watt. Elizabeth and Judith usually chose to lead family sing-alongs or recite poems, but the serious middle child, reports his mother, "liked to make speeches."

As an elementary student, Jim spent the school year in Lusk, with its population of not quite 2,000, where his father built up a flourishing law practice among the local farmers and ranchers until 1952 when Jim was in the eighth grade.

Wheatland, Wyoming

Dwight D. Eisenhower was campaigning for U.S. President when the Watts moved to Wheatland, seat of Platte County, in the valley of the Laramie River. There Jim attended Wheatland junior high and high schools, his father practiced law, and his mother managed the 30-room Globe Hotel.

It was during junior high school, Watt told me, that he became interested in politics and turned into an avid reader of current events. "I'd read two newspapers a day, and a couple of newsweeklies, too," Watt says. "I was much influenced by reading about political leaders." A conservative Republican administration was in office in those days. "My father had always been an activist, conservative Republican and was involved with the Party. I remember that Franklin D. Roosevelt's name was a cuss word in our house."

The usual biographical accounts of Watt's Wheatland High days consist superlatives—varsity athlete, honor society, Saturday nights hitting the books. I asked Watt about his scholastic ability and got a surprising answer:

I had to work hard to get through high school. I do have a good memory, but I *had* to have a good memory because I'm such a slow reader. I didn't have time to read things twice. I had to learn how to study when I was in junior high and high school, so by the time I went to college there were no shocks. But I've had to work for everything I learned.

The Spring 1981 number of *Wyoming Issues* magazine describes Watt in high school as Wheatland's "golden boy"—the citizens of Wheatland loved him, as demonstrated by quotes from old acquaintances like Don Sherard, former county attorney: "James had a reputation as being an outstanding student. James was a serious, conscientious and intelligent youngster, very deliberative and well-balanced in his thinking."

Kate Missett, who took that interview, noted that everyone in Wheatland called him James, and that all the Watt family members liked to be called by their given names. James may have been the case then, but today the political figure always introduces himself as *Jim* Watt, not James, whether in public speeches or private conversations.

Yet in high school it seems to have been "James," and James was an outstanding student. He also played on the varsity basketball and football team, was elected leader of many school clubs, and became a member of the student council, where he supported increased student rights. The American Legion Post rewarded his citizenship by sponsoring him to Boy's State, where he was elected "Governor" of Wyoming. He went on to participate in Boy's Nation.

James was probably the social envy of his peers, too, going steady with one of the most attractive girls in Wheatland High, Leilani Bomgardner. She has been described as bubbly, vivacious and as intelligent as James—which is saying a lot. In their senior year, James and Lani were king and queen of the prom.

Leilani Bomgardner grew up in eastern Wyoming, also. There is a place near her hometown of Wheatland which the adult Jim Watt likes to claim as his ancestral abode because he loves to tell a colorful story about its name—Chugwater. According to Watt, Indians used to herd buffalo over a bluff and the sound of the falling animals as they hit the river bank below—"chug"—gave the town its name. Some tender souls have cited this story as a proof that Jim Watt is a crude and insensitive animal-hater. I tend to think that Jim Watt has a down-to-earth sense of humor and these critics have none at all. In any case, many of Watt's friends today remember this story and some think he actually lived there. For example, Michael Horowitz, a Senior Policy Analyst at David Stockman's Office of Management and Budget who works closely with Watt and Interior, still calls him "Jim from Chugwater."

Laramie, Wyoming

If Jim Watt's high school years resemble a Norman Rockwell version of *American Graffiti*, the sequel reads more like an Ayn Rand novel with a sociable hero. Jim and Leilani enrolled in the University of Wyoming in Laramie in 1956. Jim entered the College of Commerce and Industry and came out with a degree four years later.

It was a busy four years. For one thing, Jim and Leilani had become serious about each other and were married November 2, 1957, during their sophomore year in college. Married life must have agreed with him, because Jim Watt stacked up a considerable pile of honors during his college career. He was elected President of the honor society in each of his last three years: Phi Epsilon (sophomore), The Iron Skull (junior), and Omicron Delta Kappa (senior). He was pledged to Alpha Tau Omega fraternity and received the Thomas Arkle Clark Award as its outstanding member in the Rocky Mountain Region. He was named to Phi Kappa Phi, the National Scholastic Honor Society, and listed during his last two undergraduate years in *Who's Who Among Students in American Universities and Colleges.* During the school year of 1958–59, he was the University of Wyoming Student Body Business and Finance Manager, budgeting and controlling the expenditure of all student government money.

Jim and Leilani met a number of people in college who would matter later: Alan Simpson, who graduated from the University of Wyoming's law school in 1958, and whose father Milward would give Jim his first crack at government work, and who would himself one day become a U.S. Senator from Wyoming; Don Thoren, who would later help Watt establish the first Management By Objectives program in the Interior Department; and others we will meet in due course.

Jim Watt finished the College of Commerce and Industry in June 1960 with a Bachelor of Science degree with honors—and he had already finished his first year of law school, working on a combined program cramming his senior undergraduate year into the same time as his freshman year at law school. Watt took a summer job as a depth interviewer for the Small Business Administration and the University of Wyoming, interviewing Wyoming business people to determine what their real business problems were, and on August 14 that summer, the Watts' first child, Erin, was born.

Watt's last two years at the University of Wyoming College of Law were busy, too. He served as Editor of the *Wyoming Law Journal,* and he took a summer job in 1961 as a Research Assistant to the Wyoming Legislative Statute Revisions Committee, recommending revisions, clarifications, and corrections of Wyoming Public School Laws.

Classmate Michael Sullivan, now an attorney in Casper, Wyoming, describes Watt during law school as "hardworking, personable, deeply religious, and dedicated to his growing family." Hardworking is hardly the word; Jim Watt not only went to law school in 1961 and 1962, but also worked both years as a part-time instructor teaching Business Law and Real Estate to upper classmen and graduate students in the University's College of Commerce and Industry. We are seeing the emergence of Jim Watt, workaholic.

On February 14, 1962, the Watts got a special Valentine: their son Eric was born. A few months later, Jim had his law degree, a Juris Doctor, and was soon admitted to the Wyoming State Bar. In June 1962 he became a 24-year-old lawyer with a wife and two children who was looking for work.

In July the first in a long series of strokes of good fortune came to Jim Watt. He went to long-time family friend Milward Simpson, who was in the midst of his primary election campaign for the U.S. Senate, and asked for a position as staff assistant. Watt's college friend Alan Simpson was serving as his father's campaign manager. The elder Simpson recalls that when he told Watt there were no campaign funds to pay for any such efforts, Watt replied, "Well, I'd like to go with you whether I get paid or not. It's time some of the young people of America got into the political fray. It's time we helped earn the privileges that we enjoy as Americans." Milward Simpson asks rhetorically, "How do you turn down a guy like that?" So Watt joined the campaign, doing opposition research, planning, and organization.

Simpson's election team included Douglas Baldwin, who today serves as Watt's Assistant to the Secretary and Director of Public Affairs, while the younger Simpson would one day serve as a U.S. Senator himself and figure prominently in Watt's nomination as Secretary of the Interior—two friendships of lasting importance.

The elder Simpson won his Senate seat. It was both a beginning and an end for James G. Watt. His Washington career was beginning. But even though it would remain his legal residence for many years, Watt and his family left Wyoming.

Washington, D.C.

In November 1962 Jim Watt became a man who was *in* the East but not *of* the East. Even today, after many years' residence in Washington, Watt has strong regional feelings for the West. We shall soon see some of the reasons why.

Watt and his family took a modest house in suburban Camp Springs, Maryland, near Andrews Air Force Base, where many federal staffers made their homes. Watt settled in as Legislative Assistant and Counsel to Senator Simpson.

Doug Baldwin had also made the jump into Washington's hyperspace, serving on Senator Simpson's three-person staff as press aide. Baldwin had been a newsman and freelance writer in Wyoming who wrote and broadcast radio news prior to coming on board the Senator's election campaign. Before that he had served in the Marine Corps in the Caribbean and Pacific. Like Watt, Baldwin was young and ambitious, and the two learned the Washington ropes together. Baldwin stayed on Capitol Hill for many years, holding similar positions with Senator Clifford Hansen and Representative William Henry Harrison.

For the most part, Watt's job was a school-of-hard-knocks education in the ways of government. He wrote most of his Senator's speeches and screened all his visitors. He answered all the correspondence that concerned legislation, politics, and the legal problems of the Wyoming constituency. But the best lessons were learned sitting on the hard staff bench behind the Senator in Committee hearings, feeding him facts and advice on the issues Jim had researched.

The real influence of a federal legislator depends largely on his or her committee assignments. Get stuck on less important committees and watch your career shrivel away in boredom. Get put on key committees and your road to power is open. Senator Simpson's most important assignment was to the Committee on Interior and Insular Affairs (since renamed the Committee on Energy and Natural Resources), which had jurisdiction over America's public lands. The Senate Interior Committtee, as it was commonly known, also served as one of the two Congressional watchdogs over the Department of the Interior, the other being the equivalent House Comitttee. Here James G. Watt learned well the intricacies of his future Department, and got to watch Secretary of the Interior Stewart L. Udall wrestle with the Senate at first-hand for four long years.

Soon Jim Watt got his first lesson in being a Westerner in an Eastern Establishment. Watt tells the story himself:

Senator Alan Bible of Nevada was chairman of the Interior Committee's Sub-Committee on Public Lands at the time, and Senator Simpson had been debating with him over some bill or another about how it should be worded—it was insignificant what the bill was about, I don't even remember. But the two Senators said, "Let's have staff work that out," and Senator Simpson said, "I'd like Jim to work with your staff man on it."

So I got together with Senator Bible's staff man—I don't even recall his name—and the first question he asked, in the way that we Westerners have frequently been treated by Easterners, was, "From what school did you graduate?" When I told him I was from the University of Wyoming, he couldn't even believe it had a law school. He then said, "I'm from Harvard," and that was the telling blow, indicating that I was just a peon and would, of course, quickly yield to his superior judgment.

My nerves just turned steel tough. I wasn't going to yield to that guy on anything just because he was from Harvard. And we got to debating whether the word should be this or that, and it really didn't make two hoots, but I just wasn't going to yield to him. We finally decided that we'd have to report back to our principals because we couldn't get over the impasse on this innocuous word.

So I explained to Senator Simpson, who had himself graduated from Harvard Law School, that there was no difference in these two words, but this staff guy had tried to pull rank on me because he was a Harvard graduate. I told my Senator he could do whatever he wanted about the word.

When we went into executive session on the bill, Chairman Bible said, "Milward, I understand that our staffs couldn't agree on this word, and I don't see any difference. Do you feel strongly about it?" Milward pounded the table and said, "I feel very strongly about it. I think Jim's absolutely right, and if you want to take it to a vote, let's vote on it!" Senator Bible replied, "Gee, Milward, if you feel that strongly about it, go ahead and put it your way."

We can see a great deal about Jim Watt in this story. Defeat on certain basic issues is not only unacceptable, but unthinkable. Tom Garrett, a Wyoming rancher and conservationist close to Watt, told a *U.S. News & World Report* writer that "His idea is not to roll with the punches. One sure way of not changing him is to fight him." Another thing we can see about Jim Watt from this story is his emerging ability to evoke loyalty from those. around him, even from his superiors.

In 1964, Jim Watt attended a gospel meeting of businessmen in Washington, an event of pivotal significance in his life; although he was already deeply religious, he soon became a fervently committed "born-again" Charismatic Christian, and became affiliated with the Assembly of God Church. Jim Watt's beliefs can be found in the bylaws of any Assembly of God Church: That the Bible is divinely inspired but not contrary to reason, that there is one true God, that Jesus Christ is the Son of God, and the many other familiar tenets of faith of Charismatic Christianity. As former ABC news journalist Jack Casserly wrote in the December 1981 issue of *Petroleum Independent*:

Watt professes he accepted Jesus Christ some 18 years ago. He has never hidden this commitment—neither privately nor in public comment since becoming a national figure as Interior Secretary. This is not because the Westerner is righteous. It is rather because, as a fundamentalist Christian, his commitment calls for witness. Otherwise, he could see himself as hypocritical.

Even critics such as Lewis Regenstein, Vice-President of the Fund for Animals admit, "At least there's no hypocrisy with Watt."

Some have asserted that Watt's religion affects his political judgments, and perhaps even violates the Constitutional requirement of separation of church and state. I do not share Watt's fundamentalist beliefs, but I find no serious ground for such assertions. Watt has never invoked Scripture in administrative policy statements, and my interviews with all top Interior officials failed to uncover a single person who could recall Watt bringing up religion in the workplace of the Department. His political judgments are pragmatic: he counts noses and calculates repercussions. Simply because he believes God plans his life does not mean that God is making Interior policy. According to a survey in the December 1981 issue of *Psychology Today*, 48 percent of all Congressmen also believe that God plans their lives, but nobody seems too worried about it. Jim Watt, like all other citizens of the United

States, has a right to his own beliefs. But one day, his 1964 religious experience would ignite a religious war, which we will examine thoroughly in Chapter 4.

During these years on Senator Simpson's staff, Jim bought a small Grumman sailboat and spent weekends with his family sailing on the lower Potomac River or on Chesapeake Bay. His law career also advanced; in 1965 he qualified and was admitted to the Bar of the U.S. Supreme Court.

A year later, in September 1966, the aging Senator Simpson retired for health reasons, a victim of Parkinson's disease. Now Jim Watt was a 28-year-old lawyer with a wife and two children who was looking for work. And for the second time, he was in the right place at the right time. His business school background, his law degree, and his four years of experience behind the scenes in the Senate Interior Committee attracted the attention of the U.S. Chamber of Commerce leadership in Washington, and the next link in his career was forged.

Jim Watt's résumé for the years between September 1966 and January 1969 reads as follows:

Secretary to the Natural Resources Committee and the Environmental Pollution Advisory Panel, Chamber of Commerce of the United States. Responsible for coordinating the activities and interests of the National Chamber in the fields of mining, public lands, energy, water and environmental pollution. Principal spokesman for the National Chamber on these issues. Developed policies and programs.

Which is to say that he was a lobbyist for the pro-development U.S. Chamber of Commerce. It was a significant time in Jim Watt's career. He had gained a wealth of knowledge and expertise on natural resource issues as a Senate staffer; he had seen the entire process of how the Wilderness Act of 1964 was lobbied and passed into law, for example. Now he had the opportunity to hone his policy-making skills, and to develop programs of substance. He may have been a lobbyist, but the real skill he was developing was that of a manager.

These were crucial years in the growth of U.S. environmental law. In 1966 Senator Edmund Muskie headed the Public Works Committee as it passed the Clean Water Restoration Act and amendments strengthening the Clean Air Act. In 1968, the 82nd Congress (dubbed the "Conservation Congress" by critics in business) outdid all previous legislatures in passing environmental laws. Two controversial National Parks were created, North Cascades in Washington State, which shut down several patented mining claims belonging to private owners, and Redwood in California, which invoked the Fifth Amendment power of Congressional Taking to confiscate private lands for a public park for the first time in American history, and at a cost to taxpayers in excess of all other National Parks combined. The 82nd Congress also passed laws creating the Wild and Scenic River System, which was to take more and more private lands away from unwilling citizens, and the national Trails System, which dedicated massive federal funds for the construction and maintenance of hiking trails across America.

Jim Watt found himself fighting more and more losing battles for his employer. The vaunted power of Big Business to get the best government money could buy was crumbling before the lobbyists for numerous environmentalist groups. Organizations like the Environmental Defense Fund, the Natural Resources Defense Council, and the Sierra Club were discovering they could win a lobbying campaign for 50,000 dollars that would cost business 50 million to defeat. Finally, no amount of money could hold back stringent regulations and no amount of lobbying could hold back the astronomical cost of complying with the new environmental laws. But watching the Friends of the Earth, the Wilderness Society, and others outmaneuver him time and again taught Watt a great deal about how power politics works in the environmental movement.

When Richard Nixon won the 1968 election, Jim Watt once again appeared in the right place at the right time. Although Watt had not been active in the Nixon campaign, in December of 1968 the leadership of the Chamber sent his name to the President-elect's transition team, which badly needed help in getting the Department of the Interior staffed up and running under Republican leadership. Watt's transition team assignment as Special Assistant to the Secretary and Under Secretary of the Department of the Interior lasted from January to May of 1969. His main task was to prepare Walter Hickel, former Governor of Alaska and President Nixon's nominee for Interior Secretary, for his Senate Confirmation hearings. Nixon had picked Hickel because he had been a hard-line State's Rights pro-development governor who could create jobs and make America move.

The environmental movement had just come out of what is still its most successful year of Congressional lobbying, and was reveling in its new political power. They went after Hickel's reputation as a land developer with a vengeance. Wally Hickel did little to deflect their blows by showing up in Washington one morning in front of the press corps straight off a red-eye flight from Alaska with no sleep and not so much as a word of briefing. The image he projected of ignorance enshrined gave the eager Washington staffs of numerous environmental groups a cause celebre. They went to the press, chewed up Wally Hickel and spit him out in little pieces. They portrayed him as a hick from Alaska who couldn't cope with the Eastern Establishment in the Washington environment.

Jim Watt and Wally Hickel holed up in a hotel room for a week and a half, with the now-Washington-savvy lobbyist coaching his fellow Westerner on the pitfalls and chicanery of a tough Senate Committee. Watt wrote down the potential questions and drilled Hickel through five grueling days of televised confirmation hearings. But something had happened to Hickel. Jim Watt watched Wally Hickel give away the store.

Watt recalls those days and their profound impact on him:

Wally Hickel was so brutalized by the environmentalists that he must have said to himself, "I'm going to prove to these guys that I'm an environmentalist, too." Once he was confirmed, Wally tried to outrun them to the left. He was no longer a State's Righter. He was no longer a hard-liner. He was no longer pro-development. He wasn't experienced enough in the Washington scene to realize that you can't outrun an environmentalist to the left, that they will always stay ahead of you and demand more from you.

Hickel made many crucial concessions to the Senate during his confirmation hearings, and finally won his appointment as Secretary of the Interior. As the months went on, headlines noted again and again the "surprising" preservationist turn of the Hickel Secretariat. His advocacy of centralized federal power to deal with environmental problems and the quota mentality he brought to enforcement by arbitrarily stepping up citation of polluters set him at odds with the Republican administration. Hickel then put his job in peril by outspokenly defending the student movement of the day, playing to the press with "leaked" letters to the President critical of administration policy. It was suggested that he was actually aiming for the Presidency and would be wiser to resign from Interior and run again for Governor of Alaska. He did not resign. Finally, President Nixon fired him on November 25, 1970. Hickel subsequently made several runs at the Alaska governorship, but was so rebuffed by his constituents for changing stripes in Washington that he never even won a gubernatorial primary election.

But back at the beginning of the Nixon Administration, newly-confirmed Secretary Hickel was both grateful for Watt's help and impressed with his abilities. Watt's reward was appointment as Deputy Assistant Secretary for Water and Power Resources, a job on the "production" side of Interior (as contrasted with the "preservation" side, which includes such things as the National Park Service and the U.S. Fish and Wildlife Service).

To get some idea of Watt's new rank, you have to know a little about the leadership structure of the Department of the Interior. First, The Boss and Head Honcho is the Secretary of the Interior, with the Under Secretary second in command. Then, under these two top executives are ranked eight senior executives, all with the same status, including six Assistant Secretaries and two other key officers, the Solicitor (the chief law officer) and the Inspector

General (the chief auditor). All of these executives are appointed by the President and require the advise and consent of the Senate.

Next, these eight senior executives each have a number of Deputies, junior executives who are appointed by the Secretary and do not require the advise and consent of the Senate, but they're still political appointees. As Watt says, "While all the senior executives are out giving speeches and being big shots, the Deputies actually run the Department." Jim Watt was one of those Deputies, a Deputy Assistant Secretary, from May 1969 to June 1972.

From 1969 onward, we will see Jim Watt as an executive, as a man with the power and responsibility to make policy and see to its implementation. From now on, he's one of the fellows who's running the show.

As Deputy Assistant Secretary for Water and Power Resources, Watt was a line officer (i.e., he had real command power, unlike a staff officer) over seven Interior Department agencies which designed, constructed and operated water and power systems such as reservoirs, water distribution systems, and electric power transmission systems. His agencies also marketed electric power and water and conducted desalting research and development. It was a fantastic opportunity to gain in-depth experience in federal development activities, and he jumped in.

His style as a bureaucrat was marked by diligence and by more concern with substance than appearance; he always arrived a few minutes early and left a few minutes late, leaving a clean desk at the end of the day; he preferred plain offices, plain writing and plain talk; he demanded a fair day's work for a fair day's pay from his subordinates. But he rarely worked nights or weekends. In the rush of career achievement, he did not forget his family.

In this new position, Watt began to meet more and more of the people who would one day figure prominently in his management team as Secretary of the Interior. Doug Baldwin was still working up on the Hill, now as administrative assistant to Representative John Wold, and still kept in touch. Derrell P. Thompson, an Aerojet-General Corp. vice-president who would one day manage Interior's Western Field Office as Special Assistant to the Secretary, met Watt in the course of business. In late August 1969 a young man named Don Hodel interviewed with Jim for the job of Deputy Administrator in the Bonneville Power Administration's Washington office. Hodel got the job and worked closely with Watt for the next three years. Neither of them knew that they were destined to become the two top executives of their employer, Secretary and Under Secretary of the Interior.

On April 1, 1970—All Fools Day—a young man named Stephen P. Shipley walked into Jim's office and said, "Well, here I am." Shipley had packed his wife and baby and moved from Cody, Wyoming, on blind faith. Watt had a few weeks earlier received a telephone call from a mutual friend in

Cody asking whether there was an opening in Interior for a young law student. Fortunately for Shipley, Watt had said yes, remembered the call, and had already located a vacancy in a minor position as an advisor on water and power matters—a "go-fer" who mostly dug up information. But that was just like Watt, according to Shipley: if he said he'd do something, he'd do it. And fortunately for Watt, Shipley turned out to be a topnotch legal mind when he finished the University of Maryland Law School, for he went on to render able service as Jim's Vice-President at Mountain States Legal Foundation and today is the indispensible Executive Assistant of the Secretary. The organization chart says he's responsible for overseeing Interior's Office of Congressional and Legislative Affairs, the Office of Public Affairs, and the Executive Secretariat (the Secretary's correspondence office), but Jim Watt says, "He's wherever he needs to be, and really acts as the Chief of Staff for both Under Secretary Hodel and me—a very important relationship."

In mid-1970, Watt attended the annual Pageant of Peace held on the Ellipse in front of the White House, where the master of ceremonies was Russell Dickenson, Director of National Capitol Parks. Watt came as a Representative of the Secretary of Interior and for the first time met the man who would one day be his Director of the National Park Service.

A year later a new Assistant Solicitor for Procurement by the name of Moody Tidwell III was given a task that brought him into contact with Jim Watt. Hickel had been fired by then and Rogers Clark Ballard Morton was Secretary. Interior had earlier become involved with a power and desalting complex to be built in Saudi Arabia—Interior is responsible for strange and wonderful things—and there were $8.5 million worth of legal claims in dispute over the plant, which was being built by the Dutch contractor Continental Engineering. Things were obviously not going well, and Secretary Morton was inclined to set them right. He sought out two of his best troubleshooters and separately told them: "Watt is in charge as policy maker, and Moody Tidwell is the lawyer for procurement. This project is a mess and you're going to fix it." They met on the first of a series of transatlantic flights, and out of their travels and travails in fixing the project grew a lasting friendship. Today, Moody Tidwell III is Deputy Solicitor of Interior, second in command of all legal work.

Tidwell is one of the few people who has routinely seen Jim Watt away from home, from family, from headquarters. "Jim and I never got to Saudi Arabia at the same time," Moody says, "but we went to Europe several times together for conferences with the powers that be at Continental Engineering. That's where we got to know each other, and that's where I became a true fan of James Watt. It was his personal thoughtfulness and his sense of fun that made him a great traveling companion and boss."

Tidwell gives a typical Watt story:

We were in London once, and Jim wanted fish and chips because he'd read about eating fish and chips in the traditional English manner—wrapped in a newspaper from a street vendor. We asked at the hotel where we were staying—they obviously did not cater to people who ate fish and chips—and they didn't even know where to send us. So we went to the theater district, found a little restaurant, went in and ordered fish and chips. The waiter grabbed a plate and said, "Comin' up!"

Jim had read enough to know that you don't eat fish and chips from a plate. He told the waiter, "No, I want it in a newspaper." The waiter looked at him funny and said, "Nobody in London eats fish and chips in a newspaper anymore!" Jim calmly replied, "I want it in a newspaper."

Luckily, the guy's father, who owned the restaurant, had overheard the exchange and came smiling out of the back room with two newspaper cones folded the old-fashioned way. He took the fish and chips off the plate, put it in the newspaper, and gave us some malt vinegar to top it off.

So we went outside, leaned against a lamp post and ate our fish and chips, feeling *so* cosmopolitan. Of course, the crowd walking by wondered what kind of weird people we were. We had a great time watching them watching us and trying to figure out whether we were just hicks straight out of the countryside or Americans.

Another of Tidwell's close encounters with Jim Watt is more telling, and involves two sides of the same story. A new subordinate was assigned to accompany Watt on a trip to Holland. He had heard that his new boss was deeply religious and was a teetotaler. Not wanting to get off on the wrong foot, and not wanting to miss his booze, the new hire decided to excuse himself during the long flight, got up and went aft, supposedly to the toilet. He then explained his situation to a stewardess and asked her to give him vodka in his soft drink even though he would only ask for a soft drink. The stewardess was helpful and the flight went on uneventfully with Watt taking soft drinks and the new hire taking harder stuff.

Some weeks later, this new employee related the story to Tidwell, enthusing about how helpful he had been to his new boss upon landing in Amsterdam, seeking out the luggage, telling the inexperienced Watt how to get a cab in a European city, and handling the details of hotel registration, not realizing that Watt had already told Tidwell the story about this new guy who went back to ask the stewardess to slip some vodka in his soft drinks and got so bombed that Watt had to get their luggage, pour the guy into a cab and put him to bed at the hotel.

The fact that Watt was amused rather than outraged and that the new man enjoyed a long and productive career with him tells us something about his alleged religious intolerance.

Jim Watt gained substantial expertise during his tenure as Deputy

Assistant Secretary. He was a U.S. delegate to the Economic Commission for Europe in Geneva and traveled to Israel to take part in a conference on desalination. But his greatest lesson from these three years was the discovery that Deputies run the Department of the Interior, a lesson he would not forget when eight years later he would staff the Department as Secretary.

In July of 1972 Watt was transferred from the production side of Interior to its preservation side. Secretary Rogers C. B. Morton had been suffering growing political embarrassment by the Bureau of Outdoor Recreation; it had been ordered by Congress to produce a Nationwide Outdoor Recreation Plan, and the plan was nearly five years overdue. Secretary Morton thus picked one of his most capable young managers to crank that plan out right now. Once again, Watt was in the right place at the right time, and was appointed Director of the Bureau of Outdoor Recreation (BOR).

As a Bureau head, Watt enjoyed a slightly higher rank than a Deputy Assistant Secretary, and much higher visibility. At 34, he was rising to the level where political infighting becomes serious and managerial ability becomes crucial. He was now the chief executive of a federal bureau of some 500 employees, with 7 regional offices and a headquarters staff in Washington. He was responsible for a $300 million annual budget of matching funds for federal agencies and state governments to acquire and develop recreation lands and facilities. He was also responsible for assisting federal, state and local agencies with land-use planning, and became a principal Nixon administration spokesman on recreational and conservation matters before Congress and interest groups. Not bad for a kid from the sticks of Wyoming. But the kid was about to find out what it's like to be the target of a slander campaign for the first time.

You don't just leap into a new bureau and create a document that's almost five years late. First you start to cure the reasons why it was five years late. And in doing that, Jim Watt put some noses out of joint. But he cured the problem, and this is how he did it:

He sized up the Bureau of Outdoor Recreation and discovered that he had a unique bureau, one with a specialized mission. It had people who were very talented in their recreation resource and wildlife disciplines, but they were not managers. That was the problem and that was the reason why Secretary Morton had put Jim Watt there: the bureau needed strengthening and Jim Watt was a strong manager.

Watt knew from his education and past experience that a widely used and well-known business management technique would solve the bureau's problems if properly applied, a technique known in the jargon of the trade as "Management By Objectives" or MBO for short. In essence, MBO is a method of getting the responsible leaders in an organization together, letting them thrash out and finally agree upon what their objectives are, having them write these objectives down, and then setting their own timetable for the accomplishment of their objectives. Top managers can then track each task as its "time tag" comes up showing that such-and-such should be accomplished by now. In short, MBO is a way to get a group to set its own goals, set its own timetable, and then live up to its commitments. There's nothing either miraculous or diabolical about it, but it requires skillful implementation.

Watt wanted to do something else to beef up his bureau's capability, and that was to install an automated accounting system to keep better track of where all the money was going. Obviously, he was running a tighter ship than the BOR was used to. Most employees were glad somebody was finally in control of the situation, but, as always, there were some few who did not appreciate the faster tempo of work and resented being held accountable for getting things done on time—and one of them would later try to derail Watt's career.

Jim first looked over the Interior Department's in-house capability for putting an MBO program into effect, and was not impressed with the track record. This put him in a bind. An old college friend, Don Thoren, had gone into the consulting business and had built up an outstanding MBO track record—but he was an old friend, and the appearance of wrongdoing was a potential problem. Watt called Interior's lawyers in the Solicitor's Office and asked whether there was any problem with his hiring someone he knew personally as a "sole-source contractor"—a contractor hired without putting out bids. The Solicitor told him that as long as he had no financial interest in his friend's business that the laws of the United States gave bureau heads discretion to issue sole-source personal service contracts as they saw fit; 45 of them had been issued by the Bureau of Outdoor Recreation in the 7 years before Watt arrived. With this answer in hand, he issued over the next two years a total of $60,000 worth of MBO contracts to Don Thoren for training and implementation, a fact that would one day be plastered all over the headlines. And over the next two years, the Bureau of Outdoor Recreation got its work done on time, saving many times more than the $60,000 investment required to put the program in place.

But for now, in October 1972, the MBO program was starting up, things were getting under control, and it was time to tackle that long overdue National Outdoor Recreation Plan. Watt assigned Assistant Director Fred Jones to the job first. Jones is a top professional in the substantive areas of outdoor recreation planning. In November 1972 Watt interviewed candidates for editing and writing the report, and hired GS-5 civil servant Emily DeRocco, a journalism graduate from Penn State working on a Master's Degree in public administration from George Washington University. Today Emily serves Secretary Watt as Assistant to the Secretary, a position she affectionately refers to as "Dumpee," the doer of things nobody else in the Interior Department can—or will—get done. And she's also finished the law degree Jim Watt encouraged her to get.

The three of them—Watt, Jones, and DeRocco—worked together personally day by day, and by late 1973 the long-awaited report was finished: *Outdoor Recreation—A Legacy for America*. It was well-received in the conservation community; the Nature Conservancy and many other professional leisure time organizations wrote glowingly of the report in their journals.

On April 9, 1975, President Gerald R. Ford appointed Jim Watt to be a member of the Federal Power Commission, a position for which he had become well qualified by three years as Deputy Assistant Secretary for Power and Water Resources and by three more years of demonstrated management skill in the BOR. Once again he had been in the right place at the right time. But now an obstacle was thrust in his path, and in a manner that was to show up again in later years: an anonymous accusation was made.

A party or parties unknown sent an unsigned letter to the General Accounting Office (a federal agency in the legislative branch that is responsible to Congress) alleging that James G. Watt had been guilty of wrongdoing in letting consulting contracts to a friend—evidently an effort to sabotage Watt's confirmation hearings before the Senate for his Federal Power Commission job. A full investigation was carried out, no wrong-doing was discovered, and in November of 1975, Watt was confirmed with the advise and consent of the Senate.

But it is instructive to see how environmentalist critics distorted Watt's Bureau of Outdoor Recreation years during and after his confirmation as Secretary of the Interior. The most telling commentary came in an article from the May 8, 1981 issue of *Audubon* magazine. This article had to say about the 1975 Senate hearing on his nomination to the Federal Power Commission: "Watt agreed that he had made a serious error in turning to an old friend and explained that he had been 'trying to get results' in a hurry. Watt's cool explanation was in essence a challenge to the Senators to do anything about the incident, and they backed down. He learned another valuable lesson: Congress respects decisive action."

In fact, the record of those Senate hearings, held September 8 and 26, 1975, does not show any of this. Watt did not agree that "he had made a serious error in turning to an old friend." The record does show him saying, "I have memoranda showing I have done what was legally right. I have articles and plenty of support showing it was a fantastically successful result. I'm very proud of what was accomplished with Mr. Thoren and the Bureau."

But when the question arose, "Would he do it again?" Watt's answer was, "No." The answer was "no" since that would avoid the slightest *appearance* of wrongdoing. The record shows that Watt did say he was embarrassed. Embarrassed because of any wrongdoing? No. Embarrassed because of his answer to "Would he do it again?" Watt said, "I am a little embarrassed about the answer because it calls for discrimination against friends." That's what's on the record. If he had done any wrong, the Senate would not have confirmed him to the Federal Power Commission.

In another illuminating passage, the same *Audubon* article also thumps on the overdue report, *Outdoor Recreation: A Legacy for America,* which Watt had held up at his Senate confirmation hearings as Secretary of the Interior in 1981, saying the document "continues to represent my philosophy and my commitment to recreation, to preservation, and the multiple use of the resources of America." And again, we get anonymous accusations: "One former high-ranking official calls the plan a 'joke' and says he was 'flabbergasted' that Watt gave it to the Senate committee. He says that at the time the plan was being written Watt didn't 'give a hoot what was in it so long as it was published by the deadline.' "

The article goes on to say, "Furthermore, he charges that Watt was not even responsible for the finished product. The document produced by Watt's bureau was so 'god-awful' the official says, that top Interior officials 'didn't think it should see the light of day.' The plan was rewritten by a higher-level member of the Interior Department, who substantially 'changed the thrust and policy direction.' "

These charges are utter fabrication; what is more, they are not even internally consistent. If some higher-level official had fixed the report, why would it be so flabbergasting to give it to the Senate? You can't have it both ways. But the fact is, Watt did give daily policy direction to the report, Fred Jones did supply the professional expertise, and Emily DeRocco did edit and write the report as it stands. And Secretary Morton signed off on it. Watt had only three superiors in Interior at that time: his immediate boss (the Assistant Secretary for Fish and Wildlife and Parks), the Under Secretary, and the Secretary himself. No one in these top executive positions is going to waste a lot of time rewriting some Director's report, regardless how botched up; they'd send it back for revision. Besides, none of these three top executives has claimed Watt did not produce the report. If the report had been such a joke, the environmental community of the day would not have received it so warmly. Obviously, the anonymous accuser is merely assassinating the character of a man who couldn't be allowed to appear in any way sympathetic to preservation.

Jim Watt left the Interior Department in November 1975 to join the Federal Power Commission, beginning a profoundly technical job that gave him expertise in the energy field. Meanwhile, more future colleagues showed up. Watt hired a lawyer during this time whose name was Elisabeth Pendley and put her to work on the FPC staff. He soon discovered that she and her lawyer husband Perry were both graduates of the University of Wyoming law school, and on several occasions thereafter Jim and Leilani made a foursome for lunch with Elisabeth and Perry Pendley. Today Elisabeth. is an attorney with the Federal Energy Regulatory Commission (the old FPC), and Perry is Watt's Deputy Assistant Secretary for Energy and Minerals in the Interior Department.

In January 1977 Jim began serving as the FPC's Vice-Chairman and soon found himself faced with a tough and controversial decision. A local utility company in Appalachia's Canaan Valley had applied for a permit to construct a hydroelectric dam on the Blackwater River. Environmentalist group leaders strongly opposed the project, but the majority of the local citizens supported it. There were no endangered species involved, no wilderness areas in question, no National Park lands at stake. It was a simple issue of pro-development versus anti-development, growth versus no-growth, aesthetics versus economics. Jim dug into the issue, saw the local support and the Washington-based opposition, and decided in favor of the dam. An avalanche of lawsuits came thundering down to stop the dam, including one brought by Secretary of the Interior Cecil Andrus.

Jim Watt also led the fight in the FPC for deregulation of natural gas prices, urging his fellow members to permit market forces to prevail and attract capital to gas production as a step in the U.S. energy self-sufficiency program, and here he succeeded. Jim Watt, conservative, was becoming recognized as a powerful force fighting for private enterprise and individual liberty and initiative. Advocates of centralized federal power such as Ralph Nader's consumerists loudly condemned his actions.

In July 1977 the FPC was merged with the newly organized Department of Energy. The Carter administration had no room for an activist conservative and Jim Watt got the boot. Now he was a 39-year-old lawyer with a wife and two children who was looking for work.

Denver

Once again Jim Watt showed up at the right place at the right time. In 1976 Joseph Coors, the Colorado brewing heir known for his unstinting support for conservative causes, had teamed up with the Washington, D.C.-based National Legal Center for the Public Interest (NLCPI) to establish the Mountain States Legal Foundation in Denver. NLCPI and Joe Coors, Chairman of the Board of the new Mountain States Legal Foundation, both put up money to get their fledgling outfit on the road. By the time Watt found himself at liberty, the new non-profit public-interest law firm had garnered pledges for enough money to get it going, a little over $200,000, from numerous Western sources, farmers, ranchers, labor groups, businesses, other foundations, and many private citizens who supported their conservative cause. It was time to hire their first president and chief legal officer. Political friends in Washington had circulated Jim's name for the new post and the Mountain States board jumped at the chance to engage his services.

Jim Watt had never met Joe Coors before 1977, but Leilani had met Joe's wife Holly in the religious context of the Fellowship Group, a Washington, D.C., gathering of Christians. Jim had met Holly, and supported her appointment to the Board of Directors of A Ministry in the National Parks, an organization which sponsors interdenominational church services and resident ministers in the National Parks. When Joe Coors came home one night and told Holly, "I've just met the greatest guy for the top spot in our new Mountain States Legal Foundation—his name is Jim Watt," Holly asked in amazement, "*My* Jim Watt?" and proceded to tell her husband about their fellow Christian.

The Watts took a modest home in the Denver suburb of Englewood. Jim's parents lived in nearby Aurora. The family joined a local Assembly of God Church, bought a recreational van, and settled into their new lives.

The background of Watt's new organization is interesting. On March 3, 1975, the first predecessor of all conservative public-interest law firms opened its doors in Sacramento, California: Pacific Legal Foundation. Its organizers were a number of former California state attorneys who had been detailed during the Reagan governorship to carry out a controversial major reform effort curbing welfare fraud, and were highly successful. These young conservative attorneys, including PLF President Ronald A. Zumbrun, quickly proved that you could represent the public interest without being a liberal espousing the usual consumerist, environmentalist, and welfare causes, and you could do it successfully in court. PLF racked up an impressive track record of court cases won in defense of private enterprise, property owners, and even labor unions, consumers, and other traditionally liberal clients.

Immediately, the traditional liberal public-interest groups launched a barrage of criticism. Robert Gnaizda of the liberal Public Advocates, Inc., in San Francisco, according to *Newsweek* insisted that "True public-interest firms represent the views of the unrepresented and the corporate view is already being fully expressed by big, well-financed corporations," and Carlyle Hall of the Center for Law in the Public Interest in Los Angeles said that PLF is "at best superfluous and at worst parasitic."

These complaints are based on a number of false assumptions. In the first place, judges may only rule on the record before them, and if liberal views are the only ones presented in the public interest, an obvious imbalance will quickly impact the court system. Also, many small businesses cannot afford legal representation and genuinely need conservative public-interest defenders—especially considering the massive numbers of government regulations that constantly raise legal questions. Then, too, the traditional liberal public-interest movement itself has been installed in the government as their former lawyers were appointed to key Civil Service positions, so the viewpoint of the bureaucracy has become seriously one-sided, clearly creating the need for counterbalancing conservative public-interest viewpoints. And many public agencies ignore and penalize middle-class values, which again shows the true need for conservative public-interest law firms.

A typical Mountain States case will demonstrate these premises. Of the 47 cases that Watt took on, only 6 of them dealt with businesses. They were not all big oil and other "fat cats," as the case of *Valdez* v. *Applegate* amply substantiates. In this case, better known as the "Rio Puerco Case" for its locale in New Mexico, the Bureau of Land Management had prepared Environmental Impact Statements to establish new range-grazing allotments which tell permitee ranchers how many head of cattle they are privileged to run per acre on the land they lease from Interior. But the Bureau had based its new allotments on the condition of the range in only one year, 1975, which was one of the worst years on record. Allotments resulting from this EIS would have made 30 percent, 40 percent, and 50 percent reductions permanent, regardless of how well the range recovered after fresh rainfall. Most of the permittees affected were very small ranchers, many of them unschooled, most of them Spanish-Americans, many of them dependent on their grazing allotment as their sole source of income. Interior told these small businessmen there was no appeal, and Mountain States stepped in with Watt protecting their economic well-being from Interior's arbitrary stance. Watt won in court. The range recovered. The ranchers survived.

Liberal public-interest law firms for over a decade have pushed to promote causes rather than clients, and openly admit it. In a January 1980 conference called *Public Interest Law: The Second Decade,* a noted speaker, Abram Chayes of Harvard, bluntly said: "I think all of us know that there is an ideological element in public-interest law and thank goodness there is. This is not a neutral enterprise. We are for social change. We are for social change in a particular direction. We are attempting to secure redistribution of our goods and power from those that have to those that have not." The principal tool of this movement has been support for ever-increasing centralized federal power.

The idea of a pro-free enterprise counterpart to Nader's Raiders and the Sierra Club stirred conservatives to spread such organizations nationwide. The National Legal Center for the Public Interest (NLCPI) in Washington, D.C., was the result. NLCPI did not go to court; instead it acted as a clearinghouse and provided seed money for regional centers: Mid-Atlantic Legal Foundation in Philadelphia, Southeastern in Atlanta, Mid-America in Chicago, Great Plains in Kansas City, and Mountain States in Denver. Jim Watt and Mountain States later reaped all the publicity, but they weren't alone by a long shot.

The motto of Mountain States Legal Foundation is: "In the courts for good, defending individual rights and sound economic growth." Critics, of course, seem unconcerned about individual rights and evidently do not believe there is any such thing as sound economic growth. But the growing Sagebrush Rebellion in the West indicated that at least somebody was upset at the growth of federal power. Mountain States Legal Foundation and Jim Watt took on only those cases that had some public interest at stake; individuals and corporations able to defend themselves were referred to private attorneys.

Mountain States began by taking on relatively simple cases, as is prudent when breaking new legal ground. The first was a friend-of-the-court (amicus curiae) brief supporting Ferrol C. Barlow, owner of a small plumbing business in Pocatello, Idaho, who got tired of inspectors barging in when no complaint had been filed and refused to allow government inspectors from OSHA (Occupational Health and Safety Administration) to enter his property without a search warrant. Barlow insisted, "No complaint, no warrant, no entry." He won an injunction from a three-judge Idaho court ruling that warrantless searches were indeed unconstitutional, which enjoined the Secretary of Labor from inspecting Barlow's premises without a warrant. The government appealed this ruling all the way to the U.S. Supreme Court, with Jim Watt and his Mountain States Legal Foundation acting as friend of the court. Barlow prevailed in a five-to-three decision. It was a major victory for private enterprise and a resounding defeat for proponents of centralized federal power.

The next few cases Watt took on were also friend-of-the-court briefs, one of them arguing against reverse discrimination at the University of Colorado. Then Mountain States grew bolder and struck out with its own lawsuits with Jim as the attorney of record, defending middle-class gas customers from being forced to pay more than the cost of service in order to subsidize low-income customers in Utah and Colorado, and in another case, supported the States of Arizona and Idaho in their right to rescind ratification of the Equal Rights Amendment—a major case in which Mountain States was the architect and contractor of the issue. Soon, Mountain States under Watt's leadership took on the Environmental Protection Agency, the Sierra Club, the Environmental Defense Fund, and the Department of the Interior—47 cases in all—and won enough times defending citizens against excessive regulation to scare the opposition out of its wits.

In September 1980 a conservative named Ronald Reagan was compaigning for President. Jim Watt joined the campaign, acting as Reagan spokesman to the American Association of Blacks in Energy, telling the group, "Everything this nation does focuses back on the need for a strong energy base." And according to a *New York Times* article by Philip Shabecoff, "The leaders of the major environmental organizations have joined—for the first time, they say— to endorse a Presidential candidate." It was not Ronald Reagan. The Sierra Club formed a political action committee to fund its political support activities, a step previously unheard of among conservationist groups. Many environmental groups are tax-exempt and therefore barred from engaging in overt political activity. On November 4, while Jim was in Denver working on a number of important cases, Ronald Reagan won the election.

Senator Paul Laxalt of Nevada, a close Reagan friend and powerhouse in the Presidential campaign, came forward so the story goes and asked for two rewards for his faithful service: "I want to pick the Secretary of the Interior and I want to play tennis on the White House courts." The story also goes that he got to do both.

Former Senator Clifford P. Hansen of Wyoming was the President's first choice for the Interior spot. Watt had known Hansen for years, had even campaigned for him when he ran for Governor of Wyoming in 1962, and supported his Senate bid too. The word of Hansen's nomination spread fast among his close friends, and Jim and Leilani offered to help Hansen and his wife Martha any way they could.

Watt was eager to help the new Reagan Administration. He called asking for a position on the transition team to help formulate Interior Department policy, even calling upon the political backing of several influential Reagan friends, but was astounded by his rejection for being "too conservative." It made him recall an earlier bid to help the Reagan team in the summer of 1980: He had flown to Washington to help the conservative think-tank, the Heritage Foundation, on their massive transition study, "Mandate for Leadership." Watt was appointed chairman of the Foundation's committee on Interior matters, but quickly discovered that his information on policy and personnel was five years out of date. He handed over the gavel to Sam Ballenger, an aide of Senator Laxalt, and flew back to Denver. He was thwarted even when the rough draft of the study was sent to him later for his editing and comments; he had been sent two copies of even-numbered pages and none at all of odd-numbered pages. Watt later joked about his predicament to an audience during a speech, saying, "I didn't know enough about Interior to serve on the Heritage Foundation committee and I couldn't get on President Reagans's transition team to help set Interior policy, so the only thing left for me to be was Secretary of the Interior," which drew roars of laughter and minutes of applause.

One late November day Jim and Leilani opened the mail and found a letter from their old Washington friend Doug Baldwin, who was now Director of the Office of Communications at the Interstate Commerce Commission. The letter contained a clipping from page B9 of the November 18, 1980, issue of the *New York Times*. It was a story by Seth S. King quoting outgoing Secretary of the Interior Cecil Andrus as saying that the incoming Reagan Administration "will be able to make few, if any, major changes in the next four years in the slow, cumbersome way the nation's natural resources are developed and regulated."

Watt read the newspaper article, "And I agreed with it," he says. "So Lani and I fastened this clipping with little magnets to our refrigerator door, to remind us to pray for the man who would have to face this frustrating job. We had known Cliff Hansen for many years, and he was a dear friend." And the Watts did pray for the man who would take on the thankless task of Interior Secretary.

As Clifford Hansen, former U.S. Senator from Wyoming, sat at home that night and the next few days looking over his potential conflicts of interest, it became obvious that there were going to be some overwhelming problems. He held long-term grazing leases with the Bureau of Land Management, an agency he would control as Secretary of the Interior. Hansen recalls, "It appeared to me that I just couldn't take the job without going out of the cow business." The leases he held had been in the family for many years, and were the mainstay of his family's future. On December 2, 1980, Hansen made an agonizing decision. On December 3, word went out to President-elect Reagan's transition team to "look for a new face."

Two days later, Jim Watt got a telephone call from the White House. He had no way of knowing it, but he had been praying for himself.

CHAPTER 2
ENVIRONMENTAL AMERICA

Who will guard the guards? —Juvenal

Here we come to the first even-numbered chapter of analysis. While I have striven for factuality in these analyses, they possess a definite viewpoint for which I take complete responsibility.

One of the purposes of these even-numbered chapters is to offer a coherent critique of the environmentalist movement. I spent many years at the grass-roots level of the movement, serving on the Conservation Committee of the Sierra Club's Puget Sound Group in the 1960s and '70s, and as an elected trustee of the Alpine Lakes Protection Society (ALPS—a nifty acronym), which is a single-purpose group concerned with Washington State's Alpine Lakes Wilderness Area. I gave dozens of presentations to schools and community groups on behalf of the Sierra Club and produced a number of audio-visual features under their aegis. As my involvement grew deeper, it became apparent to me that the movement was concerned with more than simply protecting environmental quality. I began to see deliberate alarmism, calculated political moves and a difficult attitude toward basic American values such as individul liberties and private property. I left the movement quietly but finally in 1972. The conflicts between economics and ecology concerned me deeply and became a major study; I have consulted many experts in relevant disciplines and over time have assembled a number of findings that I think will be of interest to all Americans.

Environmentalism Rising

As late as 1964 a survey conducted for *Psychology Today* magazine could discover that the top item in Americans' personal hopes was "A better or decent standard of living." Of the 11 items most important to those polled, 4 dealt with economic well-being. Concern for the environment showed up exactly nowhere. What changed us?

At first glance back over those years, there seems to be no pattern, it all looks like a bewildering hodgepodge of social shocks: assassinations, trips to the moon, an energy crisis, a Presidential resignation and a well-meaning peanut farmer in the White House. On the environmental scene, a crazy-quilt of ecological crises somehow merged into the environmentalist movement. But if we look very carefully, we can see more than a dozen separate trends in American life that got welded into the environmentalist amalgam around Earth Day, April 22, 1970, some as much by accident as by intention.

Among the earliest signs of an incipient environmentalism was the anti-pollution outcry against the "killer smogs" in Donora, Pennsylvania, in 1949. Then in the mid-'50s came the nuclear fallout scare from atmospheric testing of atomic weapons, with headlines screaming "Strontium-90 in Babies' Milk!" It was a shocking way to discover that an event in a remote and isolated location could spread to affect the entire planet. We were getting our first lessons in the interconnectedness of ecology, although "ecology" would not become a kitchen-word for more than a decade.

Rachel Carson then dramatized the pesticide bugaboo in her epoch-making 1962 classic, *Silent Spring,* which, among other things, spurred the ban on DDT in 1973. Here we have the first popular work in what was to become the favored genre of environmentalist writers: alarmism. The word "alarmism" implies a faulty or untrue outcry over a perceived problem, and although Rachel Carson's work is still widely admired as the tocsin over toxins that brought political action to the environmental field, it has also been severely criticized by scientists for its use of over-emotional color-words and its outright inaccuracies.

Claus and Bolander, respectively a microbiologist and a clinical psychologist, critiqued Carson's book in *Ecological Sanity:* "She consistently misues the word 'mutagen'; she miscites or misinterprets the writings of medical authorities"—particularly annoying to Claus, who holds two PhDs and an MD—"she gives credence to cancer theories which are either highly speculative or have already been discarded; she describes many chemicals as carcinogenic which are very unlikely to be genuine cancer-causing agents; and, most important of all, she describes chemicals in general as 'the sinister and little-recognized partners of radiation in changing the very nature of the world—the very nature of its life.' " Even biologist LaMont Cole, who was one of Carson's greatest admirers, could not abide her purple prose and challenged her assertion that pesticides generate "super-insects" by inducing over-resistance.

Of course, scientists employed by the chemical industry were among Carson's most vociferous critics for rather obvious reasons. However, there were many, many complaints from her friends such as Cole and from disinterested parties such as Claus and Bolander who financed their own researches in writing *Ecological Sanity*. This intra-scientific controversy of claims and counterclaims, however, became a standard feature of the later environmentalist movement in full bloom: the technical issues were so complex that reputable scientists looking at the same data could come to completely contradictory conclusions, which wrought havoc with public understanding and confidence in science. Laymen tended to accept the views of scientists who came closest to expressing their own worldview and lifestyles, and to dismiss out of hand those of opposing views, which is an unfortunate miscarriage of education that came on the heels of environmentalism.

The older conservation movement from Teddy Roosevelt's era made a new mark with the passage of the Wilderness Act of 1964. This major turning point in American law was the result of 15 years of lobbying efforts by the Wilderness Society and the Sierra Club. Howard Zahniser of the Wilderness Society provided much of the language of the bill: "A wilderness, in contrast with those areas where man and his own works dominate the landscape, is hereby recognized as an area where the earth and its community of life are untrammeled by man, where man himself is a visitor who does not remain." While wilderness preservationists rejoiced at this legislative affirmation of their beliefs, ranchers, farmers, miners and forest industry leaders felt that it was a violation of the "multiple-use" concept which reconciled competing uses for public lands such as grazing, timber, watershed management, recreation and wildlife protection. Wilderness designation means no roads, no motorized vehicles including floatplanes, and no logging or other commodity use for such lands, with the exceptions of certain highly constrained grazing rights and severely restricted mineral exploration and mining, which was permitted to continue until December 31, 1983.

As William Tucker remarked in a *Harpers* magazine article of March 1982 entitled "Is Nature Too Good for Us?" "The wilderness concept appears valid if it is recognized for what it is—an attempt to create what are essentially 'ecological museums' in scenic and biologically significant areas of these lands. But 'wilderness,' in the hands of environmentalists, has become an all-purpose tool for stopping economic activity as well." Environmentalist group leaders hotly deny Tucker's allegation, but the facts back up his argument.

A quick sketch of the results of the Wilderness Act of 1964 is illustrative: The law gave the U.S. Forest Service 10 years to review those lands previously designated "primitive areas," a total of 34 areas and 5.4 million acres, for "suitability or nonsuitability for preservation as wilderness." The National Park Service and the U.S. Fish and Wildlife Service were also given 10 years to study all roadless areas in excess of 5,000 acres under their jurisdictions for possible wilderness designation. Thus it was hoped that the entire wilderness process would be complete by 1974, and the enormous investment decisions over timber, minerals, energy, water and agricultural development in disputed areas could go ahead. Environmentalist lobbying and lawsuits killed those hopes.

While the 1964 Wilderness Act began the National Wilderness Preservation System with 9.1 million acres of land, preservationists soon insisted that *all* roadless areas in Forest Service jurisdiction be studied for possible wilderness values. These lands were called *de facto wilderness;* the idea was that because they had not yet been developed for resources, they should never be developed. The Forest Service inventoried 56,174 acres of potential wilderness in 1,449 areas. Regional Foresters were instructed to recommend by June 30, 1972, which of these areas should become wilderness. The complicated process of evaluating these lands for wilderness was called Roadless Area Review and Evaluation (RARE) and used sophisticated mathematical formulas to judge mineral, timber, potential water development, scenic, scientific and other values. But the Sierra Club did not like the final recommendation that 274 areas totalling 12.3 million acres become wilderness, and initiated a 1972 lawsuit charging that the Forest Service's Environmental Impact Statement was inadequate and had been done too quickly. The Forest Service argued that time was of the essence, that prolonged deliberation would unnecessarily delay orderly development and that uncertainties over resource development would seriously harm local economies. The Sierra Club won, and the process was started all over again in 1977 with RARE II.

RARE II studied about 62 million acres for possible wilderness, while, separately, the Bureau of Land Management studied 24 million. The BLM will not complete its study until 1991, but the 1979 RARE II recommendation offered 15 million acres for wilderness, 11 million for "further study" and 36 million to be released for development and multiple use. Every recommendation that any acreage be released for commodity use has been challenged, lobbied, or litigated against by various environmentalist groups including the Sierra Club, National Wildlife Federation, National Audubon Society, and the Natural Resource Defense Council. Tucker's charge that environmentalists use wilderness as an all-purpose tool for stopping economic activity is well documented by this alone, but there is considerably more to the story.

While the RARE I and RARE II studies and the BLM study progressed, no timber sales could be offered on these public lands. Between 1972 and 1980, the stumpage price of a Western douglas fir tree increased 500 percent, primarily because of the supply-demand effect of tying up huge timbered areas in studies. Then, too, mineral values have been tied up. The 1964 law mandated that all lands were supposed to be surveyed for valuable mineral resources before being put into wilderness, but no area has received more than cursory assessment and most have not been inventoried at all, even though by 1976 the original 9.1 million acres of wilderness had swollen to 14,443,705 acres, and today encompasses about 20 million acres not including those in Alaska. What's more, despite the fact that the 1964 law demanded that established wilderness be surveyed for mineral wealth "on a planned, recurring basis," environmentalist threats and lawsuits have backed down every previous Secretary of the Interior from pressing mineral inventories, and nearly 20 years later the job is barely begun. Even slant drilling methods, which use oil rigs well outside wilderness boundaries and enter wilderness areas far underground with no surface disturbance whatsoever have been repeatedly thwarted by environmentalist lawsuits and public outcry.

The wilderness feud has another dimension, what some critics call "wilderness sprawl." Although the 1964 Wilderness Act set no upper limit for wilderness acreage, its strict standards left about 208 million acres of any kind as potential preserves. But in 1975, environmentalists lobbied the Eastern Wilderness Act through Congress, which allowed smaller and less pristine areas into consideration for zero-development status. Now millions more acres are potential wilderness, which led Jim Montgomery, executive director of the Southern Forest Institute, to remark to me one day, "These environmentalists have finally come up with a 'Bottomless Pit Theory' of wilderness preservation."

But Congress is not the only target: environmentalist pressure on administrative agencies such as the Department of the Interior has raised the question, "How big is a wilderness?" Not satisfied with the size of Congressionally designated wilderness, environmental groups insist on administrative designations of "buffer zones" permitting no development in a half-mile- or one-mile-wide strip around the perimeter of existing wilderness. If a mile-wide buffer strip were to be imposed around the smallest wilderness allowed by the 1964 Act, 5,000 acres, it could add 12 or more square miles of effective wilderness to the original area, depending on the shape of its perimeter. Thus, zero-development has been brought to vast new acreages *outside* the legal boundaries of wilderness areas at the insistence of environmentalist lawyers.

Environmentalists have also sought other statutory designations to prevent economic development. In 1968, the Wild and Scenic Rivers Act was passed which could prevent logging, dams, mineral development, and watershed management on an indefinitely expandable number of river basins. The "Bottomless Pit Theory" has also been extended to our National Park System.

In the 1950s, the first private lands were condemned by the federal government to create new units for parkland, and in 1968, Congress confiscated the first large tracts of private timberlands for use as a public park with the establishment of Redwood National Park in California. This trend to "purchase" private lands for National Park use through government condemnations and "takings" has created a virtually limitless supply of new parks—by law, no private property is safe from eminent domain or Congressional taking, and an environmentalist publicity campaign has been all the trigger needed to carve new parks from the homes and farms of unwilling sellers in dozens of places, such as Cuyahoga National Recreation Area in Ohio, Mount Rogers National Recreation Area in Virginia, Buffalo National River in Arkansas, and to mount efforts to "protect" places like California's Big Sur country and Oregon's Columbia Gorge from the people who live there. This trend to condemn massive areas of private property for new parks spurred the 1978 formation of a group to fight it: the National Inholders Association, an "inholder" being anyone who owns property or equity interest in land within a government-managed area or land that is regulated by a government agency.

But the Wilderness Act of 1964 and its fallout just described was only the opening salvo of the burgeoning environmentalist movement. Other trends soon had an impact. The outdoor recreation boom of the mid-'60s came on the crest of new affluence and leisure time, and provided a new rationale for preservationist demands that ever-increasing acreage be devoted to recreation areas. Another powerful trend was the perception of pollution problems. Public opinion was swayed by television news coverage of such events as the Cuyahoga River in Ohio catching fire from petrochemical pollution, and the Santa Barbara Channel wellhead blowout that gave us photos of hundreds of dead and dying oil-soaked birds. The National Geographic Society's 1966 television special of Jaques Cousteau's dirge over the death of the ocean from man-caused pollution spread genuine alarm about the possible immediate collapse of all ecosystems and the end of life on earth. The "Doomsday Syndrome" had begun.

An interesting contemporary footnote on the gloom and doom of the late 1960s came from the 1982 conference of the United Nations Environment Program (UNEP) in Nairobi, Kenya: marine biologist Stjepan Keckes, director of ten regional seas programs for UNEP, said "Reports of the ocean's death are greatly exaggerated," paraphrasing Mark Twain's wry comment on reports of his own demise. "To talk about the seas dying is nonsense; it's like talking about death when you have a bad tooth." Keckes scoffed at Cousteau's "alarmist" warnings, saying, "As far as oil pollution goes, there haven't been the effects people predicted in the 1960s. Even though thousands of birds have been killed in particular incidents, there has been no impact on total bird populations at all." Even Eric Eckholm, who has tended to be one of the "alarmists" himself, particularly in his 1976 book for the Worldwatch Institute *Losing Ground—Environmental Stress and World Food Prospects,* said, "Overall, available data suggest that most ocean life has scarcely been affected by pollution."

Hindsight, as the saying goes, is 20/20, but apocalypse seemed right around the corner in the 1960s, and the war in Vietnam did little to ease the tensions. In retrospect, the Vietnam war contributed several things to the environmental movement, two of which still carry some influence: anti-herbicide sentiments due to the Agent Orange debate, and the counterculture. The counterculture did more than happily advocate long hair, beards and "doing your own thing;" it did more than enjoy folk music, rock concerts and the ecology songs of John Denver, Joan Baez and Gordon Lightfoot; it did more than delight in the "inner trip" of psychedelia and sexual liberation. The counterculture became keenly and permanently aware that ethical and religious systems outside the Judeao-Christian tradition existed, which fertilized the growth of the "environmental ethic."

Theodore Roszak in *The Making of a Counterculture* was incisively on target: "Ironically, it is the American young, with their underdeveloped radical background, who seem to have grasped most clearly the fact that, while such immediate emergencies as the Viet-Nam war, racial injustice, and hard-core poverty demand a deal of old-style politicking, the paramount struggle of our day is against a far more formidable, because far less obvious opponent to which I will give the name 'the technocracy'. . . ." Anti-technology was to become a main theme of the symphonic poem of the environment.

The counterculture also prompted a good deal of embarrassing hucksterism from the traditional conservation groups in trying to recruit young activists to the cause. Listen to this from Sierra Club executive director Michael McCloskey in *Ecotactics: The Sierra Club Handbook for Environment Activists*: "We are cheering at the sight of fresh reinforcements from the nation's campuses. And we are waving a new flag. It is this handbook. Take it. Use it. . . ." The handbook contained rambling essays with such titles as "The Ecology of Revolution," "A Challenge to the Law," and "Sic 'em, Kids."

Another trend that added to the environmental movement in the '60s was consumerism. The consumer movement had been around since at least 1936 when Consumers Union was founded, but it gained notoriety when former C.U. employee Ralph Nader hit the road—and the automotive industry—with *Unsafe at Any Speed* and later helped get the Public Interest Law movement rolling wtih groups such as the campus-based Public Interest

Research Groups (PIRGs), along with other activists like Charles Halpern of the Center for Law and Social Policy. Consumerist interests touched the environment movement's at junctures such as the energy crisis, smog and air pollution, health foods without chemical additives or pesticide residues, public transportation, recreation for inner city youths, and similar issues.

In 1972, it seemed to some observers that all the stops had been pulled out. America was rudely awakened to the finite resources and limited carrying capacity of the earth through the Club of Rome's doomsday warning, *The Limits To Growth,* a computerized Malthusian proof that everything was going to collapse in less than a hundred years, all based on elaborate "world system" models and high mathematics. This, along with Paul Ehrlich's *The Population Bomb* and Barry Commoner's *The Closing Circle,* scared people half to death with vivid nightmare images of the imminent destruction of the total environment, the collapse of civilization and the end of all life on earth. It seemed for a few years that scientists were elbowing each other in the rush to publish the most horrifyingly definitive Apocalypse possible. It also seemed to some observers that certain scientists were getting a little free with the truth, perhaps because doomsaying was accompanied, as John Maddox wryly put it, "by such a merry jingle of the cash register."

There were some scientists who were willing to accept stretching the truth because of the potential social benefits of corrective action, among them Eric, Lord Ashby, one of England's distinguished biologists, who asked in his book *Reconciling Man With His Environment,*

Is it morally defensible to use shock tactics, to exaggerate, to distort the facts or color them with emotive words, or to slant the television camera in order to excite the public conscience? My experience leads me reluctantly to believe that *in the present social climate* some dramatization is necessary. Without Rachel Carson, public apathy about the hazards of pesticides might have persisted for a decade longer. Without the computerized jeremiads published by Meadows and his associates [*The Limits To Growth*], the public might not yet have been alerted to the ominous consequences of unregulated consumption in affluent countries. . . . Rachel Carson's biology can be faulted, and she uses cunningly the technique of a storyteller in her opening chapter. Meadow's computer simulations deserve the description attached to them by one reviewer: "The computer that printed out W.O.L.F." And yet, if these writers had been coolly rational, if they had stuck meticulously to uncolored verifiable facts, would they have made any impression on the public conscience? I doubt it. . . .

Lord Ashby's conclusion was shared by many scientists, but somehow, as a layman, I have always wondered when confronted with this argument if the question shouldn't be, "If these writers had told the whole truth, would there be any cause for alarm?"

Another British scientist, John Maddox, editor of the prestigious journal *Nature,* got fed up with all the ranting and raving and in 1972 wrote *The Doomsday Syndrome,* a politely scathing denunciation of environmentalist Cassandras who seemed to enjoy perverting the truth for fun and profit. Maddox systematically destroyed all the arguments of Commoner, Ehrlich, Rachel Carson, the Sierra Club, the Friends of the Earth, and many others, going into great detail but always maintaining the understated dry British wit. He suggested, for example, that "The doomsday cause would be more telling if it were more securely grounded in facts, better informed by a sense of history and an awareness of economics and less cataclysmic in temper." In response to Rachel Carson's solemn warning against the overuse of DDT as written in *Silent Spring:* "A few false moves on the part of man may result in destruction of soil productivity and the arthropods may well take over," Maddox pondered how DDT, an insecticide, could possibly kill all vegetation as Carson insisted, and puzzled over her choice of horrible fates by inquiring, "What would the ecologists suggest that the arthropods would feed upon when the vegetation had been killed off? Was Miss Carson afraid that too much explanation of these points would make her tale less alarming?"

In the mid-1970s, several intellectual trends became solidly entrenched in the environmentalist movement, among the most obvious being what engineer Samuel C. Florman identified as anti-technology in his book *The Existential Pleasures of Engineering.* Anti-technology, Florman informs us, preaches that our machines, aside from polluting the world to death, have become our masters, forcing us to do tedious and degrading work, to consume things that we really do not want, and that a technocratic elite is taking over control of society. Florman spends the remainder of his text poking neatly engineered holes in each of these assertions, in what the *Wall Street Journal* called "an urbane, witty, intellectually far-ranging, large-spirited hymn to homo faber."

But the anti-technology trend seriously impacted environmentalism. The seminal works such as Siegfried Giedion's *Mechanization Takes Command,* Jaques Ellul's mournful tale of "the essential tragedy of a civilization increasingly dominated by technique," *The Technological Society,* Lewis Mumford's infinitely historical *The Myth of the Machine,* and Herbert Marcuse's jolly hatchet job on industrial civilization, *One-Dimensional Man,* found expression in such environmentalist books as the Sierra Club's *This Is The American Earth,* which not only sang the praises of wilderness, but was at pains to criticize industrial civilization as well. The anti-technology philosophy was soon reflected in action; industrialists' attempts to offer compromises and mitigations were scorned as "mere technological fixes," and demands soon emerged for coercive "behavioral fixes" and strict rigid regulation by a centralized federal government. Ralph Nader told us that "We're going to rediscover smallness. People will get back to the earth, grow their own gardens, listen to the birds, feel the wind across their cheek and watch the sun come up." Yippie Abbie Hoffman told us, "We have got to stop science and scientific progress. This is not what America needs." The Friends of the Earth told us, "We will strike lightly along the soft energy path. We will be less populous and more decentralized, less industrial and more agrarian. Our acquisitive consumer society must give way to a severe conserver society."

Another important intellectualization that infused the environmental movement is the trend I call "anti-civilization." It has several facets. The idea that man's basic nature is thwarted by the constraints of civilized living is not new; it was seriously examined, for example, by Sigmund Freud in his 1930 opus *Civilization and Its Discontents*. The related notion of the Noble Savage goes back at least to Jefferson's time in the writings of Rousseau. But during the rise of modern environmentalism, anti-civilization grew into an achingly romanticized nostalgia for our roots in the earth; it was in part the inspiration for the hippy communes. It prompted the "Survivalist" movement which simply left civilization to live off the land and later became a clutch of self-sufficiency advocates living in rural areas and squatting on federal lands, and who have stocked up on foodstuffs against the Apocalypse. They are also armed to the teeth, supposedly to protect themselves from hungry friends and neighbors, but from what I have seen of them, I rather suspect they also enjoy playing soldier-cum-Daniel Boone. Anti-civilization is also at the heart of Theodore Roszak's grandiose vision in *Person/Planet: The Creative Disintegration of Industrial Society,* which longs for the total dismantling of industrial civilization and the pleasures of pastoral life.

Survivalist and creator of *The Whole Earth Catalogue* Stewart Brand painted this picture of his preferred future in the November/December 1980 issue of *Next* magazine: "We have wished, we ecofreaks, for a disaster, or for dramatic social change to come and bomb us into the Stone Age, where we might live like Indians in our valley, with our localism, our Appropriate Technology, our gardens, and our homemade religion, guilt-free at last." Such delight in the collapse of civilization is rare in print although common-place in environmentalist conversation.

No account of the environmental movement would be complete without addressing the dark strain I call "anti-humanity." Environmentalist leaders protest this is a hoax devised by vicious opponents, but my years of experience in the movement tell me anti-humanity feelings among environmentalists are real and powerful. The mildest anti-humanity literature in the movement comes from John Muir, one of the 1892 founders of the Sierra

Club, who wrote, ". . . if a war of races should occur between the wild beasts and Lord Man, I would be tempted to sympathize with the bears."

Anti-humanity in environmentalism has been recognized and berated by many. Richard Neuhaus wrote the 1971 *In Defense of People* as "a polemic against the ecology movement." He cried, "The presumably radical eco-tacticians of the 1970s are in large part the heirs of a conservationist history that, in a thousand variations, has peddled the proposition that 'only man is vile.' It is also clear, when conservation is transformed into a passion for population control, that some kinds of men are more vile than others."

In 1970, Robert Chrisman, editor of *The Black Scholar,* wrote an article for the now-defunct *Scanlan's* magazine called "Ecology, a Racist Shuck." He said,

Ironically, today's ecology enthusiasts do not seem to like living things. Life must be limited, they say, else it will destroy itself. We must have a small population and a lot of space. People corrupt things. They breed, they eat, they shit, they need clothing, they need shelter, they need fuel. We must eliminate people; otherwise they'll *use* the earth.

Chrisman's visceral hatred for environmentalists is shared by many lily-white, blond, blue-eyed miners, loggers, construction workers, and manufacturing laborers whose jobs have been destroyed by wilderness designations and land condemnations for parks. Chrisman also complained of the movement: "It is mired in the 19th-century theories of population and energy, and that in itself represents a willful and reactionary desire to return to the past, completely ignoring contemporary knowledge."

Chrisman's assessment is borne out in environmentalist distrust and condemnation of humanity's intelligence. Zero-population growth advocate Paul Ehrlich said in the November 5, 1979, issue of *Fortune,* "Giving Society cheap, abundant energy at this point would be the equivalent of giving an idiot child a machine gun." Economist E. F. Schumacher in *Small Is Beautiful* complained that "In the excitement over the unfolding of his scientific and technical powers, modern man has built a system of production that ravishes nature and a type of society that mutilates man." Most stunningly, the late Robert Van Den Bosch came out with the bottom line in *The Pesticide Conspiracy:* "Our problem is that we are too smart for our own good, and for that matter, the good of the biosphere. The basic problem is that our brain enables us to evaluate, plan, and execute. Thus, while all other creatures are programmed by nature and subject to her whims, we have our own gray computer to motivate, for good or evil, our chemical engine." This is not an anti-intellectual statement, it is an *anti-intelligence* statement, deploring the biological fact that reason enabled us to become the dominant species of earth.

Environmentalist anti-humanity is frequently directed to suggestions that humans should somehow apologize for being the dominant species on this planet, as Mark Satin recommended in *New Age Politics:* "We should practice species modesty." One who has followed the advice is Paul Watson, a founder of Greenpeace ("The Warriors of the Rainbow") and now a pirate who sinks the ships of whalers with whom he does not agree. Watson was quoted in the February 1981 issue of *Omni* magazine as saying of his childhood experience in a Canadian be-kind-to-animals group, "I got the impression that instead of going out to shoot birds, I should go out and shoot the kids who shoot birds."

One of latest trends to inform environmentalism is a wave of eco-terrorism, assaults, wilderness bridge-burnings, spray-helicopter bombings, and power station sabotage traced or attributed to environmental activists in the Western states. In the spring of 1980 a ground crew applying herbicides with spray backpacks for brush control in the Siskiyou National Forest were attacked, their gear removed, and their crew leader forced to sign a statement that the Forest Service would not spray there again that year. The *Grants Pass Courier* in southern Oregon reported that the attack had been initiated by counterculture elements using an elaborate system of citizen's band radios to locate the spray crew. Later in 1981, a few miles away at Cave Junction, Oregon, a spray helicopter was destroyed during the night by a person or persons unknown. On February 2, 1981, the Franklin bridge leading to the Rattlesnake Wilderness Area near Missoula, Montana, was burned. The sheriff suspected hikers, because of a long-standing feud between them and trail-bikers who enjoyed using the road and bridge to ride to the boundary of the Wilderness Area (where the road ends anyway, and motorized vehicles are forbidden inside wilderness). Hikers had been known to scatter roofing nails on the Franklin road to discourage bikers. June 3, 1981, near Toldeo, Oregon, masked women calling themselves the "People's Brigade For A Healthy Genetic Future" claimed responsibility for blowing up a forestry spray helicopter, calling in television reporters for the purpose. Numerous power stations in the West have been bombed by saboteurs. Many other incidents of eco-terrorism have shaken California, Oregon, Washington, Idaho, and Montana.

Eco-terrorism has its advocates. A *Denver Post* article of July 5, 1982, reported nationally acclaimed environmentalist author Edward Abbey's speech to a Jackson Hole, Wyoming, group in protest of exploratory oil drilling in a proposed wilderness area. When told of $5,000 in damages suffered by Getty Oil from vandalism to surveying equipment, Abbey responded, "I'm not advocating illegal activity, unless you're accompanied by your parents, or at night." Reporter Mike Calabrese described Abbey as "the radical author and essayist who came to national prominence with his book *The Monkey Wrench Gang*, about a group of people who became saboteurs in defense of nature." Power stations were one of the major targets of the fictional ecotage crew in Abbey's 1975 novel.

The rationale of this wave of "eco-tage" (coined from "ecology" plus "sabotage" by the anti-utility Environmental Action handbook *Ecotage*.) was summed up in a terrorist note claiming responsibility for the May 31, 1982, bombing that did $6 million in damage to a power substation in British Columbia, Canada. An agent of the Royal Canadian Mounted Police provided me with a copy:

On May 31, we bombed four 500 k.v. transformers at the Dunsmuir substation on Vancouver Island. This substation is part of the $1 billion Cheekeye-Dunsmuir transmission line project being built by B.C. Hydro. This project, if completed, will provide electricity for a wave of industrial development planned for Vancouver Island. We are opposed to any further industrial development and to any expansion of the power grid which will facilitate such development.

We reject both the ecological destruction and the human oppression inherent in the industrial societies of the corporate machine in the West and the communist machine in the East. In the last two hundred years industrial civilization has been raping and mutilating the earth and exterminating other species at an ever accelerating rate. We say this is not right. Jobs, progress, standards of living—nothing is sufficient justification for the horrible damage being done.

Already in this province, half the forests have been logged and many rivers dammed. The valleys are littered with highways and power lines, the estuaries are paved and polluted, the water is poisoned, mills and smelters belch noxious fumes, and nuclear power and acid rain are soon to come.

While being in complete opposition to further ecological destruction, we also oppose the human oppression resulting from the economic and political systems throughout the world that are based on power and profit. In fact, ecological destruction is directly related to the human oppressions of sexism, racism, hierarchy and imperialism. The desire for power, the insensitivity to the suffering of others and the need to feel superior are the sinister bonds that underlie all these oppressive human relations.

Centuries of patriarchy and imperialism have created oppressive power relations that now permeate most societies and their institutions. As a result, people today have internalized these characteristics; however, this does not negate the ultimate responsibility of the ruling classes that control and direct these institutions.

The same ruling classes and multinational corporations who relentlessly destroy the environment, also control the repressive dictatorships and governments of democratic façade throughout the capitalist world. The repression and economic exploitation that result are an inevitable consequence of societies that function in order to fulfill the profit and growth demands of a corporate economy.

Within the capitalist world, a growing number of liberation movements have created a situation in which the industrialized societies can no longer depend for their supply of strategic materials on these potentially "unstable" regions of the so-called third world. And so during the late 70s and now into the 80s, the industrialized societies are attempting to become less energy dependent on these regions by exploiting coal, oil, gas and nuclear energy and resources from regions that meet international security objectives. Canada, at this time, meets these objectives.

We must make this an insecure and uninhabitable place for capitalists and their projects. This is the best contribution we can make towards protecting the earth and struggling for a liberated society.

Canadian authorities consider the note authentic. This remarkably literate terrorist letter reveals the intimate link between environmentalism and social change that swept the movement during the 1970s. William Tucker's analysis in *Progress and Privilege: America in the Age of Environmentalism* that the movement is a leisure-class effort to maintain the status quo is inadequate in this light. Eco-terrorists are not preservers of the status quo, or even "New Luddites" anxious about technology stealing their jobs, but rather deeply primitivist activists opposed to industrial civilization itself.

Environmentalism as Politics

In 1976, Jimmy Carter was elected President of the United States. Among the many pieces of political fallout was the appointment of hundreds of former environmentalist group activists to the new Administration. In the President's Council on Environmental Quality were placed Gustave Speth, founder of the Natural Resource Defense Council, in which he personally handled environmental lawsuits against the government, Gerald Barney from Environmental Agenda, and Marion Edey of the League of Conservation Voters. The White House staff itself became home to Kathy Fletcher from the Environmental Defense Fund and Daniel Beard from the Congressional Research Environmental Department. In the Environmental Protection Agency, Administrator Douglas Costle came from Connecticut's Environmental Protection Department, Deputy Administrator Barbara Blum, a psychiatric social worker, had strong Sierra Club ties, Counsel Sheldon Novick was the publisher of *Environment Magazine*, and Assistant Administrator David G. Hawkins came from Natural Resources Defense Council.

In the Department of Agriculture, Assistant Secretary M. Rupert Cutler, boss of the Forest Service, came from the Wilderness Society, as did Director of RARE II George Davis. And among Department of the Interior appointments, Deputy Under Secretary Barbara Heller came from the Environmental Policy Center, Assistant to the Secretary Cynthia Wilson came from the Audubon Society, Assistant Secretary for Energy and Minerals Joan Davenport came from the Environmental Protection Agency, Assistant Secretary for Land and Water Guy Martin had numerous Alaskan environmental group ties, Assistant Secretary for Fish and Wildlife and Parks Robert Herbst came from the Izaak Walton League, Executive Assistant to the Secretary Charles M. Parrish had been closely involved in several Georgia environmentalist groups, Associate Solicitor John Leshy came from the Natural Resources Defense Council, and in the Land and Water Section, Joe Browder had been director of Ralph Nader's Environmental Policy Center.

Others in key positions included James W. Moorman, Assistant Attorney General in the Justice Department, formerly director of the Sierra Club's Legal Defense Fund; former Natural Resources Defense Council attorneys included Angus C. Macbeth, Justice Department Pollution Control Section head, and Richard Cotton, executive secretary for Health, Education and Welfare. Environmental Defense Fund graduates included Leo M. Eisel, a member of the President's Water Resources Council.

Llewellyn King of Washington's *Energy Daily* said of these and hundreds of other Carter appointments:

Carter introduced into public service a new kind of individual not a part of the Washington scene. They are the environmentalists, the consumerists and others from the counterculture. They came from a gaggle of organizations and felt possessed of a moral legitimacy. They feel that any kind of compromise is a moral stain. They have an utter disregard for traditions of courtesy among rivals and the little ceremonies that make Washington life tolerable. It all leaves an unpleasant taste in the mouth. There is a feeling that bigotry, clothed in righteousness, is fouling the process of government.

It is amusing to note that, while environmentalists during Watt's Senate confirmation hearing resisted his appointment because his former connection with Mountain States Legal Foundation was a *conflict of interest*, no one seemed to recall the hundreds of similar skeletons in the closet of the Carter Administration that led King to write his bitter assessment. The swarm of environmentalists into public service became known among Washingtonians as the "termite infestation."

Many commentators began to have grave misgivings about environmentalists in power and the interests they represented. Irving Kristol in *Two Cheers For Capitalism* warned of a "New Class" of well-educated and affluent individuals moving into the public sector, including environmentalists. Kristol said, "Though they continue to speak the language of 'progressive reform,' in actuality they are acting upon a hidden agenda: to propel the nation from that modified version of capitalism we call 'the welfare state' toward an economic system so stringently regulated in detail as to fulfill many of the traditional anti-capitalist aspirations of the Left." Nobel economist Milton Friedman observed, "The new class, enshrined in the universities, the news media, and especially the federal bureaucracy, has become one of the most powerful of the special interests." The new class seemed intent upon replacing material values with amenity values, and upon "defining and dominating society," as Kristol put it.

As Carter's Cabinet appointees made their sub-Cabinet appointments, who in turn made their own appointments, and then those sub-sub-appointees made their own, Dr. H. Peter Metzger, Manager of Public Affairs Planning for the Public Service Company of Colorado, researched the "termite infestation" and found that environmental activists were using tax dollars to train young people in "the style and techniques of radical politics," obtaining government funding for already wealthy environmentalist groups such as the Sierra Club, and arranging for government-paid organizers to create new environmentalist groups on single issues. He became alarmed by the literally thousands of environmentalists in the federal government who appeared to be dismantling America's industry. He carefully documented these charges in a paper entitled *The Coercive Utopians: Their Hidden Agenda.*

Metzger discovered that Carter's ACTION agency head, Sam Brown, formerly a militant environmental activist, had given $470,475 in federal grants to ACORN, the Association of Community Organizations for Reform Now, a large (25,000 families claimed), national (600 chapters in 17 states), and well-financed ($1 million annual budget, but nonethless a client of the federal government) activist group. The "People's Platform" of ACORN reads like something written by Lenin or Mao: "In our freedom, only the people shall rule. Corporations shall have their roles producing jobs, providing products, paying taxes. No more. No less. They shall obey our wishes, respond to our needs, serve our communities. We have nothing to show for the work of our hands. Our patience has been abused. . . . Enough is Enough." ACORN called for "neighborhood control" of the private sector, much like the Soviet system, complete with "self-criticism meetings" with compulsory attendance for all citizens.

ACORN, it seems, had teamed with Chicago's Midwest Academy to train young radicals, including VISTA volunteers (the "volunteers" got about $4,000 a year in subsistence payments from the federal government), paid for by federal grants from ACTION agency in the amount of $596,315, as verified by a House Appropriation Subcommittee investigation led by Congressman Robert H. Michel in 1979. The Midwest Academy was founded by Saul Alinski, author of *Rules For Radicals.* Midwest's training manual— paid for at taxpayers' expense—offered this advice to its students from VISTA and ACORN:

Give people a "taste of blood." Push your opponents so hard you can see them squirm. You may want to assign some people to be "inciters" and move about to heat up the action getting people angrier and encouraging them to show their anger. Make what the opposition is doing or not doing sound scandalous. Stunts can help. . . . Civil disobedience . . . is not generally a good mass recruitment tactic [but] there are some exceptions. The Third Principle of Direct Action organizing is that it attempts to alter the relations of power between the people's organizations and their real enemies. The enemies are unresponsive politicians, tax assessors, utilities, landlords, government agencies, large corporations or banks.

Metzger also uncovered substantial federal payments to Ralph Nader's Public Interest Research Group (PIRG) network in the amount of $646,042 from Sam Brown's ACTION agency. The PIRGs are also funded by a "negative option" add-in to student fees at universities, a tactic once condemned by Nader himself when he was attacking book clubs. PIRGs fund anti-nuclear literature and demonstrations ("No-Nuke Teach-Ins"), and media events.

I have independently discovered that the Environmental Protection Agency, according to an internal memo of 1980, paid out $756,262 to various environmental groups for what EPA described as "information development, coalition building and problem solving" on toxic substances, including more than $48,000 to the Sierra Club for training materials.

It is also of interest to note that environmentalist groups obtain vast funding from private foundations. The Foundation Center on West 57th Street in mid-town Manhattan keeps records of all foundation transactions in the United States. Their service called Comsearch Printouts has a volume entitled *Environmental Programs* which showed that in 1980 alone, the Atlantic-Richfield, Ford, Mellon and Rockefeller Family Foundation interests gave more than $18 million to environmentalist groups. In 1979, it was over $20 million.

By 1980, Metzger could write: "Already accomplished is the virtual paralysis of new federal coal leasing, conventional electric generating plant licensing in many areas, federal minerals land leasing and water development, industrial exporting without complex environmental hearings, and the halting of new nuclear power plant construction."

A front-page story in the October 28, 1980, *Wall Street Journal* sized up the impact of four years of "termite infestation": a study had revealed that 48 major companies had laid out $2.6 billion *over and above* what good corporate citizens would normally have spent on environmental protection. Economists estimated that all businesses paid an extra $100 billion merely plowing through red tape. The impact of this excess cost, which generated no products, no real income and no environmental protection, is shown by lowered productivity and high inflation rates.

While today's public is generally unaware of the radical aspect of the environmental movement, it firmly supports protection measures, and with surprising fervor. A 1978 survey by Washington, D.C.-based environmental think-tank Resources For the Future found that when presented with 3 alternatives, 53 percent of their respondents chose the one which read: "Protecting the environment is *so important* that requirements and standards cannot be too high, and continuing improvement must be made *regardless* of cost" (emphasis in the original). This finding was confirmed in 1980 (42 percent) and in 1981 (45 percent).

The political nature of the environmentalist movement became evident during the Carter Administration. Since 1960, over 100 "political ecology" laws had been lobbied into existence, over 500 environmental lawsuits had been litigated, and some 3,000 environmentalist groups claimed 5 million members of record, with the top 10 groups receiving over $55 million in annual income. A small sector of the public had vastly influenced America's social and economic course. Yet despite the detailed discoveries of government-funded activism, there seemed to be no pattern, no tracery of cause and effect, no understanding of the dynamics of environmentalism. The most coherent ideas about the direction and intent of the movement came from the more astute environmentalists themselves and from their intellectual critics.

Alexander Cockburn and James Ridgeway offered a few hints in their introduction to a collection of essays entitled *Political Ecology: An Activist's Reader On Energy, Land, Food, Technology, Health and the Economics and Politics of Social Change:*

The scattered environmental interests eventually came together over the central question of energy. . . . While the issue of energy was the central question, more profound was the gradual realization of all the various groups within the movement . . . that the word "ecology" implies the indivisibility of total systems, and that all their disparate concerns were connected: that matters of energy, agriculture, health, transport, land use, and so forth were not susceptible of separate solution or even reform but implied structural attack on the political and economic system itself.

Jim Watt evidently had a point when he said, "The battleground is not what our critics would like you to believe it is, protecting the environment. It is over ideology, over forms of government that lead to a centralized, socialized society."

An insightful commentary on environmentalism came from the German Marxist Hans Magnus Enzenzberger in his essay *A Critique of Political Ecology*:

On the whole one can say that in the ecological movement—or perhaps one should say movements—the scientific aspects, which derive predominantly from biology, have merged in an extremely confused alliance with a whole series of political motivations and interests, which are partly manifest, partly concealed. At a deeper level one can identify a great number of sociopsychological needs, which are usually aroused without those concerned being able to see through them. These include: hopes of conversion and redemption, delight in the collapse of things, feelings of guilt and resignation, escapism and hostility to civilization.

As clearsighted as it is, even this commentary is frustratingly incomplete. Why did the science of ecology become so confused with political motivations? Why can't environmentalists see through their own "sociopsychological needs"? Why do some of these people "delight in the collapse of things"? We may see the "hows" ever so plainly, but the "whys" elude us. And that's what really matters—why?

Environmentalism as Social Dynamics

In 1977 a brilliant researcher began to make sense of the changes in our society that nourished the environmental movement. After examining the hodge-podge and crazy quilt with powerful analytical tools, a political scientist named Ronald Inglehart of the University of Michigan found that there was a pattern to it after all. He published his findings under the title: *The Silent Revolution: Changing Values and Political Styles Among Western Publics*.

The real changes of the last two decades boiled down to two things: values and political styles. This much was clear from the massive surveys taken in Europe and North America over a number of years that Inglehart used as a data base. And the direction of those changes was definite. As Inglehart put it: "The values of Western publics have been shifting from an overwhelming emphasis on material well-being and physical security toward greater emphasis on the quality of life." And, "An increasingly large proportion of the public is coming to have sufficient interest and understanding of national and ·international politics to participate in decision-making at this level."

Inglehart discovered six major causes or forces behind these shifts. *Technological innovation* is the motor of change and the historical thread that ties all the other changes together. New technology from World War II was applied to our domestic economy in the late '40s, and the result was unprecedented productivity. This productivity in turn spurred unprecedented economic growth, and affluence came to the majority of Americans; even the "pre-affluent" minorities were better off. Technology enabled fewer and fewer to supply all the goods for more and more, which created changes in the occupational structure—"total goods" producers (30%) are now outnumbered by service sector workers (70%). This new service majority needed more technical skills; technology had made expanded education both affordable and necessary. New technology also created mass communications, which linked us together in new ways with instantaneous and shared information. The distinctive experiences of the generation that grew to maturity during this time caused them to hold vastly different values from their parents, and gave them the political skills to put their values into practice.

Economic growth was a force for change with unexpected results. We didn't realize that higher incomes would also reduce our concern with material values. We didn't realize that affluence would lead many of us to emphasize lifestyle and the quality of life over and above economic concerns. We didn't realize that we would evolve into "post-materialists," in Inglehart's terminology. We didn't realize that these new concerns would lead to an increased demand for participation in decisions affecting that quality of life, whether in schools, universities, welfare agencies, offices, or factories. And we didn't realize that differences in lifestyle would generate furious disputes over everything from protection of the environment and the role of women to the redefinition of morality, drug use, and broader participation in the political process.

But we could see the obvious impacts of economic growth. Rapid industrialization and urbanization had drastic effects on air and water quality. Pollution of all kinds, physical and psychological, became impossible to ignore. It was also obvious that rising expectations would lead the less fortunate to feel that existing institutions were no longer adequate—business corporations and government itself suffered a crisis of legitimacy while disappointed minorities rioted in Detroit and Watts and elsewhere.

Changes in occupational structure also brought unforeseen changes in our values. We couldn't see that displacing masses of industrial jobs into the service sector, particularly into the knowledge industry, would create serious divergences of outlook between the new technical, professional and scientific majority and the old managers who were attached to profits, economic growth and their individual firms or bureaucracies. But that's exactly what happened. The new "Post-Industrial Society," as Daniel Bell calls it, is also buffered from and unaware of the problems of goods production and natural resources except in the most theoretical way.

Other researchers, particularly Herman Kahn, respected futurologist of the Hudson Institute, discovered that despite the service majority's higher education, its vision had narrowed to see only its own goals and problems. Kahn called this problem "educated incapacity," by which he meant "the acquired or learned inability to understand or see a problem, much less a solution." Increasingly, Kahn says, the more expert, or at least the more educated, a person is, the more likely he is to be affected by educated incapacity.

Because the service majority cannot understand the problems of the "total goods" producers, we have a new kind of "class warfare," not between the haves and have-nots, but between the knowledge class and the producer class, who possess radically different views of what the world is really all about.

The expansion of education was a direct result of economic growth and the rise of the service sector. Not only could more of us afford higher education for personal advancement, but America also needed it to train workers in the more demanding technical skills of a service society. But there's a problem: as dozens of studies have shown, higher education does not simply add information to the student, it changes values as well. Two social scientists, Kenneth Feldman and Theodore Newcomb, summarized the impact of college: college students have passed the stage of maximum family influence, and higher education makes them more liberal, less dogmatic, less authoritarian, more interested in political matters, and teaches them to think independently. In the middle '60s, students got some practical lessons in politics, not in the classroom, but in campus protests.

The development of mass communications was the real sleeper. Television has been the center of endless disputes over whether or not it influences behavior; for example, the familiar fight over the presentation of sex and violence and its impact on the young. Specifics may be debatable, but Inglehart discovered that some impacts of television are quite real. For one thing, television is nationwide—and, as one wag put it, half an inch deep—which means that local traditions are constantly being invaded by alien viewpoints. This clearly makes it tougher for many parents to pass their values on to their children in unaltered form. News coverge is a particular force for change by presenting dissatisfaction, alternative lifestyles and other dissonant signals to viewers—a fact that protesters quickly grasped, and thus made every effort to plan their activities for maximum publicity value, as we shall see later in the Sierra Club's secret memo planning the "Dump Watt" campaign as a media circus.

Conservatives charge that the media managers are themselves the products of colleges which liberalized their views. "The liberal media" is a catchword of disgruntled conservatives who find their views missing or distorted in news coverage. A 1981 study by S. Robert Lichter and Stanley Rothman for the Research Institute on International Change at Columbia University revealed that this liberal bias in the media is real. They talked with 240 journalists and broadcasters and 76 percent completed the study questionnaire. Almost all had college degrees, two-fifths came from the Eastern

Establishment—from New York, New Jersey and Pennsylvania upper-middle-class families, more than 80 percent voted liberal in the last four Presidential elections, and more than half agreed that "the U.S. exploits the Third World and causes poverty." What is astounding, however, is that more than half agreed that the use of natural resources by the United States is "immoral." As a group, the study concluded, media people are overwhelmingly for abortion, affirmative action, women's rights, sexual freedom and environmental protection.

Distinctive generational experiences—the famous "generation gap" of pop psychology—had more influence on our changing values than we realized. For one thing, the older generation who presided over the 1960s had all known total war in one form or another—not many missed out on World War II who were living then. But the younger generation of the '60s had never known total war—war was something that happened only in other countries. Thus an entire generation of young Americans grew up in this affluent, highly-educated, communications-rich society with unprecedented physical security. They had less concern about economics and put much more emphasis on lifestyle and the quality of life—and ideology—than their parents. They were willing to endure and impose economic penalties in order to obtain environmental values.

These six forces for change reveal the cause-and-effect patterns of shifting values and political skills. Now Inglehart looked for the mechanism that would explain *why* such drastic shifts in values would occur in the direction that they did.

Inglehart found his mechanism in the work of psychologist Abraham Maslow. Maslow's professional interest was the age-old desire to know what makes people tick, to grasp what motivates people, what shapes their personality. After years of clinical research, he came out with a landmark study called *Motivation and Personality*. In it he laid out his theory of the "needs hierarchy." Inglehart was quick to grasp the fundamental importance of this needs hierarchy, which for the first time showed a way to predict the direction in which values will change under given circumstances.

In basic outline, here is what Maslow discovered: First, the physiological needs, the food, clothing and shelter needs take top priority as long as they are in short supply, and physical security comes next in importance. Nothing much new there, anybody could have told him that.

But Maslow was smart. He then asked the question: "What happens when people get enough of the basics? What happens when people are well-off enough to afford enough food, clothing, shelter and safety?" He discovered something very peculiar: the basic material and safety needs, once satisfied, no longer motivate as powerfully, discontent sets in, and new, higher-level needs arise. These new higher-level needs arise in more or less regular order, and they have this in common: they are all needs for non-material things.

The first of these new needs is for love and affection, followed by the need for a sense of belonging, then the need for self-esteem, and then for what Maslow called "self-actualization," by which he meant the need to be "all that one can be."

Then Maslow got another surprise: when these higher-level needs themselves are gratified, they too cease to motivate as strongly, a new discontent sets in, and final, highest-level needs arise: the knowledge needs (which might also be called the curiosity needs or the intellectual needs), and finally the aesthetic needs (the need for beauty, for beautiful surroundings or to create beautiful things). These two highest-level needs would also encompass spiritual or philosophic needs.

Inglehart was delighted with Maslow's theory: better than any other hypothesis it explained the facts he had so laboriously confirmed. So the story of America for the last few decades is the story of a nation becoming wealthy enough to climb all the way up the needs hierarchy, pure and not-so-simple. Environmentalism had been explained.

But there's a catch. And even Inglehart missed it. If you read on in Maslow's *Motivation and Personality,* and go a few pages past the aesthetic needs, you will find that Maslow also discovered some serious consequences of rising up the needs hierarchy.

The first consequence, Maslow found, is that once we have gotten one or two stages into the non-material needs, we begin to feel an "independence of and a certain disdain for the old satisfiers and goal objects." The lower-material levels begin to look boring and then even repulsive. Material things are not good enough any more. An insidious change comes over our minds, a change we cannot see through: the higher we go, the more we tend to reconstruct our view of the world, and we overestimate the value of the higher ungratified needs, and underestimate the value of the lower-level satisfied needs. As Maslow warned:

In a word, we tend to take for granted the blessings we already have, especially if we don't have to work or struggle for them. The food, the security, the love, the admiration, the freedom that have always been there, that have never been lacking or yearned for tend not only to be unnoticed but also even to be devalued or mocked .or destroyed. This phenomenon of failing to count one's blessings is, of course, not realistic and can therefore be considered to be a form of pathology.

Maslow gave this pathology a forbidding name: "postgratification forgetting and devaluation," and predicted, "This relatively neglected phenomenon of postgratification forgetting and devaluation is, in my opinion, of very great potential importance and power."

Today America is seriously afflicted with "postgratification forgetting and devaluation." We are seriously afflicted with educated incapacity that blinds us to economics and makes us accept all problems and reject all solutions. The needs hierarchy alone does not explain environmentalism. These two treacherous pitfalls of forgetful devaluation and learned inability to see economic problems have twisted environmentalism from a sane and insightful protection of the whole environment, civilization included, into a mad scramble for political power and economic control by self-appointed saviors who don't care what it costs.

And this is the background against which James Watt received and accepted the nomination as President Reagan's Secretary of the Interior.

CHAPTER 3
THE CONFIRMATION BATTLE

Neither to change, nor falter, nor repent.
—Shelley

The final selections for nearly half the Reagan Administration's initial Cabinet positions were worked out by seven top advisors: Vice-President George Bush; James Baker III, the President-elect's Chief of Staff; Edwin Meese III, Presidential counselor; Michael Deaver, appointments and scheduling; E. Pendleton James, transition team personnel director; William Casey, designated Director of the Central Intelligence Agency; and Senator Paul Laxalt of Nevada, probably Ronald Reagan's closest personal friend. Senator Laxalt had selected former Senator Clifford P. Hansen for the Secretary of the Interior spot, but when Hansen bowed out it fell upon Laxalt to find another candidate—quick.

Hansen had not declined the Interior position until the first week in December. Time was growing short; the President-elect wanted his Cabinet filled before Christmas if at all possible. On Thursday, December 4, 1980, Senator Laxalt asked four fellow Western Senators to his office in Room 315 of the Russell Senate Office Building: James McClure of Idaho, Chairman of the crucial Senate Committee on Energy and Natural Resources that would hear confirmation testimony on the Secretary of the Interior-designate; Alan Simpson and Malcolm Wallop of Wyoming; and Pete Domenici of New Mexico.

A number of people were considered. Among those in the running were Representative Manuel Lujan of New Mexico, ranking minority member of the House Interior and Insular Affairs Committee—who could not be spared from his Congressional role; Representative John Rhodes of Arizona; retiring Representative Jim Johnson of Colorado; Utah GOP leader Richard Richards; Colorado House Speaker Bob Burford, regarded by many as practically "Mr. Colorado"; former Interior Solicitor Ken Frizell; and former Bon-

51

neville Power Administrator Don Hodel, whose name had been tossed into the ring by Oregon Senator Mark Hatfield.

The five Senators knew the kind of man they needed. He had to be knowledgeable about Interior problems. He had to be tough enough to take the inevitable abuse from environmentalists. He had to be strong enough to make the Department run in the best interests of all the Nation.

Senator James McClure asked, "What about Jim Watt?"

Senator Simpson smiled and, in typical Simpson fashion, said, "Well, I'll be . . . I'm stunned at the brilliance of the idea."

Senators Wallop and Domenici agreed. But Senator Laxalt did not know Jim Watt. Senator Simpson filled him in: "Jim Watt is the man who can grab that monster by the throat and make it behave. He knows where all the bones are buried. He knows where the deadwood accumulates. He knows where all the blockage systems are built in. He knows where all the conduits and shunts and leaks are. He knows the bureaucracy!"

Laxalt asked: "But will he take the job?"

On Friday, they detailed a mutual friend to ask Jim Watt that question, and when the answer came back 'Yes,' Watt received another telephone call inviting him to Washington to meet Senator Laxalt the next working day, Monday, December 8. When Watt arrived in Washington Sunday night before the day of his Laxalt meeting, he checked into the University Club on 16th Street N.W., a few blocks north of the White House. It would be tough enough to avoid bumping into friends in this city where he was well known, and the University Club offered more privacy than a public hotel.

Monday morning at 7:30, Watt's long-time Washington friend Perry Pendley, then working as Minority Counsel for the House Interior and Insular Affairs subcommittee on Mines and Mining, got a telephone call. Hearing Watt's voice, Pendley was both surprised and delighted, and asked, "It's awfully early out there in Denver, isn't it, Jim?"

"The older I get, the earlier I get up," answered Watt noncommitally. "I've only got a few seconds, and what I called for was to ask you an important question about minerals policy."

A few months earlier Watt and Pendley had roomed together at the Rocky Mountain Mineral Law Institute for four days in Sun Valley, Idaho—part of their continuing education requirements as lawyers. Pendley's room reservation had been cancelled out from under him by the hotel. Watt, who was standing nearby, said, "Come on and share my room." Thus they spent the four days attending law classes, talking minerals policy, renewing old acquaintances, and watching the televised Republican National Convention at which Ronald Reagan became the GOP candidate for President of the United States. This morning, Pendley assumed that Watt was merely consulting his opinion for some Mountain States Legal Foundation case, as he had done occasionally in the past, so he gave him the answer, not realizing that Watt was already turning over in his mind what to do if this week turned out to be a success, who to call upon for his own transition team.

Late that morning, Watt met Senator Wallop of Wyoming, and the two joined Senator Laxalt for a two-hour lunch. Laxalt and Watt hit it off together immediately. The Senator from Nevada grilled Watt on every issue in the book, National Parks, water development, Wilderness Areas, sheep and cattle grazing leases, predator control, territorial affairs, the Indian issues of self-determination and economic development, the Carter Administration's thrust to run Interior with the lawyers of the Solicitor's office, and hundreds of details of Department business. They also covered in detail Watt's career and any bombshells that might come up to ruffle the confirmation hearings. Watt played devil's advocate, spelling out for Senator Laxalt every difficulty that might cross his path at Interior.

As Watt recalls the meeting, "I put the most harsh interpretations on everything I had done in my career. I made it plain that I wasn't trying to sell myself to the Reagan Administration. If they wanted me they'd have to buy me, but I wasn't going to play salesman." Jim told Laxalt everything he could think of that might be used against him, the Don Thoren Management-By-Objectives contracts that had drawn such heat at his Federal Power Commission hearings, and every case that Mountain States Legal Foundation had handled which might bring down the wrath of environmentalist groups. For Jim Watt it was a very arduous two hours.

Paul Laxalt is fully as decisive as Jim Watt. When the luncheon was over, he picked up the phone and called President-elect Reagan. "I've found the man for Interior," Laxalt told Reagan. "His name is Jim Watt—you haven't met him—and he's razor sharp. He's a steely manager who knows the Department, and he can take the pressure—he's got the hide of a rhino. What's more, he's clean as a whistle. He's our man."

Now the careful checking began. Watt was instructed not to go on any rounds of courtesy calls, not to visit with anyone on Capitol Hill, not to see anybody. An FBI clearance was run on Watt's background. Even with the urgency of time pressing the Cabinet selection process, a thoroughgoing security check was carried out.

When Tuesday dawned, Watt knew there would be no official business today, no appointments, just waiting for the checkout to be completed. But it was evident from Senator Laxalt's enthusiasm that he was more than in the running, he was the likely choice. So he called a real-estate friend, indicating that a close associate was being considered for a high position in the Reagan Administration and would need a house close in. Thus, Watt spent the day driving around looking at houses, and spotted the home on Massachusetts Avenue where he and Leilani now reside.

But Wednesday morning Watt ran into an old friend who was also staying at the University Club, Stan Hulett, an associate from earlier days in the Interior Department who had for the past few years served with the California Forest Protection Association. They breakfasted together and Hulett confided that although he was in Washington working on the Reagan transition team, he was actively seeking the appointment for Under Secretary of Interior. By this time, Jim had mulled over his own choices for several top spots in the Department should he be selected, and had already decided that Don Hodel, former administrator of the Bonneville Power Administration, would serve as a perfect foil for him as Under Secretary.

In an utterly straightforward manner, Watt said to Stan Hulett, "I don't think you should be Under Secretary. I think there's another job you ought to be interested in, and that's Director of the Office of Congressional and Legislative Affairs."

Hulett replied, "That's a top staff job. What makes you think the Secretary would appoint me?"

Watt only said, "I just think you ought to be interested in the Congressional and Legislative Affairs spot."

Hulett did not pursue the point further and the conversation turned to other things. When they said their goodbyes and Hulett went to his office in the Reagan transition building at 1776 M Street N.W., he picked up the phone, called his wife at their home in California and said, "I just had breakfast with the next Secretary of the Interior."

Watt received instructions to go for an interview with several key transition team members Wednesday afternoon. He realized how crucial these meetings would be; the support of the five Western Senators who already backed him would have to be seconded by the Reagan political advisors and staff members such as Ed Meese, Jim Baker and Fred Fielding. It was late afternoon before Watt was admitted to the conference room to face Meese, Baker, and Fielding.

He had been checked out by the FBI, he was told, and had come up clean on paper. His new friend Senator Laxalt had been highly impressed, he was told. The political advisors had been pleased with his conservative 'Republican credentials, he was told—but remembered his rebuffed attempt to join the transition team and his rejection for being too conservative. It was obvious that the decision had already been made. It was obvious that the real turning point had already come: the Monday luncheon with Senator Laxalt. Laxalt and the President-elect had clearly made up their minds. Today's meeting with these transition team members was a pro forma affair, more an opportunity to get acquainted with the troops than a command performance to stand inspection. Jim smiled and joined wholeheartedly in the polite chit-chat and was not at all surprised when he was invited to meet with Ronald Reagan at noon the next day.

By Thursday morning the news began to break. A *Denver Post* headline was typeset announcing "Denverite Heads List for Top Interior Post," followed by an article outlining Watt's biography and devoting nearly ten column-inches to his role at Mountain States Legal Foundation. Joe Coors had been interviewed and was quoted as saying that if Watt became Interior Secretary, he would "do a fine job," and that Watt was "tremendously capable and qualified."

At noon, Jim was ushered into a room at Blair House on Pennsylvania Avenue. In the room were Jim Baker, Michael Deaver and the President-elect. When Watt and Reagan met for the first time, there was instant rapport: both were long-time, bone-deep conservative Republicans, both were from the West, both had a bold vision for America's future. With the genial manner of the born leader, Ronald Reagan invited James G. Watt to accept the nomination as Secretary of the Interior, and Watt accepted.

Then it was down to business. First came the matters of policy. Within a few minutes, the two men had settled on five major Interior objectives: first, to open America's public lands once more to multiple use; second, to reduce our national energy dependence; third, to establish a strategic minerals policy; fourth, to restore the National Parks which had been allowed to seriously deteriorate; and fifth, to provide strong leadership for the Department.

When Jim Watt and Ronald Reagan had agreed upon the issues, the subject turned to personalities. "Mr. President," Jim said, "I'm committed to your program and to making it work for America whatever price I personally have to pay. You're going to have to back me and back me, and when you can't back me any more, you're going to have to fire me."

Ronald Reagan smiled, and patted Jim Watt on the back. "Jim," he said, "I'll back you all the way. Sic 'em."

Total elapsed time during the meeting: just under 20 minutes. In that short time they had laid the groundwork for setting American natural resource policy back on course.

(For skeptics, there is another version of Ronald Reagan's response to Jim's comment about having to "back me and back me and then fire me." It is told that Ronald Reagan smiled and simply said, "Jim, *I will*." not specifying whether he would back Watt or fire him.)

Thursday afternoon Watt met discreetly with several of his Western

Senator friends to chart strategy for the coming confirmation battle. The Reagan transition team had been given strict orders not to comment on the Watt nomination until formal announcement could be made later in the month. Senator McClure made every effort to schedule Watt's hearing as early as possible in conformance with Senate rules. Watt was going to have to spend the next three weeks cramming for the biggest final exam of his life, and one of the tasks was to size up the opposition he could expect.

There was little doubt among Watt's advisors that Senator Dale Bumpers of Arkansas would be the most outspoken critic during confirmation hearings, and everyone agreed that the big question was going to center on Jim's feelings about preservation, particularly the National Parks. Watt and Mountain States had been prominent in a number of lawsuits with the Secretary of the Interior, but one would almost certainly concern Senator Bumpers: the Foundation had come to the defense of concessioners offering motorized expeditions down the Colorado River within Grand Canyon National Park in Arizona. Environmentalists had sued Interior to ban motors on the large river rafts used by the concessioners, complaining that motors were unnatural and spoiled the experience, interfering with "the sounds of silence." (Somehow, environmentalists think motorless rafts are perfectly natural even though less safe and controllable, and they don't seem to mind the 100+ decibel noise of the rapids, particularly Granite and Crystal Rapids, which can be heard from the Canyon's South Rim five miles away.) The truth of the matter was blurted out in 1972 by Sierra Club director Martin Litton in *Time-Life Books'* volume *The Grand Canyon*: "The only way we can save any wilderness in this country is to make it harder to get into, and harder to stay in once you get there." Litton expressed contempt for motor rafting because it's too easy, like climbing a mountain with the aid of a helicopter.

The first call Watt made that Thursday afternoon was to Doug Baldwin, Director of Communications at the Interstate Commerce Commission. Watt impressed upon him that discretion was imperative, asked if he would join the team, and had his public affairs man.

Now he needed a policy man for substantive issues, and Perry Pendley had proven he was on top of minerals policy just last Monday. When Watt's calls finally caught up with Perry on a speaking tour in Minnesota, the immediate reply was, "Of course I'll join your team. How can I help right now?" Watt had his policy man. Pendley and Baldwin would get together and begin the tedious process of digging out materials on past nominees and their confirmation experiences in order to brief Jim in the days to come.

In the next few days Watt called upon others. He needed help from someone familiar with his Bureau of Outdoor Recreation days. Emily DeRocco agreed to join his team, telling him, "I said you'd be back in Washington."

An old friend from earlier Interior days, William S. Heffelfinger, also agreed to help Jim with his confirmation briefing.

For a lawyer, Watt called upon Moody Tidwell III, who had been booted out of Interior by Cecil Andrus, and was now working in the Department of Labor. When Jim contacted him, Moody said, "I'll be delighted to join your family and come back to the real world." Senator Laxalt agreed to permit his own Legislative Assistant Sam Ballenger to take some time helping with Jim's briefing. Dave Russell, a Professional Staff Member of the Senate Committee on Energy and Natural Resources was tapped for his procedural expertise. With Steve Shipley who had been working with him back in Denver at Mountain States, Watt now had the solid core of a crack transition team. They were committed, but wouldn't really get rolling until the formal announcement of Jim's candidacy, which was now set for Monday, December 22.

Watt flew back to Denver the day after his meeting with President-elect Reagan with one main task in mind: to avoid the press before his formal nomination. Reaction would soon be filling the headlines, making for plenty of controversy without Jim adding to it. He resolved to avoid the pitfalls Hickel had fallen into.

It was no mean task. When Jim landed at Stapleton International Airport, Denver's *Rocky Mountain News* headlines blared "Denverite Is Top Candidate for Interior Post," much as the *Denver Post* had the day before. The Watt home in Englewood was swamped with calls and Jim's office at Mountain States was beseiged with reporters. Watt says of the time,

The pressure from the press was incredible. I couldn't get in or out of the office to close up my affairs there without practically being pushed to the ground by reporters. They tried everything—I wasn't even safe at home. It was one of the most awkward times of my life. I absolutely couldn't say anything until the President made the announcement.

By mid-week, the press realized they weren't going to get anything out of Jim Watt, and evenings he had some some quiet time for contemplation. Jim and Leilani would miss the West. They were old Washington hands, both of them, and had no qualms about handling the new assignment, but the life where they were was so good. They reminisced together, recalling their outdoor life in the Rockies most poignantly. Only last September they had spent many days in the wilderness. From the Bar Convention in Jackson Hole, Wyoming, they had floated the Snake River, then stayed in the high Rockies at a guest ranch for a couples Bible study retreat. Jim had gone on alone to run the Colorado River through Grand Canyon—in a motorized raft.

As he retold his adventure bounding down the Colorado between the sheer walls of Marble Canyon, real-life storm clouds were gathering in the headlines. Critical statements were moderate at first; regional Sierra Club representative Bruce Hamilton of Lander, Wyoming, said "In almost every legal action that we have taken up and down the Rockies, Mountain States has intervened on the other side." Then Bob Turner, regional representative of the National Audubon Society said, "I'm very concerned. I hope it doesn't mean a giveaway of the nation's resources."

While Jim recounted his experience camping by the clear blue pools at the base of the cliffs beside the mouth of the Little Colorado river, environmentalist rhetoric picked up a few octaves. William Turnage, director of the Wilderness Society said, "The appointment is disastrous. It appears that Reagan is paying off his political debts to the right wing with the environmental issue." Rafe Pomerance, director of the Friends of the Earth said, "I am astounded at the prospect. Watt has only represented those who want to undo the careful systems of wilderness protection so long in the making."

As Watt remembered his rest at a small oasis in the sere desert climate of Grand Canyon's Inner Gorge close by Deer Creek Falls, Bill Cunningham of the Wilderness Society in Helena, Montana, was saying, "Watt represents a naïve and simplistic philosophy. He represents the blind faith in technology of the large corporations who believe that we can develop our way out of resource scarcity." And a group of 12 large environmental groups sent a telegram to President-elect Reagan asking him "to find a nominee who can better try to represent the public interests in managing and conserving the nation's economic, cultural and natural resources."

President-elect Reagan acknowledged Watt's candidacy in a casual interview while carting some beef from a storage locker, saying, "Jim Watt has only opposed environmental extremists. I think he's an environmentalist himself, as I am."

Watt's candidacy was to be formally announced Monday, December 22, in Washington. When dawn broke that day, Watt met first with two of his transition team members for an extensive briefing. Doug Baldwin and Perry Pendley had gotten together a week earlier to begin the long and tedious process of gathering all the facts, scanning the public statements of past candidates, and putting together a clear set of introductory remarks. They warned Jim of the reactions to his candidacy that had already surfaced, and prepared suitable responses for the press conference that was to follow the announcement. Then there were phone calls to make and more people to gather for the transition team. The problem of finding the right Assistant Secretaries and Deputies was closing in.

The formal announcement would include five Cabinet selections: John R. Block to be Secretary of Agriculture; Samuel R. Pierce, Jr., to be Secretary of Housing and Urban Development; James B. Edwards to be Secretary of Energy; Jeane J. Kirkpatrick to be United States representative to the United Nations; and James G. Watt to be secretary of the Interior. Alexander Haig and Raymond Donovan, who had been named the preceding week, were also in attendance, and took part in the press conference.

And now America had its first public look at the future Secretary of the Interior. His opening statement was quiet and factual, with no hint of confrontation. Among the points he made were these:

The tremendous complexities and statutory requirements vested in the Secretary's office fill that job with conflict and controversy. The Secretary must have the ability, and the judicial perspective and temperament to evaluate conflicts. Acting under the law, he must choose actions that will insure common sense, balanced perspectives in managing lands and waters subject to the multiple-use concepts which have been hammered out by Congress.

My record will demonstrate my adherence to principle and my commitment to the fundamental values of America. My record will demonstrate that I have the balanced perspective necessary to manage America's natural resources.

Watt went into some detail outlining his career as an Interior officer for both the development and preservation side of the House. He also described his work with Mountain States Legal Foundation, saying "The foundation is to counterbalance those who use our judicial system to restrict economic growth and to defend individuals and the private sector from illegal and excessive bureaucratic regulation."

Watt closed his statement with these words:

I am a concerned Westerner, a concerned American. I want the federal and state governments to strike a balance between the development and protection of our natural resources. We can have reasonable development of our energy resources and preserve our natural environment, if we are given an opportunity to phase in, with proper safeguards, the expansion being demanded by the nation.

The press conference was not hostile; there were no loaded questions. When the show was over, Watt huddled again with Perry Pendley and Doug Baldwin. Baldwin gave him advice on an upcoming Wednesday press conference to be held in Denver, and Pendley made arrangements to fly to Denver the following week to brief Watt on confirmation matters. The transition team was to begin work in earnest, Watt instructed, making preparations for a full-day briefing session here in Washington just a day or two before the Senate hearings, which Senator McClure had by now scheduled for Wednesday and Thursday, January 7 and 8, 1981.

While Watt was flying back to Denver that evening, a *New York*

Times article presented excerpts from his opening statement and noted that William Turnage of the Wilderness Society had called him "a joke" and "a caricature of an anticonservationist" and said, "You would have to go back to Teapot Dome to find a Secretary of Interior so totally out of step with society."

The next day in Denver, Watt granted an interview to a reporter from the *Rocky Mountain News,* in which he was quoted on many policy changes he would bring to Interior: preventing the bureaucracy from usurping the power to manage public lands, stopping the delays in energy development that had stifled the Department in the past, his commitment to "the preservation of the best that remains in God's creation," and commenting on environmental groups, "I'll be able to work with those who have not damaged my hearing." Some of these remarks would be questioned by the Senate Energy Committee.

On Wednesday, Watt held a press conference at the Denver Hilton, speaking more substantively than at his public debut two days earlier. For one thing, the Indian issue had heated up: leaders of 176 tribes meeting in San Diego the previous Friday had endorsed a letter of protest against his nomination. They had been alarmed by Watt's amicus briefs in two cases, particularly *Merrion* v. *Jicarilla Apache Tribe* which asked the court to give non-tribal members equal rights with Indians in contracts covering tribal natural resources. Watt told reporters that he knew who his new boss was, and promised to urge the President to give Assistant Secretary rank to Indian Affairs, and to deal with tribes on a "government-to-government" basis (both promises have been kept completely). There was virtually no press notice, however, of the fact that numerous Indian tribes had supported Watt's nomination. Norm Wilson, tribal chairman of the 15,000 member Rosebud Sioux Tribe in South Dakota said the Indian opposition had been due to the fact that "some of our chairmen are staunch Democrats, and they're going through a period of crying in their beer, so to speak." The Rosebud Sioux, Colville Confederated Tribes, Papago, Coushatta, Tule River, Eastern Cherokee, San Carlos Apache, The Inter-Tribal Council (19 tribes), the Inter-Tribal Assembly (27 tribes), and many others including the Eskimos were enthusiastic Watt supporters. In the end, virtually the entire Native American community backed him once they heard his hearing testimony.

During this press conference Watt also told reporters that he would speed up the mineral inventory process which Congress had authorized years before to determine what mineral values our public lands held in reserve—an inventory that had never been carried out. He stressed, too, that water policy would not be run under his administration "with a hit list" as President Carter had done, "with bureaucrats from Washington calling the shots." He also instituted his "good neighbor" policy, saying "a good neighbor does not come in and dictate like an oppressive landlord," which Interior had done in recent years.

When asked about the growing environmentalist opposition, Watt replied, "They never supported President-elect Reagan and they probably never will." And referring to a *Washington Post* story by Dan Balz, Jim said, "An eastern paper identified me as an ideological soulmate of Ronald Reagan, and I can't think of a more flattering compliment." The question session was sharp, but not particularly hostile, and when Watt closed the conference, he and Steve Shipley quickly left the room, refusing to answer further questions by saying, "The issues are too sensitive to be discussed now. Any public comments should not jeopardize my ability to carry out President Reagan's wishes in changing the Department."

Reports had been coming from Interior staff members that they feared reprisals and massive firings, and environmentalist groups pumped up these reports as a confirmation issue. As Watt strode briskly down the hall, a reporter stuck a microphone in his face and asked, "What's your strategy for the confirmation hearing?" He smiled and replied curtly, "To be responsive."

The last week in December Perry Pendley flew in to Denver from Washington and stuffed Watt's mind with facts and figures. There was only one small respite from this information overload, and it was no picnic. Watt had put a high priority on arranging a meeting with environmental group representatives to see if some kind of detente could be worked out. His old friend and opponent, Tony Ruckel of the local Sierra Club, had agreed to arrange a breakfast meeting Tuesday, December 30. He knew Ruckel from several cases, and in one instance, Jim had copied some language from several Sierra Club complaints and combined it into a single lawsuit against the Secretary of the Interior about wild horses overgrazing public lands, and had asked the Sierra Club to join him in the suit to fight together for a change. Ruckel had said, "Jim, I don't want to get into that case with you. It would hurt my fundraising, but I'm sure you can handle the case and do a good job by yourself."

A mob of aggressive reporters got wind of the meeting and tried to force their way in with the 16 environmentalists who showed up. All parties to the meeting firmly told the press to leave their hotel meeting room, which they did. After introductions all around, breakfast was served and Watt invited the environmentalists to tell or ask him anything that might be on their minds, promising to be absolutely candid. For two straight hours he listened and answered. On some questions, such as the acid rain issue, he found himself embarrassed and frankly told the group that he was uninformed on the subject, but would be willing to listen to their views. After exhaustive probing on policy, on his background and on his intentions, both sides were satisfied with the session. It looked like a bridge could be built.

Watt told the group that he was not going to talk to the press outside: "This has been too important a meeting to me," he said, "but you do what you want." As the environmentalists worked their way through the waiting barrage of cameras and microphones, they had the opportunity to denounce him—but did not. Ruckel answered questions with generalities: "Mr. Watt does not know many of the leaders of the environmental community, and this was a get-acquainted session to exchange views." He added that everyone had paid their own way at $5.00 each for breakfast. In parting, Ruckel remarked, "I'm still looking forward to the Senate confirmation hearing. I want to hear more." Watt was to learn from this experience that the local groups of large environmental organizations are much more pragmatic and reasonable than the centralized paid staffs, and later came to count on these local people for input and practical discussion throughout the United States.

Sunday, January 4, 1981, Watt was in Washington. He had soaked up as much as he could from Pendley's briefing sessions. Now he was in the center of power. The confirmation vote was looking very favorable. Only an unexpected bombshell or gross mishandling of the hearing could keep him out of office. But James G. Watt was determined that he would not give the store away. He hoped the Senate would take him whole or not at all. And that would require unprecedented preparation.

Today was the day for that preparation. His transition team had devised a mock hearing, an advance practice session that would come as close as they could to the actual questions and comments likely to come from the Senate Committee on Energy and Natural Resources only two days later. Seven team members were present: Doug Baldwin, who had researched all press releases on candidates for Secretary of the Interior going back to Stewart Udall; Sam Ballenger, Legislative Assistant for Senator Laxalt, who had been detailed to provide legislative expertise; Emily DeRocco, who had dug up all the confirmation hearing testimony of past candidates and analyzed it for mistakes and blunders; William S. Heffelfinger, an old friend from earlier days at Interior (he is now Assistant Secretary for Management and Administration in the Department of Energy); Perry Pendley, for advice on minerals policy; Dave Russell, who had come from a Professional Staff Member spot on the Senate Energy Committee with extensive procedural savvy; and Moody Tidwell III, an outstanding legal mind.

The mock hearing team gathered at the Hay-Adams Hotel on the corner of 16th Street N.W. and H Street, a venerable building overlooking Lafayette Square to the south, and the White House beyond. The team had discovered that so many issues were likely to be raised that it would be impossible to address them all, much less do an in-depth briefing—but that Sunday morning Watt intuitively saw the right answer. He said:

Pick the issues of widest national significance. Brief me in-depth on those. Don't tell me a thing about the Alaska National Interest Lands Act, for example: we could hold an entire hearing on that alone. And someone's likely to try to push me into a corner on issues that we can't decide upon yet. Brief me on what matters to America most and brief me on the problems we can solve wisely. The rest we'll leave to Interior's career professionals and future deliberations.

So they did. The transition team opened the mock hearing with Jim's prepared statement, which emphasized his experience in Interior, his qualifications to run the Department, and fully disclosed his activities with Mountain States Legal Foundation.

Ballenger and Russell, both Senate-wise veterans, knew which Senators would come on strong, and tried to anticipate some of their questions: What about oil drilling off Georges Banks near the Massachusetts coast? The U.S. Geological Survey says there are 128 million barrels in that deposit, which is only a 7-day supply for America, but the fishery there could be destroyed by a well-head blowout like the one in Mexico's Campeche Bay which polluted the Texas coast a few years earlier. And what about the windfall profits tax on petroleum producers benefiting from crude oil price deregulation? And what about the severance tax on coal that is levied by several Western States, and which raises the price for customers in other states?

And what about the wily Senators who would undoubtedly try to get Watt to disqualify himself from any Interior business that might relate to Mountain States Legal Foundation to avoid any possible conflict of interest? How could their thrust be resisted?

Then there were the procedural details: Had Jim submitted his financial disclosure report? Had he shown that his net worth was only $65,000, second lowest in the Reagan Administration's millionaire Cabinet? Had he sent everything necessary to the U.S. Office of Government Ethics?

The mock hearing wore on and on and the practice issues and answers piled higher and higher. Lunch was brought in, and then dinner. One after another, the team tried to nail Watt down on issues that would lure him into inflammatory statements or into making concessions that might limit his ability to run the Department. It was late evening before everyone was satisfied that their candidate was properly briefed. They had covered everything from keeping professional leadership in the National Parks to plans for the Office of Surface Mining to the qualifications that should be required for

Eastern Wilderness Areas, and everything in between. As Emily DeRocco later said, "Jim Watt was the best briefed candidate for any Cabinet position in American history. I'd recommend it highly for anybody going before the Senate." Even so, there were to be a few surprises and unanswerable questions on Wednesday.

Watt spent the Monday and Tuesday before his hearing paying last-minute courtesy calls to key Democratic Senators, going over any problems or concerns they might like to discuss with him. It is common Congressional courtesy for Senators to discuss their points of attack privately with Cabinet candidates ahead of time to give them fair warning; only rarely does some shocking revelation hit a Cabinet designate cold. Watt spent an hour with Democratic Senator Gary Hart of Colorado, who later said of the meeting, "He wasn't a rigid ideologue. In person, Watt is more pragmatic than his image, and he understands that his responsibility as Secretary will be different from his responsibilities as head of a legal advocacy group." But Senator Hart was still undecided about how he would vote on Watt's confirmation, and he did not warn him about a little bombshell that he planned to drop in the hearing, a bombshell he was tipped off about from two environmentalists, Ron Wolf and Tim Lange.

Watt also visited Senator Jackson, Senator Tsongas and Senator Bumpers. Senator Bumpers welcomed the nominee into his office and had a very candid conversation with him: "In fairness to you," said the Senator from Arkansas, "so that you won't think I am springing on you tomorrow, I would like to tell you what my concerns are so you can be thinking about it before you appear before the Committee tomorrow," and gave Watt a laundry list of issues that worried him, including the Sagebrush Rebellion's insistence on transferring federal lands to state ownership, and Jim's plans for the National Parks. As it turned out, even though Senator Bumpers was Watt's harshest critic in the hearing, he was as good as his word and presented no surprises.

Senator Henry M. "Scoop" Jackson had passed the gavel of the Energy and Natural Resources Committee to Senator James McClure as a result of the 1980 elections that brought a Republican majority to the Senate. But Senator Jackson would still be the ranking minority member of Watt's confirmation committee, and it was essential to stand inspection before this vastly experienced and exceedingly professional legislator.

The private meetings of ideological opponents in government are not always the icy or heated confrontations of television melodramas. In fact, cordiality and courtesy are the hallmarks of true professionals in the trade, regardless of their genuine commitment to their causes or their public statements. The little ceremonies and social graces are the grease that makes it possible for the wheels of Washington to turn at all, even if with somewhat deliberate speed. Watt found Senator Jackson to be a true professional, and their discussion focused mainly on Jim's connection to Mountain States Legal Foundation and the avoidance of any conflict of interest.

Among the last visits in Watt's round of courtesy calls was one paid to Senator Paul Tsongas of Massachusetts. The White House guide who had accompanied him on these Senatorial visits said "You two are going to have an instant dislike for each other: your philosophies are at opposite poles." Watt gritted his teeth and decided, "Okay, we'd better get it over with." It was 6:30 P.M. on Tuesday night anyway. There was to be a white-tie reception for the nominee at the Library of Congress Annex Reception Hall, but he had decided not to go—he'd save his strength for the ordeal tomorrow. He'd try to be friendly with Tsongas and get home to rest as soon as possible.

When they were shown into the Senator's office and shook hands, a highly unlikely event took place. Watt says, "We took an instant liking to each other. It shocked him and it shocked me and it shocked my White House guide. I really did like the guy."

Their conversation rambled over many subjects, with light spots of humor and shared chuckles, but they both realized they were men of deep if opposing principle, and Paul Tsongas seriously asked Jim to imagine himself four years from now at a farewell dinner, and to describe how he'd like to be remembered by those imaginary conservationists and developers gathered to bid him a hypothetical farewell.

Watt insisted that such a farewell might just be eight years away—to the amusement of Paul Tsongas—but addressed himself to the question, giving this answer in a way that only Jim Watt can convey ideas, evoking a certain austere beauty of thought embracing man and nature:

Senator Tsongas, I would first like the conservationists to say upon my retirement from the Department of the Interior that "Here was a man who loved the land that nurtured him. He believed deeply in stewardship and conservation. He did address his charge as a good steward. While we did not agree with him entirely, we understood what he was doing and we respected the integrity and commitment he brought to the job."

Then I would like the developers to say, "You, Mr. Watt, were a hard-knuckled administrator and you made things happen in a land-developing agency upon which so much of America is dependent."

And finally I would like America to say, "You, James Watt, were the catalyst to bring together the forces within our system to put together a meaningful strategic minerals policy that made America a better and stronger nation. Your friends were right: we had no reason to fear you."

Senator Tsongas was impressed, and replied, "Jim Watt, I'm going to frame that answer and save it for that dinner, so don't you forget what you said."

Wednesday, January 7, dawned clear and cold. Watt was scheduled to appear only one day if everything went well. Thursday would be filled with testimony from other witnesses. This would be his only chance to convince skeptics, his only chance to defend himself prior to committee recommendation and floor debate in the Senate later in the month. This was it.

The Committee convened at 10 A.M. in Room 3110 of the Dirksen Senate Office Building across from the Capitol. The room was an incredible jam—dozens of still photographers, dozens of reporters carrying tape recorders, hundreds of observers. Out of the roar of voices an aide of Oregon Senator Mark Hatfield was heard to say in open-mouthed amazement: "I've never seen 17 television cameras at a Senate hearing before, never!" It was the most heavily reported and attended confirmation event of the Reagan Cabinet selection process, and perhaps of all U.S. history.

Chairman McClure gaveled the meeting to order and made the opening statement. His words set the tone for the entire hearing: "We are a great and powerful nation, with vast intellectual, natural and spiritual resources. Yet we are a nation literally and figuratively held hostage today by our crippling dependence on foreign oil and gas. We are also a nation already dramatically dependent upon foreign sources for critical and strategic minerals. This dependency will only increase to more dramatic and crippling dimensions in the decade ahead, given our current posture." There was no doubt whose side he was on in this hearing.

Ranking minority committee member Senator Jackson warned that the role of the Secretary of the Interior had changed radically in the past two decades: "No longer is he the guardian of narrow Western interests, but is now the steward of public lands for all Americans."

Then began the long purple patches of introductory rhetoric that precede the business of these inquisitorial get-togethers. Friends and allies in the Senate rose to give Jim an introduction which was understood as an endorsement of his candidacy: Senators Wallop, Domenici, Melcher—a Democrat who mostly wanted to get the IRS forms on Mountain States proving their tax-exempt status, but who did say he was "inclined" to support Jim's nomination—Murkowski and Simpson spoke eloquently of Jim's abilities.

Although not on the committee, Senator Armstrong of Colorado and Congressman Cheney of Wyoming also spoke up for their friend, Jim Watt. Senator Warner, seeing these Westerners at the same table with Jim, asked, "Are all men from Wyoming tall and bald?" More than two hours elapsed before the subject of all the adulation got to say a single word. Then, in typical Watt fashion, the nominee started out on a light-hearted note: "If it were appropriate, Mr. Chairman, I would like to move that the committee adjourn and act on the record that has just been presented."

Chairman McClure, replied, "I don't blame you for that request, but I rather suspect the record will be amplified before we get to that point."

Watt was sworn in, and read his opening statement in its entirety, repeating many of his comments from the December 22 announcement of his candidacy, but going into considerable detail on his role at Mountain States Legal Foundation (MSLF), which as expected, was to raise serious questions from the Democrats of the hearing committee. Watt had an aide pass out to the hearing committee an analysis of all 47 cases handled by MSLF under Watt's leadership. Each case was named and the public-interest issue it turned on was described.

The first to question Jim was Senator Jackson, who began an insistent push to make Watt disqualify himself from any case affecting Interior and MSLF, past or future, asking, "Would it be wise for you to participate in making a decision where the foundation is a party?"

Time and again in this hearing, Watt would try to deflect this thrust. He replied, "Simply to tie your hands behind your back because at some future time something might come up and then be unable to assume the responsibilities you would have taken an oath to do would be disrespectful of the office and not a proper approach at all."

To which Senator Jackson retorted, "I disagree with you."

Here we see a strategic decision. Watt knew full well that he could not prevail over Senator Jackson's demands. He also knew that he could not afford to make such a vital concession at the very outset of his hearing—it would multiply the pressure from other Senators on more crucial issues. The next day Watt sent a written agreement to recuse himself from all past and future cases between Interior and MSLF—but not cases involving firms that had contributed funds to the foundation. ("Recuse" is a legal term meaning to disqualify one's self as a judge.) The written agreement satisfied most critics.

Issue after issue was put to Watt. Senator Domenici brought up Jim's attitude toward the Indians, making sure that he understood correctly Watt's intent to follow President-elect Reagan's policy of self-determination and economic development for all American tribes, to which Watt replied, "Without reservation." Gales of laughter erupted at the unintended pun, and Jim sheepishly said, "May we back up on that? I want the Indians to have control of their reservations and I support it enthusiastically—maybe that's better!" More laughter and applause.

Many Senators who were not on the Energy and Natural Resources committee submitted written questions that Watt was required to answer, 204 queries in all, which kept Watt, Perry Pendley and a core staff busy for more than a week after the hearing.

The introductions had taken so long that only two Senators had time to question the nominee before lunch break. The fact that mobs of people were jamming the halls outside the hearing room prompted Chairman Mc-Clure to move the afternoon session to room 1202, which was much larger.

When the hearing reconvened at 2 P.M., the real battle began. Senator Bumpers led off with probing questions, thinly concealing his opposition toward Watt's candidacy. He said, "This is not an adversary proceeding, but obviously there are some things about your background that cause me some concern," and proceeded to interrogate Jim on many hard issues, but not before he read into the record an 1855 letter from the eponymous Chief Sealth, for whom the city of Seattle was named, written to President Pierce, which stands as a masterpiece of eloquent nature writing:

The Great Chief in Washington sends word that he wishes to buy our lands. How can he buy or sell the sky? The wealth of the land? The idea is strange to us.

We don't own the freshness of the air, or the sparkle of the water, so how can he buy them from us? Every part of the earth is sacred to my people; every shining pine needle, every sandy shore, every mist in the dark woods, every clearing and humming insect is holy in the memory and experience of my people.

We know the white man does not understand our ways. One portion of the land is the same to him as the next, for he is a stranger who comes in the night and takes the land, whatever he needs.

The earth is not his brother, but his enemy. When he has conquered it, he moves on. He leaves his father's grave and his children's birthright is forgotten. There is no quiet place in the white man's cities; no place to hear the leaves of spring or the rustle of insect wings. . . .

Whites, too, shall pass. Perhaps sooner than other tribes. Continue to contaminate your bed and you will one night suffocate in your waste.

The sacred corners of the forest are heavy with the sons of many men, and the views of the ripe hills blotted by talking wires. Where is the thicket? Gone. Where is the eagle? Gone.

And what is it to say goodbye to the swift and the hunt, the end of the living and the beginning of survival?

This haunting message from the past contains the essence of modern environmentalist sentiments about industrial civilization: only a destroyer, nothing more. But there is a missing concept in this plea that Senator Bumpers offered the committee: Sealth was saying goodbye to *his* culture, not to ours; to a way of life that modern environmentalists would be loath to endure for long, regardless how idyllic; a way of life with disadvantages as well as benefits, like ours; a way of life with annual hunger and death and endemic diseases; a way of life full of violence and slave raids, even possessing a carved club known as a "slave killer" from its use by disgruntled chiefs taking out frustrations on captives; a way of life built around the Potlatch custom in which wealth was used as a weapon to shame those who could not give as great gifts as others; a way of life without official Wilderness Areas—which are artifacts of civilization—without lawyers, without books, without all those things which are used but not appreciated by environmental advocates. It is easy to yearn for Sealth's world and his wisdom; it would not be so easy to live it—it was not easy for him either. But this vast cultural abyss was ignored by Senator Bumpers, who accepts the picture of Sealth's wisdom but would quickly reject living as Sealth lived. The Senator bore down, demanding to know what kind of policy he could expect from Interior in the next four years, particularly concerning preservation and selling off federal lands to Sagebrush Rebels. The Senator was astonished at Watt's answers:

One of the proud agencies with the Department of the Interior is the National Park Service. It would be my commitment and intention to keep it at the highest professional level.

I do not see the need now for massive transfers of land. The Sagebrush Rebellion is caused by the arrogant attitude of certain bureaucrats. Good management will defuse the Sagebrush Rebellion.

Then in turn, question after question came raining down from many Senators:

Senator Bumpers: Do you favor the Wilderness Act?

Mr. Watt: Absolutely.

Senator Ford: What is your definition of an environmental extremist?

Mr. Watt: An extremist is one who is intolerant and unwilling to consider another point of view, or recognize the need to balance the viewpoints in making a decision.

Senator Warner: What did you mean in the *Rocky Mountain News* interview by "I will be able to work with those who have not damaged my hearing"?

Mr. Watt: I think people can become so shrill that they lose their credibility and you cannot hear them. If someone is just continually screaming for their extreme position not recognizing any balance, you become immune to that.

Senator Humphrey: I would like to know your general feelings on exploration and development of the Outer Continental Shelf, especially in the Northeast.

Mr. Watt: Senator Johnston of Louisiana talked this morning about 30 years of successful offshore drilling experience in the Gulf of Mexico. I think with the technology and knowhow gained there that the dangers to the environment are much less.

Senator Bumpers: On the question of motor boats on the Colorado River and Grand Canyon, you know you will have to make that decision. You brought a lawsuit, and we know what the foundation feels. How do you feel?

Mr. Watt: I think before anyone makes a decision on that, they should have a hands-on experience so they know what they're talking about. I can address it because I floated that river in September. We need to allow motors on some of the boats, and we need to allow some to go down the river without them. There ought to be freedom of choice.

Senator East: We can have economic growth and if we don't have it we will not have a strong country, we are' not going to have a strong policy to compete effectively in a world of international policy.

Mr. Watt: My response to that is Amen.

Senator Melcher: Are you in favor of states having the right to their own siting act of energy facilities as a control?

Mr. Watt: Absolutely. I do not feel that some bureaucrat in Washington has the ability or the wisdom to make such decisions.

Senator Hart (who is not on the committee, but was granted the right to question the candidate): Your foundation filed an amicus brief having to do with the question of racial quotas and so on. I would offer you the opportunity to respond to a quote from a local newspaper in Denver dated October 6, 1977, on a racially-related issue: "As a white man, in 10 years I will be very hesitant to allow a black doctor to operate on me because I will always have the feeling that he may have been carried by the quota system." Do you want to identify the accuracy of that quote or add anything to it? (This was the bombshell Senator Hart's environmentalist friends planted)

Mr. Watt: I can certainly identify that it did happen. I stand against discrimination and I do not like the quota system. Nothing is to be gained by arguing with that quote yes or no.

Senator Hart: I think there is a lot to be gained if you didn't say it.

Mr. Watt: I can say it then. I think we ought to let it rest where it is and not try to make too much of it. It was your choice to bring it up, and it has been brought up, and it has been addressed, and there it rests.

In a *Denver Post* article headlined: "Denver Black Raps Hart for Racism Challenge of James Watt," Mr. Clark Watson took Hart to task for being a liberal who only thinks of blacks in a welfare context but never in an entrepreneuer setting. Watson said,

What Hart should have known was that Watt had been endorsed in December by a national black publication, *Energy Scene*. It is doubtful Gary Hart consulted anyone in the black community about their perceptions of Watt. Perhaps it did not suit the purposes of his environmentalist friends. He may have felt more comfortable consulting two early '60s vintage white radicals on black issues—Tim Lange,who heads a campus-oriented newspaper in Boulder which has never employed a black reporter . . . and Ron Wolf, part of the management of the now-defunct *Straight Creek Journal* [publisher of Watt's remarks about black surgeons], which too never employed blacks during its 7-year tenure. These tactics suggest Hart should more closely examine his own attitudes about race before accusing others of insensitivity.

On many hard questions, Watt would not allow himself to be pinned down or lured into an inflammatory answer. He had studied well the record of past nominees who had been manipulated into making concessions that strangled their ability to manage the Department. Thus he would give no hard-and-fast answers on oil shale development, federal water policies, Alaska policy, and he would not reveal the names of contributors to Mountain States Legal Foundation, just as the Sierra Club and Wilderness Society do not reveal the names of their funding sources. Senator Wendell Ford of Kentucky criticized him for "vagueness and evasion" but ultimately voted to confirm him.

When Watt's testimony was being wrapped up, Senator Bumpers was impressed: he said to Watt, "You have scored heavily with me two times: one is on your feelings about the Park Service; and the other is that you do not feel these lands ought to be sold or transferred to the states. Both of those came as very pleasant surprises."

Senator Tsongas said to Watt, "It is very easy for an environmentalist—and I consider myself one—to vote against you. The difficulty is crossing. I began a week ago disposed to vote against you. If I should end up voting for you, it is for one reason and one reason only, and that is I believed what you told me last night." Tsongas asked Watt to repeat for the record his remarks from the previous evening, and Jim accomodated his request.

Near the end of the day, environmentalists came forward to denounce Watt's candidacy. The environmental lobby is politically among the most savvy there is. They had counted the votes on Jim's confirmation and knew full well there was no possibility he would not be confirmed. Yet they decided, unquestionably with full deliberation and awareness, to savage Jim Watt's reputation. Did they expect better treatment after his confirmation? No. Did they expect their vilification of him to change his mind? No. I have seen similar matters deliberated from the inside of the movement; to me the answer is plain. A doomsday warning about Jim Watt is an opportunity to seize the moral high ground, and to perpetuate the myth that Interior has but one role: to preserve and never develop resources—and to rake in the money. As Tony Ruckel of the Sierra Club said in refusing to join Watt in a lawsuit against Interior, to cooperate would hurt his fundraising. The converse is also true: to create conflict with manufactured crises helps fundraising, but you have to paint Jim Watt as an environmental ogre first. However, some observers were not convinced. Senator Armstrong of Colorado said, "Critics who charge that Watt is an environmental ogre will find that their stance is not credible." And James Kilpatrick said it all in a *Washington Star* column: "The environmentalists found themselves cast in the unconvincing role of the pot that calls the kettle black. Mr. Watt, they cried, was an extremist. As the saying goes, it takes one to know one."

This is what a few of the environmentalists had to say—Brock Evans of the Sierra Club:

How can James Watt be a steward when he had spent the last three years attacking agencies which have been trying to advance stewardship? How can he suddenly find balance when the record is so one-sided? How can he now judiciously weigh competing claims when the language in favor of one side is so injudicious? How can he faithfully execute laws that he has derided and attacked?

David Brower of the Friends of the Earth:

Raymond Dassman, one of the world's best ecologists, said we are already in World War III, and we are winning it. It is the war against the Earth. From what I found out in looking at Mr. Watt's record, and hearing him today . . . were he to become Secretary of the Interior . . . the war against the earth would step up in pace and this country and the globe are not likely to reach the year 2,000 intact.

Russell Peterson of the National Audubon Society:

Mr. Watt's background makes him imminently unsuited for this position of guardian of our nation's natural resources. His actions and statements identify him as an aggressive, shortsighted exploiter, rather than a far-sighted protector, of the nation's air, land and water. Mr. Watt has distinguished himself as one of the most dedicated anti-environmentalists of the decade.

Gaylord Nelson of the Wilderness Society (who appeared Thursday):

Let me state our position at the outset: We are strongly opposed to this nomination and we are very gravely concerned for the future of America's wilderness and environmental integrity if Mr. Watt is confirmed.

At 7:15 P.M. the Wednesday hearings were recessed. The next day, Thursday, January 8, 1981, 23 people testified for Watt's confirmation and 5 testified against. Tom Kimball of the National Wildlife Federation claimed he was testifying neither for nor against and then proceeded to tear Watt up on one issue after another.

On the 14th of January, the Senate Committee on Energy and Natural Resources voted Watt's confirmation out of committee 16 to 0, with Senator Tsongas abstaining, recommending that Jim be confirmed by the Senate as a whole.

On January 22, two days after the inauguration of President Ronald Reagan, Watt's confirmation was debated on the Senate floor. Senator Bumpers warned that Watt "could do irreparable harm to our sacred lands." Senator Metzenbaum of Ohio predicted that Watt's confirmation would "send the wrong signal to the country, indicating a change of direction in favor of business interests." The Senate then voted to confirm James G. Watt as Secretary of the Interior by a margin of 83 to 12. The 12 dissenters were all Democrats; the supporters strongly bipartisan.

When Watt heard the news, he realized that the real confirmation battle had not been fought in the hearing chambers of the Senate, or in the Energy Committee's executive session, or on the Senate floor, or in the offices of various Senators, or in the mock hearing, or in press conferences, or in the councils of the environmental movement. It had been fought in the hearts and minds of men and women throughout America, and he had won. He was the Secretary of the Interior of the United States of America.

CHAPTER 4
THE RELIGIOUS WAR

The Religion of one seems madness to another.
—Sir Thomas Browne

The House of Representatives has no power to accept or reject Presidential appointees as does the Senate. However, it is traditional for each newly confirmed Secretary of the Interior to give an "Orientation Briefing" to the House Interior and Insular Affairs Committee to share his views, exchange ideas and get to know everyone. In mood, this orientation briefing is much the same as a Senate confirmation hearing, with the Congressmen doing the asking and the new Secretary the answering.

Watt went to his introductory session with this powerful House Committee on February 5, 1981, exactly two weeks to the day after his Senate confirmation. It was at this orientation that he made the now famous remark about his religious beliefs that led the press and environmentalist organizations to wage The Religious War: ". . . I do not know how many future generations we can count on before the Lord returns. . . ."

Of all the remarks that Jim Watt has been attacked for making, this one prompted one of the most incredible and unfair distortions of his career. What was he talking about? What actually went on in that session?

The orientation began at 9:50 A.M. in room 1324 of the Longworth House Office Building, with Congressman Morris Udall presiding. Jim's notorious comment came after more than two hours of interrogation by the whole committee, and it came in response to some queries by Congressman James Weaver of Oregon.

Mr. Weaver: Do you want to see on lands under your management, the sustained yield policies continued?
  Secretary Watt: Absolutely.
  Mr. Weaver: I am very pleased to hear that. Then I will make one final

74

statement. I happen to be one who thinks that while we made great strides in this nation to right the imbalances we are talking about, there is still imbalance on the other side in many ways, in many areas. I believe very strongly that we should not, for instance, use up all the oil that took nature a billion years to make in one century.

We ought to leave a few drops of it for our children, their children. They are going to need it just to eat, not to drive around in gas-guzzling cars, just to produce the food they will need.

I wonder if you agree, also, in the general statement that we should leave some of our resources—I am now talking about scenic areas or preservation, but scenic resources for our children? Not just gobble them up all at once?

Secretary Watt: Absolutely. That is the delicate balance the Secretary of the Interior must have, to be steward for the natural resources for this generation as well as future generations.

I do not know how many future generations we can count on before the Lord returns, whatever it is we have to manage with a skill to leave the resources needed for future generations.

Mr. Weaver: Mr. Chairman, I wanted to conclude, if I might, seeing the Secretary brought up the Lord, with a story.

The Chairman: The conversation will be in order.

Mr. Weaver: In my district, Mr. Chairman, there are some who do not like wilderness. They do not like it at all. I would try to plead with them. I go around my district and say do you not believe—I would plead with their religious sensibilities—that we should leave some of our land the way we received it from the Creator?

I have said this frequently throughout my district. I got a letter from a constituent right in the most conservative area in my whole district—and it is conservative. He said, "Mr. Weaver, if the Lord wanted to leave his forest lands, some of them in the way that we got them from Him," he said, "why did He send His only Son down to earth as a carpenter?"

(Laughter)

Mr. Weaver: That stumped us. That stumped us until one of my aides, an absolute genius, said that the Lord Jesus before He determined His true mission spent 40 days and 40 nights in the wilderness.

(Laughter)

The Congressmen were obviously not attacking Watt's beliefs. The session had been pointed, but not vicious. As the record shows, there was good humor all around. And Secretary Watt's comments were quite the opposite from the way in which they were later characterized in the press.

The *Washington Star's* religious editor Jim Castelli wrote: "Environmentalists already critical of Watt's policies saw the remark as a signal that he did not care about preserving the earth's resources for future generations."

The *Washington Post's* razor-tongued Colman McCarthy became positively livid, saying that if he got the theological drift of Watt's "pastoral vision," it was that all public lands were under "divine mandate to be bulldozed, levelled, drilled, mined and leased down to the last holy square yard." He called Jim's remarks "yawping preachments" and accused him of "baptizing his pro-exploitation policies in the waters of his selective Christianity."

Former Secretary of the Interior Cecil Andrus responded on National Public Radio to Watt's remark, "When we do have the Second Coming, I do not believe the Lord expects his place to be a barren desert used up by man."

Environmentalist journals uncoiled their own brand of attack. *Audubon* magazine of May 1981 published an article entitled "God, James Watt, and the Public's Land," written by Ron Wolf—the same environmentalist who, had written the article containing Watt's remarks about black surgeons that Senator Hart tried to drop as a bombshell in the Senate confirmation hearing. Wolf wrote, "Ronald Reagan may be his temporal leader, but Watt, by his own admission, will be receiving instructions for managing the 548 million acres under his control from God as well as the President," and repeatedly referred to Jim's religious beliefs in a caustic vein. Wolf's article drew many angry protests from Audubon Society members.

The Sierra Club's periodical *Sierra* also panned Watt's religious beliefs in their July/August 1981 issue:

Watt seems to think he has divine sanction for his efforts to turn our natural resources over to concessioners and developers. He has been quoted in *Time* magazine as saying, "My responsibility is to follow the Scriptures, which call upon us to occupy the land until Jesus returns."

Virtually every major environmentalist journal had something to say about Watt's religion, all of it scurrilous and abusive. Why did environmentalists so ferociously assail Jim Watt's fundamentalist Christian beliefs? The answer is that in the last 20 years environmentalism itself has become a religion in a real and structural sense. When Jim Watt raised the environmental debate above mere crass economics, he presented a competing moral belief system in the market place of ideas. Environmentalist leaders can tolerate crass economic arguments against their proposals, and even deign to use them in their own efforts to stop development—it does not threaten their moral high ground. But competing moral belief systems are intolerable. To environmentalist leaders, any opposing morality means war, religious war. Jim Watt simply happened to be standing first in line.

What do I mean by environmentalism becoming a religion in a "real and structural sense"? I mean that environmentalism over the past two decades has taken on more and more of the concrete features we find in traditional faiths until today it displays most if not all the behaviors of a religion. I mean that environmentalism has acquired the outward forms of ritual and worship on a secular plane that standard religions possess. If the particulars are different, the basics are not; remember that our word *religion* probably came from the Latin *religare*, to bind back, to tie to beliefs; environmentalism certainly contains beliefs its leaders want us bound to.

Nearly 20 years ago I noticed that environmentalist periodicals such as the Wilderness Society's *Living Wilderness* and *The Sierra Club Bulletin* were publishing an increasing number of articles with titles such as "A Theology of Earth" by the noted biologist Rene Dubos, "Ecology and Theology" by theologian Gabriel Fackre, and "The Spiritual Aspects of Wilderness" by naturalist Sigurd Olson.

I also found that even scientific studies of "wildernists" such as the U.S. Forest Service's *Wilderness Users in the Pacific Northwest—Their Characteristics, Values and Management Preferences* were applying such measurements as "esthetic-religious" to identify feelings hikers had about their experience in the backcountry.

When I first encountered this kind of belief, I could not precisely identify it; I have since realized that it is an example of the large family of beliefs called "nature mysticism."

As time went on, I noticed other symptoms of environmentalism shifting ground into a religious mold: it began to claim the powers of salvation and healing in very specific ways. Salvation was announced in 1962 by a posh Sierra Club coffee-table book with text by Thoreau called *In Wildness Is The Preservation Of The World,* displaying gorgeous nature photographs by the master Eliot Porter. About the same time, numerous articles in environmentalist journals began to pound the theme that active wildernists enjoy better physical health, gain a sense of renewal, and obtain relief from the emotional and psychic tensions of "dirty civilization." This amounts to a "psychic safety valve" theory of environmentalism, and was explored in detail in an article by psychiatrist Donald McKinley, M.D., entitled *Why Wilderness?* in the February 1963 issue of *Forest Industries* magazine.

McKinley's clinical experience included treating environmentalists, and convinced him that "In the wilderness, competition and suspicion seem to fade. . . . In the wilderness, man loses his identity from the man-made chaotic world and he forms a new perspective on his relations to other people and the environment around him," a more relaxed perspective. But the most significant point was McKinley's statement that "The emotional aspects of a wilderness experience might be compared to a religious experience. It is particularly valuable for those people whose unconscious associations of pain and discomfort in relationships to man render a deity in human form impossible. Christianity is unacceptable to some people because of the use of the human symbol, but some who can't accept Christ can gain a tremendous sense of peace from relating to uncontaminated areas." Dr. McKinley's insights begin to unfold a new perspective on environmentalist attacks on Jim Watt's fundamentalist Christianity.

And what about a missionary service? Do environmentalists try to convert and redeem The Great Unwashed? You bet they do. They publish attractive books and magazines to interest potential converts, they offer nature activities that set up and facilitate the "commitment event," they stir up negative feelings about "devilish" development, and they stage "revivals" at annual meetings and in membership campaigns with big-name endorsements from the inspired leadership like this one for the Wilderness Society by rich and famous nature photographer Ansel Adams: "I have witnessed one beautiful wild area after another destroyed by commercialism, political maneuvering and the distressing indifference of many of our citizens. . . . Please join me in this epic struggle against the selfish objectives of material gain."

One of the functions of religion is to provide feelings of moral superiority, and environmentalism certainly does that. We can see evidence of such feelings in Ansel Adams' arch remark about the "distressing indifference" of the unholy to his righteous cause. We see implications of moral superiority in an *Audubon* magazine article from July 1981 by Peter Steinhart called "Tough Times," which says that environmentalists "are elitists in that they fear a life in which men substitute speed for curiosity, sensation for knowledge, and mass culture for individuality."

Environmentalism also has a considerable body of dogma and ethical writings. The two central dogmas, as close as I can tell, are the "land ethic" of naturalist Aldo Leopold, and the "environmental ethic" that varies from writer to writer and has never been fully codified.

Aldo Leopold in the late 1940s suggested that the West needs a "new ethic" and explained that the history of moral judgment could be divided into three stages; first, the Ten Commandments which taught man's duty to other individuals; second, the later philosophies that taught man's duties to society; and third, the still lacking ethic that teaches man's duties to the land and its living things. His new ethic conceived of land not as a commodity that we own, but rather as a community to which we belong. He stated it thus: "It is inconceivable to me that an ethical relation to land can exist without love, respect and admiration for land, and a high regard for its value. By value, I of course mean something far broader than mere economic value; I mean value in the philosophic sense."

The land ethic was very influential in the environmental movement, but Leopold's statement is actually almost a definition of any kind of ethical treatment, and would be just as meaningful if the word "land" were replaced with some other noun, for example "industrial civilization." Consider: "It is inconceivable to me that an ethical relation to industrial civilization can exist without love, respect and admiration for industrial civilization, and a high regard for its value."

The environmental ethic is much tougher to define. It varies depending on who's writing about it. The clearest statement to date was made by Ian Barbour, a professor of both religion and physics, in his *Western Man and Environmental Ethics*. Two other commentaries may be of interest: Garrett Hardin's thoughtful *Exploring New Ethics for Survival,* and the somewhat wild-eyed version in *Environmental Ethics* by the Science Action Coalition with Albert J. Fritsch.

Ian Barbour boiled down the diverse historical sources of the environmental crisis to four root causes. Here is a paraphrase of his causes and comments:

1. *Attitudes toward nature.* Our attitudes have been influenced by Western religion and culture, and have contributed to man's devastation of the earth.

2. *Economic institutions since the Industrial Revolution.* Industry creates ecological destruction and must be changed by legislative and political means.

3. *Technologies.* The use of raw materials and creation of waste products must be improved to conserve natural resources, reduce pollution and recycle wastes.

4. *Growth in population and living standards.* Ever-increasing environmental demands consume natural resources; growth is a problem. Stability demands changes in values and social institutions.

With this stage setting, Barbour proposed five themes of the environmental ethic that were basically a reaction to the environmental crisis. To paraphrase:

1. *Interdependence.* There is new recognition of man's dependence on the environment, and awareness of the limited capacity of the earth to absorb the by-products of civilization.

2. *Man's unity with nature.* Man is inseparable from nature.

3. *Finite resources.* There are fixed amounts of all natural resources, tillable soil, oil reserves, mineral ores, air, water, and so forth; these limits can be exceeded by the demands of exponential growth to the detriment of man and nature.

4. *The control of technology.* Uncontrolled technology is the main threat to the earth, and many feel that individual liberties must be sacrificed to meet social responsibilities; the social costs of any product must be paid by users, strict controls must be put on air and water effluents, materials must be recycled, and new technologies must be assessed politically before they can be permitted to become vested interests.

5. *Social justice*. Poverty and pollution are linked as products of our economic institutions such as private property. Changes in political power are necessary before technology can become an equitable instrument for human welfare.

This summary of the environmental ethic was gleaned by Barbour from the writings of all the major environmental commentators; it is not his original thesis, but it is the most honest statement of the ethic I have seen, and the most understandable. It is obvious that certain aspects of the land ethic and the environmental ethic are incompatible with numerous American ideals, for example, the protection of individual liberties and an open society. Social and political changes are envisioned by these ethics that would harm those ideals, a fact which some environmentalists try to deny, hide or confuse. What would happen, for example, to the economic and political structure of our society if land were not a commodity that could be owned, bought, and sold?

By 1970, environmentalism thus had all the trappings of a religion: inspired leaders and true believers, revered dogmas and irreproachable beliefs, a system of ethics, standards of personal morality (voluntary simplicity), a sense of awe and cosmic unity, community bonds, a sense of distinctiveness and moral superiority to non-believers, promises of salvation and healing, the urge to convert and redeem others as expressed in a missionary service to unbelievers, apocalyptic visions of the end of the world—and even a number of denominations preaching variations on the central dogma: the Sierra Club, Wilderness Society, Audubon Society, National Wildlife Federation, Izaak Walton League, National Parks and Conservation Association, and other houses of nature worship, in the exact sense of worship as respect, admiration or devotion to an object of esteem. This is not to say that environmentalism is only a religion: it is not. But it does have many religion-like features and behaves in many ways exactly like a religion.

Ultimately, the religion of environmentalism made nature sacred, and that idea is rejected by many Christians including Watt—only God is sacred in their view, yet the earth is to be "kept and dressed" by good stewards as well. Watt's fundamentalist Christianity *had* to be attacked, because the idea of a sacred nature has certain political advantages: if nature is sacred, any environmental issue becomes a moral issue, and since most of us want to be moral, the issue is easier to win from the moral high ground. Thus the truth of the matter is that behind the doctrinal wrangling of The Religious War raged an intense political war.

The truer truth, I think, lies in what really happened on the way to modern environmentalism, and that can only be given to us by a patient and perceptive historian of the movement. Fortunately, such a person has shown up and devoted a good many months of study to the records, notes, personal memos, correspondence, and bulletins of several key environmental groups, some dating from the last century. Her name is Susan Schrepfer and she discovered that traditional Christian thought had a powerful shaping impact on the Sierra Club, the Save The Redwoods League, and other groups—a fact which may come as a surprise even to their modern leaders.

In the April 1980 issue of the *Journal of Forest History,* Schrepfer's article "Conflict in Preservation" told an illuminating story. "Historical narration," Schrepfer began, "often neglects the fact that the politics of individuals and groups reflects their philosophic assumptions and that, when beliefs change, behavior changes." In this manner she introduced her discovery that the Sierra Club and the Save The Redwoods league once shared the common vision of a progressive and benevolent world which gave them similar attitudes about the function of a park and the need for economic development and political moderation. Schrepfer found that when the battle to create a Redwood National Park erupted in the 1960s, the Sierra Club had lost its earlier vision and was drawn to a premonition of environmental doom in a universe that lacked order and direction, and had adjusted its politics accordingly—only to find that its old ally, the Save The Redwoods League, had not changed its worldview and had now become an antagonist.

When the Sierra Club was founded in 1892, Schrepfer explained, Christians were still reeling under the assault of Darwin and the theory of evolution. Many of the Club's founders were both Christians and scientists. One Club founder, Joseph LeConte, a University of California paleontologist, tried to reconcile his idea of God with his knowledge of natural law. LeConte saw God as having both a real, independent existence and a presence in nature. He saw man as having two natures, the animal and the spiritual. And he saw nature as the result of design. His study of the fossil record as a paleontologist convinced him that long spans of time had indeed elapsed since the world was formed, but he saw it as God's work. To him, evolution was creation, "the conception of the one infinite, all-embracing design, stretching across infinite space." The universe to LeConte had a direction; the very existence of man proved that evolution moves toward greater physical and spiritual development.

LeConte was not alone in his view of progressive design in nature: Sierra Club officers such as naturalist John Muir, business leader Duncan McDuffie, professor of theology William Badè, and Stanford University President David Starr Jordan influenced the organization with similar conceptions. When the Save the Redwoods League was founded in 1918, its leaders were of the same persuasion. The two groups were headquartered across the street from each other in San Francisco; they were close physically and spiritually.

Their religious beliefs, which were based on traditional Christianity, had definite policy consequences. League president John Campbell Merriam preached reconciliation of religion and evolution like LeConte, and saw science verifying the existence of a central, moral vision in the universe. If the world was progressive and the human intellect was the highest product of directional evolution, then our mastery of the world must be beneficial. These men in the Club and the League felt that parks were temples within which to worship the creator of a universe of continuity and design. They had faith in divine will and faith in human progress and thus balanced their preservationist philosophy with respect for technology. Bordered, improved and well-traveled parks would complement a rapidly industrializing civilization in a universe that tended toward the good. Man was not the destroyer of worlds—rather he was the enhancer of life. In their official view, most lands would be used. Only unique examples of the greatest scenic wonders would be saved. And that, believe it or not, is the way the Sierra Club thought and behaved for more than two-thirds of its history.

Until the late 1940s, in fact, the Sierra Club rarely came into conflict with resource users; indeed they acknowledged no polarization between the preservationist and the entrepreneuer. Industrial corporations were not necessarily evil. Bestor Robinson, a Sierra Club president and director in the '30s and '40s, said this: "Never let your love of nature overshadow your concern for human needs. I want wilderness to contribute to the American way of life." One should fight for wilderness, in this view, but know when to compromise, based on the priorities implied by purposeful, progressive evolution.

But in 1949, "Young Turks," led by Richard Leonard and David Brower, in the power hierarchy of the Sierra Club began to challenge this balanced and reasonable approach to preservation. Despite charges from board members that they were going against founder John Muir's wishes, these two young radicals succeeded in deleting from the bylaws of the Club its original intent "to render accessible the mountains," and mounted a hardnosed campaign to block all proposed roads into new areas. These two men saw that roads brought more people into areas of wild country, and saw it leading to crowded parking lots and heavily-peopled campsites. The prospect infuriated them. The Club had previously supported roads throughout the Sierra Nevada of California, up Tenaya Canyon into Little Yosemite, across Kearsarge Pass and into Kings Canyon National Park. Now the Club vigorously opposed any new access. The new leadership also encouraged the spread of the Club into neighboring states, accompanied by deep misgivings from the Board; the very nature of the Club was shifting to something else.

By 1960 the Sierra Club was national in scope. No longer young, David Brower was now executive director. He deliberately advocated extremism, saying, "In today's world one must be either paranoid or naïve." He was not naïve; he refused to sanction even limited progress or the perpetrators of such. As historian Schrepfer said, based on Brower's private memos and public statements: "He relished being called an extremist. *Extremism* meant distrust of authority, public attacks on misguided expertise, and avoidance of compromise." Now the Club began to reject the leadership of those members active in industry who had long supported it financially. The Club also rejected its old policy of cooperation with developers in the selection of alternative sites.

What had brought such drastic changes within a single decade? Was it the increasing population pressure on wilderness use? Was it increasing abuse by developers? Only partially, says historian Schrepfer. Her in-depth study says it came as a result of changes in philosophic outlook. During the 1950s and '60s, the traditional view of a progressive universe of divine design had been replaced with a kind of philosophical naturalism. While the older view demanded faith in a higher intelligence, empirical evidence only supported the belief that randomness characterized the universe. The natural sciences no longer seemed to offer proof that man's brain and technology were the crowning achievement of evolution. Biology only revealed interdependence, specialization and adaptation, but allowed no judgment as to superiority of species. Man was now seen as an accident of the chance-filled course of genetics. Man was no better than a grasshopper or an amoeba. The vision had been lost.

Club member and naturalist Loren Eisley gave poetic expression to this new view in many publications. Man, he said, was not the master of the cosmos; he could not escape nature. Wilderness held answers to more questions than man yet knew or might ever know how to ask. The role of the scientist is only to understand, never to seek to master nature. Man's outward thrust must be merely a programmed response, a natural mechanism as a means of spreading, as with spores, disease. To Eisley, the disease spores were the "ticky-tacky" housing that Pete Seeger loved to sing about and the Sierra Club saw "obliterating fields, orchards, meadows."

And again, the Club's basic philosophy controlled its concrete policy. Now the Sierra Club saw federal power as the only answer strong enough to preserve what was left. Lobbying Congress to pass the Wilderness Act became the top priority, and building a strong centralized government became an explicit part of policy. In 1968 the Club convinced Congress to seize private lands for a public park for the first time in American history. From then on the thrust was to forge an environmental empire and to foster the social and political change necessary to bring it about.

The story of the Save The Redwoods League is entirely different. The League from its very beginnings in 1918 directed its efforts to private fundraising and the purchase of prime parklands from willing sellers. As Schrepfer notes, "The League shunned publicity hostile to the lumbermen and went to great lengths to acquire lands through negotiation rather than through eminent domain. . . . They believed that Americans should earn their parks through philanthropy and state funding." In fact, the League of the 1930s felt that the New Deal was creating parks without adequate consideration and was spending money too freely. Schrepfer writes: "League members were disgusted by the 'cheap showmanship' of the National Park Service, its rampant acquisition of low-quality parks, and the sapping of states' rights" by federal takeover of state lands.

The League successfully lobbied the California legislature in 1929 to establish a state park system and authorize the first park bond issue. Together, the state and the Save The Redwoods League established Humboldt, Prairie Creek, Jedediah Smith, and Del Norte Redwoods state parks. When the Sierra Club in the 1960s was preparing to fight for a Redwood National Park, they came to the Save The Redwoods League to work again with their old friend—but found a new enemy.

The Sierra Club wanted to seize private timberlands for a public park. The League stuck to its honorable principles of putting their money where their mouth was; they preferred to buy private lands and then donate them to government bodies for permanent management. The Club wanted a 90,000-acre park in remote Redwood Creek. The League argued that Redwood Creek's steep slopes sprouted even-aged stands a mere 400 years old and were mixed with Douglas fir and other species—and besides, it was in a watershed that would only be half in public ownership at best, and forever be subject to erosion from the industrially owned forests upstream. The Club wanted Congress to authorize $160 million in court settlements to the firms from which the new park would be seized. The League argued that their site in Mill Creek near Highway 101 was pure redwoods nearly 1,000 years old, and their 42,000-acre park would cost only $60 million, a more likely sum since Congress had never appropriated more than $35 million for a single park purchase. The bickering was endless, and the Sierra Club finally decided to ignore the League's expertise and began their planned campaign to besmirch the reputation of the businesses that owned the land they wanted for a park in order to gain public support for their position, a move which disgusted members of the League.

In early 1967, the Sierra Club began a masterful pressure campaign. They hit the theme "The Last Redwoods" hard, even though the original 2-million acre forest was still growing redwoods—all but about 4 percent (which were in parks) were owned by individuals or lumber companies. The Club held out for the big remote Redwood Creek park, even though President Johnson favored the League's Mill Creek park. The Club ran ads in six major newspapers, saying, "Mr. President: There is one great forest of redwoods left on earth; but the one you are trying to save isn't it."

Here the Sierra Club sang for the first time the song that America would make into a hit again and again: So what if it's private property? We want it, and we're going to get it. As Schrepfer described the Club's campaign:

Club leaders also believed their "extremism" to be justified because this was a clear case of the people versus the interests. Their publicity urged Americans to stand up for their rights and provided coupons to convey this popular will to Congress. A rejection of Redwood Creek would place the interests of the "powerful and wealthy" above those of the American people.

The Sierra Club won, and the American people won, and Redwood National Park was established in 1968. Then in 1977 the whole battle was fought again, this time to expand the park to twice its original size. Once more the Sierra Club won and the American people won. The "powerful and wealthy" weren't so powerful after all—and not so wealthy by about 70,000 acres of timberlands. The original price tag of $160 million went over the top to more than $1 billion. But the Sierra Club didn't have to pay for it; when you promote a billion-dollar park for the American people, the American people get to pay for it. More than 2,400 American people paid for it with their jobs and their way of life. It was a genuine golden fleece. The dollar price tag is still going up for that park because it's still in court after all these years, and to add insult to injury, Redwood is one of the least-visited National Parks in the system.

The Redwood National Park issue couldn't have come out any other way; it too was a religious issue to the American people. We didn't care about economics. We didn't care that there was an alternative site available from the Save The Redwoods League at a lower dollar price and no job loss price. It was a power play based on religious fervor. The tactic was used in dozens and dozens of other areas. Santa Monica Mountains National Recreation Area will likely cost over $1 billion before its seized lands are paid for. National Park Service expert Ric Davidge says there is a $3.2 billion *backlog* of debts authorized by Congress for Park acquisition with funds not yet appropriated, much of which will go eventually to pay off thousands of victims of environmentalist land grabs—eventually, eventually.

From 1968 to today, when these victims have spoken up to protect their lives and property, environmentalists have chided them for being selfish. The classic comment of this type came from scientist Denis Puleston in an article for *The New Scientist* complaining about "anti-ecologists": "By the use of such specious arguments as the loss of jobs, the lowering of living standards, and the raising of prices, they are endeavoring to turn the citizens away from those who are striving to save a viable environment for future generations." Environmental Protection Agency Administrator Russell E. Train was right, I think, when he said in 1977, "Environmental activists must become more sensitive to the real-life concerns of others, particularly when it comes to jobs, economic well-being, and adequate profits."

The religious fervor of environmentalists is a fact America must face up to. It is revealed in uncompromising demands that preservation always come before economics. It is revealed in emotional pressure campaigns that knowingly distort the facts, the options and the consequences of preservation. It is revealed in the unbroken string of legislative and litigative victories chalked up by environmentalist groups since the Wilderness Act of 1964. The symbols of environmental sanctity must be made clear and understood if we are to avoid being made the unwitting pawns of devout but unwise advocates who could destroy today in the name of building a better tomorrow.

As a Sierra Club president once said, "Never let your love of nature overshadow your concern for human needs." America is unaware of the tremendous acreage that is now off-limits to economic use, and clings to an outdated image that developers have ravaged all but "the last redwoods," or "the last mountains," or "the last desert." We forget that in exactly the same sense, we are "the last humans." We are inviting a changed form of government and economic disaster by letting environmentmental extremism go without checks and balances. But only an informed public can build a wise set of checks and balances. Perhaps we cannot develop our way out of resource scarcity without conservation, but we certainly cannot conserve our way out of the daily need for food, clothing and shelter without development. May our wisdom prevail over our fervor.

Now that we have approached The Religious War from several angles, we can see more clearly the forces that had been gathering and were ready to spring on Jim Watt when he said ". . . I do not know how many future generations we can count on before the Lord returns. . . ." We can see more clearly the substance beneath all the furor. We can see more clearly that one can indeed be a fundamentalist Christian and be a good steward of the earth. We can see more clearly the weakness of the environmentalists' moral high ground when they stooped to attack Jim Watt's religious beliefs—and for their own ends twisted his words to the exact opposite of his intent.

In all, the environmentalists' attack on Watt's religious beliefs had no useful purpose. The right of environmentalists to their beliefs is unquestionable. But Jim Watt's right to his beliefs is also unquestionable. So long as he does not propose policy on the basis of religion, his beliefs are a personal matter. I doubt that many Americans would be swayed by Watt's assertion that some political policy was God's policy even if he did make such a claim. Most Americans by my experience tend to look upon federal land policy, private property rights, and other Interior Department issues as having no particular religious flavor. Merely insulting Jim Watt's beliefs did not change him in any event. He had a job to do: he was the new Secretary of the Interior.

CHAPTER 5
SECRETARY WATT

Nothing is so powerful as an idea whose time has come.

—Victor Hugo

The watchword of the Reagan transition team was "We'll hit the ground running!" When James G. Watt was sworn in as Secretary of the Interior at the White House on Friday, January 23, 1981, he had already hit the ground and had been running for two weeks. He had been planning strategy, assembling his management team and outlining policy changes since the day of his Senate hearing January 7th.

The Secretary of the Interior cannot be just one person; in a figurative and a literal way, he must be a team of immensely capable people with widely divergent talents. If his personality cannot stretch to encompass many people and inspire their loyalty, his programs are doomed to drown in the bureaucracy. Nobody knew this better than Jim Watt. His mission meant bringing major change to a vast 80,000-employee Department. He could eliminate 80 Carter political appointees, but budget constraints would allow him to replace them with only 35 of his own. He absolutely had to choose the right team.

While supporters and opponents gave the Senate their views on the Watt nomination January 8th, the nominee was busy searching for the right team. A capable and experienced young lawyer named J. Robinson West— known as Robin—had been assigned by the Presidential transition team to help get Interior staffed up. West immediately went to work telephoning candidates for the Department's political positions, inviting them to Washington at their own expense for job interviews with Secretary-designate Watt. Several showed up within 24 hours, among them Dick Harris and Bob Broadbent, who were later tapped for the respective directorships of the Office of Surface Mining and Bureau of Reclamation.

88

During the next few days Watt interviewed candidates for his leadership team and handled a myriad of other tasks. For one thing, there were 204 written questions from various Senators that demanded written answers for his confirmation. Perry Pendley and a small corps of helpers were taking care of that with frequent advice from Watt. For another, Robin West was running Watt through the total organization chart of Interior, studying problem areas, planning reorganization strategy, and trying to anticipate program budget cuts.

Getting his top leaders on the scene in a hurry was Watt's first priority. He knew how much he needed help in bringing about the changes he saw as necessary for America. He and the Presidential transition team had made good headway putting together a list of candidates for the senior executives and bureau heads: Under Secretary, Solicitor, Inspector General, and six Assistant Secretaries (senior executives), and directors of a dozen or so bureaus and offices such as the Bureau of Land Management and the Office of Water Research and Technology. These people had to be nominated by the President and confirmed with the advise and consent of the Senate, and the selections were technically out of Watt's hands. However, tradition and the Reagan management style demanded extensive delegation of this authority, and Watt was given a virtually free hand in picking these senior managers.

One of the first men Watt needed was his Under Secretary, his alter-ego, the man who would serve as Acting Secretary in Watt's absence, and who would be one of his key assistants. The Under Secretary has full authority except for a few matters reserved only to the Secretary, and Watt's first choice was Don Hodel, energy consultant of Portland, Oregon. Hodel stipulated that he would serve only if there was no one else who could adequately fill the job, and Watt promised to look elsewhere. But near the middle of January Hodel answered the phone to hear Watt say, "This is that call you were dreading." Don Hodel was in Washington the next day, nominated by the President within a week, and confirmed by the Senate on February 5.

The first Assistant Secretary Jim wanted to bring on board was Fish and Wildlife and Parks because his program for preservation—contrary to the assertions of environmentalist opponents—was one of his primary political and strategic commitments. The candidate lists coming from the White House were crammed with names for each position with one exception: the candidate list for Assistant Secretary for Fish and Wildlife and Parks had exactly one name on it: G. Ray Arnett. Ray Arnett is a distinguished conservationist, having served as director of the California Department of Fish and Game during the Reagan governorship, and possessing a long string of conservation credentials including 17 years as a director of the National Wildlife Federation. But Watt had never met him, and insisted that he be able to get along with the man who would occupy this crucial position. Arnett was invited to interview with Watt by Robin West, who called on Saturday, January 17, and asked, "How soon can you be back here in Washington?" Ray Arnett was just getting ready to go hunting with his youngest son when he got the call and replied, "I'd like to stay until duck season is over, how about sometime in February?" Robin laughed and said, "How about tomorrow?" Ray Arnett showed up the next day. After he got together with Watt, the Secretary-designate said, "Ray Arnett would have been my choice if there had been a hundred names on that list. Everything in his career and personality testifies to his devotion to America's outdoor heritage." Arnett stayed on the transition team, was nominated February 18, and confirmed by the Senate May 13, 1981.

The public is generally unaware of the awkwardness of Presidential transitions. Senior managers and Cabinet officers have no budget, no authority, and no power before their confirmation and swearings-in. Senior managers are commonly hired by newly-confirmed Cabinet officers as "consultants" while waiting for the Senate to act, which is the time-honored method of coping with such delays. However, Secretary-designates do not even have that option. The Presidential transition team provides some help with office space, but little more. Until he was sworn in, Watt was just an ordinary citizen, and that created particularly severe stresses during his two weeks waiting for Senate confirmation.

For political and tactical reasons, Watt had refused any briefings from anyone at Interior for his confirmation hearing. Politically, it would have been too risky letting the bureaucracy close enough to begin controlling him during a vulnerable time. Tactically, Watt did not want to know some of the Carter Administration's answers on specific issues; he wished to remain purposefully vague to avoid closing off administrative options before he had time to study them with command power as Secretary of the Interior.

The graspings of the bureaucracy are many and subtle, and Watt sensed that with the major changes he knew must be made in the Department, it was important to keep his distance during the entire transition period. Outgoing Secretary Andrus offered Watt a car and driver and the other complimentary perquisites that go with the office, but Watt refused them, unlike other Reagan Cabinet-designates. He says, "I didn't want the Department to own me in any way when I came in. I wanted to come in with authority and power."

Things had been touchy enough during the first week of transition in the Presidential offices on M Street, but on January 15, the day after the Energy and Natural Resources Committee voted his confirmation out with the recommendation that the whole Senate approve it, Watt found it necessary to move his growing crew into the Interior Building on 18th and C Streets N.W. Now things were distinctly uncomfortable. The dozen or so people on his transition team were crammed into three bare rooms on the 7th floor with a single typewriter and a few phones. Watt found the tentacles of the bureaucracy reaching out for him in his office, in the halls, in the elevators, even in the rest rooms. He quickly made it a policy to engage in no conversations with Interior employees and to keep moving, shuttling back and forth between Interior and the Presidential transition building.

During this chaotic time, the first bonds formed between the new management team—they first realized they were an entity, a "something" that was new and real and important. The blossoming friendship and loyalty made it easier to live and work in the cramped space. Don Hodel made himself welcome by beginning to write down all the tasks that Jim assigned; by now there was so much to do nobody could keep up with it any more. Hodel also began attending to such details as: Who will make the room assignments for the new crew as it arrives?, How will correspondence be handled until the new leadership is firmly in place some months from now? Where are the pencils and paper kept? Hodel's lists were soon to expand to include the dates when assigned tasks were due for completion, and everybody kept shuffling through his flipcharts trying to remember what they had committed themselves to do. Emily DeRocco sorted tasks; Perry Pendley got the new minerals policy begun; Moody Tidwell began reviewing reams of Solicitors' opinions from the Andrus years; Robin West grew from appointment-maker to general administrator; Steve Shipley helped chart strategy for the first days after confirmation; Doug Baldwin prepared press releases and managed news contacts.

Special circumstances brought many on the new team together and cemented the growing bonds of friendship. Don Hodel had left his wife and consulting partner Barbara in Portland to close up their business and sell their house; Steve Shipley had likewise left his family in Denver to sew things up. Don and Steve shared a rented apartment while waiting for their wives, and with no family duties, the two spent virtually all their waking hours at work, arriving early after jogging together, and staying late, often until 10:00 or 11:00 P.M. In a short, intensive time, the new and burgeoning Watt family took shape, absorbing dozens of diverse personalities eager to perform far beyond the bounds of duty.

Inauguration Day, January 20, 1981, saw a festive Washington jammed for the changing of the guard. After the ceremony that publicly installed Ronald Reagan as President of the United States, arrangements had been made for the new Chief Executive to attend a joint swearing-in ceremony for his Cabinet, but the Senate had not confirmed any of them. After sitting at his Oval Office desk for the first time and looking in the drawers, saying "I wonder if they left us anything. . . . Well, they've left me some paper clips," President Reagan took the time to meet his Cabinet and their families, pose for group portraits, and generally get acquainted.

The next day, Wednesday, the Senate confirmed five Cabinet members and on Thursday voted for eight more, including James G. Watt for Secretary of the Interior. In a hurry-up ceremony on Friday, ten Cabinet members including Watt were rushed to the White House and without publicity or fanfare were sworn in by an anonymous clerk who administered the oath and scurried back to his job. The President was not in attendance! They had missed their big party and the message was clear: get to work, folks.

Watt's first official act that Friday was to appoint his long-time friend and confidant Steve Shipley as Executive Assistant to the Secretary, the pivotal staff officer who serves as major-domo and factotum to the top executives of Interior, and whose job description could not possibly be written down, so broad is his staff responsibility.

Now James G. Watt was free to act. Now he had the authority and power. Now it was time to get to work on the Department of the Interior. On the last Monday in January he began the task.

By 8:30 that Monday morning, Secretary Watt had already taken decisive action to put his administration firmly in place. He had issued a directive reaffirming the President's hiring freeze. He ordered a freeze on all but the "most essential" travel; everyone in the leadership was to stay on the job for the first crucial six months. This strategic decision had two aims: one, instead of going out and making speeches telling America what the Watt Secretariat was *going* to do, they would wait and tell what they *had* done; and two, it would help make sure that the Watt administration controlled the bureaucracy rather than the other way around. Secretary Watt had ordered a survey of all consulting contracts in force, he had ordered a review of all proposed foreign travel by Departmental officials, and he had written letters to the governors of the 50 States pledging his Department to "excercising its responsibilities in full and complete recognition of the vital role of the States in the federal system." This "good neighbor policy" letter asked the governors to communicate directly with Jim about their ideas and concerns, and offered a meeting with Interior officials during the next month's National Governor's Conference in Washington.

Down on the first floor in the Interior Auditorium Watt held 7 introductory meetings one after another for nearly 700 employees at a time. Striding to the onstage podium and standing before the huge mural "Western

Lands" by Louis Bouche, Secretary Watt told his Department exactly what they could expect:

It was an honor for me to be named by President Reagan to become Secretary of the Interior and confirmed by the Senate. It is a special thrill to be back at the Department and I'm excited about the challenges and opportunities.

One of the finest things that has been afforded me is the opportunity to work with a President who understands the goals and missions of Interior. When he interviewed me for this job, President Reagan used our jargon and talked about the USGS, BLM, the Endangered Species Act, and the Bureau of Reclamation—he, too, has not learned the new name [Water and Power Resources Service]. And so we have the privilege of working with a man who has been involved in public land issues, a man who cares and who has some ideas about what we ought to be doing.

On November 4, the people of America spoke with great clarity. They called for a dramatic new beginning and a change in our course of government. It will come as no great surprise, I am sure, that I am hereby accepting the resignations of all appointees of the Carter Administration. The fact is that you were terminated on November 4, and I am simply putting the decision of the American people into effect. I expect you to be prepared to depart at the end of work today.

The changes President Reagan has commanded me to bring to the management of our environment and our resources will be exciting for those of you committed to the multiple use of our lands, for those of you committed to preserving the best values of our natural and cultural heritages, and for those of you committed to using the lands for people of this generation and future generations. To those of you who do not share this commitment, you will be happier if you seek employment opportunities elsewhere.

My experience in the past here in the Department has been that when there have been foulups or failures, it has been because of inept direction and leadership from the political side, not the career side. I will rely upon the professionalism which is in the bureaus and is the strength of the Department. This is where the people are located who really understand the mission and the resource base we are charged with managing.

In less than five minutes, Jim Watt had fired the Carter appointees, urged those who opposed the new Administration's goals to leave Interior, and affirmed his faith in the professional career people, making it clear that his own leadership team was on notice not to blame mistakes on the bureaucracy. Now he continued his introduction by laying out eight points of his program for Interior: (1) a balanced perspective between economic use and preservation of America's public lands; (2) the development of America's energy resources in an environmentally sound manner; (3) removal of excessive regulations; (4) the "good neighbor" policy between federal land managers and the states—Watt emphasized that this policy would be a reality, not just lip service; (5) the development of a strategic minerals policy; (6) a more aggressive program to bring self-determination and economic development to the American Indians; (7) the protection and preservation of wildlife habitat, parks, recreation areas and refuge lands by improvement of existing facilities rather than the rapid expansion and over-extended budgets of the past decade; and (8) the address of water resource development needs for agriculture, industry and domestic use.

In a brief talk, Jim Watt had made his intentions unmistakable; no one was uncertain of Interior's future course. It is illuminating to compare Jim's statement with that of Cecil Andrus when he took over the office four years earlier. Among Andrus' remarks were these:

I am a part of the environment movement and I intend to make Interior responsive to the movement's needs. We intend to break up the little fiefdoms which have divided Interior for years. For too long, each of the interests— grazing, mining, timber and so forth—has had its own domain. The place was like a centipede with each little pair of feet scuttling off in its own direction. That is going to change.

Policy-making will be centralized and it will be responsive to my philosophy and the philosophy of President Carter. And, our philosophies do not include allowing developers to crank up the bulldozers and run rough-shod over the Public Domain.

If development can be accomplished without harm to the environment, we'll side with development; but if it cannot be accomplished without destruction of the environment, the environment must be our highest priority.

It would be several days before Watt interviewed the career professionals from the development side of the house, in Energy and Minerals, in Land and Water Resources, and discovered to his horror just how literally Secretary Andrus had meant his last sentence. Watt was to find that development had been gutted. He was to find that the smallest environmental disruption had been eagerly sought out in every project proposal and then used as an excuse to ban the project. He was to find that mineral scientists in the Bureau of Mines, once respected throughout the world, had been fired or suppressed and were utterly demoralized. He was to find that the development side of the house had been tortured into the prevention-of-development branch of Interior.

But that Monday morning, as Watt jumped down from the stage to greet people after his 8:30 meeting, throngs of employees crowded to shake his hand and welcome him to the Department, some out of sheer relief, some out of sheer panic. Career employees from the development side of the house came forward in delight. And dozens from the preservation side of the house also came forward happily, saying how tired they were of trying to manage infinite expansion on a microscopic maintenance budget. The vast majority wholeheartedly supported his coming to the Department. Those less pleased slunk out looking glum, but not all of them sought employment elsewhere·

some stayed on as leaks and shunts and conduits to the environmental movement.

One poor soul lingered on after that 8:30 meeting, pressing others ahead of him to meet Watt. Finally he approached Watt with a look of disbelief on his face. He was a bureau head who had come in with Cecil Andrus, and had even served in a state post when Andrus was Governor of Idaho. He said to Watt, "I can't believe you've terminated me! I'm a career bureaucrat, I'll take orders from anybody. I never took that political appointee business seriously."

Now it was Watt's turn to look in disbelief. Had this man forgotten that Secretary Andrus had done the same thing four years earlier and fired nearly all the Republican appointees from the Ford and Nixon Years, just as every new Administration has done since the Department was created in 1849? Had this man forgotten about his own Republican predecessor who got the boot to make way for a Democrat? Watt marvelled at the man's naïveté and simply said, "I'm sorry. We're going to bring in a whole new team. I expect you to be gone tonight with all the other Carter appointees."

The media seldom make clear what this traditional housecleaning is all about. The top spots at Interior and all other Cabinet Departments are political appointments. They are confidential and policy-making positions. Critics of every new Administration complain about the bloodbath and make it sound as if career civil servants were being given an unceremonious heave-ho. This is not the case. Everyone Watt fired that day had been personally appointed by Jimmy Carter or Cecil Andrus to replace former Republican appointees. Washington insiders are perfectly aware of what these mass firings mean: the changing of the guard is in the leadership, not in the career professional spots.

The media treatment of the event, however, was typified in the October 15, 1981 issue of *Rolling Stone* in an article entitled "After James Watt What?" Writer Howard Kohn said, "Perhaps the shrewdest move Watt made was to fire everyone he could when he took office. It was like a Russian purge. Though the people Watt has appointed are far less visible than he is, they have been moving to take control of the Interior Department." The implication is that Watt didn't fire those he couldn't, which is true: he didn't fire any GS-rated civil servants.

The most ironic reference, however, is ". . . like a Russian purge. . . ." It was Cecil Andrus who promised centralized control a la the Soviets; Jim Watt had promised decentralized decision-making and reduction of government powers. And there had been no *Rolling Stone* coverage when Secretary Andrus went down the halls of the development side of the Interior on February 22, 1977, and fired 43 people, including career civil servants, with an hour and a half's notice. What Secretary Andrus said in public about it was, "At Interior we have begun to make sweeping institutional and policy changes to end what I see as the domination of the Department by mining, oil and other special interests."

If by "special interests" Secretary Andrus meant people who were out to make a healthy profit, he was absolutely right. Miners and oil companies and cattlemen and loggers and irrigators and farmers don't take things away from the public and keep them, however. They process those raw materials into products and make them available to the market place, where any American who's willing to trade value-for-value can have oil, metal, food, clothing, shelter, and other material goods. The special interests are the only ones who provide those necessities to us. It's the special interests, as Andrus so indignantly called them, who keep us alive.

Watt did hold over one Carter appointee, in a critical spot: Russell Dickenson remained as Director of the National Park Service. In the last decade, political jockeying and the tendency of the Park Service to become a land-grab agency has brought contention to the office. A single Presidency might see two or even three National Park directors come and go as the Secretary tried to find someone agreeable to shifting Park policy. This trend had deeply troubled Jim Watt. He felt it was largely responsible for the terrible deterioration in National Park visitor facilities; endless expansion rather than care for existing properties had become the rule. Watt wanted to bring stability to the position of Director of the National Park Service. Although he had kept away from Interior during the transition period, Jim had tried to send some personal signals to Russ Dickenson, hoping he would hold off on any decisions about seeking a new post until the new Administration was in place.

As soon as Watt had a free moment, he paid Dickenson a visit. The two men had worked together closely in the early 1970s when Watt was Director of the Bureau of Outdoor Recreation. Dickenson had only been appointed Director of the Park Service in 1980 and, in effect, was still settling into the office, but Watt knew him as a strong professional manager and wanted to keep him if at all possible. Watt quizzed Dickenson on his view of the policy directions the Park Service should take. Russell Dickenson had been saying for several years that the rapid expansion of park properties should be curtailed in favor of consolidation—a point on which he and Watt saw eye to eye. But Dickenson wanted more money to repair the Parks and bring them up to at least meet the deficiencies discovered in a General Accounting Office report. Increasing the Park Service budget during the Reagan Administration might be a tough thing to do, but Jim had already determined to do just that. Dickenson also thought that superintendents should have more job stability: current policy was to shuttle them from one Park to another every couple of years to prevent them from becoming too chummy with concessioners. What the policy really accomplished was to give every Park a new man on the job all the time; as soon as a superintendent began to really understand his facility, he was transferred to another one. Watt saw the merits of stability and supported it, too. Jim Watt and Russ Dickenson were not too far apart on policy.

Now Watt laid down several conditions on Russ' continued employment as Park Service Director: he must be able to work with the new leadership; he must adopt whatever management system the Watt administration eventually came up with; he must leave all political decisions to Ray Arnett, his boss as the Assistant Secretary for Fish and Wildlife and Parks. If he was willing to abide by these stipulations, he could keep the job. Russ Dickenson told me, "I'm a professional career bureaucrat, my degree is in Business Administration, and I've never been a political person of any kind, so it was easy to meet these conditions."

Watt's choice for Solicitor, William H. Coldiron, had been a director and vice-chairman of the Montana Power Company. As *Rolling Stone* carped: "Montana Power owns a huge coal strip mine, has litigated against air-pollution controls, and has been among the contributors to the Mountain States Legal Foundation." Coldiron's firm won a number of its air-pollution control suits, however, which indicates that the courts thought Montana Power was right. And Bill Coldiron's name appeared on the President's own candidate list; Jim Watt selected him from the other candidates because he knew the man's abilities at first-hand. Jim has said, "Bill Coldiron has had a distinguished career in the law and public utility management, and has developed special skills in resource use and management." Critics never mention that Coldiron was a professor of law at the University of Montana, or that he is a Fellow of the American Bar Foundation.

The Solicitor of the Department of the Interior is the principal legal adviser to the Secretary and the chief law officer of the Department. He is responsible for and has supervision over all legal work except that performed by Interior's office of Hearings and Appeals and the Office of Congressional and Legislative Affairs. This officer is the only person in the Department who can stop a Secretary dead in his tracks by issuing a formal legal opinion on a given subject or by informing a bureau that they do not have to follow certain directives of the Secretary. Therefore, Interior Secretaries are usually quite careful about who they put in such a powerful place, and Watt was no exception. Bill Coldiron is as professional as they come, but at the same time he is a devoted "Wattsman," a label often used by Interior employees to describe themselves.

Much has been made of Jim Watt's firing of 51 Solicitor's Office employees on March 19, 1981, but reporters did not explain the reasons behind Watt's move. The March 30, 1981, issue of *U.S. News & World Report* wrote it up this way: "On March 19, he fired 51 Interior employees who he said were victims of Jimmy Carter's 'blatant disregard of the budget and hiring laws.' " That's all they said. *Rolling Stone* wrote it up like this:

Coldiron became solititor after Watt eliminated fifty-one employees, most of them lawyers, from the solicitor's staff. These same lawyers had built cases against violators of the strip-mining law and had fought, most often with success, against suits brought by Watt when he was at Mountain States. While the rationale for getting rid of them was the budget crunch, some of the vacancies are now being filled with Watt's own men.

The facts of the case are somewhat different. Carter Administration Solicitor Clyde Martz in 1979 hired 51 more people than he had budget to pay, a totally illegal action with criminal penalties for violation of the Anti-Deficiency Act. Jim Watt was not the first person to object; Secretary Andrus' own Assistant Secretary for Policy, Budget and Administration, Larry Meierotto, responded by revoking the Solicitor's personnel authority, an exceedingly harsh action against a fellow Democrat. But Secretary Andrus did not fix the problem; he left it for Jim Watt. Upon investigation, newly-appointed Deputy Solicitor Moody Tidwell found that if Interior continued the Andrus staffing level, they would be $1.3 million in the hole. Jim promptly fired 14 full-time lawyers, 4 part-time lawyers, and 33 clerks. It was not "mostly lawyers," and there was much more to it than *U.S. News & World Report* indicated. In truth, the whole thing had been dirty work left over for Watt to do. When Watt's own budget was approved, he hired four people for the Solicitor's office—and he had the money to pay them.

Another favorite whipping boy of the press was Watt's pick for Director of the Bureau of Land Mangement, Robert F. Burford, a working rancher and former speaker of the Colorado House of Representatives. Bob Burford came on the scene February 2 from Grand Junction, Colorado, where he held grazing rights on 33,614 acres of BLM land that were transferred to his son to satisfy conflict-of-interest laws. Critics like to point to Bob and call him a disciple of those who will practice the "Three Rs," rape, ruin and run, on the BLM's 175 million acres in the lower 48 states. It does not seem to occur to them that a man who is a long-time rancher and permitee with grazing rights passed down from his father who got them when the Taylor Grazing Act was passed in 1934, and who has served for years on state and district grazing advisory boards, might also know a thing or two about properly using public lands. As Burford says, "I'm not going to tear up the land that I love, and I think there's a correct way to use it as well as preserve it. I think we can address the energy needs of America and help with the balance of payments and produce more coal and oil and do it in an environmentally sound way. I've looked at those strip mines in western Colorado that are being revegetated and they've all got more vegetation on them now than before they were mined."

Burford has also been rapped for being a staunch conservative. In his slow and friendly way of speaking, he responds, "I'm as liberal as a graduate of the Colorado School of Mines, a World War II Marine Corps veteran, and lifelong rancher could be expected to be." One day in early 1981 Bob took on Congressman John Seiberling of the House Interior and Insular Affairs Committee who had accused him of taking away federal lands from all the people and giving it to miners and cattle and sheepmen. Burford asked, "Aren't miners and ranchers people, too? Where do you think your nice wool Brooks Brothers suit came from?"

Another Watt appointee who was raked over the coals in the press was James R. (Dick) Harris, Director of the Office of Surface Mining. A *Wall Street Journal* front-page article accused Harris of making huge profits on parts of reclaimed strip mines he bought from two large coal companies by improper procedures. After two full FBI investigations and a Senate committee investigation it was found that he had done nothing wrong whatsoever. As Harris says, "In fact, it was discovered that I was the buyer of last resort rather than somebody who was getting a big deal out of it. It was determined that I had paid Peabody 22 percent more than the professionally appraised value of the land, and on the Amax tract, the FBI found they had been trying to peddle it for two years and again I paid more than the appraised value. The Senate vote on my confirmation was unanimous both in committee and on the floor. After the facts came out nobody had any objections to my candidacy. But it's shocking to wake up one morning and find out you're a bad guy on the front page of the *Wall Street Journal*."

But the really remarkable news story is the one that never got written. When it came time to staff up the Indian Affairs part of the house, Watt selected Kenneth L. Smith, general manager of the Confederated Tribes of Warm Springs, to be Assistant Secretary for Indian Affairs. For the first time in history an Indian from a reservation was directing the Indian Affairs program. Smith says, "I was confirmed by the Senate on my birthday, March 30, 1981—but that was the same day President Reagan was shot. You can guess what happened to the confirmation story."

Smith's two Deputy Assistant Secretaries are also Indians, Roy H. Sampsel, a Choctaw Indian from Portland, Oregon, who has served in numerous federal and Indian government posts, and John W. Fritz, a Cherokee Indian from St. Paul, Minnesota, who had been serving as senior corporate counsel for Minnesota Mining and Manufacturing Company (3M).

And what about the ubiquitous Mr. Robin West, telephoner of the transition team? He had proven himself to be a talented administrator, and Watt recommended that President Reagan nominate him as Assistant Secretary for Policy, Budget and Administration, which he did, and West was subsequently confirmed by the Senate.

Another top Watt selection who has received very little press is Prof. Garrey E. Carruthers who serves as Assistant Secretary for Land and Water Resources, one of the most important development spots in the house: he's the boss of the Commissioner of the Bureau of Reclamation, the director of the Bureau of Land Management, and the directors of the Office of Water Research and Technology and Office of Coal Leasing Planning and Coordination—a highly critical task. He has received so little notice because no one can find a bad thing to say about him. He was formerly a full professor of agricultural economics at New Mexico State University, has served as a White House Fellow, which is a distinguished honor, and is the author of more than 30 publications on multiple-use of natural resources and land and water resource economics. Since Carruthers came from academia, Watt was especially hard on him during his job interview, insistently asking him how he was "tough." Carruthers replied that the way he manages things he didn't have to be tough, he could always find a consensus. But Jim kept at him, asking, "How do I know that when it really comes to a tight situation you're going to be strong enough?" And Carruthers again replied that he'd never had to be tough, but Jim came back at him with an edge of anger in his voice and said, "How do I know that you're tough?" At which Garrey Carruthers leaned over Jim's circular work table, looked him in the eye coldly and said, "Quite honestly, I win more times than I lose, but if you ever beat me you won't get a virgin. I can handle myself."

Carruthers remembers the meeting and smiles, "By that time he'd triggered some emotion in me, and that's what he'd intended to do, and he said back to me, 'Garrey, I can tell you're tough by your eyes.' And ever since then, when Jim wants to elicit a response from me he just says something like, 'I can tell by Carruthers' eyes that he's not with us, or he's not going to buy off on this project,' and I believe that one of the chief reasons why Interior under Jim Watt is so successful is the chemistry between him and all the people around him in the Department. It's that personal chemistry that makes our management team unbeatable."

Another irreproachable Watt selection was Dr. Dan Miller, one of the world's most highly regarded oil and gas geologists, as Assistant Secretary for Energy and Minerals. Dan was previously the Wyoming State Geologist and Executive Director of the Wyoming Geological Survey for 11½ years. He has written or edited more than 35 scientific publications on mineral and energy resources. He is the boss of the directors of the Bureau of Mines, U.S.

Geological Survey, Office of Surface Mining, and Office of Minerals Policy and Research Analysis.

Jim's selection for Director of the U.S. Fish and Wildlife Service is likewise irreproachable and for that reason has received scant press notice: Robert A. Jantzen, a former director of the Arizona Game and Fish Department, and a man who has spent his entire career in the wildlife management profession, holding his Arizona position from 1953 to 1981. Jantzen, 54, proved his professional dedication in his Deputy Director appointment as well, choosing Dr. F. Eugene Hester, a career employee of the Fish and Wildlife Service since 1963. Dr. Hester had been appointed by Jim as Acting Director until a suitable candidate could be found, in accordance with the Watt pledge to use career bureaucrats in as many "acting" positions as possible during his candidate search.

Jantzen had been contacted for the Director's job by Ray Arnett, who would be his boss, and when Watt interviewed him, as Jantzen says, "Jim Watt got to the bottom line very quickly. He wanted to know very little about my personal background, but was keenly interested in my professional outlook, to see what my philosophy of fish and wildlife management was, whether the preservationist view or the conservationist view. Conservation, you will recall, is a word coined by the first chief of the U.S. Forest Service Gifford Pinchot to mean 'the wise use of resources,' and not the perpetual preservation of resources with no extractive use. I made it plain that I was a staunch conservationist and had been all of my career."

When Watt described his feelings about Bob Jantzen, he said,

We determined that we would have professionals managing the natural resource agencies in this Administration, and Bob Jantzen for 30 years has earned the respect of other professionals. When I first took office, I made the commitment to overcome health and safety deficiencies in the National Parks. Since then I have learned that for too many years the political managers of the Interior Department overlooked similar deficiencies on the National Wildlife Refuges and Ranges managed by the Fish and Wildlife Service. We're determined to overcome these deficiencies, and to carry out this commitment we need a professional manager like Bob Jantzen.

We shall meet more of the people Jim Watt selected for his management team in later chapters (see also Fig. 4 in the Appendix), but all of them share the depth of ability and commitment of the leaders we have just examined.

CHAPTER 6
A QUESTION OF BALANCE

A dissenting minority feels free only when it can impose its will on the majority; what it abominates most is the dissent of the majority.
—Eric Hoffer

When Secretary Watt released his first policy directives in the spring of 1981—the moratorium on further National Park land acquisitions, proposals to establish a new Office of National Water Policy, to turn over strip mine regulation to the states, to open up more federal land to mining and logging, to establish a stockpile of strategic minerals, to increase leasing of offshore oil and gas, and other moves—his intent was to restore balance to the preservation and development of U.S. natural resources.

Watt had sympathized with business and industry being stifled by excessive regulation and its sinews weakened by set-asides of vital raw materials. However, as we have seen in earlier chapters, many Americans during the environmental revolution came to feel that any development was too much development, that in the new Age of Limits there were only limits and no freedoms, and that the use of natural resources was "immoral." They were not particularly sympathetic to business and industry. Watt's early policy initiatives were seen by these forces as "anti-environmental," and Watt's rhetoric did little to turn away that criticism.

But, as in most matters political, there is more to that than meets the headlines. Watt was less concerned with his reputation than with the substance of his policy. He saw the need to curtail excessive federal spending and reduce inflation. He saw parks, minerals and energy policy being administered in many cases contrary to Congressional intent in the name of environmentalism. In the area of National Parks he even had in hand General Accounting Office reports pointing to health and safety violations that would

102

cost $1.6 billion to set right. In minerals he had seen Department personnel demoralized by years of suppression and neglect. These were realities. Watt's early claims of restoring balance may have been perceived as a mere sop for the public or rhetorical window dressing to hide rapacious intent, but in this chapter we will examine the record of imbalances and abuses that had damaged the civil rights of many citizens and the economic stability of the nation.

The National Parks

Much of the news coverage featuring Secretary Watt's early National Park policy was superficial and raised nearly nonsensical issues. For example, the May 11, 1981, issue of *Time* magazine noted: "Watt has declared a moratorium on the acquisition of more national parkland, despite the fact that parks are now being used by more people than ever. In 1970 more than 172 million visited the country's national recreation areas; last year at least 300 million toured places like Yosemite, Yellowstone and Glacier."

A little reflection will reveal how superficial this argument is: How many places are there like Yosemite, Yellowstone, and Glacier? There is no substitute for a unique resource, no more of these crown jewels to be added; all were long ago given protected status. And where are the visitors thronging? According to the Park Service's Denver Service Center Statistical Office, of the top ten attractions in 1980, four were city parks, two were roads (National Parkways), three offered beaches or water recreation, and exactly one was a scenic National Park (Great Smoky Mountain). Ranked by visitors, they were (1) Golden Gate National Recreation Area in San Francisco (18.4 million visits); (2) Natchez Trace Parkway in Mississippi, Alabama and Tennessee (10.6 million); (3) Gateway NRA in New York City (9 million); (4) Great Smoky Mountain National Park in Tennessee (8.4 million); (5) Colonial National Historical Park, Jamestown Island, Virginia (6.3 million); (6) George Washington Memorial Parkway, Virginia and Maryland (6.2 million); (7) Lake Mead NRA, Arizona-Nevada (4.9 million); (8) Cape Cod National Seashore, Massachusetts (4.7 million); (9) John F. Kennedy Center for the Performing Arts, Washington D.C. (4.2 million); (10) National Capitol Parks, Washington, D.C. (4.0 million). The Lincoln Memorial had more visitors (3.3 million) than Yosemite (2.4 million), Yellowstone (2.0 million), or Glacier (1.4 million). The *Time* report was grossly misleading; the moratorium was not intended to exclude outstanding scenic or ecological treasures, since a substantial cross-section of each representative type is already preserved in the system.

In fact, the moratorium issue has little if anything to do with letting great natural areas slip through our fingers; it is more nearly a question of how many more city parks we put in the federal system. A more legitimate concern is whether National Park Rangers with degrees in environmental science ought to be directing traffic, baby-sitting on swing sets, arresting drug pushers, and picking up trash on the street.

A few critics of Watt's National Park policy dug deeper. Writer Elizabeth Drew noted in the May 4, 1981 *New Yorker* that many dispassionate observers, "who include conservation-minded Democrats, maintain that Congress has got in the habit in recent years of authorizing the purchase of parks that could not be described as 'national jewels'—that a bit of pork barreling was going on."

A useful understanding of the National Parks issue can only come from an historical perspective. When Congress created the National Park Service in 1916, it gave the new agency a conflicting set of rules: protection and preservation on the one hand, and provision for appropriate use and public enjoyment on the other. The resulting tensions have never been successfully resolved. Preservation advocates assert that wilderness is at the heart of the National Park concept, while use-oriented partisans claim just as loudly that public enjoyment is the core of the idea. The law is silent on this point; as far as the legislation is concerned there are two cores, protection and appropriate use, preservation and public enjoyment. Resolving the dichotomy is left to the National Park Service.

By the time the National Park Service was established in 1916, some of the parks had been going concerns for nearly half a century, one of them much longer. Hot Springs Reservation in Arkansas had been set aside April 20, 1832, but was not dedicated to public use as a park until June 16, 1880. The Yo-Semite Valley Act of 1864 granted Yosemite to the State of California for use as a park, thus setting a precedent for scenic reserves, but Yellowstone in Wyoming was the first and largest National Park, established March 1, 1872, "dedicated and set apart as a public park or pleasuring-ground for the benefit and enjoyment of the people," and "for the preservation, from injury or spoliation, of all timber, mineral deposits, natural curiosities, or wonders . . . and their retention in their natural condition." Although the two purposes of public use and natural preservation are clearly spelled out in this excerpt from Yellowstone's enabling act, a preservationist faction in the modern National Park Service attempted to modify that legislative mandate without the consent of Congress in writing the Master Plan for Yellowstone: "the original purpose must be translated in terms of contemporary connotations; as such it should read:

To perpetuate the natural ecosystems within the park *in as near pristine conditions as possible for their inspirational, educational, cultural, and scientific values for this and future generations* [emphasis in the original].

The 1960s and '70s saw increasing amounts of such administrative tampering with Congressional intent; one at a time, imbalances stacked up in favor of preservation and against public use and enjoyment.

Other National Parks that had already been established when the National Park Service was created in 1916 include Sequoia (1890), Yosemite (1890), Mount Rainier (1899), Crater Lake (1902), Wind Cave (1903), Mesa Verde (1906), and Rocky Mountain (1915). They were soon joined by Lassen Volcanic (1916), Hawaii (later redesignated as Haleakala and Hawaii Volcanoes) (1916), Mount McKinley (renamed Denali) (1917), Zion (1919), Acadia (1919) and Grand Canyon (1919). Grand Canyon had been designated a Forest Reserve in 1893, a National Monument in 1908, and was administered by the Forest Service, U.S. Department of Agriculture, until transferred to Interior August 15, 1919.

These early parks had two things in common: first, they were carved from the vast public domain lands in the West which were for the most part considered worthless for economic pursuits; and second, they had within their boundaries tracts of land that had already been homesteaded or were otherwise withdrawn for private uses such as mines, visitor accommodations, and so forth.

These embedded private tracts, known as "inholdings," have aroused terrible conflict from the very beginning of the National Park Service. Secretary of the Interior Franklin K. Lane wrote to Stephen Mather, first Director of the National Park Service, on May 13, 1918:

There are many private holdings in the national parks and many of these seriously hamper administration of these reservations. All of them should be eliminated as far as practicable. This should be accomplished in the course of time either through Congressional appropriations or by acceptance of donations of these lands. Isolated tracts in important scenic areas should be given first consideration, of course, in the pursuit of private property.

As Secretary Lane's bounty hunters set out in "pursuit of private property," they were quickly ambushed by howls of protest from inholders who took the Fifth Amendment's Constitutional private property protection clause seriously. Secretary Lane's intentions were partially thwarted; condemnation proceedings were slow. Only a few strategically located sites were acquired to prevent private development. Funds were short, and as current Park Service Director Russell Dickenson says, "the uses being made of the private tracts remained for the most part harmless to the natural and other values of the areas of the system."

The National Park system grew rapidly: Bryce Canyon was added in 1924, followed by Shenandoah (1926), Great Smoky Mountains (1926), Mammoth Cave (1926), Grand Teton (1929), Carlsbad Caverns (1930), Isle Royal (1931), Everglades (1934), Big Bend (1935) and Olympic (1938). The Eastern Parks were assembled largely through the efforts of philanthropists and state governments.

A reorganization in 1933 brought battlefields and historic places into the system. Virtually all of these areas had private property within their boundaries, yet its distribution did not unduly disturb operation and management of the affected units. But a dramatic shift in national policy came with the authorization of Minuteman National Historic Park in 1959 and Cape Cod National Seashore in 1961. Both of these areas had to be assembled from predominantly private lands before they could be made available to the public. Congress followed this lead by the quick authorization of three National Seashores: Padre Island (1962), Point Reyes (1962), and Assateague Island (1965), plus a host of preserves in other categories, all comprised of predominantly private property. In 1968, Redwood became the first National Park to be made up primarily of appropriated real estate.

The Land and Water Conservation Fund was approved by Congress in 1964, providing monies for federal and state acquisition of private lands for preservation uses, and sealed the new trend in National Park policy: no longer would the nation's "public pleasuring grounds" be hewn from the public domain with small private inholdings, but henceforth were to be taken primarily from private citizens, with or without small parcels of public land included. Whether one regards this new trend as an abuse, an imbalance or a sound direction, it definitely marks a drastic change in historical U.S. land policy.

A substantial amount of the United States is administered by the National Park Service, and National Parks are not the only thing you will find in the system. There are more than 20 different kinds of Park Service areas, and this multitude of classifications is divided into three major categories, Natural Areas, Historical Areas, and Recreational Areas. Although the National Park system is best known for its great scenic parks, and justly so, more than half the areas in the system preserve places and commemorate persons, events, or activities important in America's history.

Natural Areas include National Parks, National Monuments, Wilderness Areas (most, however, are administered by the Department of Agriculture's Forest Service), National Environmental Education Landmarks, National Preserves, and Registered Natural Landmarks. A National Park is usually large in area and contains a variety of resources; a National Monument is normally smaller than a National Park, lacks its diversity, but preserves at

least one nationally significant resource, such as Devils Tower in Wyoming, /
the first National Monument, established September 24, 1906, and made
famous in the 1977 science-fiction movie *Close Encounters of the Third Kind*,
which brought hordes of visitors the following summer.

Historical Areas include National Historic Sites, National Historical
Parks, National Memorials, National Military Parks, National Battlefields,
National Battlefield Parks, National Battlefield Sites, National Cemeteries
and National Historic Landmarks. This bewildering array of titles includes
vastly different things; the home of Abraham Lincoln in Springfield, Illinois,
is a National Historic Site, but the Lincoln Memorial in Washington is a
National Memorial. The obvious military titles preserve diverse areas important in American history, although other areas such as National Monuments
may also include forts and other items of military interest.

Recreation Areas include National Parkways, National Recreation
Areas, National Seashores, National Lakeshores, National Scenic Trails, National Scenic Riverways and National Wild and Scenic Rivers. The Parkways
are mere ribbons of land flanking low-speed roadways with 35- to 45-mile-
per-hour speed limits for leisurely driving through scenic areas, such as Blue
Ridge. National Recreation Areas were originally units surrounding the
reservoirs impounded by federal dams, but now include both natural and
urban areas—some NRAs are administered by the Forest Service or by the
U.S. Army Corps of Engineers. Wild and Scenic Rivers preserve ribbons of
land bordering free-flowing streams which have not been dammed or channel-
ized, or otherwise man-altered, and are used primarily for canoeing, hiking,
or hunting.

By 1980 there were 323 separate areas authorized in the National Park
system, 319 of them fully established: 132 Natural Areas (41%), 131 Historical Areas (41%), and 56 Recreational Areas (18%), covering 77.0 million
acres, or 117,000 square miles, an area nearly twice the size of the six New
England States or larger than Arizona, sixth largest state in the Union.

The growth of the National Park system during the preservationist
decades between 1960 and 1980 gives us a useful perspective: The number of
units in the system was 185 in 1960 compared to 319 in 1980 (72%
increase); acreage grew from 25.1 million in 1960 to 77.0 million in 1980
(207% increase); the staff of the National Park Service increased from 4,036
in 1960 to 15,349 in 1980 (280% growth); and visitation rose from 73.6
million to 300.3 million (a gain of 310%). But Congressional funding tells
the story Secretary Watt was talking about when he described the deteriorated
condition of the parks after years of expansion: in 1960, the land acquisition
fund was a mere $5.28 million compared to 1980's $152.9 million (dollar
figures are adjusted by the Consumer Price Index to compensate for the effects

of inflation). On the other hand, construction funds in 1960 amounted to $127.04 million but had shrunk in 1980 to $108 million inflation-adjusted dollars, or $127.7 1980 dollars. These figures were provided by Ric Davidge, Special Assistant to G. Ray Arnett, Assistant Secretary for Fish and Wildlife and Parks, and were gathered for an Interior Department in-house (unpublished) document, *Trends in National Park System Management*. Davidge, a recognized expert on federal land acquisition and the application of eminent domain law, feels that these numbers and others substantiate claims that land-grabbing had seriously overbalanced caring for what the system already owned during the preservationist years. Davidge is chairman of Interior's Lands Policy Work Group, which was established by Secretary Watt to develop a clear and positive national policy outlining the proper federal role in open-space conservation.

The land acquisition policy of the Park Service during the preservationist era between 1960 and 1980 was centered around obtaining title in what real estate people call "fee simple" ownership. Fee simple is absolute and unqualified ownership, the highest and most ample estate of ownership known to law, out of which all other kinds of title are taken or "carved." The government's right of eminent domain has long provided for confiscation of fee simple ownerships of private property for public use. The particular method of asserting eminent domain used in most National Park land acquisition during this time was either Congressional Taking by which the federal legislature exerts its Fifth Amendment right to take anything it wants from any citizen so long as it pays for what is taken, or the Declaration of Taking issued by the Park Service. The Declaration of Taking is a particularly harsh step: title changes immediately to the United States government. The landowner need not be notified in advance. The landowner must sue the new owner to get his land back. The government can give you 90 days to get off the property; 90 percent of the "approved appraised value," set by the government, becomes immediately available to the dispossessed owner. It is a frightening thing to have happen to you.

In 1978, disgruntled inholders got together and formed the National Inholders Association, which describes itself as "a public interest non-profit group formed to protect the rights of Americans on lands owned or regulated by government." This inholder group was invited to testify in Washington at a "Workshop on Public Land Acquisition and Alternatives" held by the Subcommittee of Public Lands and Reserved Water of the Senate Energy and Natural Resources Committee in October 1981. National Inholders Executive Director Charles S. Cushman described 'many of the problems his constituents had with the Park Service, beginning with the problem of agreeing on a price for condemned inholdings: "There seems to be a good case that the Park

Service has been less than candid with the Congress in setting values for certain projects."

Cushman cited a specific instance: "The *Los Angeles Times* released a Park Service memo which indicated that it would take $667 million to complete the Santa Monica Mountains National Recreation Area if all the money were obtained in 1982 and Declarations of Taking were used to freeze values. Experts familiar with the situation feel the ultimate price will be at least $1 billion and probably much more. The authorized price was $155 million and that didn't inflate to over $1 billion in two years. That increase, it appears, is not due so much to inflation as to faulty value setting motivated by political considerations in order to get the legislation passed." However, a House Committee, not the Park Service, set the original $155 million price tag.

A very real example of politically motivated low estimates came from the expansion of Redwood National Park in 1977: Sierra Club projections for taking 48,000 acres of timberlands were in the $200 million range. Congress authorized $335 million, which has already been spent to pay for *one-third* of the land; the ultimate price tag will obviously exceed $1 billion, and for one of the least-visited Parks in the system, which consists of more than 38,000 acres of land that had been cutover and replanted in young seedlings by its former commercial timber firm owners in decades past—hardly the image of the magnificent National Park.

Because of such deliberately low estimates, the $3 billion backlog of incomplete projects acknowledged by the Park Service will probably exceed $10 billion in cost overruns.

Low valuation problems have another aspect: Cushman testified that the Park Service has gone "appraisal shopping" to find the lowest figure available in settling property claims. One Inholders Association member, Cushman says, caught the Park Service flatfooted when a "shopped" appraisal was adopted and the landowner's was judged to be faulty. Cushman says, "The only reason the landowner became aware of the different appraisals was that he didn't recognize the name on the appraisal he saw. He was never given an opportunity to accompany the appraiser as is required under Public Law 91-646." Here are further points brought up in Cushman's testimony:

An Inholders member in Florida suffered another injustice: coercion. A Park Service agent told this family they would receive more money for relocation benefits if they would agree to a lower settlement price for their house. A California member had been denied access to a roadway that had been promised him and was told he might not get back 53 acres of his property that had been seized but was later found to lie outside the Park

Service boundary unless he agreed to a lower price for the property within the boundary.

An Arkansas farmer who was dispossessed waited so long for payment that he could no longer find another farm for the amount he received—a victim of inflation and delays. In a Minnesota case involving the U.S. Forest Service, a landowner wanted to widen a road over government land so that an oil truck could deliver heating oil and the family could remain in their home during wintertime. Cushman testified that "The official of the agency said within hearing distance of witnesses he was not aware of that 'things happen—the agency has been known to burn down houses.' This house was on fee title land. This family has never escaped the fear of that statement." Three years later, the family still did not have winter access and were slipping into bankruptcy from the cost of finding winter accommodations.

Cushman pointed up the magnitude of the problem: 70,000 parcels of land have been acquired by the Park Service in the last 14 years, he says, and in 1979 alone, 21,000 condemnations were in process, nearly half of them by the National Park Service. It must be remembered that Mr. Cushman is an advocate, and may tend to overstate his case as much as environmentalist advocates. In checking his numbers with Willis Kriz, Chief of the Land Resources Division of the National Park Service, the total number of private tracts acquired from 1965 to 1980, inclusive, was 87,155; 45,200 of those resulted from the addition of Big Cypress National Preserve in Florida, mostly subdivision lots, which is why the number is so large. Thus, without Big Cypress, the Park Service has condemned 44,955 private properties since 1965. Many of these sales were by willing sellers, but without doubt, many more were accompanied by hardships, emergencies, severe economic dislocation, culture shock, and emotional trauma. The Park Service, you see, classifies anyone as a "willing seller" who sells prior to a judge rendering a decision, even those who do so under threat of condemnation.

Totally aside from the individual suffering, Cushman warned against overzealous administration of these takings and attitudes that fly in the teeth of our ideals, of proper forms of government, of individual liberties. His prime exhibit was the Environmental Impact Statement for Fire Island National Seashore, stated in the Park Service's own words:

Impacts on the Socioeconomic Environment

Opportunities for additional development in the development district of the Seashore would become progressively more limited as the federal government acquired more land within the communities and held it in reserve as undeveloped open space. The density of development would slowly decrease, resulting in a general decline in the population that the communities could support. As the population declined, commercial establishments providing goods and services to residents would realize progressively lower profits, and the number of closings would increase. Development within the commercial districts would slowly be acquired by the federal government and the land converted to open space. Ferry service from the Long Island mainland would become less profitable and more limited as population declined. With access progressively more restricted, goods and services more difficult to secure, and the land progressively more fragmented into a mosaic of developed and undeveloped parcels, the communities would become less desirable places for some residents to live; these residents would sell their properties to the federal government. Eventually, a small cadre of residents would remain. These would be self-sufficient people willing to endure the considerable inconvenience of living in isolated enclaves with a matrix of federal land.

When I read this EIS it sounded hauntingly familiar. I then realized it was virtually a synopsis of events in Ayn Rand's novel, *Atlas Shrugged*, without a John Galt, and with the federal government serving as the man who "stopped the motor of the world." It also brought to mind a vision of America's future prophesied in many environmentalist writings from Ernest Callenbach's *Ecotopia* to E.F. Schumacher's *Small Is Beautiful*, from Gerald Barney's *The Unfinished Agenda* to William Ophuls' *Ecology and the Politics of Scarcity*, which asserted that modern civilization has outlived its usefulness and that we must be "governed by implacable ecological imperatives." Then the really chilling realization set in: the same mentality that had written the Fire Island EIS had been ensconced in hundreds of jobs in the Carter Administration, what Llewellyn King of the *Energy Daily* dubbed "the termite infestation." And how coolly that mentality had laid out the destruction of commerce and communities on Fire Island!

The General Accounting Office of the legislative branch in the federal government issued a number of reports on Interior Department land acquisition practices that point to abuses and injustice. A GAO report issued May 8, 1981, bore the title *The National Park Service Should Improve Its Land Acquisition And Mangement At The Fire Island National Seashore*. The summary on the cover of this report said: "The National Park Service's zoning standards at Fire Island National Seashore are too restrictive and permit land to be acquired that is not needed to achieve the purposes of the Fire Island National Seashore Act. The National Park Service should revise its zoning standards, establish criteria for acquiring properties, and sell back to private citizens land it acquired but does not need." In the body of this report, GAO officials took the Park Service to task for their extreme interpretation of zoning powers in a neatly understated remark: "Zoning should be an alternative to, not a means of, fee simple acquisition." The environmentalist formula for putting the lights out on Fire Island has been overturned by new 1980 standards of resource protection for the area, under which no new condemnations have been executed.

Another important General Accounting Office study was requested by none other than Democratic Representative Phillip Burton of San Francisco. Burton is second-ranking majority member of the powerful House Interior and Insular Affairs Committee which rides herd on Interior and these days on Jim Watt. Congressman Burton was one of those who has forged the sawtooth edge of national land acquisition policy. In the summer of 1979, Congressman Burton and Interior Secretary Cecil Andrus, and a few others, determined to dispossess all 36,000 inholders from the National Parks within four years, to do in one Presidency what had not been accomplished since 1916. Recalling that the General Accounting Office is normally friendly to its legislative clients, Congressman Burton, as the Chairman of the Subcommittee on National Parks and Insular Affairs, asked them to look into the matter of federal land acquisition, hoping their report would bolster his position against the fledgling National Inholders Association. GAO complied with the request.

On December 14, 1979, Congressman Burton received "A Report by the Comptroller General of the United States." But the title of the report dismayed him: *The Federal Drive to Acquire Private Lands Should be Reassessed.* A banner headline in the *San Francisco Chronicle* announced: "Burton Stung by GAO Study Made at His Request." A paragraph on the cover of the GAO report said:

"The National Park, Forest, and Fish and Wildlife Services had been following a general practice of acquiring as much private land as possible regardless of need, alternative land control methods, and impacts on private landowners." Congressman Burton may have been appalled at this lack of support, but GAO's recommendations were a worse blow to his intentions for the inholders:

GAO recommends that the Secretaries of Agriculture and Interior: (1) jointly establish a policy on when lands should be purchased or when other protection alternatives, such as easements, zoning, and Federal controls, should be used; (2) critically evaluate the need to purchase additional lands in existing projects; and (3) prepare plans identifying lands needed to achieve project purposes and objectives at every new project before acquiring land.

Among the many abuses this GAO report cited were a number that had appeared on the National Inholders Association's list: "Agencies have regularly exceeded original cost estimates for purchasing land. The cost of many projects has doubled, tripled, even quadrupled from original estimates and authorizations. Also, agencies have bought land without adequate consideration of the impact on communities and private owners."

The report cited a specific example of insensitivity:

When a 52-mile section of the Lower St. Croix River was made a component of the Wild and Scenic River System, local zoning ordinances were changed to provide protection. The Park Service, however, viewed this as only a temporary measure until it could purchase titles and restrictive easements to all the lands in the Park Service's 27-mile section. Costs have increased from the initial legislated ceiling of $7.3 million to the current ceiling of $19 million. This attitude toward zoning has antagonized local communities and landowners.

Congressman Burton was not really surprised by GAO's response to his request: he knew that on May 22, 1978, GAO had released a report entitled *Federal Protection And Preservation Of Wild And Scenic Rivers Is Slow And Costly*. GAO reported that Congress had passed the Wild and Scenic Rivers Act in 1968, designating 8 rivers as components of the system. By 1977, 11 rivers had been added to the system and 58 more had been identified as potential additions—the bottomless pit aspect of such laws was rearing its ugly head. However, states had been reluctant to nominate rivers "because national designation contributes to increased river use, with attendant problems of deterioration of scenic values and increased administrative costs." The report also complained that "Acquisition of lands and easements as a preservation strategy has proven controversial, time consuming and increasingly costly."

On January 22, 1981, the very day Jim Watt was confirmed as Secretary of the Interior, the GAO published a report called *Lands in the Lake Chelan National Recreation Area Should Be Returned to Private Ownership*, which asserted that Congress had intended that land acquisition costs in this Washington State scenic area "be minimal, the private community of Stehekin in the recreation area continue to exist, existing commercial development not be eliminated, and additional compatible development be permitted to accommodate increased visitor use." GAO not only complained that the Park Service had violated the intent of Congress in its management of the area, but also that it had wrongfully dispossessed landowners and should sell back certain areas to private individuals.

The pressure for the National Park Service to continually acquire new lands comes from two main sources: large national environmental groups such as the National Parks and Conservation Association who feel a proprietary interest in enlarging the public domain, and local environmental groups and governments who pressure Congressmen to obtain federal funding for what are essentially community uses. Underhanded tactics have been used in numerous cases to deprive landowners of their rights to use private property being considered for federal classification. A most notorious case involves the local government effort to include a private tract known as Wolfback Ridge in the Golden Gate National Recreation Area in the San Francisco Bay region.

This horror story was brought to my attention by Joseph Gughemetti, co-author of *The Taking*, who had come across it while researching his book. Then, among the many files provided for my inspection by Ric Davidge of the National Park Service, I discovered a folder of correspondence about Wolfback Ridge that tells a story of collusion and unconscionable government intrusion into the life of private citizens.

Golden Gate National Recreation Area was one of two "experiments" in federal urban park formation—the other was New York harbor's Gateway NRA—both of which were established October 27, 1981. Golden Gate NRA was conceived as a long playground stretching north and south of San Francisco and including a long strip of waterfront real estate in Congressman Phillip Burton's district. The northern extension was to include parts of the city of Sausalito, where three families, FitzSimmons, Lynch, and Melchoir, owned a 160-acre parcel on a mountain crest known as Wolfback Ridge, commanding some of most magnificent views in the Bay Area. The owners were unaware of it, but on May 10, 1972, City of Sausalito Mayor Mrs. Robin R. Sweeny wrote a letter to Congressman William S. Mailliard concerning their property.

Mayor Sweeny was concerned about a large 1,800-acre tract known as the Marincello property, near Wolfback Ridge that was slated for addition to Golden Gate NRA (GGNRA). It seems that a good price could be negotiated with its owners because there was no recent comparable sale for an appraiser to use in setting a higher price. But Mr. FitzSimmons had just thrown a monkey-wrench into the deal by submitting plans to subdivide the jointly owned Wolfback Ridge property and sell it, which would give any appraiser a very exact idea of what the Marincello property was really worth, and that posed a great difficulty. As Mrs. Sweeny wrote to the Congressman, "Since the U.S. Government is required by law to pay the appraised fair market value for any lands it acquires, the sale of the FitzSimmons property into residential lots would create high, recent and very comparable sales which no appraiser could ignore when valuing the Marincello lands for sale to the Unites States." That could not be allowed. It would threaten inclusion of the Marincello property in GGNRA. The answer was obvious: all you had to do to prevent the Wolfback Ridge sale was to add it to GGNRA too.

As Mayor Sweeny put it, "For this much additional cost due to the FitzSimmons subdivision, it would certainly make more sense to the United States to acquire the FitzSimmons property for inclusion in the Golden Gate

NRA." The owners were not notified of this letter, which strongly suggests that the ensuing entanglement had nothing to do with the desirability of the Wolfback Ridge property for a National Recreation Area on its own merits, but was merely to prevent any unacceptable increase in price on the Marincello tract.

In the autumn of 1972, Congress authorized Golden Gate NRA, but did not include Wolfback Ridge. The Marincello price tag could still go up if FitzSimmons sold the land, and the game was still on. Democratic Senator Alan Cranston wrote Mayor Sweeny on October 13, 1972, to apologize in advance that "Unfortunately, the Wolfback Ridge area was not included in the bill," but offered, "If there's any other way in which I can help with the preservation of the Wolfback Ridge area, please don't hesitate to let me know."

By now FitzSimmons had made several applications to subdivide the land and had been put off each time. Mayor Sweeny began to panic; she knew that there was no basis in law for denying FitzSimmons' request. She contacted Washington, D.C., governmental affairs consultant Jonas V. Morris for advice, and in a letter dated October 17, 1972, Morris wrote,

I suggest that right away, preferably before the election, you get Maillaird, Cranston, Tunney and if possible Burton to agree to introduce in January legislation amending the GGNRA by including the Wolfback Ridge property. Get the commitment in writing, if at all possible. . . . If you lay the ground work, I think you have a very good chance of getting Wolfback included in the NRA in another year or so. I hope you can hold off FitzSimmons that long.

But Ed·FitzSimmons kept at it, trying to get the subdivision approved, and a number of local government agents were becoming increasingly nervous over his persistence. The chances that he would discover their collusion and begin legal proceedings grew with every passing day. On February 12, 1974, Acting Superintendent of Golden Gate NRA Jack Wheat responded to a request from Lari Sheehan of the Local Agency Formation Commission in the Bay Area asking that the Park Service act to stop FitzSimmons from subdividing his land. To his everlasting credit, Wheat wrote, "Until such time as this property is authorized for acquisition by the National Park Service, we can in no way restrain Mr. FitzSimmons from pursuing his legal rights."

The federal government approached the Wolfback Ridge owners to see if a price could be negotiated. The owners made it clear they would not accept less than $25,000 per acre, or about $4 million for the entire tract. Nevertheless, environmentalists interested in the Wolfback Ridge acquisition told the federal government that the fair market value was in the range of $260,000 which was less than half of what the Marin County Assessor had valued it for in 1971!

By mid-1974, the Sausalito city council had denied development rights for the sixth time for a 311-home subdivision on 156 acres of Wolfback Ridge. By the end of the year, however, Congress came through and finally added Wolfback Ridge as an authorized acquisition target for the Golden Gate NRA. Yet the owners still had the property and continued to demand their rights. In May of 1975, the City of Sausalito slapped an outright moratorium on any development on Wolfback Ridge.

As Gughemetti and Wheeler note in their study, *The Taking*, "In September 1975 the federal government offered the Wolfback Ridge owners $1 million for their property." Then on July 12, 1976, "the United States filed a condemnation action to acquire the Wolfback Ridge property. Despite the fact that the government had already offered the owners $1 million for their property, the government's testimony as to the value of that property was reduced to $300,000. . . ." This was an outrageous offer for prime-view residential property and the owners sued; in June 1977 they prevailed in federal court, obtaining a jury award of $3.8 million. The federal government appealed this award, but after a year and a half of further delays and haggling, dropped their appeal and finally paid the owners their "just compensation" in December of 1978. It came too late for owner Frank Lynch: he died of cancer while waiting for the government.

But that is not the end of the story. The fact that several members of the federal government, Congressman Phillip Burton for one and Senator Alan Cranston for another, acted with full knowledge of the City of Sausalito's intent to prevent the Wolfback Ridge owners from excercising their property rights may very well constitute a conspiracy to deprive citizens of their civil rights under an obscure law known as the Civil Rights Act of 1871. This law provides "That if two or more persons within any State or Territory of the United States shall conspire together . . . and if any one or more persons engaged in any such conspiracy shall do, or cause to be done, any act in furtherance of the object of such conspiracy, whereby any person shall be injured in his person or property, or deprived of having and excercising any right or privilege of a citizen of the United States, the person so injured or deprived" has the right to obtain damages in court.

The concept that property rights are civil rights has struggled to the fore in recent years, against such environmentalist views as those expressed by the Wilderness Society's William Turnage: "I don't see that there is anything sacred about private property. I think human rights are more important than property rights." One exponent of property rights as civil rights, Dr. Frank Schnidman, visiting scholar in residence at Harvard Law School, discussed the issue with me at length. He feels that in the future, questions of federal land use policy will be increasingly shaped by concerns of developers and landowners over their civil rights. He points out that the courts have repeatedly stated since the 1971 case *Lynch* v. *Household Finance Corporation*, "that there is no real dichotomy between personal liberties and property rights, and that rights in property are basic civil rights." Schnidman also notes that "The civil rights law provides a federal judicial forum to examine the actions of local government, and a civil rights case can be made against the government officials holding them personally liable for damages, as well as holding the municipality liable." The Wolfback Ridge owners have not to my knowledge sought damages from the City of Sausalito and Mayor Sweeny, but they evidently could. Schnidman's words should stand as a caution to Turnage and other post-materialist environmentalists. Interesting consequences may ultimately flow from their unreasonable and uncompassionate views of private property and the working people who cherish ownership as a moral ideal.

Minerals and Energy Policy

Industrial civilization runs on minerals and energy. Secretary Watt's early policy directives in these areas drew sharp criticism from environmentalists who feared that their hard-fought victories since 1960 might be swept away in the face of a national minerals shortage. Yet Watt's own concerns had been aroused by previous Administrations that had tended to ignore minerals policy and to propose weak energy policy. One of the prime missions of his Secretariat, he felt, was to be the construction of a sound strategic minerals policy; Congress had ordered the Executive branch to do so since the Mining and Minerals Policy Act of 1970, but it had never complied.

In 1970 only 17 percent of federal land was closed to mineral entry. By 1980, the Department of the Interior acknowledged 42 percent to be absolutely closed and an additional 25 percent to be "highly or moderately restricted." Restricted or closed lands include military installations, Indian reservations, National Parks, National Forests, National Trails, Wild and Scenic Rivers, National Seashores and Wilderness Areas.

Also, 20 different federal departments, agencies, councils and commissions create policy and programs which significantly affect nonfuel minerals supply and consumption. There are 80 different laws, executive orders and regulations which deal with non-fuel minerals. In 1980 there was no federal policy which controlled, directed, or coordinated these activities.

A "Nonfuel Minerals Policy Report" issued by the Carter Administration in August 1979 failed to assess and evaluate the serious problem areas of import dependency, strategic minerals stockpiles, or critical shortages. As natural science editor Robert C. Cowen wrote in a January 1982 *Christian Science Monitor* article, "U.S. dependence on imported strategic raw materials—resources essential to its industry and defense—is as much a continuing threat to the U.S. economy and national security as is reliance on imported oil. Yet this has aroused nowhere near a comparable degree of public concern." But more than half a million scientists and technicians whose professional societies make up the umbrella-group Federation of Materials Societies (FMS) are deeply concerned.

The Federation has declared, "The United States depends heavily on foreign imports of more than . . . 90 percent of our total annual requirements of columbium, manganese, chromium, cobalt, bauxite [an aluminum ore] and platinum metals; between 75 percent and 90 percent of our requirements for tin and nickel; and between 50 and 75 percent of our requirements for zinc, antimony, tungsten and cadmium."

In November of 1979, Harry J. Gray, Chairman and President of United Technologies Corporation, parent company of Pratt & Whitney Aircraft, a leading jet engine manufacturer, laid out four hard realities to the American Society for Metals meeting in Chicago:

One: The United States is a have-not nation when it comes to certain critical metals. Two: From 1950 to the present, our raw materials situation has deteriorated drastically. We have *never* been self-sufficient, and today we are frighteningly vulnerable to overseas producers. Three: For certain critical metals, such as chromium and cobalt, we are close to 100 percent dependent on imports. Four: Our primary sources for these critical metals are unstable or unfriendly.

Hopes for resolving critical minerals shortages and vulnerabilities through domestic production have been dashed in the last decade, not only for the five most sensitive materials, (cobalt, chromium, manganese, platinum, titanium), but also for 22 others among the 36 minerals that are strategically critical to U.S. economic and security interests. The mining industry says it is discouraged by excessive environmental regulations such as certain clauses of the Clean Air Act which are too restrictive on smelters, driving refinery production to foreign countries. The three cures for the problem, recycling, conservation and discovery of substitute materials, have not lived up to their promise. Freight rates are far higher for scrap steel than ore, which discourages recycling. The once bright vision of "garbage into gold" has in fact turned into a quagmire of 700 million tons of iron and steel scrap now on hand that we are nowhere near being able to use economically. Conservation techniques, using less metal to make equivalent products, have already pushed the frontiers of metalworking knowledge to their limits, but as Oleg D. Sherby of Stanford University warned Congress in 1980, "Metalworking research facilities are either primitive or nonexistent at universities in the United States. And education in metalforming is not being emphasized." New materials and alloys are being discovered all the time, but for the most part have been mere tradeoffs of one critical mineral for another, with few real breakthroughs in finding substitutes for vital product uses. Vacillating and unpredictable federal land policy has also discouraged mineral inventories, mineral exploration, and mineral extraction and processing. For example, although the Wilderness Act of 1964 clearly demands a mineral inventory of all lands under consideration for inclusion in the National Wilderness Preservation System, not one area has been thoroughly studied to discover what mineral resources it contains. Worse, in several cases, Congressional committees with environmentalist biases have proposed that known sources of critical strategic minerals be forever removed from economic use.

The U.S. energy resources on federal lands are well-documented, but a General Accounting Office report estimated it would take 50 years to complete a mineral assessment of government properties. This is an intolerable situation in light of the fact that our nation is largely dependent on unreliable foreign sources for materials that enable us to travel, to receive medical care, to work at jobs that put groceries on the table, to grow the produce we put in grocery bags and to manufacture the bags themselves. Representative Jim Santini of Nevada, Chairman of the House Mines and Mining Subcommittee, sees this dependency in the light of "resource wars." He has said, "The Soviet Union has moved into the international resource arena armed with a strategy of confrontation that extends beyond economic competition, but which falls just short of conventional military conflict." Santini notes the USSR's own mineral self-sufficiency and the Soviet penetration of such critical areas as those near South Africa, a major U.S. supplier of minerals. Representative Don Fuqua of Florida, chairman of the House Science and Technology Committee, sees the Soviet bloc maneuvering to starve the Western world of minerals. Environmentalist groups such as the Sierra Club and Audubon Society are suspicious of these views and Watt's as an excuse to relax pollution control laws and open wilderness lands to mining, even though, as we shall see in later chapters, Watt advocated only an *inventory* of Wilderness lands in accordance with the Wilderness Act of 1964, and has *never* advocated *mining* in Wilderness (or National Parks, for that matter), although he has advocated opening other federal lands to mining.

National energy policy was not in much better shape when Watt took office. Less than 15 percent of federal onshore lands were under lease for oil and gas development. No oil and gas leases had been issued in Alaska for 15 years. Only 4 percent of the entire Outer Continental Shelf (OCS) had been made available for oil and gas exploration, and less than 2 percent had been leased. Less than 1 percent of federal coal lands were under lease and new leasing had been at a virtual standstill since 1971. No tar sands leases had been issued since 1965. Geothermal energy development had been stifled by administratively imposed delays and a Department apparently unwilling to issue new leases. The areas of minerals and energy had clearly become severely imbalanced during the environmental revolution in favor of preservation and against economic use.

General Environmentalist Imbalances

Examples of administrative bias toward preservation and against development can be found every place there is federal land. The place where there is most federal land is Alaska, which was 95 percent federally owned or controlled in 1980. While environmentalists spread the image that Alaska was nearly as developed as New Jersey and that bulldozers were poised to push over the last landmark in its 375 million acres, the fact is that there are fewer people in the entire State (407,000) than inside the city limits of Seattle (470,000), and less than 3 percent of Alaska's area is privately owned (600,000 acres). The state was granted 103 million acres of federal land in its Statehood Act, but has not received it all yet. When the Alaska National Interest Lands Conservation Act of 1977 proposed to designate 83 million acres as immediate Wilderness and another 45 million acres for Wilderness study, most citizens of Alaska strongly objected, not only to the vast extent of these preserves, but also to their strategic locations. In 1978, among the strongest statements I heard in Alaska were those of a normally soft-spoken man who is widely respected throughout his state: Lew Williams, publisher of the *Ketchikan Daily News*. He told me,

If you look at the environmentalists' wilderness areas, you'll see that they put one at the end of every road in the state to prevent any further development whatsoever. Somehow, they got hold of our Chamber of Commerce list of projects and programs and put a stop to every single one. Not just some of them; every last one. They took away our power supply by preventing any hydroelectric dams. They took away our timber supply by locking up the most productive forest lands. They took away a molybdenum mine [a critical mineral] in Misty Fjords, the largest known deposit on earth. They blocked the Unuk River access corridor so we can never tie our roads into the Alaskan highway, which isolates us here on the coast in Ketchikan with only slow barge or high-cost air transport forever. These environmentalists have no conscience about the economic well-being of their fellow human beings. Their plan [which was adopted] is a disaster for nearly everybody in Alaska. I look upon these environmental groups as organized crime.

This is not the kind of thing you usually hear from a responsible community leader, but I heard it repeated in every town in Alaska, by mayors, by bankers, by schoolteachers, by university professors. A small cadre of locals and the big political clout of national environmentalist groups has permanently stopped much significant development in Alaska.

In other cases, it is not a single action such as Wilderness withdrawal that poses the imbalance, but rather subtle interconnections between a law here, a study there, a set of regulations someplace else that adds up to a nightmarish web of restrictions. A particularly dumbfounding case involves the ripple impacts of the National Forest Management Act of 1976 (NFMA), its regulations, which were created by a Committee of Scientists, and its interlocking features affecting the Roadless Area Review and Evaluation study number two (RARE II), which carried on in 1977 a Wilderness study begun in 1972, this one affecting 62 million acres in the "Lower 48." The impacts on national timber supply were so complex that special studies had to be carried out, sorting administrative classifications, Code of Federal Regulations (CFR) citations, RARE II study area timber volumes, and dozens of technical forestry criteria. I discussed the impact on the nation's timber supply in 1980 with Dennis Teeguarden, professor of forestry at the University of California at Berkeley, who had also served as chairman of the Committee of Scientists which had developed the regulations for the NFMA. Dr. Teeguarden told me: "The United States has lost from 20 to 25 percent of its annual allowable harvest of timber as a result of the National Forest Management Act of 1976 and its regulations. But the problem is so complex that I am unable to determine whether this loss is a part of, or in addition to, the losses we will suffer from RARE II." Dr. Teeguarden is one of the best qualified forest scientists in the United States. His frank admission of uncertainty in this crucial issue is testimony to the complication and strangling complexity of many environmentalist-inspired restrictions on our economy.

Inequities in Wilderness Area additions and restriction of public land use were studied by agricultural-and-forest economist Frederick W. Obermiller of Oregon State University. Dr. Obermiller found that the benefits of these restrictions flowed predominantly to remote urban dwellers of middle- and higher-income levels and the costs were borne primarily by local economies, firms and households. In his report, *The Local Costs of Public Land Use Restrictions* (1980), Obermiller said "From the point of view of local resource users and dependent communities, a decision which is efficient in the national context may be viewed as quite inequitable by local people if they must forego benefits in the interests of greater net benefits at the national level." This trend to place the burden of environmentalism on producers and local communities is widespread throughout the United States, but particularly devastating in the Western states.

Obermiller's analysis, *An Economic Interpretation of the "Sagebrush Rebellion"* (1981) stated that "The federal government is perceived to have failed to invest sufficiently in the public domain; to have have allowed the productivity of public land resources to diminish through improper management; and to have neglected to consider the opportunity costs to traditional users of land use decisions designed to preserve or enchance environmental quality." Western supporters of the "Sagebrush Rebellion" generally agree with the Public Lands Council, a resource group, that

. . . all regulations and laws pertinent to the grazing, management, and development of public lands be either honestly enforced, properly amended, or repealed in such manner as (1) to expedite, fund, and maximize the programs of range improvement and range research; (2) to protect the land and domestic livestock from damage by pests, predators, and other influences which would detract from orderly increasing food and fiber production; and (3) to minimize or prevent adverse impacts of military activities, wildlife refuges, wilderness, wild and scenic rivers, or other government activities which could reduce or materially interfere with livestock production.

Obermiller notes that other supporters emphasize mining or timber harvesting, but that common concerns have united producers and households as well as local governments to demand fair treatment. Local governments are concerned since tax payments derived from productive use of public lands are lost when Wilderness Areas are added or restrictions are placed on land management. Obermiller suggests that cash reimbursement of local victims of environmentalism would be in order so that "America could accept responsibility for the burden those limited-use designations impose on local people living in public land-dependent communities."

Other examples of public land imbalances can be found in the Carter Administration water project "hit list" of 1977 in which 18 major federal water projects were held up "for reconsideration." Five of these water projects were the responsibility of the Bureau of Reclamation in the Department of the Interior. Secretary Andrus had recommended they be killed: Auburn on the American River in California, Fruitland Mesa on Crystal and Curecanti Creeks in Colorado, Narrows Unit on the South Platte River in Colorado, Oahe Unit on the Missouri River in South Dakota, and Savery-Pot Hook on Savery Creek in Colorado and Pot Hook Creek in Wyoming. Federal water projects are commonly dubbed "boondoggles" by the environmental movement, and seen merely as ways to enrich local business tycoons. The National Wildlife Federation, for example, in its July 31, 1981, *Conservation*

Report editorialized about "Waste Wins Again" in the passage of funding for the Tennessee-Tombigbee Waterway, calling it a "pet project" and "pork barrelling." Never in these criticisms is the small farmer beneficiary acknowledged to exist; never is the general economic benefit in more abundant food and fiber and jobs acknowledged to exist.

In the general society, an immense array of post-materialist desires has cropped up that adds more and more pressure to further burden the economy: "Animal rights" advocates push for restrictions that would lower our output of food; "conscience cooking" advocates seek to remove meat from our diet and destroy an entire livestock industry; anti-pesticide advocates have succeeded in limiting pest control even in cases where chemical means have been shown repeatedly to be safe; "aquarian conspiracy" advocates who admire Marilyn Ferguson's fascinating book on social and personal transformation press for hundreds of post-materialist causes that may ultimately come home to roost in public policy—and further restrict America's economic vigor. The ramifications are endless. Our economy is not.

Such stories of the crippling of the U.S. economy from within are legion. We have bit by bit impaired our productivity with excessive and unwise restrictions on forest and rangelands, on water and agriculture, on construction and manufacture, on energy and minerals, *on every material value upon which our society is built*. Serious problems have arisen from a multitude of these restrictions. Most of the problems were unexpected side effects of genuine attempts to improve our quality of life. The impacts of this well-meaning but devastating movement are so widespread that even experts cannot calculate the ultimate economic destruction. Just as we once learned from ecology that all nature is interconnected, so we are learning that the same thing is true of a society's material economy: tamper with it here and it will lash back and strike you in an unexpected "there." Some of the tampering hits the headlines, but most of it creeps silently like a slow-motion version of the Russian Revolution of 1917 or like the curse of Caliban in Shakespeare's *Tempest* to "make us inchmeal a disease."

When Jim Watt held his House Interior and Insular Affairs Committee orientation briefing in February 1981, Chairman Morris Udall of Arizona led off by asserting that "most conservationists think they have the balance and you are extreme." Secretary Watt responded by reminding Chairman Udall that his Senate confirmation had seen "shrill Senate voices" quoting from the Federal Land Policy and Management Act of 1976 about the Interior Secretary being the "guardian of our natural resources," and that Watt had chided them for failing to read on in the law to where it says "the Secretary is also made responsible for resource development." Balance is indeed a highly subjective judgment. But this chapter has perhaps revealed something of what Jim Watt meant in his final reply to Chairman Udall: "Environmentalist special interests read only what they want to, and press the Secretary to do only what they want him to."

CHAPTER 7
TAMING THE BUREAUCRACY

The secret of success is constancy to purpose.
—Disraeli

As we saw in Chapter 5, Watt spent his first weeks in office interviewing and gathering his management team. But there was a great deal more going on. The confusion that usually comes with a Presidential transition was compounded in 1981 by the Reagan Administration's intent to bring major change to American government. For the Department of the Interior during that winter and spring, the confusion at times verged on chaos. However, the confusion was quiet and the chaos sedate; there were no temper tantrums or shouting matches despite the pressures for rapid change—bureaucrats are well accustomed to periodic adjustment. Many in the Department who had worked with Watt during his previous years at Interior welcomed him back, not just to curry favor with the new boss, but out of real friendship. While almost no one was surprised at Jim's housecleaning of all the Carter appointees, or at the retention of Russell Dickenson as Director of the National Park Service, there were those who watched Watt's every move for signals about the future. It was a corridor conversation topic when Watt kept Secretary Andrus' driver and five of his six private secretaries, but brought in Kittie Smith, saying, "I picked her because she's as abrupt as I am." Senior Executive Service rules protect the jobs of upper-level administrators for 120 days while they prove they can work with the new boss. A few asked for transfers, and a number of lower-level ultra-environmentalist employees fled like rabbits, but most held tight, hoping for the best. Bureaucrats may be accustomed to periodic change, but they can't read minds.

Jim Watt's biggest problem was getting his new management direction across to the Department while juggling the tasks of budget preparation, training his new crew in "the government way," setting policy in half a dozen

125

areas of major national interest, testifying before Congressional committees, and continuing to interview and select the bulk of his appointees.

Within a week of his confirmation as Interior Secretary, Watt instituted a radically innovative program to get his management direction across to every political appointee in the senior and junior appointive echelons and every senior manager in the career professional civil service of the Department.

Perry Pendley, Secretary Watt's long-time friend and now Deputy Assistant Secretary for Minerals and Energy, tells of this first management initiative:

Those of us in the transition team had already agreed that everyone at headquarters should stay in Washington for the first six months, primarily to make sure that we ended up controlling the bureaucracy instead of it controlling us. It also saved some budget, but that was not the real point. Under Secretary Hodel and Steve Shipley, Jim's Executive Assistant—in fact, most of us—came up with that idea separately.

But then came the question of what to do while we stayed here in Washington. Jim saw the answer intuitively. You have to understand that Jim Watt has a very unusual mind for a bureaucrat, you might even say unique. He doesn't spend a lot of time figuring things out and finding all the rationale. Don Hodel does think that way, getting every last detail lined up, and that's why he's the perfect foil for Jim as Under Secretary. But Jim thinks intuitively, almost instinctively, and he's right more often than he's wrong. His answer to putting us in control of the bureaucracy was simple and totally unprecedented: he would personally establish routine contact with every senior manager in the Department through a series of regular meetings. Stupidly simple, but it works.

Each Monday morning at 8:00 A.M. sharp, Jim Watt walks into the Secretary's Conference Room on the fifth floor of the Interior Building's southwest wing and spends 45 minutes with his political appointees, those 15 or so people who were nominated by the President and confirmed with the advise and consent of the Senate in senior appointive positions, and those 20 or so more named by Secretary Watt to junior appointive jobs, such as Deputy Assistant Secretaries like Perry Pendley. All of these people are what could be called "Reaganites," and their meeting agenda includes not only Interior's technical business, but also the political issues of the day. Watt may also discuss matters of interest to Interior appointees who must testify before Congress, a continuous obligation. Watt may bring up news events concerning Interior. He may just talk. During the first month or so of Watt's tenure, none of his political appointees had been confirmed by the Senate—Don Hodel was the first, receiving confirmation as Under Secretary February 5th, but the next senior appointee confirmation did not come until the last of March, most waited until May and June, while the last stretched to December— and in the interim none of these nominees had any authority or power. Yet they had already arrived on the scene, had been hired by Interior as "consultants" in the time-honored way of coping with such transitional delays, and had begun their "on-the-job training" which was handled entirely by Jim Watt. Watt had named a career civil servant from Interior's professional ranks to serve in "acting" capacities for each appointee awaiting confirmation. However, he treated the unconfirmed appointees as if they were fully on board, giving them areas of responsibility, assigning tasks, asking them to meetings, checking their progress, giving advice. Law forbids unconfirmed nominees from certain actions, for example, signing paperwork or participating in budget decisions, although Watt allowed them to observe budget deliberations.

This awkward situation threw everyone off stride. As Secretary Watt recalls,

We laughed about our predicament frequently, because I'd tell some appointee like Ray Arnett or Garrey Carruthers to do such-and-such, and they really didn't have the authority to do it, so they would give my instructions to the career guy who had the "acting" authority. Then later I would get uptight about some job not being finished and jump on my political appointees who wouldn't know what had been done. Then it would come out that some GS-13 civil servant had done the appointee's job but didn't know who to report back to. So it was confusing to the whole Department at first because I ran things as if all the political appointees had been sworn in from the very beginning. I was determined to make them effective managers and get them into the work stream as soon as possible.

It took several weeks to get all the confusions sorted out so the civil servants knew what was going on. During this time, Watt was cagey about not letting his appointees overstep the bounds of law; the lawyer in him, no doubt. He didn't want anything coming back to haunt his people during Senate confirmation hearings. Much of the informal training Watt's new appointees received came from the eight o'clock Monday morning meeting. But there was much more to the Watt management initiative.

Each Monday morning at 9:00 A.M. sharp Jim Watt walks into the conference room of one of Interior's bureaus, for example, the Bureau of Land Management or the Office of Surface Mining, and meets with its senior management staff. There may be 5 or 6 political appointees in the room and 40 to 50 career professionals who are responsible for the work of the bureau. In these bureau meetings, Watt goes into fine detail on specific tasks assigned to the agency, monitoring their progress, checking the disposition of each duty, listening to problems and discussing solutions. Anyone in the room may say anything.

Forty-five minutes later, Watt goes to another bureau and does the same thing; then another and another. Thus Watt spends each Monday morning making personal contacts. In half a day, Watt sees all of his top-echelon political appointees and 200 or so career professionals at the senior manager level (which begins just below the political appointee level and spreads downward in rank). Watt rotates the bureaus that he meets with on a weekly basis. For example, he may meet with the Energy and Minerals bureaus on the first Monday of the month (Bureau of Mines, U.S. Geological Survey, Office of Surface Mining, and Office of Minerals Policy and Research Analysis), then with the Land and Water Resources bureaus on the second Monday of the month (Bureau of Reclamation, Bureau of Land Management, Office of Coal Leasing Planning and Coordination). As it works out, every senior manager in every bureau of the Department, about 800 of them, has personal contact with the Secretary once each month. But that's not all of the Watt management initiative.

Each Tuesday morning at 7:45 A.M. sharp, Jim Watt walks into the Secretary's Conference Room on the fifth floor of the Interior Building's southwest wing and spends 45 minutes with all the political appointees that he saw Monday morning, plus the top-ranking member of each bureau who happens to be in Washington that week (Watt relaxed his travel restrictions after the first six months of his Secretariat). This Tuesday morning meeting, known as the"Bureau Heads" meeting, is not a mere replay of the Monday morning meeting with more folks involved. The "Bureau Heads" meeting includes all the "Reaganites" plus other "cuts," as bureaucrats call "types": the senior managers of the bureaus are not all political appointees, some are career bureaucrats covered by the Civil Service Act and the Hatch Act. A civil service employee cannot be fired solely for political reasons, but only for cause and only under rigidly controlled conditions, which is not to say that political motivations may not be behind some firings of civil servants. Employees who have been "Hatched," that is, brought under the Hatch Act, may not participate in political activities beyond voting; they may not campaign for candidates or issues, electioneer, or discuss political issues in the workplace. Therefore, the Watt Tuesday morning agenda does not range over the political landscape like that of Monday morning, but sticks to the strict technical business of Interior. Actual subjects discussed may be instructions from Watt on how to handle specific Congressional requests for oversight information, or descriptions of news events and instructions on responses to the press, or inter-bureau conflicts, and so forth.

One Tuesday morning agenda item in those early months provides us with an almost diagnostic example of the Watt management style. It concerns the matter of leaks. The only overt resistance to Watt's policy initiatives that came from within the Department itself took the form of leaks. Internal memoranda from the National Park Service and the U.S. Fish and Wildlife Service were dropped by parties unknown over the transom and into the waiting lap of the *Washington Post*. While the memos themselves in every case consisted of terse questions and a list of places, elaborations and creative twists from the leaks led the newspapers to bill the memos as "hit lists" of National Parks that James Watt surely intended to de-authorize. The impression was that Watt was about to pave Yosemite or sell the Grand Canyon for a sanitary land fill site. No mention was made that only Congress can de-authorize a National Park, or for that matter, that such things have been done in past adminstrations: Platt National Park in Oklahoma was de-authorized March 17, 1976 and demoted to a National Recreation Area, the Chickasaw, without so much as a squawk or a headline.

Watt's response to these leaks and this furor is illuminating. Russell Dickenson, Director of the National Park Service, brought up the issue during a Tuesday morning "Bureau Heads" meeting and got this reply from Secretary Watt:

I've made a conscious decision, Russ, to ignore these people. Don't go around trying to find out who they are. In any government there's always going to be that 5 to 10 percent of the crew that's hostile to you, no matter who you are. If you fight 'em, they feed off of it, because they're getting the attention that they really want. So we're just going ahead with our agenda. If we let these "5 percenters" distract us, we'll end up playing the *Washington Post's* agenda, and if we do that, we lose. We will not yield to this thing. Nothing will deter us from our agenda.

By way of the Tuesday morning "Bureau Heads" meeting, top-level civil servants come into personal contact with the Secretary not only once a month when their bureau comes up for its Monday morning meeting, but also every week. But that's not all of the Watt management initiative. Every Friday afternoon at three or four o'clock, Watt holds an "Assistant Secretary Level Meeting" with only the senior executives of the Department (the six Assistant Secretaries, the Solicitor, and the Inspector General). Four others sit in on this meeting with Watt: Steve Shipley, Jim's Executive Assistant, Doug Baldwin, Public Affairs Director, Stan Hulett, Congressional and Legislative Affairs Director, and Under Secretary Don Hodel. This meeting is held around the big conference table in Ickes' "Secretary's Office," that great, pretentious bastion of officialdom that Jim Watt rejected for his own personal use. These Friday meetings give the top executives a blank check on the Secretary's time so they can air problems, initiate discussions, argue, complain, cajole, plan, squabble, learn, decide, or do whatever else is important in the day-to-day business of running the Department.

Every day in the late afternoon, Watt schedules what he calls "Free Time," during which any senior manager can come in with a problem, an idea, or just to shoot the breeze, to get the Secretary's full attention in a small group setting with no agenda. Free Time may find one or two people or six or eight talking with Watt, and it occasionally turns into a downright bull session of wideranging ideas, of fascinating explorations of concepts, running well past quitting time. Free Time exists in part simply to cement the bonds of loyalty.

This routine series of meetings began immediately after Watt's confirmation and continues as a Secretarial tradition. It was the first decisive mechanism Watt used to gain control of the bureaucracy. The idea was to give every top manager in the Department access to the Secretary, something that had never been done before. As Watt says, "When I was working here in the Bureau of Outdoor Recreation and in Water and Power Resources, I know that months went by without an Assistant Secretary seeing the Secretary. Bureau heads would go long periods of time without seeing the Secretary. They might see him on TV or giving testimony up on the Hill, but not in one-on-one conversations."

Taming the bureaucracy, however, could not be done by mere personal contact, and the Interior Department was not the only bureaucracy that Watt had to cope with: there were the other Cabinet-level natural resource people to deal with, Congress to worry about, and the Governors of the 50 states to work with.

Very early in Watt's Secretariat he was appointed Chairman of the Cabinet Council on Natural Resources and the Environment, which extends his authority in a limited way over the Environmental Protection Agency run by Anne Gorsuch, the Department of Energy's Secretary James Edwards, and the Boss of the U.S. Department of Agriculture's Forest Service, Assistant Secretary John Crowell. Watt also impacts other Cabinet-level decisions by his membership on the Food and Agriculture Cabinet Council, and by his Chairmanship of the statutorily created independent Advisory Commission on Intergovernmental Affairs—President Reagan personally appointed Watt to this Chairmanship. Watt is also a member of the newly-created Cabinet Council on Legal Affairs, and sits in on meetings of the Economic Affairs Cabinet Council, even though he is not an official member.

The Interior Department budget was one of Watt's highest priorities. President Reagan had scheduled his Administration budget proposal for release on February 18, 1981, which was only three weeks after Watt's confirmation as Secretary. But time pressure was not only the reason that the budget was a high priority: it had become obvious that Watt would have to shape Interior policy largely through the budget and appropriations process. This intricate and controversial Watt maneuver deserves thorough examination.

Watt's alternative to setting Interior policy through the budget and other administrative means would have been a legislative program. In the strictest sense, only Congress sets policy through legislation. In practical terms, the Executive sets policy in many ways, through its own Constitutional power and through legislative programs it submits to Congress. Watt could have chosen to use the traditional legislative pathway to policy, but it would be fraught with pitfalls for his program. With a Republican majority in the Senate, Watt could have expected and obtained approvals for most programs he wanted, but not for all; in the Democratically-controlled House, and especially in the environmentalist stronghold of the House Interior and Insular Affairs Committee, anything Watt sent in that did not smack of centralized federal power or a preservationist land grab would likely be rejected out of hand.

On one occasion, Jim Watt actually did encourage Congress to move favorably on a bill that would help his program; the response was predictable. It happened on May 14, 1981, when the Subcommittee on Public Lands and National Parks of the House Interior and Insular Affairs Committee held an oversight hearing on federal land management policy. Secretary Watt had been called upon to testify, and after more than an hour of grilling by Congressman Burton (California), Byron (Maryland), Clausen (California), Udall (Arizona), and Young (Alaska), Watt encouraged the subcommittee to favorably report out New Mexico Representative Manuel Lujan's House Resolution 3586, a bill that would authorize Land and Water Conservation Fund monies specifically earmarked for land acquisition to be used instead for maintenance and improvement of National Park facilities. Subcommittee Chairman John Seiberling, replied, "Don't hold your breath."

That attitude prevails in the whole Committee on Interior and Insular Affairs. Thus, if Jim Watt were to submit a legislative package to this committee, the ideological differences would be too great; no Watt policy package would likely win their cachet. Every bill relating to the Department of the Interior must pass through this committee, so there's an end to it.

However, even though he knew he was stymied in Congress, Watt could still act administratively. Many of the programs that the Reagan Administration had found most objectionable would be easy to squelch: much of the over-regulation and land-grabbing of past years had been done contrary to the intent of Congress in the first place. Rectifying these abuses would require no new laws, only respect for existing ones. And, since most of Watt's goals consisted of eliminating governmental powers rather than enlarging them, he could refuse to exercise discretionary powers and still remain true to the intent of Congress. One way to do that would be to set budget levels for Interior programs according to their merits as seen in terms of his policy. His budget itself would require the approval of Congress, but they could hardly reject that: to do so would bring Interior to a halt. Congress could restore some of the cuts he would make, but only at the risk of appearing to be irresponsible big spenders during hard times. And once Congress approved his budget, they would have automatically put their stamp of approval on his policy.

But that approval would have to be purchased at a terrible personal price: Watt had yet no Assistant Secretaries confirmed to help with budget decisions; he could hardly take the risk of accepting the unexamined budget recommendations of a bureaucracy he had just taken hold of; he would have to make every budget decision personally. In practical terms, that meant going line by line through the entire budget of 8 major divisions, 11 major bureaus, 13 major offices, hundreds of programs, and 80,000 employees. But that is exactly what Jim Watt did in late January and early February 1981.

Watt called upon each budget manager and sat down with them one by one, along with Watt's own advisers, mostly Deputy Assistant Secretaries who did not require the advise and consent of the Senate, and with selected career professionals who could give him substantive information on programs by which to judge budget levels. He went through every budget sheet in the Department of the Interior, line by line, item by item, asking pointed questions, demanding studies and documentations to prove questionable budget needs, streamlining here, chopping there, adding some other place. Fourteen- and 16-hour days and 7-day weeks were routine. "Keeping up with Watt" became the name of the game.

Watt transmitted his preliminary budget projections to President Reagan in time for the February 18 announcement. On March 10, 1981, the Reagan Administration released its budget proposal with firm dollar figures to follow up the programmatic February 18 statement. A detailed look at the Interior Department's portion of that budget will reveal exactly how Watt used the budget process to shape Interior policy. In overall terms, Watt reduced the Carter Administration's Fiscal Year (FY) 1982 budget request by $877 million to a total of $5.76 billion, as well as recission of $383 million in FY 1981 funds.

Specifically, Watt established a funding moratorium on grant programs for recreation and historic preservation (state land acquisition grants were reduced by $185 million, urban park grants by $75 million, and historic preservation grants by $28 million). A moratorium on federal land acquisition from the Land and Water Conservation Fund (LWCF) was designed to save almost $400 million in the following 19 months. Watt also asked for an increase of $105 million for National Park restoration and improvement, with funds to come from the LWCF, which would require legislative approval. The Heritage Conservation and Recreation Service was consolidated into the National Park Service (not eliminated, as critics complained). The Youth Conservation Corps ($60 million) was abolished altogether.

Watt's remarks on this small section of the budget explain his policy intent: About the moratorium on recreation and historic preservation funding, Watt said:

We took this action because the states, volunteer agencies, and private sector are able to do these jobs without federal funding. State and local government funding for recreation in 1981 is about $5.7 billion; our total moratorium is less than $300 million. The nation will not be without recreation opportunities while this moratorium is in effect.

On the federal land acquisition moratorium and the increase in maintenance and improvement funds for the National Parks, Watt said:

No decision I made more clearly illustrates this Administration's change of course. This Administration is determined to be a good steward of what we have before reaching for additional lands whose national significance may be questionable. The General Accounting Office has documented the deterioration of park facilities. We want to see the truly national parks improved so that they can be used by the people, and not held for the exclusive use of the elite who disdain all but the most rugged recreation. We understand fully that there must be management to assure that use does not in itself destroy our parks. We will channel the funds "to the ground" to get the most from our management investment.

On the consolidation of the Heritage Conservation and Recreation Service into the Park Service: "It provides a good opportunity to absorb skilled personnel from HCRS into the Park Service where a substantial number of vacancies exist. I believe the affected programs will benefit from this consolidation."

Watt said of the Youth Conservation Corps, "This program meets a limited national need for federally financed employment. It is proposed for termination, saving up to $116 million over the next two years."

It is noteworthy that Watt retained $4.7 million for the National Trust for Historic Preservation. But the Reagan Administration also felt that the private sector should take a larger role in historic preservation, pointing out that Mount Vernon, George Washington's estate, and Monticello, Thomas Jefferson's home, have always been privately owned and operated, and are among the best managed facilities in the nation.

Further details of the Watt budget for fiscal year 1982: Watt proposed to eliminate funding for the Office of Water Research and Technology and the Water Resources Council. Eight Bureau of Reclamation Projects, among them the Central Arizona Project and the Yuma desalting complex, were reduced, with $36.6 million of their $652.6 million total postponed. Watt proposed to establish a new Office of National Water Policy ($2.5 million). Bureau of Land Management funds were cut $35.4 million to $388.3 million; $10 million in cuts were slated for Outer Continental Shelf studies, $7 million was cut from wilderness planning and mineral surveys, and $6 million in construction and maintenance costs were deferred. Watt proposed to redesign and fund at $45 million the Payment In Lieu of Taxes program which had been proposed for elimination by the Carter Administration.

Watt's comments on these Land and Water Resources budgets:

As a nation we clearly need to rethink our approaches to conserve water resources. The emphasis should be on respect for state water rights and management of their water resources. I believe that neither the Office of Water Research and Technology or the Water Resources Council properly focuses on national concerns for development of water policies and programs; many of their functions should be the responsibility of the states and private industry.

All our bureaus will go through belt tightening, eliminating lower-priority programs and ones that can be conducted by private industry or state and local governments, streamlining programs, and reduction or postponement of funding.

We have received many inquiries about the Payment In Lieu of Taxes program which reimburses governments for their loss of tax revenues because of federal ownership of land. We feel this is an important program to county and state governments and should not be terminated.

On the Energy and Minerals front, the Watt budget slashed $66.6 million from the Office of Surface Mining, leaving a $179.8 budget. Funding for regulatory enforcement was cut $10 million, reflecting Watt's intent to stress State primacy in surface mining enforcement. Funding for the Abandoned Mine Land Fund, which is used to reclaim lands disturbed by past mining and then abandoned, were increased by $35.5 million. No money was requested for mineral institutes, which had received $9.6 million in fiscal 1981. The U.S. Geological Survey budget was chopped by $37.7 million, including withdrawn requests for increases in oil shale programs, earthquake and geologic research, mapping modernization, and curtailment of travel and personnel accounts.

Watt's remarks on Energy and Minerals:

Most economists point to the costs of complying with regulatory excess as a significant factor in the decline of American productivity. As an example of what this Administration intends to do about it, let me point to the Office of Surface Mining. Anyone who has seen Appalachia realizes the need for proper control of surface mining. On the other hand, anyone who examines the reams of regulations issued by OSM will conclude there has to be a better way of meeting the intent of Congress. Regulations on returning land to its approximate original contours may have to be reformed to offer alternatives such as contouring for farming, recreation and other uses. Our regulatory approach will stress flexibility and innovation rather than command and control.

We intend to move ahead on a broad front in the leasing of oil and gas in the Outer Continental Shelf; oil and gas leasing onshore, including the National Petroleum Reserve in Alaska; and leasing of coal, geothermal, oil shale, and tar sands. We intend to develop and enhance our domestic sources of energy and to do it with adequate environmental safeguards.

The mineral institutes program did not produce a significant return of federal funds. When the government balances its budget, America will have a stronger economy and mining industries will flourish.

State regulatory programs and reclamation grants for surface mining were either retained at Carter Administration levels or increased; environmentalist claims that Watt was letting miners "rape, ruin and run" were somewhat overstated. Watt surprised the mining industry by being tougher about important regulations than his predecessors, and downright mean when it came to royalty payment reporting; Watt never promised them removal of *all* regulation, only of *excessive* regulations. There is still some dispute as to exactly what is excessive.

What Watt actually said about regulation in general was this: "In the past, all too frequently a perfectly reasonable intention of balancing environmental values with other values has led to unnecessary red tape. Well-intentioned procedural safeguards and regulations seem to have become ends unto themselves, rather than a means to an end. President Reagan and I believe that we can reform the regulatory system and remove unnecessary burdens while protecting the environment and the basic values of our nation, especially if such reforms are made in a reasoned way." Watt's retention of state regulatory funding should have been predictable to those who listened to that last sentence.

Watt's Indian Affairs budget proposal was reduced, but the reduction was cushioned by cutting down overhead. Watt consolidated a number of Indian programs into a single bloc-grant program with greater flexibility for tribes, even though at a reduced funding level. Watt identified over $160 million in the Carter Budget as being adaptable to a bloc-grant approach. He also proposed reduction of up to 400 positions in the Bureau of Indian Affairs. Watt retained sufficient funding of both operating programs and support for construction programs for schools, building rehabilitation, roads and irrigation projects.

Watt's comment: "This approach will give tribal governments much more say in the final allocation than is traditionally the case. It is my hope that tribal leaders will view this as an important new opportunity for them in their pursuit of self-determination. In my discussions with tribal leaders they have indicated a strong desire for less administrative burden and more program flexibility."

Territorial programs received some budget decreases; $20 million earlier budgeted for a program to assist the governments of Guam and the Virgin Islands to eliminate their budget deficits was eliminated; $18 million was also reduced in financial assistance to three entities in the Trust Territory of Micronesia for the construction of new capitals, leaving $3 million for preparatory work and deferring the balance until 1983.

Of his Territorial responsibilities, Watt said, "Our basic objective in all these areas Guam, American Samoa, the Virgin Islands, the Northern Mariana Islands, and the Trust Territory of the Pacific Islands (Micronesia), is to aid in the development of educational, economic, social, and political programs that will enable the people to have greater local control of their affairs."

Watt also substantially reduced funding for his own Office of the Secretary.

It should be obvious from the foregoing that any Secretary of the Interior cannot help but make policy through budget decisions; Jim Watt raised a ruckus because he plainly said that he was going to do so. At a Conference of National Park Concessioners, for example, Watt bluntly told them, "We will use the budget system as the excuse to make major policy decisions." Gasps of horror subsequently rippled through the environmentalist community. Newsweeklies and opinion-leader magazines such as *The New Yorker* commented upon his tactic as if it were illegal or as if Watt had invented the ploy; neither is true. Watt's only crime was to say clearly what other politicians cloak in euphemisms. Remember, Congress still had to approve this budget. Watt proposes, Congress disposes. As it turned out, they eventually gave him most of what he wanted without need of a legislative program.

Congressman John Seiberling of the House Subcommittee on Public Lands and National Parks was so angered by Watt's remarks that he began to bring up the subject at every hearing at which Watt was present, even after Seiberling himself had voted to approve Watt's fiscal 1982 budget authorizations. Their exchanges became so predictable that it developed into a standing joke on Capital Hill.

Seiberling: You did say publicly that you were going to change Interior policy through the budget?
   Watt: Yes, I said that.
   Seiberling: Don't you realize that policy is made by Congress?
   Watt: Yes, I realize that.
   Seiberling: Then you don't really make policy changes?
   Watt: No, Congress does that by voting for my budget, just like you did.

Watt's use of the budget to shape policy was also a deliberate piece of political strategy: his environmentalist opponents are accustomed to promises, white papers, legislative lobbying, and court fights. Watt's administrative moves baffled them. His refusal to exercise power was beyond their grasp. His refusal to ask for more money to acquire private land, like his appointment of pro-development personnel to the executive ranks of Interior, could not be challenged in court. In fact, during Watt's first year on the job, only 138 lawsuits were filed against the Department of the Interior, compared to 197 filed against the Andrus administration in 1980, a reduction of 30 percent.

Environmentalist cries of alarm went up: "Watt doesn't announce policy statements; he just acts administratively and through the budget." To which Watt responds: "There aren't a lot of handles they can use to grab us."

In all, this is another example of Watt sticking to his own agenda. He knew that Interior was more than a romping ground for environmentalists and acted that way to meet his total spectrum of responsibilities—preservation and development. His remarks about the criteria he used in budget reviews with bureau heads and budget officers show clearly his intent:

I screened their proposed budgets with the following three questions in mind: (1) Was there a compelling reason why the government should exercise its power to do the activity or could it be done by the private sector? (2) If it were properly a governmental function, should it be done by the federal government or could state and local governments do it? (3) If it were a federal responsibility, was it being done well or was the federal government, in fact, a part of the problem? No programmatic decisions were made without the full support of the professional career managers, who rely on the best available scientific data.

Staying Together

It took Jim Watt about five weeks from the date of his confirmation to get his act together to the point that a management system could be envisioned. He had begun his regular personal contact meetings and established that pattern immediately. He had gone through the budget and gotten that gargantuan task out of the way. In the process he had testified before six Congressional committee sessions, and soon had to make two presentations on minerals policy and one on his California offshore oil and gas leasing proposal. Each session required hours of preparation. Watt also personally briefed his "acting" Assistant Secretaries from the career ranks for their obligatory visits to Capitol Hill for various types of testimony. Watt had known from the beginning that he would install some type of Management By Objectives (MBO) system into his administration, and at lunch with Executive Assistant Steve Shipley and Under Secretary Don Hodel on February 16, while Watt was still buried in the budget, the subject of an MBO came up in serious discussion for the first time.

Under Secretary Hodel describes the discussion:

We knew that the standard way you put an MBO system into place is to hire an outside consulting firm. They come in, they interview all the managers. They decide what it is everybody's doing, and what they want to do, and what they're supposed to be doing, and how they're supposed to inter-relate. And that takes about three months.

Then the consultant writes up a report, laying out a matrix and a system. They come in and say, "Now here's what each of you is supposed to do, and here are the forms you need to follow, and here's how you fill them out." Report writing and presentation takes another three months.

Then it takes six months to a year's training to get onto the system. We didn't have that kind of time.

Hodel realized that he had already started the core of a Management By Objectives system in those assignment lists and flipcharts he made in January to help everyone keep track of what they ought to be doing. These lists were soon put in Interior's computer with dates behind each task, then a week or so later this list was arranged in chronological order by completion dates so Watt could punch a button and see at a glance everything that should be done by such-and-such a date.

By the first week in March, Watt felt it was time to move on their management system, and that it was hopeless to hire an outside consultant. They would have to create their own MBO. Don Hodel was elected to make it happen. Watt says, "I feel strongly that the MBO idea will not work if the top man is not intimately involved from the beginning. It will also fail if he does not act as policeman on a regular basis." Watt worked closely with Hodel.

On Saturday, March 7, 1981, the six Assistant Secretary-designates, Ray Arnett (Fish and Wildlife and Parks), Garrey Carruthers (Land and Water Resources), Dan Miller (Energy and Minerals), Ken Smith (Indian Affairs), Robin West (Policy, Budget and Administration), Pedro Sanjuan (Territorial and International Affairs), plus Solicitor William Coldiron and Inspector General Richard Mulberry met with Shipley, Hodel, Public Affairs Director Doug Baldwin, and Legislative Affairs Director Stan Hulett in an Interior facility outside the headquarters building so they would not be disturbed by telephone calls, and there they created the Department of the Interior's Management By Objectives system.

Every Management By Objectives system begins with a Mission statement, a brief description of what the firm, government agency, or what-not, is agreed to be all about. The next two lower levels, which spell out the

Mission in progressively greater detail, are labeled either Goals and Objectives or Objectives and Goals, depending on where you went to management school. Thus, the intrepid Interior crew took four or five minutes deciding which it would be; they then agreed to proceed from (1) Mission, to (2) Goals, to (3) Objectives. But the first substantive decision they had to make immediately reared its contentious head: What is the Mission of the Department of the Interior? This is no trivial question: from the exact statement agreed upon by these dozen or so people, all lower goals, objectives, tasks, duties and jobs of an 80,000-employee department of the United States would be determined.

Under Secretary Hodel describes what they did:

For the mission statement, we worked from what the Secretary had said in his confirmation hearings, and all these policy makers in the room then began suggesting statements of what the Mission really was. Before too long, we were fighting over every word, shearing away unnecessary ideas, homing in on exactly and only what the Mission was. It took us an hour, but we got it down to 52 words, precise, concise, complete:

The mission of the Department of the Interior is to manage properly the trust responsibilities of the United States and to encourage and provide for the preservation, development and management of the natural resources of the United States for the use, enjoyment and security of its people, now and in the future.

Every task of the Department of the Interior, every intention of its managers, is there. If it's not included, it's not the Mission of Interior.

The next step was to define the Goals of Interior, those intermediate-level statements of intent that set forth the purposes of the primary divisions within Interior. After several hours, the dozen people in the room decided upon this statement:

It is a goal of the Department of the Interior to act with common sense and environmental sensitivity to:
1. Open federal lands to public access for appropriate use or uses.
2. Manage, preserve and restore our National Park System for the benefit and use of people.
3. Increase domestic production of energy and minerals resources.
4. Increase the supply of quality water in cooperation with user groups.
5. Promote the development of the economic and social resources of Indian tribes and trust territories.
6. Create balanced ecosystems through the proper management of wild plants and animals.
7. Establish and implement sound management concepts and practices.

This Mission and Goals statement was signed later by Secretary Watt, Under Secretary Hodel, the six Assistant Secretaries and the Solicitor, and is a key document of the Watt Secretariat. Every policy maker had participated in its creation. Watt had been there to give the proceedings his authority.

Next, as Under Secretary Hodel says, "As a result of that meeting, I told these people, 'Each of you go back to your area and start listing what the things are that you have to do to carry out those goals,' that is, start listing the third-level statements, the Objectives." Each Assistant Secretary-designate came up with a list of Objectives, which was then broken down into detailed Tasks required to accomplish the Objective, and the Tasks were themselves further broken down into Subtasks required to accomplish the Tasks, and so on down to the finest level of detail. At each stage, the people involved in the actual work were brought in to participate in the definition of Objectives, Tasks and Subtasks, so that ultimately, the Management By Objectives system of Interior was constructed by all the managers who had to carry it out.

One of the unexpected virtues of the MBO system, as Watt discovered, is that it can easily be extended out beyond headquarters managers into field office locations throughout the nation so that everyone down to the lowest management level can eventually get on the system to define their own goals and make their own commitments, which is an excellent tool for decentralizing control while keeping central accountability.

On February 25, 1981, Watt chose his long-time friend Derrell P. Thompson to manage the Western Field Office as Special Assistant to the Secretary, with headquarters in Denver, Colorado. Watt had brought Thompson to Interior in 1972 as Mid-Continent Regional Director of the Bureau of Outdoor Recreation, later known as the Heritage Conservation and Recreation Service. Watt felt that Thompson's experience in the public and private sectors, including 14 years with Aerojet-General Corp., would make a significant contribution to the Department.

By February 1982, most Assistant Secretaries were totally in control of their divisions, and Watt had only to check with them every Monday, Tuesday, and Friday to keep tabs on how they were doing. I had a long conversation with Ken Smith, Assistant Secretary for Indian Affairs in his office on the fourth floor of Interior's southwest wing, two floors directly below the Secretary's office. Like Watt, Smith uses the circular work table in the center of his gold-carpeted office when talking to visitors rather than his large, formal desk on the west wall. The wiry Smith talks easily about his job.

Just like Jim built his team, he let each one of us Assistant Secretaries build our own team. I went out and chose Roy Sampsel to be my Deputy in charge of policy and John Fritz to be my Deputy in charge of operations. Roy chose some of the people on our staff, and I chose some, so if things go haywire, we got no one to blame but ourselves. We have less money and less people to work with than previous Administrations; we don't have a big bureaucracy in Assistant Secretary offices any more. There used to be 36 here, but now we're down to 14.

I was familiar with Management By Objectives since I instituted one when I was general manager of the Warm Springs Reservation. It worked okay, but you had to bear down to make it happen. At first everybody resented it, but when top management keeps at it, they know you mean what you're saying. You have to spend time going through it, asking about target dates, are we on target, and continuously use it, because if you stop, everybody else will just go back to the easy way.

But Interior's MBO is working a little better. We think we're having better luck because for the first time the Head Honcho has said, look, this is what our objectives are. In Indian Affairs we run the MBO a little differently because our policy is to work on a government-to-government basis; that was President Reagan's campaign promise, and that's how it is. So we feel that tribal governments should be making a lot of these decisions. I've found that like most organizations, they love to make the decisions but they don't like the responsibility, and I say to them that they go together. If they mess up and things go wrong, it's their fault, and we don't baby them.

We're trying to run our MBO down further in our organizations to get the local managers up to speed. We have a lot of weak tribal government out there. We've been too easy on them in the past, and that's not good management. Nowadays, if they don't perform under some contract, we'll pull the contract and say to them, "No, no contract until you get your shop in shape. We'll help you get there. If you got a weak link in your organization, tell us. If you need a better accounting system, tell us. We'll give you technical assistance and support, we'll help to beef up your organization, but you tribes, you got to get your own shop in shape. Learn how to work with your banker. Learn how to run your tribal enterprises more profitably. Learn how to create a tribal government atmosphere to make things happen, to make your economy grow."

Ken Smith is a tough manager much in the Watt mold. He is responsible for 12 area offices, 82 agency offices, 18 satellite offices and 16,500 employees. He works much like Watt at creating loyalty by giving loyalty. He maintains close communication with tribal leaders, and never lets them forget he's one of them—the first Indian with Reservation management experience ever to serve in the Indian Affairs top spot. He says,

I think we got pretty fair loyalty. There might be a few exceptions, but I get along with most Indian leaders. There's been no jealousy, unless maybe when I give them a "No." And they know they can't fool me. I've been in their positions on Reservation government for 22 years, and I know how you can roll the system back here in Washington, too. I let them know that I want their input, but I'm responsible for the final decision.

The other Assistant Secretaries told me same thing about their MBO systems: They set their own objectives, they commit to their own completion dates, they run their own shop—Watt gives them a totally free hand but holds them totally responsible for success.

By June of 1981, the Management By Objectives system was in place and operational at headquarters. There was now no chance that the policy makers would be captured by the bureaucracy, and taming the bureaucracy had not been a matter of "shouting down orders," but of installing a sound system, getting participation and firmly managing the entire Department with close personal contact.

But by June of 1981, the environmental movement was about to launch the largest attack of its entire history. Watt's real trouble was just beginning.

CHAPTER 8
REGULATIONISM

I will o'errun thee with policy.—Shakespeare

Public land policy has been one of the major issues in U.S. history from the very beginning. In America, as in Europe, land was the basic form of wealth, but it was not to be concentrated into the hands of great landlords. Nor did the early U.S. government choose to manage it as a capital asset. The original plan was to turn it over to private hands as soon as it was surveyed. This resource of staggering value was to be denationalized as soon as possible. Many see in this move the influence of ideology, of government support for free enterprise, but there was much more to it, and the seeds of the shift toward keeping the public domain that came later in the 19th century were inherent in the original policy of selling off the public domain. True, the Founding Fathers had read their Locke well. John Locke's *Second Treatise of Government* taught that property was one of the basic human rights, that land was a basic property, and that improvement or development of land was a basic act in securing title; development represented the earned result of one's own labor—earned liberty. In fact, Locke took America to task for *not* developing its land. He said:

Americans are rich in land and poor in all the comforts of life; whom nature having furnished as liberally as any other people with the materials of plenty, i.e., a fruitful soil, apt to produce in abundance what might serve for food, raiment, and delight, yet for want of improving it by labor have not one-hundredth part of the conveniences we enjoy. And a king of a large and fruitful territory there feeds, lodges and is clad worse than a day-laborer in England.

Adam Smith's 1776 *Wealth of Nations* urged governments to heed the marketplace, to realize that laissez faire was the best policy; supply and demand, along with the enlightened self-interest of the entrepreneuer, unreg-

143

ulated by government, would serve society better than governmentally-mandated programs. The American Revolution itself was an expression of one nation's demand for economic independence from another; our nation's very existence was a symbol of independence and free markets.

While the Founding Fathers enshrined the individual profit motive and property ownership in the Bill of Rights—"nor [shall any person] be deprived of life, liberty or property without due process of law; nor shall private property be taken for public use without just compensation"—the first few Presidents were not intent upon selling off the public domain solely to benefit free enterprise. As Lawrence M. Friedman notes in *A History of American Law:*

Divestment was never the whole policy, nor even the sole *reason* for policy. The professed social goal was not to make government weaker or smaller; but to create a country of free citizens, living independently on their land. Where strict market principles seemed to clash with this goal, these principles had to yield. Government was never merely a passive umpire of the market; it did more than chop the land into units and market it. It used land as a lever of policy.

But in fact, during most of the 19th century, there was little swerving from the basic land disposal policy. However, there were constant battles over how it should be done: Jefferson envisioned a nation of yeoman farmers and advocated selling off small tracts, giving farmers and veterans preference. Hamilton wanted to sell off the public domain, too, but he didn't give a whit for farmers, yeoman or otherwise. His national treasury was empty and he wanted the money; he wanted the land sold in great wholesale blocks to cash buyers. And when it came to mineral rights, the government fought tooth and nail against the free market, seldom letting mineral rights into private hands; the Land Ordinance of 1785 authorized sale of public land, but reserved "one-third part of all gold, silver, lead and copper mines" to the government. The law of 1796 held back "every salt spring which may be discovered." In 1807, Congress insisted that lead-bearing lands be leased and not sold. The government's early offerings of big chunks of land didn't sell well, and section minimums were reduced to half-sections, quarter-sections, and even 40-acre plots. Then regional feuds ignited: the new raw Western states such as Ohio and Michigan wanted low land prices because they were cash poor; Eastern speculators wanted high prices for obvious reasons. The basic disputes over public domain lands that riddle the Department of the Interior today began over 50 years before there even was a Department of the Interior; as early as 1812, a House committee recommended a Home Department to deal with such problems.

When the Interior Department was created in 1849, westward migration was well under way, the Eastern seaboard was becoming industrialized, and the government was ready to begin making land grants to railroads. In 1850, the federal government gave to the states of Illinois, Alabama, and Mississippi alternate sections of land for six miles on either side of a proposed line of tracks from Chicago to Mobile.

Two years later, the first regulatory agency was created with the Steam Boiler Act amendment, which sought to strengthen an 1838 law designed to stop explosions of steam boilers on river boats that had plagued water transportation since about 1817. The 1838 law and its 1852 amendment had been lobbied by a citizen activist group, Philadelphia's Franklin Institute, casting shadows of things to come. It is significant that the first U.S. regulatory agency, a board of nine supervisors for boiler inspection, was lobbied into existence by a citizen organization for health and safety reasons.

But a year before Interior was created, the seeds of the future conservation movement were planted without fanfare. In 1848, the American Association for the Advancement of Science (AAAS) became the first substantial group to take note of water supply, forest protection, and land use issues and later went on to become the largest general scientific organization in the United States. While most scientists of the day were development advocates of the "wise use" variety, and not preservationists in any way, the moral and ethical aspects of environmentalism that would shape future conservation groups had begun to stir in literature and the arts.

In 1851, Henry David Thoreau made his renowned remark during a lecture, "In wildness is the preservation of the world," a theme he had cultivated from his association with the New England transcendentalist writers, particularly Ralph Waldo Emerson, whose 1836 essay "Nature" had given the movement its original impetus. Emerson himself had been influenced by William Cullen Bryant, who in 1811 wrote America's first nature poem, "Thanatopsis," which found moral and religious significance in "the continuous woods where rolls the Oregon" (which at that time was thought of as a mythical river rather than simply a territory). By 1825, Bryant was ready to give nature worship a niche in American thought in his poem "A Forest Hymn," asserting that "the groves were God's first temples." The year 1825 also saw the rise of the "Hudson River School" of landscape painters which influenced generations of cultured Americans. The wild romantic landscapes of Thomas Cole and Asher B. Durand, among others, were the first visual interpretations of nature as somehow sacred and imbued with moral meaning, and their infinitely detailed technique stressed the richness and complexity of the natural world.

What was going on culturally in the first half of the 19th century in America had an important bearing on the eventual development of environmental regulationism. The Enlightenment under which the Founding Fathers were educated had stressed confidence in mankind's advance over ignorance and the uncivilized, and the belief that scientific and material progress was inevitable and endless. John Locke's philosophy of individualism, property rights, and freedom from excessive government which had so influenced Franklin and Jefferson was the epitome of rational Enlightenment thought. The Constitution of the United States is itself an exemplary Enlightenment document, despite its peculiarities of compromise and its imprint from the Federalist debates. It is supremely rational and trusting in men's ability to govern themselves by reason. But the Rationalism and industrialism of the 18th century provoked a severe reaction in the 19th century: Romanticism.

The Romantic Movement is the direct ancestor of the modern environmental movement. Although Romanticism varied from country to country, it has these common threads: freedom of imagination, the free expression of emotions and passions, the rejection of strict rules in the arts, interest in social reform, love of nature, and an urge to return to the primitive life as symbolized in the idea of the "noble savage." This could easily be a definition of the Counterculture of the American 1960s and '70s.

In 1762, Jean Jaques Rousseau had given Romanticism its social and governmental treatise, *The Social Contract,* suggesting that man originally lived in a state of nature, unhampered by laws, and agreed to a social contract in order to survive, in the process becoming moral man by leaving behind solely selfish desires to want what is best for all.

And so Rousseau influenced Wordsworth, who influenced Bryant, who influenced Emerson, who influenced Thoreau—and by 1854 *Walden, Or Life in the Woods* began its long history of influencing legislation, primarily by influencing literate and thoughtful public figures. Thoreau's work touched writers and practical men of affairs. In 1862, the same year Thoreau died, George Perkins Marsh, a Vermont lawyer and former U.S. diplomat, finished the manuscript of *Man and Nature; or, Physical Geography as Modified by Human Action.* When it was published in 1864, it alarmed people with its dramatic prophecy that the inexhaustibility of the earth was a myth, and that man disrupts the fundamental harmony or balance of nature. Marsh's book became the fountainhead, as close to being *the* source of the conservation movement as any one book can be, although some professional environmentalists claim direct descent from William Bartram (1739–1823), American naturalist whose 1791 account of travels through the South influenced Romantic writers. Bartram was in no sense a conservationist like Marsh, but rather a practical botanist who also wrote picturesque descriptions of places he visited.

Marsh spoke with sufficient technical expertise, even though he was an amateur scientist, that important Americans took him seriously. Annual Reports of the Departments of Interior and Agriculture routinely referred to

Marsh's lectures on the ethics of land use and his concern for future supplies of timber and water. Another who took Marsh seriously was Frederick Law Olmstead, a landscape architect and early advocate of urban parks—he designed the U.S. Capitol grounds and New York City's Central Park. He saw parks as a means of resisting the "vital exhaustion" and "nervous irritation" of the city. In 1865, the year after Marsh's book was published, Olmstead said, "We grow more and more artificial every day," and proposed that patches of "wild forest" be preserved near metropolitan centers.

The 1860s and '70s were a watershed for American land policy. Law after law encouraged settlement and development: there were land grants to states, to railroads, to homesteaders, and developers; and to serve farmers the Department of Agriculture was created. 1862 was the vintage year for most of this activity: the Department of Agriculture was established; the Morrill Act of 1862 gave states huge tracts of land to be used in establishing and supporting "Colleges for the Benefit of Agricultural and Mechanic Arts:" the Homestead Act of 1862 ended all pretense that federal land was being sold to stock the federal treasury, since anyone who would pay a filing fee and prove up the land could have 160 western acres in 5 years; and Congress passed a law in aid of the Union Pacific, granting lands directly to the railroad instead of to the states as in 1850.

In the 1870s came more giveaways: The Timber Culture Act of 1873 gave 160 acres to anyone who would plant trees on 40 of them. The Desert Land Act of 1877 sold cheap land to whomever would irrigate it within three years. The Timber and Stone Act of 1878 authorized sale of nontillable public timberland to private individuals. Conservation was no part of the intent in any of these laws; Congress plainly intended to develop the West as rapidly as possible and to meet the needs of the settlers and developers. However, abuses of these liberal provisions were legion. The Department of the Interior in 1884 established Division P to protect public land resources from timber rustlers, corrupt federal officers who agreed upon fines with thieves in advance, buyers who pulled boats on wheels over dry land to enter swamp land illegally, small farmers conspiring with lumber companies to enter 160-acre claims and sell them for logging. A whole fraudulent economy grew up; dummy entrymen for false claims could be had for $50 to $125; you could buy a witness for $25. As historian John Ise put it, fraud was a frontier way of life. The Revolutionary War suspicion of any government was institutionalized by the pioneers in honoring federal law in the breach. Historian Harold K. Steen notes, "To make a show of curbing these frauds and abuses, Congress legislated a number of efforts which were perhaps half-hearted at best; most congressional interests, after all, lay with placing the West in private ownership rather than in impeding progress by intensive policing."

But things had changed by the 1890s. George Perkins Marsh's message was getting across: the earth was not inexhaustible. The national domain was visibly vanishing. The frontier that had been the psychological safety valve for questing, striving generations was gradually filling up, closing up, ending. The first pangs of future scarcity were being felt, and concerns for efficient management came forward a little at a time.

While the pioneers had been settling the tillable land, scientists and explorers had been charting mountain, forest and desert in recognition of the fact that proper management required exact knowledge and careful classification of resource lands. One of the earliest was Major John Wesley Powell, Civil War hero who had lost an arm in the battle of Shiloh. In 1869, Powell had made a daring reconnaisance with nine others of the unknown Colorado River and its Grand Canyon, despite frightful Indian legends of mile-high waterfalls and endless underground caverns that swallowed up the torrent and all it bore. Three who abandoned the rapids to walk out of the Canyon died at the hands of hostile Indians; those who braved the remaining raging rapids survived to gain renown. Powell became an influential voice in government, serving as the first director of Interior's new 1879 agency, the U.S. Geological Survey. Although his difficulties with underbrush reputedly led him to say that "the best thing to do for the Rocky Mountain forests is to burn them down," Powell spoke for conservation, recommending in 1878 that mineral, timber, coal, irrigable and grazing lands be classified for their highest and best use.

Millions of Easterners became aware of scenic America in the 1870s when Congress commissioned landscape painter Alfred Bierstadt to depict the great West in gigantic canvases of fantastic panoramic detail, romanticized in the tradition of the Hudson River School. A steady stream of conservation groups began with a trickle and then grew to a storm: the American Fisheries Society in 1870, the American Forestry Association in 1875, the Appalachian Mountain Club in 1876, sportsman Teddy Roosevelt's Boone and Crockett Club in 1888, the Sierra Club in 1892, the Mazamas of Portland, Oregon, a mountaineering club, in 1894, and in 1900, the American League for Civic Improvement and the Society for the Preservation of Historical and Scenic Spots. Yellowstone had become the first wilderness-like National Park in 1872, but not without some stiff objections from Westerners worried that their territories would become a playground for effete Easterners. In 1875 Congress passed the first law protecting a wildlife species, the buffalo. Ironically, President Grant vetoed it, as the buffalo hunters were better at starving the Plains Indians than the Army was at killing them in combat.

By 1890 the U.S. public was growing edgy about the end of the frontier, and federal policy was taking a definite turn toward restricting and retaining rather than disposing of the national lands. Already in 1874 the Windom Committee, investigating railroad land scandals for Congress, had reinvoked the Steam Boiler Act amendments of 1852 which established the nation's first regulatory agency, to justify further regulation of business, resulting in the Interstate Commerce Act of 1877 and a decade later in the first large solely regulatory bureaucracy, the Interstate Commerce Commission. By now only a small minority thought that government should not regulate business.

On March 3, 1891, Congress passed the Act to Repeal the Timber Culture Laws. Most Congressmen didn't realize it, but in doing so they had also established the Forest Reserves, the forerunners of the U.S. Forest Service. Section 24 of that law, giving the President authority to "set apart and reserve" appropriate "public land bearing forests as public reservations," was added as a rider at the last minute in a Congressional conference commit-tee by the personal intervention of Secretary of the Interior John W. Noble, but was never properly referred back to the originating committees. Euphe-mistically known today as "The Forest Reserve Act of 1891" or the "Creative Act of 1891" by Forest Service bureaucrats, the Section 24 rider evoked protest from Western Congressmen when they found out about it; they saw the reserves as threats to logging and mining. President Harrison immediately put 13 million acres into preserves and President Cleveland shortly added 5 million more, but said he would add no more until real protection measures could be enacted on the ground—timber rustling was still widespread.

One evening in July of 1893 at a program during the Columbian Exposition in Chicago, a young professor from Wisconsin named Frederick Jackson Turner read his paper, "The Significance of the Frontier in American History." He said that America's most cherished institutions owed their being to the western frontier, the place misfits could always get away to, the purifying crucible in which strength could be gathered, the soul toughened, the sinews of the great-hearted nation tested and proven. Turner told his audience that "out of his wilderness experience" the American "fashioned a formula for social regeneration—the freedom of the individual." Then Turner said what many had uneasily sensed: "the rough conquest of the wilderness is accomplished." The frontier was closed.

In newspaper and magazine articles, Turner's message rippled through the nation: no more cheap resources, a drastic adjustment of economic, political and daily lives ahead. America's psychological horizon darkened perceptibly, and troubling questions flitted through people's minds: If urban-industrial civilization was replacing the wilderness that made us strong, where would our strength and resolve come from now? Where the wilderness had brought forth sobriety, honesty and hard work, would the growing city spawn ultimate decadence, immorality and squalor? Pacifists wondered whether

America's frontier thrust would now be turned to the conquest of the world. Nostalgic regret crept over America.

Americans rushed to form a cult of the wild and an anti-business bloc. The Sherman Anti-Trust Act had already been passed in 1890. The Organic Administration Act of 1897 favored "withdrawal" of public land from private sale, establishing national forests "for the purpose of securing favorable conditions of water flows, and to furnish a continuous supply of timber for the use and necessities" of the nation. Nature writers such as John Muir, John Burroughs, and Jack London became popular. Teddy Roosevelt's second State of the Union address asserted that "forest and water problems are perhaps the most vital internal questions of the United States." Boston *Post* headlines sensationalized the 60-day stunt of part-time illustrator Joe Knowles, who one August day in 1913 stripped naked and trudged into the Maine woods to live off the land "as Adam had" (he succeeded). The Boy Scout movement of Sir Robert S. S. Baden-Powell was founded to retain the invigorating influence of wilderness in modern civilization.

During the 1890s a great debate arose over just exactly what conservation was really all about. Foresters such as the Department of Interior's Bernhard Eduard Fernow, chief of the Division of Forestry, and Gifford Pinchot, first Chief of the U.S. Forest Service when it was transferred to the Department of Agriculture February 1, 1905, insisted that Forests were for use, not reservation from use. The very term "conservation" was coined by Gifford Pinchot to mean "wise use of resources." His Forest Service for many years was a strictly economic bureau providing timber revenue while protecting public property from damage and theft. Others of a more naturalist bent felt that preservation of resources in their natural condition was the true role of forest reserves. This dispute came to a head in 1908 over a proposed reservoir in Hetch Hetchy Valley near Yosemite to supply water for San Francisco. John Muir of the Sierra Club demanded that the area remain forever wild, but Pinchot advocated construction of the reservoir. Muir lost, the reservoir was built, and smouldering hatred among preservationists fueled their resolve to future activism.

In the aftermath, Pinchot's term "conservation" was gradually expropriated by Muir's faction to mean only "preservation." The argument still rages; today one can find "wise use" advocates like Jim Watt calling themselves conservationists and decrying the betrayal of the term by land-grabbing preservationists, and "perpetual protection" advocates like Michael McCloskey of the Sierra Club calling themselves conservationists and railing against the destroyers and rapists who don't think development is a crime. Historian Samuel P. Hays asserts that the record clearly shows conservation from 1890 to 1920 was a scientific movement led by a small group of men whose objective was the orderly, efficient use of resources under the guidance of experts, and not a popular defense of the public domain against "big business," as documented in his study, *Conservation and the Gospel of Efficiency: The Progressive Conservation Movement, 1890-1920*.

Legislation marched forward to further restrict the conduct of business. The Pickett Act of 1910 weakened the disposal of public lands by authorizing the President to make "temporary" withdrawls of sales for a variety of purposes. The Clayton Act of 1914 tightened "restraint of trade" provisions in the anti-trust laws, and 1914 also saw the creation of the Federal Trade Commission, which regulated a growing range of business and industry activities. Land regulation and preservation were forwarded by the founding of the National Park Service in 1916. In 1924, a U.S. Forest Service officer named Aldo Leopold successfully fought for establishment of the world's first official Wilderness Area in New Mexico's Gila National Forest. The Sierra Club (1892) and Audubon Society (1905) were joined in 1935 as preservation advocates by U.S. Forest Service officer Bob Marshall's Wilderness Society. Their advocacy furthered land use restrictions and regulationism in the early 20th century.

By 1922, the problems of regulationism had become so pervasive that many wondered whether the Constitution's basic protection of property rights from government abuse still had any force. The question was brought up in a famous U.S. Supreme Court case heard by Justice Oliver Wendell Holmes: *Pennsylvania Coal Company* v. *Mahon*. The particular dispute is virtually forgotten; the general principle in the case established an important precedent. Justice Holmes' majority opinion said: "The general rule at least is that while property may be regulated to a certain extent, if regulation goes too far it will be recognized as a taking. . . . When it reaches a certain magnitude, in most if not all cases there must be an exercise of eminent domain and compensation to sustain the action." The Fifth and Fourteen Amendments still worked.

American life was becoming tremendously complex. Government regulation continued, challenging the Holmes decision. The Taylor Grazing Act of 1934 spread regulationism to grazing lands and made it more difficult for public lands to pass into private ownership. Franklin D. Roosevelt's New Deal took regulationism to new heights, and World War II brought emergency suspension of many Constitutional rights.

In 1964 the Public Land Law Review Commission (PLLRC) was created by Congress to study land policy and make recommendations for its future course. The Commission's report, *One Third of the Nation's Land, a Report to the President and to the Congress by the Public Land Law Review Commission*, made it clear that America's original direction had been reversed, the long-standing statutory preference for land disposal was at an end. Now, "maximum benefit for the general public" was the new goal. The PLLRC report recommended that "environmental quality should be recognized as an important objective of public land management" on the 725 million acres of remaining public land, one-third of the Nation's total area. The trouble was and is that when the land disposal program slowed down, the oldest states had reaped their golden harvest of private land, with ample acreages in state and local government control, while the 28 land grant states received wildly unequal percentages of their total areas in federal land grants. For example, Florida received 64.3 percent of its total area in federal land grants, while Utah received only 13.7 percent, Oregon 11.2 percent, California 8.7 percent, Wyoming and Idaho 6.8 percent, Montana and Colorado 6.6 percent, and Nevada 3.8 percent. The Public Land Law Review Commission was frankly afraid of raising the specter of further land grants to the states, saying, "any attempt to equalize land grants among the states in some fashion is neither feasible nor practical. . . . To bring all the public land states, past and present, up to the same percentage of its area as Louisiana (36.2%) would liquidate every acre of the remaining public domain, including the major conservation programs of the National Park Service, the Forest Service and the Fish and Wildlife Service." Those Easterners who thumped Jim Watt for speaking strongly in regional terms pitting Eastern interests against Western interests are apparently unaware of the terrible unfairness of existing public land distribution and burdens.

By the mid-1960s, dozens of laws were pouring out of Congress each year tightening the grip of regulatory authority over land policy, corporate practice, and agency powers. The Multiple Use/Sustained Yield Act of 1960 became one of the first post-materialist laws in America. While establishing the idea of something for everyone in the Multiple Use concept, and protection of forest resources in the Sustained Yield idea—cutting no more timber volume in any given year than grows back—the Act also laid down a rule that deliberately rebuked economics: Forest Service lands would provide timber, watershed, wildlife, recreation, grazing, and other values, "with consideration being given to the relative values of the various resources, and not necessarily the combination of uses that will give the greatest dollar return or the greatest unit output." Efficiency in management and cost-effectiveness in programs was no longer the ruling principle in land management. The environmental lobby had driven the first wedge into American productivity.

"Political ecology" laws also created numerous regulations required to enforce those laws. Environmental groups quickly learned to pressure the administrative agencies responsible for creating regulations. The Sierra Club *Political Handbook* edited by Eugene Coan instructs members, under the title, "Hassling Administrative Agencies," that "An important function of political activity is seeing that the administration . . . does not issue regulations which you oppose," and explaining how to get Congressmen to pressure administrators: "Agencies jump when they get a phone call or a letter from a legislator, and once they do it is up to you to keep them jumping." And during the 1960s and '70s, the top ten environmentalist groups did "keep them jumping."

By 1976, with the passage of the Resources Conservation and Recovery Act and the Toxic-Substances Control Act, all the loopholes had been closed: Congress had given itself authority to regulate every substance in existence and most business activities. The environmental movement bore down with its lawyers and lobbyists and shaped the regulations on all aspects of American life, quietly, efficiently. America had become a thoroughgoing Regulation State, thanks in no small measure to the efforts of environmentalist organizations.

Although every aspect of industrial civilization was affected by environmental regulations, one small segment's troubles will duly illustrate the harm that unreasonable restrictions have done, and that is the utility industry. In a 1981 document by the President's Task Force on Regulatory Relief entitled *Federal Land Use Regulations Adversely Affecting the Western Utility Industry*, dozens upon dozens of regulations were evaluated, their costs and benefits calculated, and appropriate revisions suggested that would adequately protect environmental values, yet leave industry able to survive. Among the regulations that were shaped by environmentalist organizations to handicap the utility industry, several are particularly revealing.

The "Integral Vista" idea was supposedly derived from the Clean Air Act amendments of 1977, but a careful reading of the law shows that it was not authorized at all; the Environmental Protection Agency created the "Integral Vista" in Section 40 of the Code of Federal Regulations, Part 51, at the insistence of several large environmental groups including the Wilderness Society. An "Integral Vista" was described by EPA as "a view perceived from within national parks, monuments, and wilderness areas or panorama located outside the boundary," which was to be protected from any air quality deterioration that might affect scenic views, including private lands. In effect, a utility company could not construct power lines, burn slash from right-of-way clearing, build a coal-fired power generating plant, or conduct other vital activities on their own property if it could be seen from any preserved area. The Task Force pointed out that the "Integral Vista" clearly exceeds the authority of the Clean Air Act, and recommended that all language referring to "Integral Vistas" be stricken from the regulations. Otherwise, no power project in the 11 Western states could be carried out, which may have been the intent of the environmentalist groups that pressured these regulations into existence.

Another utility industry problem was centered around the Department of the Interior's appeals board procedures, which are so tangled in regulations that many projects take three to four years for approval, by which time costs inflate to the point where the project is no longer economically feasible. A case cited showed that Western Slope Gas Company filed a "letter of intent" for a power line across federal lands in 1975 and waited until late 1979 for approval from Interior's appeals board, while project costs escalated from $14 million to $25 million. When approval was finally granted, the project had to be suspended because of cost. Delays of this sort are the "paralysis by analysis" that Jim Watt warns against, and are deliberate tactics on the part of environmentalist groups. An Alaska case was recently decided in which the environmental group plaintiff was reprimanded by Judge Allen T. Compton for openly bragging about its "delaying tactics" to stop a timber sale in the Chilkat Valley. The Schnable Lumber Company of Haines, Alaska, defendant, won the lawsuit, and Judge Compton awarded them $25,000 court costs from the environmental group. In both lawsuits and regulatory pressures, environmentalists actively pressure to kill projects by entangling delays.

Much of the thrust of regulationism comes from organizations claiming to speak for the total populace—environmentalists, consumerist, health and safety groups, and so forth. The role of these citizen activist groups in changing U.S. government and policy in the last two decades deserves a closer look.

By 1850, the French commentator Alexis de Tocqueville had published his final edition of *Democracy In America*, summarizing his travels in our nation and his keen observations of our virtues and foibles. Among his most piercing pronouncements was this: "Americans of all ages, all stations in life, and all types of disposition are forever forming associations. There are not only commercial and industrial associations in which all take part, but others of a thousand different types—religious, moral, serious, futile, very general and very limited, immensely large and very minute. . . . If they want to proclaim a truth or propagate some feeling by the encouragement of a great example, they form an association." He saw something about us that we ourselves missed: we are a nation of joiners. When strong interests emerge in our society, they are reflected in organizations—labor unions, industrial combines, farmers' organizations, occupational associations, environmental groups—all struggling for power and position. Groups have molded, shaped and dominated American law.

Therefore, knowing something about the nature of groups is vital to our grasp of regulationism in America. Groups are not formed merely for mutual aid, but also to exclude, to define the enemy, to create a reason for struggling, to make common cause against outsiders. How and why they do this has been of serious interest to sociologists of social conflict for many years. Sociologist Georg Simmel did an incredibly detailed study entitled *Conflict* and discovered that most groups exist to lay claim to status, power, allegiance, wealth, or systems of values (belief systems).

While it is easy to see that groups must promote a goal and make efforts to achieve it (such as environmentalist groups working to preserve wilderness or enlarge National Parks), Simmel found that it is also necessary to maintain internal cohesion and to enlist strong personal commitment from members by less direct means. For one thing, Simmel found that "it is useful to hate the opponent." But he also found that members must not hate out of mere personal spite; petty actions do not help group cohesion. It is necessary to fight in the name of some high principle, and the group must provide unimpeachable motives and idealistic appeal.

A modern sociologist re-examined Simmel's assumptions in light of modern techniques and developed his findings further. Lewis Coser, in *The Functions of Social Conflict*, stated his discoveries thus: "The consciousness of speaking for a superindividual 'right' or system of values reinforces each party's intransigence, mobilizing energies that would not be available for mere personal interests and goals." Coser also found that "(1) individuals entering into a superindividual conflict act as *representatives* of groups or ideas; and (2) that they are imbued with a sense of *respectability* and self-righteousness since they are not acting for 'selfish' reasons."

Coser focuses most carefully on one of Simmel's most crucial ideas about social conflict: the notion of a "struggle group," an organization that fights for a cause against some clearly identified antagonist. In commenting on Simmel's early studies, Coser says, "Following up on the idea that outside conflict increases group cohesion, Simmel now claims that struggle groups may actually 'attract' enemies in order to help maintain and increase group cohesion. Continued conflict being a condition of survival for struggle groups, they must perpetually provoke it."

"Moreover," Coser goes on, "outside conflict need not even be objectively present in order to foster in-group cohesion; all that is necessary is for the members to perceive an outside threat in order to 'pull themselves together.' "

Coser concludes: "Conflict, which the group originally engaged in as a means to a stated end, now becomes an end in itself . . . so the group's search for enemies is aimed not at obtaining results for its members, but merely at maintaining its own structure as a going concern." This analysis is intriguingly explanatory of modern environmentalist group behavior.

Environmentalists know the subtleties of social conflict—as we shall see in the next chapter—and they know the benefits their social class can gain from regulationism. They know that environmentalism is class warfare. They know that regulationism is their most powerful weapon.

It is time that all of America knew.

CHAPTER 9
BESIEGED

The fireborn are at home in fire.
—Carl Sandburg

By July 1981 the environmental movement had regained its composure after the disarray surrounding Watt's confirmation. Its executives had discussed strategy and decided among themselves that an all-out publicity campaign could remove Watt from office. And by July Watt had given them plenty of ammunition by sparking over a dozen major controversies, including plans for mineral inventories in Wilderness Areas, an increased role for National Park concessioners, the firing of 51 Solicitor's Office employees, a moratorium on further acquisition of private lands for federal parks, oil and gas leasing programs in disputed areas of the Outer Continental Shelf, staunch defense of states water rights, proposed easing of restrictions on pesticide use for public lands, consideration of a proposal to turn over to the state of Texas a National Wildlife Refuge on Matagorda Island (part of which is a wintering ground for the critically endangered whooping crane), and opening of grazing lands to wider livestock use. Former Senator Gaylord Nelson of the Wilderness Society called Watt "unfit to hold office," and the Sierra Club was collecting a million signatures demanding his ouster.

Then Congressman Jim Weaver accused Watt of approaching strip mining regulation with an attitude of "Why worry? The Lord's return is imminent," while Senators William Proxmire and Alan Cranston joined former Interior Secretary Cecil Andrus in calling for Watt's resignation.

Earlier, on the fifth of May, Watt had given a speech to the National Trust for Historic Preservation that neatly summarized his philosophy of decentralizing federal authority and putting control back in the hands of citizens. Among his remarks were these:

157

Instead of turning automatically to the bulldozer, today's wise developer looks first to see what can be rehabilitated and preserved. At Interior, we will continue to administer a stringent National Register of Historic Places. But we will expect states to carry the load with planning and survey work. The federal government can be the catalyst of historical preservation, but it cannot be the perpetual overseer and provider.

About that time, according to a Knight News Wire story by Juanita Greene, "Ken Spaulding of Rangeley, Maine . . . read that new Interior Secretary James Watt was going to cut off the money to buy national parkland. He wrapped an angry letter around a $35 check" and mailed it to help the Wilderness Society "put a leash on the mongrel Watt." On the other side of the country, Greene writes, in Redlands, California, William Emrick wrote the White House, "If Mr. Watt is retained as Secretary of Interior, I plan to devote a considerable amount of effort and money to defeat the Republican Party over the next four years." The point of this news release was that environmental groups were reporting substantial increases in memberships and contributions as a result of Jim Watt's policy initiatives.

On the eleventh of May, Watt addressed the Coal Convention of the American Mining Congress and warned them that

The mining industry must become an assertive partner in the stewardship of America's natural resources and environment. Our proposals to act according to federal law in giving states more authority over surface mining reclamation cannot be viewed as a relaxation of environmental protection. The environment and its values will be protected. This is a challenge to industry to intensify efforts to cause as little disturbance as possible and to repair any damage.

About that time, Nathaniel Reed, a wealthy Florida environmentalist who had served as an Assistant Secretary of Interior under President Nixon, accused Watt of "attempting to turn back the clock to the pre-Rooseveltian era, when everyone supposed natural resources were inexhaustible." Reed also had a few choice remarks in reponse to Watt's speech to a group of National Park concessioners in March where Jim had said: "We have a bias for private enterprise. I will err on the side of public use versus preservation. We are going to ask you to be involved in areas that you haven't been allowed to be involved in before," including tasks of greeting visitors as they arrive and giving them information, much as in the privately-owned preserves of Mount Vernon and Monticello. Reed asserted that "This was one of the most fawning, disgusting performances ever given by a Secretary of the Interior. He was so eager to please that he all but gave away the park system."

It was during this "fawning, disgusting performance" that several worried park concessioners asked whether motors on rafts would be outlawed for Colorado River runs, and whether horses and mules would be forbidden on the Grand Canyon's Bright Angel and Kaibab trails. Watt was having a good time at this meeting, and shot back the now-famous one-liner: "I don't like to paddle and I don't like to walk." It is remarkable how a quick-witted but compassionate reassurance meaning "Don't worry about these traditional services, regulations won't get any more restrictive than they already are" can be twisted by struggle groups and their media promoters to mean "I'm a crass and insensitive destroyer who couldn't care less about outdoor recreation."

On the fourteenth of May, Secretary Watt told a House Subcommittee that

This Administration has never intended, and will never intend, to change the law to allow drilling for oil in the National Parks, or mining in the National Parks, or logging in the National Parks. This Administration does not now have, nor has it had, a "hit list" of national parks or other areas which the Department would request the Congress to deauthorize. I have an "open door" policy regarding environmental groups. I think meetings with environmentalists on specific issues could be very constructive. Let me emphasize the need to work on specific problems rather than philosophical differences. I don't need to be chewed out or congratulated.

About that time, Destry Jarvis of the National Parks and Conservation Association began an interesting practice: he had looked over copies of two memoranda authorized by Assistant Secretary for Fish and Wildlife and Parks Ray Arnett which requested a survey of recent land acquisitions, acquisitions which had been opposed during the Carter Administration by Park Service personnel, specifically mentioning Santa Monica Mountains and Cuyahoga Valley National Recreation Areas, Fire Island National Seashore, and Indiana Dunes National Lakeshore. Jarvis then issued an authoritative interpretation for the press: "The Reagan Administration plans to target important units of the National Park system for de-authorization." Others soon got the idea. Audubon Society leader Russell Peterson insisted that Watt planned to drill for minerals and oil in the National Parks. Jay Hair of the National Wildlife Federation pontificated that "support for Watt in the White House has been waning in recent months." Michael Bean of the Environmental Defense Fund assured America that "Watt does not intend to list 44 endangered species that the Carter Administration found eligible for protection, or any others." Gaylord Nelson of the Wilderness Society dogmatically asserted: "The Reagan Administration is planning to reverse all the environmental laws of the last two decades." John W. Grandy of the Defenders of Wildlife preached: "The Department of the Interior is planning to disestablish 21 wildlife refuges managed by the U.S. Fish and Wildlife Service." Without further investigation, the environmental movement's friends in the media dutifully printed these pronouncements. Not one of the assertions mentioned above actually came to pass, as revealed by subsequent events.

It should be noted, however, that in response to the Sierra Club's direct attack on Watt as a person in their million-signature petition drive, Jack Lorenz, executive director of the 50,000-member Izaak Walton League rejected the tactic, saying, "We've got to go after specific programs. If we can't go after the program, we shouldn't be in business."

On the twentieth of May, Watt testified before a House Appropriations Subcommittee on National Parks budgets. The news of the day, however, centered around Watt's accelerated oil and gas leasing program for the Outer Continental Shelf. While environmentalists claimed that Watt was acting somehow illegally in opening up new offshore areas to exploration, he pointed out that "The Outer Continental Shelf Lands Act, as amended, places on the federal government an affirmative responsibility to obtain for the public the benefits of oil and gas resources. Those resources are to 'be made available for expeditious and orderly development, subject to environmental safeguards' in order to 'achieve national economic and energy policy goals, assure national security, reduce dependence on foreign sources, and maintain a favorable balance of payments in world trade.' " Watt's five-year plan included opening 1 billion acres of federal Outer Continental Shelf lands to leasing.

Response to Watt's proposal exploded into a free-for-all. Two Watt critics provide us with classic studies in politicizing the issue: California Governor Edmund G. Brown, Jr., and the Audubon Society. Governor Brown objected to specific areas in Watt's "OCS Sale 53": Eel River with 63 million barrels estimated oil, Point Arena with 28 million, Santa Cruz with 140 million, and Bodega with 11 million. Brown claimed that these sales would threaten the sea otter and gray whale, and that the risk of environmental damage from potential oil spills outweighed the benefits to the nation. Arguments for and against Brown's position erupted. Connecticut Congressman Toby Moffett brought up a National Academy of Sciences study that contradicted testimony Watt had given in April to the effect that offshore drilling was safer than supertanker traffic in the same waters. The NAS study estimated that 57,000 barrels of oil a year were "routinely discharged into marine environments during Outer Continental Shelf oil and gas explorations." The long-term effects of these discharges had not been adequately researched, the academy said. Governor Brown emphasized that "the potential environmental destruction of an oil spill far outweighs the fact that there are only a few weeks supply of oil in these sites."

Allan Fitzsimmons, chairman of the Environmental Studies Program at George Washington University, countered: "In the case of petroleum there is widespread agreement that most new and future discoveries can be characterized in terms of so many weeks' or month's worth of our total petroleum requirement. Should the don't-develop-it-because-it's-only-a-few-weeks'-worth-of-petroleum argument prevail, the nation's petroleum producing future could be significantly altered."

More to the point, however, is the fact that Governor Brown issued lease after lease in many areas near Watt's "OCS Sale 53" but in state offshore lands within the three-mile limit. Revenues from state oil lands go into Governor Brown's state coffers. Some observers think the real worry is that OCS drilling may tap the same underlying oil pool and divert revenues into federal coffers.

The Audubon Society's President Russell W. Peterson said of Watt's offshore oil and gas leases, and of Watt's plans to open up other federal lands to mineral exploration, "The new administration has shown a misunderstanding and even a contempt for the most precious things in our lives." Peterson characterized Watt's program as "a possibly disastrous assault on the nation's resources." What he didn't mention, however, was that at the very moment he stood at the microphones denouncing Watt as a "short-sighted exploiter," Consolidated Oil and Gas Company and two other petroleum corporations were operating six gas wells in the Audubon Society's privately owned Rainey Wildlife Sanctuary near Intracostal City in Vermilion Parish, Louisiana. Upon request, Audubon will even provide a pamphlet on their Rainey property to justify their actions, saying, "There are oil wells in Rainey which are a potential source of pollution, yet Audubon experience in the past few decades indicates that oil can be extracted without measurable damage to the marsh." Jim Watt couldn't have said it any better; in fact, he has used the identical argument.

Audubon's Rainey oil and gas leases generate nearly two million dollars annually, which provides their lawyers and lobbyists with the means to prevent the United States from doing on public lands what Audubon freely does on private lands. Then, too, Audubon also grazes cattle on the dry parts of Rainey for a per-head fee from local cattlemen, despite the fact that they publicly denounce Jim Watt for doing the same thing on Bureau of Land Management grasslands.

Into the offshore leasing fray jumped Atlantic Richfield Company, saying "We do not believe that the industry can respond effectively and efficiently year after year to such extensive offerings," ticking off inadequate capital, a shortage of drilling rigs, inadequate technical manpower and limited geophysical data as factors "limiting the industry's ability to participate." By this time in May, environmentalists were ready to attack Watt, and they set aside their complaints about the "multinational exploiters" to form a united front against Watt with big oil. Michael Weber of the Center for

Environmental Education was reported as saying, "It is a measure of the outrageousness of the plan that we find so much common ground between ourselves and the oil companies." Soon Exxon and several others of the "Seven Sisters," the seven giant oil companies, joined in the chorus.

However, officials from several of the 475 firms in the National Ocean Industries Association, an offshore industry trade group, said they could easily accommodate Watt's proposals. Chairman C.R. Palmer of Rowan Companies, Inc., said, "The five-year leasing program proposed by the Secretary of the Interior is well within our capability. The offshore drilling industry is capable of providing equipment and manpower to operate anywhere in the world today. We're ready to go." Quiet suggestions emerged that the Seven Sisters might not like Watt's plan because it would obviously increase the nation's crude oil supply, which in turn would have a predictable effect on gasoline prices at the pump.

No one in the media seemed to notice that Watt was standing eyeball to eyeball with big oil just as he had with big environmentalism. A *Time* magazine article criticized Watt for saying of environmentalists, "They were quite surprised and upset when we did not consult them on decisions. But we didn't need to. We knew exactly what we wanted to do." He said the same thing about big oil. His leasing plan was designed with the national interest in mind, not a specific corporate interest.

However, Watt was scrupulous about consulting with the states involved before making his final decision on offshore leasing, whether he ultimately accepted their counsels or not; it was part of his "good neighbor" policy. Critics made much of Watt's inclusion of disputed areas in his final lease offerings, particularly the "OCS Sale 53" areas Jerry Brown did not like. They shouted that Watt had broken his "good neighbor" promise. You can look at it either way. Watt had promised to consult and consider, which he did. Watt had not promised to do every last thing every Governor requested. In the "OCS Sale 53" case, Governor Brown filed suit to stop 34 of 115 leases in the Santa Maria Basin, which means that he agreed with Watt on 81 leases in that area. The basic issue boiled down to who had the authority to manage federal Outer Continental Shelf lands, states or the federal government. In Alaska, Governor Jay Hammond cautioned Watt about the pace and scope of his leasing program, particularly since 16 of the 37 areas coming to the auction block were off Alaska's coast. Watt withdrew Bristol Bay from oil and gas leasing after Governor Hammond demonstrated that more study was needed.

On May twenty-first, the House Committee on Interior and Insular Affairs went all out to get James Watt: by a 23 to 18 vote, 1-½ million acres of Montana Wilderness was put off-limits to oil and gas development, invoking Section 204(e), an emergency clause of the Federal Land Policy and Management Act of 1976. This clause provides that when "an emergency situation exists and that extraordinary measures must be taken to preserve values that would otherwise be lost," the Committee can make an immediate withdrawal of any kind, including energy leasing, and do so without the inconvenience of getting approval from the full House or Senate. Committee Chairman Morris Udall said publicly of the move, "This is the price Interior Secretary Watt will have to pay on Capitol Hill for his repeated vows to open up Wilderness to mineral exploration."

The emergency clause was invoked by Representative Pat Williams, Democrat of Montana, who justified his action thus: "The Bob Marshall—Great Bear—Scapegoat Wilderness complex, which contains 70 percent of the grizzly bears left in the U.S., has 343 pending applications for natural gas exploration or mineral leasing. This Wilderness, located in the fossil fuel-rich Overthrust Belt, has important ecological and tourism values."

As a matter of fact, many of those applications had been pending for years, and Watt had not approved a single wilderness surface occupancy mineral exploration permit. As far as the grizzly bears were concerned, wildlife biologists such as Dr. Frank Craighead, Jr., and his brother John found in 1966 that the great beasts can hold their own despite man's intrusions on their domain. The feared and respected carnivore had maintained its population in Yellowstone National Park, for example, quite well, according to their studies. That is, until National Park Service officials decided that all the grizzlies should get out of the peopled areas and go back to nature. During the Nixon Administration, Interior Department executives including Nathaniel Reed, one of Watt's most vociferous critics, rejected Dr. Craighead's advice and shut down the grizzly's favorite haunts, park garbage dumps. Soon Craighead's worst fears were realized: hungry bears attacked campsites and mauled people. First offenders were usually trapped and taken to the backcountry. Those who returned were destroyed. With a major food supply gone, the grizzlies thinned out, pushing on into neighboring National Forest land where some were bagged by sportsmen, others perished of starvation and some survived. Some wildlife scientists today estimate that the Park Service program reduced Yellowstone's grizzly population by more than half. Man's activities can indeed harm the mighty grizzly, particularly bureaucratic man. The National Park Service has killed many more grizzlies than mineral or petroleum engineers exploring for society's needs.

When Jim Watt heard of the emergency clause vote, he had an appointment with Chairman Udall to ask why there had been no hearings on the emergency withdrawal. At their meeting a few days later, the conversation went like this:

Watt asked Udall if there was some reason the leasing issue had come up so suddenly, and as Watt recalls, Udall apologized for the hasty action, indicating that the session had simply gotten out of hand. Udall agreed that hearings should have been held prior to the Committee's final decision, and Watt reassured him that there had been no emergency. "I'm not preparing any lease permits in that wilderness, Mo," Watt said. "There was no issue. It was fabricated." Udall acknowledged Watt's concerns and promised to hold hearings should similar issues erupt in the future. Watt and Udall agreed that the Committee was a highly independent bunch, and the meeting ended amicably.

One should not mistake Udall's professional courtesy in this conversation for acquiescence. If Udall had felt strongly that Williams was right, there would have been no apology. Udall does not agree with Watt on most issues, and he never caves in under pressure. Udall simply respects Watt as a person. The respect is returned; I found that every top executive in Watt's Interior, although they disagree with his politics, all hold Mo Udall in high esteem as a true professional.

On the twenty-eighth of May, Assistant Secretary for Land and Water Resources Garrey Carruthers sent an internal memo to a number of Interior executives. The memo covered a proposed *Policy Manual* change that would abolish four federal restrictions on pesticide use for public lands: no more requirements for advance notice and posting, no lists of "restricted" pesticides, no lists of "prohibited" pesticides, and no more requirement for users of public lands to get advance approval of their spray plans. Carruthers asked his fellow workers to review and comment on the changes within two days. "I realize this is a short deadline, but the Secretary has asked us to expedite handling of this proposal." Of course, the memo was leaked, this time to the Portland, Oregon *Journal*. The newspaper then told a Democrat in the Oregon State Legislature, Senator Ted Kulongoski, of the memo. Kulongoski said, "They're not only not going forwards, they have gone a long ways backwards on this policy," and "If their purpose is to keep the public uninformed, the pesticide applicators are going to be much happier."

Senator Kulongoski who had sponsored two pesticide bills requiring users to notify the public in advance of spraying, said, "This is a matter of state concern, and the state has got to be prepared to walk into the vacuum that will be created by the loss of these policies." The policies were not being lost. Watt's intent in changing Interior's *Policy Manual* was to remove a redundant regulation which was already adequately enforced by other federal agencies, the Environmental Protection Agency in particular, and by the states. Virtually all federal pesticide programs are administered by the states at the county level in the first place.

On May twenty-ninth, Secretary Watt wrote a letter to Texas Governor William E. Clements, Jr., responding to his request that control of Matagorda Island be transferred to the State of Texas. Watt said he was "inclined to transfer management responsibilities to States where possible," and that he was directing Interior's Fish and Wildlife Service and the Department's Solicitor to review the laws and policies governing the 19,000-acre portion of the Aransas National Wildlife Refuge on Matagorda Island. Watt concluded his letter, "I am very pleased with your expression of intent to emphasize comprehensive conservation and management of this property and would eagerly solicit any state proposals in that regard." Of course, the letter was leaked, this time to the Defenders of Wildlife. John W. Grandy, executive vice president of the environmentalist group, told the world that transfer of this refuge to Texas jurisdiction "will pave the way for commercial development of the island." Grandy pointed out that Matagorda is a key nesting spot for the 78 surviving whooping cranes left in the world, a population that has been increased from 15 since their wintering ground was set aside more than 40 years ago in 1937. Grandy also claimed that Matagorda is vital to the survival of the brown pelican, the southern bald eagle, arctic peregrine falcons, American alligators, and several varieties of sea turtle.

In fact, Watt's letter was a standard bureaucratic "thanks-for-the-suggestion-and-I'll-look-at-it" response that Cabinet officers routinely send. And, even if it had been a bill of sale instantly transferring title to the State of Texas, there is little evidence that Texas intended to revoke protection for the resident wildlife, or that commercial development even in massive doses on the ocean side of this barrier island would have any impact whatsoever on the lagoon side where the wildlife lives. Indeed, the U.S. Air Force operated a base and bombing range on Matagorda until 1971 while the whooping crane's population was being built back up, and bombers make considerably more racket than swimmers.

In early June, a Harris Survey showed a dramatic political turnaround in Ronald Reagan's West: Democrats showed a 55–36 lead in the region they had lost decisively in the November elections. The reason, according to Harris, was "dissatisfaction with the environmental and land policies" of Jim Watt. The Western Democratic Party Caucus called for Watt's resignation "before our region is spoiled and wasted." Mo Udall joined the Siege Environmentalists by announcing that "White House people are beginning to worry that this Department is being run by a guy so far off the mainstream that he is going to get them into all kinds of trouble." Harris' poll did not impress Westerners, however. As Bill Prochnau wrote in the *Washington Post*, "Most seasoned Western politicians, Republicans and Democrats alike, scoff at polls that show Watt hurting President Reagan in what they consider the 'real' West. They joke that the wounded cries come from the West's two antagonists, 'the two Easts' represented by California and Washington, D.C." Democratic Governors in the West rushed to Watt's defense. Colorado Governor Richard D. Lamm said, "Watt has treated us fairly and I don't want to get into a fight with him. I've got a lot riding on the guy." Utah's Governor Scott A. Matheson warned, "It would be foolish to try running against Watt in Utah."

Jim Watt was reluctant to give too many speeches during the early months of his Secretariat. It took him away from the Department and the all-important tasks of setting priorities, establishing policy, and aiming the bureaucracy in his direction. However, during mid-June Watt gave two important talks back-to-back. In Louisville, Kentucky, June 15, 1981, Watt addressed the Outdoor Writers Association of America, leading off with a frank admission of the penalty he had to pay for not making more public appearances: "We have paid a rather high price by concentrating on changes in administration, policy and programs during the early months. But in order to bring the pendulum back to the center, we necessarily set aside concern for our public image, thus we allowed our critics to run wild." He went on:

The critics have successfully confused some members of the press and the public into believing that this Administration seeks to mine and log the National Park areas. We have never proposed that. But we will better manage other hundreds of millions of acres of public lands controlled by the multiple use laws so that the benefits of these lands can be shared by all Americans, not just the select few.

The past privileged position of the select few has been terminated. New keys of access to the Reagan Administration have been passed out to all the hunters and fishermen and to all groups and people who believe in managing the lands, the waters and the wildlife for the benefit of all Americans.

This speech got almost no press coverage at all: Watt departed from his prepared script to give his audience a personal look into his true feelings about the outdoors. This is a side of Jim Watt that has been unjustly ignored:

My parents introduced me to camping, hunting and fishing as a child in my home state of Wyoming. I gave those same experiences to my two children. With my family or with friends, I've fished the creeks and streams and lakes of Wyoming. I've fished for bass in Louisiana, salmon off the Pacific Northwest coast, flounder in the Chesapeake, marlin in the seas off American Samoa, and bottom fish in the Red Sea.

My son and I have lifted our canoe onto our old station wagon on many weekends to paddle through the backwaters of the Chesapeake and the waters of the Colorado. I've paddled the Boundary Waters Canoe Area and Lake Powell; I've snorkled off the Florida Keys, and water skiied and sailed on the man-made lakes of Colorado and Wyoming. I've floated the Snake and Platte Rivers, and the Colorado in Arizona, and the New River in West Virginia.

Recreation—to re-create one's soul—is not limited to the pursuit of wildlife in my opinion, nor does it require any great skill. I'm not a very good skiier, but I love the thrill of skiing the Colorado Rockies.

My son and I have gone trail biking near Canyonlands National Park. What a thrill for us. After our first night out in the early spring, we woke up to find 12 inches of snow covering our tents and motor bikes. Getting out reminded me of a snowmobile trip in the Wind River Mountains along the Continental Divide in Wyoming. As we stood atop those majestic mountains, we could see how the very snow packs we stood on would melt to flow three ways, to the Pacific Ocean, to the Gulf of Mexico and the Gulf of California. The beauty of God's creation is captivating.

I've hiked the Appalachian Trail, bicycled across the State of Wyoming and through Yellowstone and Grand Teton National Parks. I've walked through the urban parks of many great cities and the beaches of America watching the tide roll in and out. All of these experiences have been enriching.

Watt's son Eric added cross-country ski trips to this list when I spoke with him in early 1982, yet Watt's real feelings about the outdoors were embargoed by the press. The one-liner "I don't like to paddle and I don't like to walk" got reams of coverage, but hardly a line about his true feelings was ever set in print.

The same day, Watt addressed the annual meeting of the National Coal Association in St. Louis, Missouri. Again, he made some statements that did not square well with the reporter's and editor's stereotype, and thus never made a headline. Watt said to these miners and corporate leaders:

Do not mistake our programs, policies, or pronouncements as signals that the coal industry or any industry is free to despoil the land and pollute the environment. This Administration is in the mainstream of the environmental movement, and we will be good stewards of our natural resources.

Your responsibility is not only to follow the rules on environmental protection, but to be constantly in search of ways to do a better job of protecting the environment while extracting coal. You must treat with care the land which serves your industry and upon which this generation and untold generations to come must depend.

You also have an obligation to the free enterprise system. People who care about free enterprise will care about the environment. People who run roughshod over the environment in the name of free enterprise are despoiling the free enterprise system.

This Administration believes that a healthy mining industry is essential to America's national security, to a strong economy and to our environment. We also believe that a healthy environment is essential to these goals.

Watt's talk about protecting the environment was backed up with policy decisions that denied development in sensitive areas, but these too received scant press notice. For example, within a few weeks of this Coal Association speech, Watt denied construction permits to the State of North

Carolina for two jetties that would deepen and stablize the migrating channels of Oregon Inlet so that large trawlers could safely enter access waters to the $7.6 million Wanchese Seafood Industrial Park. Watt wrote North Carolina Governor Jim Hunt telling him that the Department of the Interior had refused to grant the Army Corps of Engineers permission to anchor the jetties on beaches in Cape Hatteras National Seashore. Watt said that he must obey the Congressional mandate to protect the land in its natural state and that current policy is not to spend money protecting structures on unoccupied barrier islands. Watt also promised "to try and develop a reasonable and viable alternative to jetty construction." The *New York Times* and *Washington Post* evidently didn't think this was news.

The conflicts of May and June soon became the past that was prologue to stormy July. The pitched battles of July 1981 have no parallel in Interior Department history. The opening salvo was fired by employees of the Office of Surface Mining who filed suit to block Watt's plan to move their office to Casper, Wyoming. Watt's handling of this conflict offers an insight into his political strategy.

The proposed move of the Denver Regional Office of Surface Mining (OSM) facility was only a splinter in the beam of Watt's overall reorganization plan. Watt's goal was to rapidly shift control of surface mining regulation to the states, a step that had been mandated by Congress in the Surface Mining Control Act of 1977 which required the federal government to regulate strip mining only until states developed their own proper regulatory plans and the ability to enforce them. Watt's total reorganization would cut the federal OSM force from about 1,200 employees to about 650, and reduce the number of OSM offices from 42 to 22. Watt also intended to expedite program approval for all 24 surface mining states, finally implementing the "state primacy" principle set down in the law. The immediate response to Watt's announced intention of moving the Denver OSM office to Casper was fiery outrage.

Colorado Representative Patricia Schroeder, described by Watt as a "very leftwing Democrat," jumped on the Denver office closure to prevent 50 to 100 of her constituents from being dispersed to other states. Watt's move would have sent most Denver employees to Casper, Wyoming, but some would have gone to Albuquerque, New Mexico, and to Olympia, Washington, at a cost of $3.9 million, but Watt claimed that ensuing cuts in personnel, travel expenses and office rents would amount to $4.6 million in savings as well as putting the technical support personnel closer to the states. Congressional hearings were quickly held by several committees.

The Appropriations Committee placed a condition on the early draft of Watt's Interior appropriations bills prohibiting him from using any funds to move the Denver people to Casper. Watt says, "Every signal was given to me by all these committee people that if I would back off on the Casper move, they would simply forget the issue with no hard feelings." But Watt remembered how slyly the House Interior and Insular Affairs Committee had needlessly acted to prevent any possible mineral exploration in the Montana Wilderness emergency withdrawal, and was determined not to lose his overall Office of Surface Mining reorganization to the whims of the same hostile forces. Watt saw how the Denver office move had riveted Congressional attention so firmly, and realized that it could be the diversionary tactic to give him the time he needed for his total OSM reorganization. He also realized that he would lose the fight over moving the Denver office in the process. But like a seasoned chess player, Watt knew that a Queen sacrifice can often lead to a rapid checkmate. He says:

So, I kept the move hyped up. I kept the Denver controversy going, refusing to ever bow or compromise. My own staff just went furious with me, because it seemed like I was deliberately taking a beating from Pat Shroeder when I could have avoided it. But my strategy was to keep this issue in front of everybody while I quietly cut the federal OSM force by half and shut down 20 offices completely. By focusing attention on a move of 50 to 100 people from Denver to Casper, I gained the maneuvering room to put my total reorganization in place.

Watt lost the battle but won the war. He says:

Those people are still in Denver. From Pat Shroeder's point of view, she won a major victory. She proved she could stop Watt, and that's fine with me. But even at that, I didn't lose the whole Casper issue: I had intended to put a state office and a technical office there. I lost the technical office, which would have come from Denver, but I got my state office, which is now operating. And I totally reorganized OSM before the House committees could stop me.

By the time Watt had accomplished most of his reorganization, the House Interior Subcommittee on Energy and the Environment became alarmed and called Watt to testify, contending that he intended to dismantle the federal office altogether. On July 17, Watt appeared, armed to the teeth with charts and maps stretching the length of the committee room. Subcommittee Chairman Udall (who is also the full committee chairman) said to Watt: "If your plan is carried through, we may not have a law that is effectively enforced by either the states or the federal government. The states will be hurt, industry and citizens will be hurt, we will have more lawsuits, more confusion and less reclamation."

Watt defended his moves, asserting that he was taking the next logical step in a long process ordered by Congress itself. He said that former President Carter began the process by reducing federal inspectors from 222 in fiscal 1980 to 156 in 1981, to a proposed 97 in 1982. President Reagan's budget reduced the 1982 figure to 69, which Watt said was "a force adequate to oversee state programs." Watt also countered criticism by saying it was unfair to look only at the federal figures. The 222 federal inspectors in 1980 were matched against 297 state inspectors, and in 1981 there were 565 state inspectors, meaning government oversight of the mining industry was increasing.

Chairman Udall conceded that Congress intended to shift the regulatory job to the states, but challenged Watt that they were not ready to accept it. But what had really irked Udall was Watt's playing of their own Montana Wilderness emergency withdrawal game and failing to consult with Congress before announcing his plan. Udall said, "Many of us feel just a little bit ambushed. If you had consulted with us first, a lot of this controversy could have been avoided."

Watt responded by assuring the Chairman that authority would not be shifted to specific states before they had submitted workable regulations, and pointed out that when proposals are made to Congress first, they tend "to be studied to death."

Representative Seiberling broke in angrily, saying, "I trust the states. I don't trust the coal industry. I think you have to be sensitive to the fact that we're dealing with a bunch of people who will push just as far as they can to gain their advantage. With the disarray within OSM today, you have already given the mining industry the impression that OSM enforcement is weakened; and they're going to start taking advantage."

Congressman Manuel Lujan of New Mexico retorted that this uproar was just "much ado about nothing." Representative Richard Cheney of Wyoming called it "an unnecessary controversy." Nonetheless, Seiberling continued, accusing Watt of undermining the Surface Mining Control and Reclamation Act of 1977 and gutting the federal regulatory and enforcement role under the act. Watt replied, "We fully support the Act and its intentions. The law, as Congress intended, and as upheld by the highest court in the land, will be implemented and fully enforced."

Then Congressman James Weaver of Oregon, commented, "Secretary Watt, earlier this year you made the remark to me that 'I do not know how many future generations we can count on before the Lord returns.' I wonder if you aren't approaching the issues of surface mining regulation as 'Why worry? The Lord's return is imminent.' Does the imminent return of the Lord have anything to do with this?"

Jim Watt smiled and said, "I'm surprised at you, Congressman. My religious freedom is guaranteed under the First Amendment. I don't think this should be a subject of this hearing."

Congressman Don Young of Alaska furiously stood up and demanded that Chairman Udall rule Weaver out of order. Udall declined. Young then said to Watt, "Mr. Secretary, I apologize to you for the behavior of this committee."

Congressman Williams of Montana, for whatever reason, sided with Watt on the OSM reorganization: "I find your actions to be logical and sound on their face. I only think your actions to implement the plan might have been a little more precipitous than they had to be."

Regardless of the furor, Watt won his issue: he totally reorganized the Office of Surface Mining and no degradation in enforcement resulted. The head of the Denver office soon resigned to express his displeasure with Watt's program. Watt accepted the resignation happily; the man had been an ultra-environmental movement supporter and an opponent of Watt policies. Watt then called the Denver office to apologize to those families that had waited in suspense during the controversy for leaving them with such nerve-shattering uncertainty. He assured them that their positions were secure and the issue was closed.

The "Fire Watt" Fire

July was planned as "Dump Watt" month by the environmentalist movement. On the 5th, the Audubon Society announced its opposition to the Reagan Administration. On July 14, the National Wildlife Federation requested President Reagan to fire Watt, using a survey sent to 4,000 of their 4.5 million members as a justification. July 24, the Wilderness Society called for Watt's resignation. By spacing the announcements, the movement planned to gain maximum press coverage and keep the issue rolling to a crescendo that the Administration could not ignore. The case of the National Wildlife Federation is of particular interest.

Dr. Jay D. Hair, director of the Federation, called for Watt's resignation while claiming that his group had tried to work with Watt, but found him unyielding. Hair said he had taken his case "through quiet channels of diplomacy," and urged cooperation with Watt until he had finally proven himself "out of step, not only with the views of conservation leaders, but with the mainstream of American thought on conservation issues." The mainstream, presumably, was reflected in the opinion survey sent to 4,000 NWF members.

The National Wildlife Federation in early September, 1980, sent then-director Thomas Kimball to the White House with 21 other environmental group leaders to formally endorse Jimmy Carter's candidacy for President. These people all later claimed to have been speaking as individuals. Then, the NWF sent Kimball to Watt's confirmation hearing to express his views on the candidate. Kimball challenged each position Watt took during the hearing, questioned Watt's integrity, and criticized Watt's selection of Steve Shipley as his Executive Assistant. At the Federation's 45th Annual Meeting, which featured Kimball's farewell speech, he dwelled at length on denunciations of the Reagan Adminstration's policies and called for a concerted effort by its grassroots affiliates to defeat the Reagan program.

New Federation director Dr. Jay Hair let the cat out of the bag in a May 1981 interview when he admitted to a reporter that the Federation was really trying to "create a well-documented attempt to cooperate" with Watt. Dr. Hair said, "When we come off the fence it'll be with more and greater credibility than if we had attacked from the first." Leaked memos from key environmentalist groups, the Sierra Club in particular (see chap. 11), reveal major groups colluding to denounce Watt from the beginning, but deciding to carefully orchestrate their demands for his ouster to maximize press coverage.

Hair and nine other environmentalist leaders met with Watt May 15, presenting him with a ten-point list of demands that they wanted embraced by the Interior Secretary. After the meeting, Hair told a reporter, "To my surprise, Watt agreed with seven out of the ten points." Veteran politicos know that seven out of ten is not a bad score in Washington's compromise country. However, Watt's reasonable and mostly agreeable stand could not be allowed to interfere with the "Dump Watt" schedule. Hair later said, "Despite this harmony, there are quite frankly some fundamental, major differences with Watt."

As expected, Dr. Hair announced on July 14 that the National Wildlife Federation was calling for Watt's resignation—"sadly, because we have no personal animus against Mr. Watt, and we still want to cooperate with the Reagan Administration." Hair said he had no choice in the matter because his 4.5 million members were sending him "the same kind of signals the other groups are getting against Watt," as evidenced in the Federation's opinion survey.

In a news conference when a reporter asked Watt if he was going to resign, Watt deadpanned, "Yes." When the reporter asked when, Watt grinned and said, "As soon as my usefulness expires." Asked what he thought of the Federation questionnaire, Watt said, "It's hilariously funny. This poll is so rigged, I even voted to fire myself. I think we've dismissed it."

Shortly after the National Wildlife Federation called for Watt's resignation, three notables jumped on the bandwagon: former Interior Secretary Cecil Andrus and Senators William Proxmire and Alan Cranston. On the NBC *Today* show, former Secretary Andrus predicted an early end to Watt's regime, saying, "It is only a matter of time until President Reagan will be forced to oust this controversial Cabinet member." Andrus went on to Boise,

Idaho, where he appeared on KTVB's *Viewpoint* news program, saying that he had put a six-month embargo on himself before saying anything, to give Watt "time to get used to the chair." Now, he said, his old friend Mo Udall had been right by saying that having Watt as Interior Secretary was like "putting Dracula in charge of the blood bank." Andrus raked Watt over the coals for his "developmental zeal," and for acting unilaterally with administrative decisions.

Contrast these statements with these facts: In a secret meeting April 16, 1979, on the second floor of the Office of Management and Budget, Andrus and Presidential Assistant for Domestic Affairs and Policy Stuart E. Eizenstat met with executives from the Nation's major timber industry trade associations. As Joseph McCracken, Director of the Western Forest Industries Association describes the meeting: "Andrus sat to my left with Eizenstat on his left and the association executives all around the table. He told us that if we would support his proposal to create a Department of Natural Resources to contain the Forest Service, he would immediately release to us all of the Wilderness Study areas of the RARE II program and the Bureau of Land Management's Wilderness Study program. The representatives from the National Forest Products Association were utterly stunned, and put Andrus off as politely as they could." The industry rejected the Andrus deal, fearing the long-term timber famine that would be caused by such a Frankenstein monster. And yet this same Cecil Andrus felt self-righeously qualified to denounce James Watt for his "developmental zeal."

While the environmental movement was carefully orchestrating its "Dump Watt" symphony, Jim Watt was sticking to his agenda. Among his many accomplishments during the July Siege were these:

July 1 Watt went to court to appeal an Audubon Society victory in stopping North Dakota's Garrison Diversion project, which was to have irrigated 250,000 acres of farm land as well as providing water for municipal, industrial and recreational use. Watt considered the halt to have been illegal, since Secretary Cecil Andrus had signed a 1977 agreement with the Audubon Society to stop construction despite the fact that Congress had authorized and funded it. Watt was outraged at this "sweetheart deal," not just because Andrus had rolled over and played dead, or because the Audubon Society had no business setting American farm and economic policy, but because the Justice Department had sealed the Andrus deal. "I cannot imagine any lawyer agreeing with this Audubon Society stipulation," Watt told me. "He ought to be disbarred and run out of the country." Evidently the court thought so too: Watt won his appeal and the Garrison project is underway.

July 7th, Watt defeated the Sierra Club in the U.S. Court of Appeals for the District of Columbia in their effort to stop several proposed energy projects in Utah and Arizona on the grounds they would jeopardize "federal reserved water rights." United States law has never recognized federally reserved rights on water rising in public lands, but it was an imaginative try by the Sierra Club. Judge George E. MacKinnon wrote for the appeals court: "No Federal water rights were reserved when Congress passed the Lands Policy Act." Fortunately for America's energy future, Secretary Watt brought the Sierra Club back to reality.

July 8th, Watt showed up at a sendoff party for the U.S. delegation to the International Whaling Commission, which surprised some of the environmentalists present. He came to wish an old high school chum well: Tom Garrett, veteran anti-whaling advocate, whom Watt had nominated for the top spot on the U.S. Whaling Commission, having written to Commerce Secretary Malcolm Baldrige and then Secretary of State Alexander Haig urging them to recommend that President Reagan name Garrett delegation leader. Watt had said that whales are "gentle, beautiful creatures that must have international protection."

Some of Watt's concern for whales resulted from a new tradition Watt created at Interior: "Resource Learning Sessions." The first of these sessions was held informally at noon in July 1981 by Dr. Sylvia Earle, marine biologist of the California Academy of Sciences, who presented movies and slides of whales for the Department's top executives. The session was so well received that Bruce White of the Charles A. Lindbergh Foundation was invited to report on his efforts to protect eagles, and Dennis Baake of the Mellon Institute came to brief executives on energy conservation. The first formal evening sessions, held off Interior premises, featured Dr. Robert Ballard of the Woods Hole Oceanographic Institute, reporting on mineral-producing hyrdothermal vents. Lester Brown, president of Worldwatch Institute, later discussed world hunger and his book *Building A Sustainable Society*; others invited were Jean-Michael Costeau of the Costeau Society and economist Julian Simon, author of *The Ultimate Resource*. Watt said of the idea, "We want to hear first-hand from top scientists, researchers, academicians, and explorers about the world we live in and breakthroughs in the sciences of land, water, energy, and human resources. Most importantly, I want to ensure that my key management officials have the latest information and opinions on which to base program and policy decisions."

July 9th, Watt attended a Senate symposium on public lands and less oppressive and expensive alternatives to confiscation. July 15th, Watt authorized the Linowes Commission to develop solutions to minerals management problems, focusing on royalty accounting and oil theft. By mid-July, most of Watt's appointees had been confirmed, and his final key man was formally nominated, Pedro Sanjuan as Assistant Secretary for Territorial and International Affairs—although it would be December before Sanjuan was finally confirmed by the Senate. July 24th, Watt found his speech in Asheville, North Carolina, disrupted by the first of many noisy sign-waving demonstrations *in favor* of his policies.

It had been a busy month. It had been a busy year. The crew had stayed home the first six months as planned. They had gained full control of the bureaucracy. They had won several key court fights. They had pulled off several crucial reorganizations. The Environmentalist Siege had stormed the walls of Watt's Secretariat only to be rebuffed by White House Chief of Staff James Baker, who told the National Press Club, "We are aware that there is a great deal of tension with respect to some of these policies. The President has absolute faith and confidence in Jim Watt. This has been discussed. The President thinks Jim is doing a fine job."

Under Secretary Hodel now had the Management By Objectives system in place, but by July he was becoming uneasy. One evening after dinner, his wife Barbara and Assistant Secretary Robin West sat with him before the ever-present flipchart, trying to further elaborate the MBO. Hodel says, "We tried to see where we were going in the next six months. Our management plan just wouldn't go." After Robin West left, as Hodel lay sleepless, it hit him: the basic job was done. Interior was in order. The MBO needed to be worked further down the Department, but it was essentially complete. It was time for a new direction. It was time to deal with the public. It was time for outreach.

CHAPTER 10
THE PUBLIC INTEREST

> *Necessity reforms the poor, and satiety re-forms the rich.*
>
> —Publius Cornelius Tacitus

Much has been made of James Watt's association with Mountain States Legal Foundation, a conservative public interest legal group. Protests from the traditional liberal public-interest movement, the consumerists, the store-front lawyers, the civil rights advocates and the environmentalists, all held that Watt had only represented "special" or "merely" private interests. The policies and solutions "of the left," according to these advocates, serve the "true" public interest, and demand the enhancement of governmental, largely federal, power. This, they insisted, was the traditional meaning of the public interest.

Yet the traditional public-interest movement itself is a strikingly recent event in our history. Charles Halpern, founder of what is generally regarded as the first public-interest law center, has said that despite the longer history of the American Civil Liberties Union and the National Association for the Advancement of Colored People's Legal Defense and Education Fund, "the term public-interest law had [in 1969] not been created." And the movement has been small. According to the Council for Public Interest Law, the traditional movement's umbrella organization, during 1979-80, there were fewer than 700 attorneys employed by about 110 tax-exempt centers in public-interest law practice.

The sense of morality in acting for the public interest has carried this movement, and particularly the environmentalist portion, to a position of substantial political clout. Environmental interests today are prominently represented in federal statute and case law, and in public opinion. Everyone is an environmentalist in some sense, and everyone likes to act morally, judges

176

and legislators included. But we seldom pose those critically serious questions of the costs, methods, and results of environmental programs. Does money spent on environmental programs actually protect the environment? Does Wilderness designation actually protect wild areas? Is environmentalist participation in the decision-making process extended to other sectors of the public in fact? Are all the bans on pesticides really necessary—what crop protection are we losing versus what harm are we preventing? To what extent shall we control pollution—minimal cleanup at minimal cost, basic filtration at $1 million, best-available-technology at $100 million, remove-every-last-molecule at a cost in excess of the Gross National Product?

And aside from such questioning of the programs, what about the environmentalist movement itself? How is the public interest affected by a network of struggle groups that have substantial political clout, no constraints of governmental regulation, and whose every victory serves to allocate resources to non-goods wants? As Irving Kristol wrote in *Two Cheers for Capitalism*, "there is now considerable evidence that the environmentalist movement has lost its self-control, or, to put it bluntly, has become an exercise in ideological fanaticism. It is mindlessly trying to impose its will— sometimes in utterly absurd and self-contradictory ways, and very often in unreasonable ways—on a reality that is always recalcitrant to any such imposition, by anyone."

The Public

The truest truth I have found in thinking about "the public" was best put by law professor Milton R. Wessel in *The Rule of Reason*: "The public's interests are as many and disparate as there are people and organizations, and no one speaks for them all." So there is no "the public." There are publics. There is no "the public interest." There are publics' interests. Yet we still need to talk of ideas and actions that serve the greatest good for the greatest number, at least, if not the total public interest. So we will still use that rather inexact phrase "the public interest," but with an awareness of its limitations and the diverse realities that lie beneath it: there are publics, and no one speaks for them all.

The environmentalist public, in opposing Jim Watt, was and is adamant about asserting the total public interest, claiming Watt to be a destroyer and themselves a savior. One of the main props of their argument is the disclaimer to any motive of financial gain. The non-profit status of environmentalism has always been one of its chief pillars of respectability, and the non-profit volunteer struggle group has been the central idea behind the movement's success. All rhetoric about non-profit goals and no financial gain simply serves to hide the fact that the movement is a serious and powerful competitor for economic resources in America today.

In order to see through the rhetoric, it is necessary to understand some basic ideas about resources and economics. For example, financial goals and economic goals are not the same. The college text *Forest Resource Management* makes a rather flatfooted but crystal clear distinction between them. In discussing "money goals," the text tells us, "Such objectives are occasionally referred to as economic, but this is a misnomer to be avoided. . . . Objectives are *economic* by relating to human choice, or resource allocation, for the fulfillment of human wants." This is the crucial distinction: financial goals relate to money. Economic goals are broader: they relate to allocating resources for the fulfillment of human wants, whether money is involved or not. Thus, environmentalists may validly claim to have no financial stake in winning a Wilderness Area designation; indeed, they receive no cash if they win. However, it should be perfectly obvious that in winning a Wilderness Area designation, they have absolutely allocated public resources in the area to the fulfillment of *their* wants, which involve amenity values, while forbidding others to fulfill *different* wants, particularly commodity values. Even though the Audubon Society and others may carefully explain that the ethical content of "dispersed forms of recreation" is the real point of Wilderness designation, there is no escaping the fact that it is also economic competition for the allocation of resources. Environmentalists may validly complain that the rest of society does not understand recreational ethics, but by the same token, the rest of society may validly complain that environmentalists do not understand economics.

So we see that non-profit, non-financial goals are not really to the point in claiming the public interest. The allocation of resources to fulfill human wants is to the point. Environmentalist groups definitely compete with other sectors of the public for the allocation of resources, whether it be in establishing a Wilderness Area, or in confiscating somebody's home for a federal park, or in imposing $100 billion worth of excess paperwork on all businesses in the name of environmental protection programs. All of which qualifies the environmentalist movement as a special interest.

Another clue to the special-interest nature of environmentalism is the size of its constituent groups. By the highest estimate, under 10 percent of all Americans belong to any kind of environmentalist organization, and the large wealthy organizations such as the National Wildlife Federation and the Sierra Club, the "top ten" or a dozen, can claim less than 2 percent. These struggle groups have remarkably few members among the poor, ethnic minorities, or the goods-producing sector; the vast majority of environmentalists are middle- or upper-middle-class, highly educated, and have abundant leisure time.

Scientific studies such as the U.S. Forest Service's *The Social Characteristics of Participants in Three Styles of Family Camping* and *Wilderness Users in the Pacific Northwest—Their Characteristics, Values, and Management Preferences* consistently find that people using Wilderness Areas or remote camping sites come from the top third of U.S. income and educational achievement ranks.

Just as I think more motivates environmentalists than the public interest, I think more motivates environmentalists than merely hanging on to the status quo, than simple conservatism. There is too much political ambition evident and too much struggle for social change within the movement for that analysis to hold completely true. I think the movement in 1982 is shifting toward outright partisan political activism, supporting Democrats in specific candidacies, which has never been done before. Connecticut Congressman Toby Moffett helped the 1982 Democratic Congressional Campaign Committee set up the "Emergency Environmental Fund." A *Washington Post* article by Bill Peterson on April 20, 1982, was headlined, "Environmental Lobbyists Map New Effort: State Political Action Committees to Stress 'Green Vote.' " Peterson wrote, "Five national groups—the Sierra Club, Environmental Action, the Solar Lobby, Friends of the Earth and the League of Conservation Voters—plan major campaign efforts this year," and environmentalists "have formed 30 state political action committees . . . to raise money and recruit volunteers for candidates who support their views." This is an unprecedented shift to partisan political action.

Nonetheless, in the past 20 years, environmental lobbyists have shown furious ambition not to follow the law, but to shape it in their own image. In one legislative campaign after another, they have worked to define the public interest in their own terms. Environmentalist lawyers have assaulted the courts with much the same thrust, constantly seeking legal judgments that would explicitly state that their views *were* the public interest. They came close in the watershed case, *Sierra Club* v. *Morton*, the famous attempt to obtain legal rights for natural objects (1972). The U.S. Supreme Court heard the case, and turned away the issue of legal rights for natural objects. Technically, the Sierra Club lost that case, but many points in the opinion of the Court, delivered by Justice Stewart, broadened the right of environmental groups to sue in court, an issue known as "standing" to sue. The Sierra Club claimed that its members would be affected by certain developments in California's Mineral King area, but did not claim economic injury. They lost in part because of this, but the Court's opinion did say, "the fact of economic injury is what gives a person standing to seek judicial review [to go to court] under the statute, but once review is properly invoked, that person may argue the public interest in support of his claim. . . ." This is a tremendously important point to an environmentalist appeals court lawyer: in effect, it gives "standing" to an appellant as a "representative of the public interest," once he has followed the rules about getting into court in the first place.

Another vitally important weapon in the environmental lawyer's arsenal is the concept of the "private attorney general." "Private attorney general" is a right conferred by Congress or a state legislature upon an individual citizen that enables him, upon discovering some infraction of an environmental law, to go to court and be paid for turning in the offending business or the public agency that is required to enforce the law. Environmentalist lawyers often treat this as a "bounty hunter's license" to sue industry and be paid for it. Environmental groups have lobbied to spread this concept to as many new laws as possible. They narrowly failed to tack private attorney general provisions onto the bill that created the Trans-Alaska Oil Pipeline, for example.

A critical part of environmentalist lobbying is the skillful orchestration of public hearings before agencies, state legislatures, or Congress, particularly Congressional field hearings on proposed environmental laws. The *Sierra Club Political Handbook* (4th ed.) offers members sophisticated advice on winning hearings, explaining how hearing committees work, warning to study "the background and character of the committee members" before making an appearance, and pointing out that "some witnesses testify in full awareness that they are not changing the minds of committee members, and they aim at the public who will read about the hearing in newspapers and see excerpts of it on television." The environmentalists' paid staff members at Jim Watt's Senate Confirmation Hearing closely followed that advice.

However, there is an entire armory of strategies that environmentalists use but do not write in their political handbooks. Journalist Allan May filled in the blanks in his exposé, *A Voice in the Wilderness*, a book based on years of covering the wilderness-preservationist wars. May listed the strategies used by environmentalist groups to win hearings and influence American law: "The name of the game is to get out many times more people than the opposition and to pretend that the general population is on their side," he writes. "A major part of the strategy is to intimidate the opposition," he goes on, noting typical tactics: "They applaud friendly speakers; they boo and hiss unfriendly ones. They laugh sarcastically, *en masse*, when an unfriendly speaker makes a point. They shout insults and counterarguments. . . ." Allan May summed up his observations of environmentalists at hearings: "Silencing their adversaries is a major goal of wilderness-conservationists."

What do hearing chairmen do in hearings? It depends on who's chairing. Some, such as Senator Mark Hatfield of Oregon, tolerate very little of the usual environmentalist shenanigans and run clean hearings. Others, such as Representative James Weaver, also of Oregon, often seem not to hear, or make exasperated pleas for order which are ineffective, thus allowing environmentalists to roast the opposition. Agency hearings tend to be rowdier than Congressional hearings; agency directors have less prestige than Congressmen and no power of contempt—a number of environmentalists of the "pressure relief for personality maintenance" type go after agency heads because they know they can attack with impunity. Field hearings tend to be more unruly than Washington hearings; more dignitaries who can influence legislation tend to show up for Washington hearings and the environmentalists tend to be more polite.

Letter writing is another aspect of lobbying that environmentalist groups have mastered. Years ago when I was active in the Pacific Northwest Chapter of the Sierra Club we had a "telephone tree" arrangement that was called into play whenever a crucial Congressional vote required a letter campaign. Every volunteer for the "telephone tree" was given the names of two members. When the volunteer received a call from the person on the next lower rung of the "tree," he or she wrote the necessary letter and then called the two people on the next higher rung of the "tree." With only two people to call and one letter to write, almost everyone cooperated. This setup could crank out ten thousand letters in a week or less nationwide.

The Sierra Club *Political Handbook* also spells out letter-writing tips for Club members to keep in mind: "Write in your own words." "Don't send a postcard or form letter." "Refer to bills by name and number, if possible." "Remember when you write, *don't* mention that you are a member of the Club or that you are part of a letter-writing campaign. A letter from a 'concerned citizen' is much more effective."

Business and industry have long used independent studies to make their own cases before a legislature or court. When environmentalists began the practice in the late 1960s, a new phenomenon appeared. Milton Wessel described it in *The Rule of Reason*: "It is almost commonplace in socio-scientific litigation to hear numerous scientific experts, with equally outstanding credentials and reputations, testify one after the other, describe substantially the same data, and yet reach diametrically opposite conclusions." Scientists are alert to the treacherous nature of raw data, and fully comprehend that divergent interpretation techniques and the limited statistical reliability of most data can give rise to contradictory opinions among conscientious scientists. However, the public, when faced with such awkward disagreements, does not know whom to believe. The usual result is that laymen believe the scientist who most closely reflects their own beliefs and lifestyle perferences. I call this the "My Expert's Better Than Your Expert" syndrome; other commentators call it "Information Pollution."

Environmentalist groups have powerful friends on the right Congressional Committees. Pro-environmentalist Congressmen chair the House Interior and Insular Affairs Committee and its Energy and the Environment and Public Lands and National Parks subcommittees, the House Government Operations Subcommittee on Environment, Energy and Natural Resources, and the House Energy and Commerce Committee. Congressman Phillip Burton, an important figure on the House Interior Committee, has an interesting background as a "hardball player" in taking private lands for federal parks. He was among the first to recognize that the parks issue was a hot vote-getter in his urban San Francisco District, and gained a reputation for utter ruthlessness in his Subcommittee Chairmanship for National Parks and Insular Affairs. A story in the San Jose, California, *Mercury* for July 30, 1978, illustrates the point. The story quotes conservative Congressman John H. Rousselot as saying, " 'Burton scares people,' " and comments, "They may have reasons for fear." The case of Representative James Oberstar, Democrat from the 8th District in Minnesota, was cited. Oberstar's constituents love to ride on snowmobiles, so hated by environmentalists (one of my wildernist friends calls them "anti-terrain vehicles" although they never touch the ground and there is no real environmental damage done by them). Oberstar came before Burton's Subcommittee asking him to allow snowmobiles and motorboats on certain limited areas of the Boundary Waters Canoe Area in Minnesota, and in a protracted battle, actually won an amendment—one of the few times anyone has ever beaten Burton. The article quoted Burton as coming up to Oberstar after the vote and saying, "Jim, I'm going to get even with you one of these days. I'll make the whole [expletive deleted] 8th [Oberstar's] District a National Park." Oberstar replied, "[Expletive deleted], Phil, I thought you already had!"

Burton is also an astute judge of which way power is flowing. By early 1979, he had sensed resistance growing to the direct Congressional taking of private land for federal parks. On May 31, 1979, he quietly sent out invitations to a select few to attend "An informal seminar to consider improvements in federal land acquisition efforts related to our National Park system and related types of areas." Only environmentalist groups and strongly pro-environmentalist government officials were invited. A staff aide of a prominent Senator was invited, and upon seeing the invitation list, asked Burton whether a more balanced representation shouldn't be asked to attend. Burton was emphatic: "No one else has been invited, or will be; if they come uninvited, they will be asked to leave." Charles Cushman, executive director of the National Inholders Association heard of the seminar and requested admission; he was bluntly refused entry.

What went on in the Burton seminar was intended to remain secret; no transcript of the proceedings has been published. I obtained the following account from the staff aide of a prominent Western Senator who attended the

Burton Secret Seminar, as it has since been dubbed by insiders, held June 15 and 16, 1979, in Room 2118 of the Rayburn House Office Building, which is the Armed Services Committee Room. In attendance were land acquisition personnel from the Nature Conservancy, the Trust for Public Lands, and the National Parks Foundation, plus the Chiefs of Land Acquisition for the U.S. Department of Agriculture Forest Service, the Bureau of Land Management, and the National Park Service. Willis Kriz represented the Park Service. Congressman John Seiberling was in and out, but a key staff aide attended the entire seminar for him.

Congressman Burton opened the seminar: "We are here to figure out how to buy more land at less cost, faster. Some of the biggest problems we have are the conservative leaders in the Senate and in the Office of Management and Budget." The first panel after Burton's introductory statement was made up of land acquisition specialists from several non-profit groups that buy private land for preservation, including the Nature Conservancy. The panelists complained of the lag time between their purchase of land targeted for federal acquisition and government buy-out: interest rates and administrative costs were sapping their capital, and they asked for more direct access to federal funds.

Then Nathaniel Pryor Reed, an independently wealthy former Assistant Secretary of Interior, took the floor. Reed bills himself as a "staunch Republican," although his politics closely resemble Teddy Kennedy's, and he takes every available opportunity to knock Ronald Reagan and James Watt. Reed made some saber-tongued remarks about Watt as the banquet speaker of the Sierra Club's annual dinner May 2, 1981, where he also called National Park inholders "squatters." Reed seemed to be the real force behind the "Burton Seminar"; one attendee noted that "Burton would constantly look to Reed for signals, and guided his remarks according to Reed's affirmative or negative nods of the head. I've never seen Burton play second fiddle to anyone before." Reed stood up in the seminar and strongly recommended that the Land and Water Conservation Fund be removed from Congressional control to become, as he put it, "a self-activating land acquisition slush fund" completely at the discretion of the Secretary of the Interior. (Remember that Cecil Andrus was in office at the time.)

Among the 41 attendees, 9 were environmentalists, including Laurance Rockefeller of the Natural Resources Defense Council and Edgar Wayburn of the Sierra Club; 14 were federal agency officials, including Jim Moorman of the Justice Department (formerly of the Sierra Club Legal Defense Fund) and Malcolm Baldwin of the Council of Environmental Quality; 5, Congressional aides; 7, Congressional committee staffers; and several were state officials, including Huey Johnson of California. Attendees were invited to a reception and dinner at the Democratic Club in Washington during the seminar. Multiple-use groups were refused entry to this closed-door session, making a mockery of environmentalist insistence on "public access to the decision-making process."

These machinations of the New Preservationists to create an uncontrollable land grab slush fund and to feed public monies to private non-profit environmentalist land-buying groups are rather disturbing in themselves, but they take on new meaning in light of Congressman Burton's later behavior. After President Reagan took office, Burton resigned his National Parks and Insular Affairs Subcommittee chairmanship, but remained on the Interior Committee. His old subcommittee was reconstituted as the Public Lands and National Parks Subcommittee, Congressman Seiberling presiding. Insiders believe Burton is gearing up for another run at the Speaker of the House position by emphasizing his role on the House Education and Labor Committee— he narrowly lost to Thomas P. "Tip" O'Neill of Masachusetts in a past try.

It is worthwhile during our consideration of the public interest to focus on the activities of certain non-profit land buying organizations such as the Nature Conservancy and the Trust for Public Lands. Their groups function roughly as follows: A non-profit group identifies a parcel of land they believe should be preserved as open space. Often a piece of land is brought to their attention by other environmentalist groups, or by the property owner. The "non-profit" may then discuss the land with federal, state or local governments to determine their interest in acquiring the property. If the government says "yes," then the non-profit borrows funds against the government's pledge from private sources, and negotiates acquisition with the land owner. If the government says "no," the non-profit may still purchase the land and then lobby Congress to buy the land from them anyway. In this way private non-profit environmentalist groups set national priorities for what land should be purchased, from whom and for how much.

This rather simplified sketch of the process is in real life subject to many ifs, and or buts that wildly complicate the transactions, but the outline is essentially correct and realistic. After the non-profit buys the land, they hold it for a while, paying interest on the loan until the government is willing to acquire the land and has Congressional authorization and appropriations. The lag time can kill the deal as interest payments draw down the non-profit's capital. If all goes well, the non-profit sells the land to the government for the price at which they acquired it, *plus* the cost of their interest payments and an administrative charge to cover the cost of their administrators' and professionals' salaries. In effect, these private non-profit land preservation groups operate on real-estate commissions from selling land to the government.

These activities raise certain questions of the public interest in relation to the land acquisition policy of the U.S. government. For openers, who is making that policy? Is the government a reactor to non-profit group actions? Once the land is acquired by a non-profit, is the government legally or morally obligated to bail them out? By what criteria does the non-profit determine these lands to be "threatened," or to be of local, state or national significance, or that federal purchase would be in "the public interest"? Are there alternatives to acquisition?

Some of these same questions were raised by a September 1, 1977, *Review of Acquisition Costs of National Seashores* by the Congressional Research Service. A section on what they called "The Secrecy Option" pointed out that one of the most significant factors in raising prices that the federal government must pay for recreation lands is the openness of the entire procedure. "In the private sector, when a large parcel of land is to be acquired from numerous property owners, the proposed acquisition is seldom widely publicized," the report said.

Rather, the acquisition is made piece by piece, often by dummy or front organizations to conceal the fact that a large quantity of land may be sought until purchase of the desired parcel is essentially completed. The advantage of this strategy is that it keeps down the cost of acquisition because if the property owner knows that his land is greatly desired, he can often ask and receive a higher price for it.

The Federal government has not usually been able to employ this technique in the acquisition of park and recreation lands. It is possible that this has been done on projects of sensitive or classified nature.

The dummy corporation front was successfully used recently by a private group to acquire a series of Atlantic barrier islands and preserve them in their natural condition. The Nature Conservancy, from 1972 to 1975, used the technique when "Offshore Islands, Incorporated," a cover corporation for the Nature Conservancy, purchased most of the islands comprising the barrier chain stretching south from Assateague Island National Seashore and Chincoteague National Wildlife Refuge to Chesapeake Bay.

The *Washington Post* described the procedure in an interview: "We created it just as a front, so they"—the Conservancy—"could proceed with buying the islands," said M. Lee Payne, a Norfolk, Virginia, banker, who the Nature Conservancy said conceived the idea for the company. "Some of those islands wouldn't have been sold if the owners had known they were going to the Nature Conservancy" [and eventually to the Federal government].

Non-profit environmentalist groups have another favorite tactic: buy a piece of land and then create a political climate by public agitation for federal purchase. The Trust for Public Land has become particularly adept at land speculation using environmentalist tactics and public relations to pressure governmental purchase of their property. An interesting case in point involves an obsolete electronics facility owned by RCA within the boundaries of the Point Reyes National Seashore. RCA had no plans to develop the property and did not care whether it was sold or not, and the National Park Service had said they did not wish to acquire the inholding. However, the Trust for Public Land sent a representative to New York, negotiated an option on the property with RCA, began a strong political campaign for federal purchase of the land, and forced the United States into buying property that the National Park Service did not want, was not on their acquisition list, and yielded no benefit to the public.

The Trust for Public Land is involved in another interesting case: Sweeney Ridge, an area south of San Francisco that environmentalists decided should be included in the Golden Gate National Recreation Area (remember Wolfback Ridge from chap. 6?). Sweeney Ridge is an open hilly site of grassy slopes and swales with clustered oak copses and other tree types. The Trust for Public Land went to the owner, West Aspen Corporation, an oil and development company from the south central United States, and negotiated an option to buy Sweeney Ridge for $8.5 million, putting up no money. The Trust then hired an appraiser to put a value on the land, spending about $40,000 for an appraisal that found Sweeney Ridge to be worth from $22 to $24 million. Next, the Trust offered to sell the land to the United States government for $9.6 million. The National Park Service said, "Sweeney Ridge is not on our acquisition list, we do not want to buy it."

So the Trust for Public Land began a political campaign with other environmentalist groups to pressure Congress into buying Sweeney Ridge. Congressman Phillip Burton came to the rescue, and included the site in his bill known as House Resolution 3 in 1980, which was a cleanup bill to include everything that had been forgotten in his parks-barrel legislation from 1978, the Omnibus Parks Act. H.R. 3 passed even though the Andrus Interior Department testified that Sweeney Ridge should not be part of the Recreation Area and that they were opposed to it. Sweeney Ridge was thus authorized, but went to the bottom of the priority list. The Trust for Public Land then convinced their friends in Congress to go to the Appropriations Committee and get Sweeney Ridge added as a "line item," to be slipped into the budget without notice. The Trust failed in this effort, but the site was mentioned in an Appropriations Committee Report with no authority to overrule Interior Department priorities.

Thwarted in Congress, the Trust for Public Land created a huge media and public relations blitz, claiming that a deadline would soon arrive to escalate the price, and that this precious piece of speculative property was the discovery site of San Francisco Bay by the Spanish explorer Gaspar de Portola in 1770. Charles Cushman, executive director of the National Inholders Association, was skeptical of the Portola claim and did a title search and historical reconnaisance. He found that the actual discovery site was on a nearby tract that had been condemned by the City of Pacifica in 1971 and was already in public ownership. But Cushman also found that West Aspen Corporation had held back 50 prime acres in the midst of the Sweeney Ridge site for construction of condominiums, which had not been mentioned in the public furor. And West Aspen would also qualify for a $14 million tax deduction since their land had been appraised at $24 million and they would "only" receive $8.5 million. In sum, then, West Aspen got federal zoning for its condominium sites, a $14 million tax break, and $8.5 million in public money from this plan while the Trust for Public Land was to obtain a $1.1 million return for a $40,000 appraisal investment which amounted to a double escrow scheme. With the cloak of environmentalist holiness, a developer could get rich and a non-profit group could milk the federal treasury for a tidy "donation," all in "the public interest." James Watt's Interior Department has not agreed to go along with this plan. For this, Watt is blasted as a destroyer of the environment, and blamed for "cutting off money to buy more national parkland." It sounds different when you say, "stopping the confiscation of private property for use as a federal park," or "preventing environmentalist land speculators from profiting in a million-dollar public relations scam." It's all in the point of view.

Ah, Wilderness!

One of the little-noted facets of Wilderness preservation is the fact that Congressional designation of a new area acts as a mating call to all wildernists. Hordes of people, golden hordes of the affluent, rush to share solitude with each other. Not only do wild and remote places thus become crowded and unfit for a Wilderness experience, but they also become physically degraded with deep ruts gouged by the vibram soles of a thousand hiking boots, they are stripped of natural fuel for campfires, decorated with what the U.S. Forest Service calls "white flags" (used toilet paper on the ground), and denuded of delicate ecological treasures such as endemic plant species. The Wilderness is being loved to death by its friends. Perhaps it is a good thing that less than 5 percent of the American population ever gets into a Wilderness Area.

Environmentalists are well aware of this problem, although they are reluctant to speak of it in public. Colin Fletcher, "the man who walked through time" (the Grand Canyon, actually), and acknowledged high priest of backpacking, put the problem succinctly: "The woods are overrun and sons of bitches like me are half the problem."

Efforts to regulate wilderness entry by a system of quotas or user fees are violently opposed by the big wealthy environmentalist groups. Although they demand that business and industry pay all social costs in water projects and other developments, they balk when the shoe is on their own foot. Regulation is for the other guy, not for the environmentalist. It is amusing to read the fervent speech of Sierra Club Executive Director Michael McCloskey to the Rotary Club of Fort Worth, Texas, given March 10, 1978:

We do not believe in subsidies that distort market patterns. We have opposed subsidizing the price of irrigation water from public projects that competes with private sources. We have opposed underpricing oil and natural gas and have called for an end to depletion allowances and tax write-offs for the energy industry. We have urged user taxes on barge traffic on public waterways that benefit from public investments to compete unfairly with railroads. We believe that product prices should reflect their real, true costs and should not be held down through subsidies to create the illusion of cheap goods.

This same man and his counterparts in most large wealthy environmentalist groups furiously oppose Wilderness entry fees and many other Wilderness rationing plans.

The U.S. Department of Agriculture, Forest Service, publication *Wilderness Management* verifies this observation: "Most wilderness visitors object to fees, and it seems unlikely that Congress will grant the wilderness-administering agencies the authority to use fees as a wilderness management tool." Wilderness rationing is widely opposed as well, but has been used in a few Wilderness Areas: only 7 parties per day may float the Middle Fork of the Salmon River in Idaho; 100 persons per day for day use and 30 for overnight use may enter Linville Gorge Wilderness in North Carolina; 400 overnight campers are allowed in California's San Jacinto Wilderness; Rocky Mountain National Park limits overnight camping to 150 designated campsites and 63 non-designated cross-country travel campsites per day; Mount Whitney access in California is mainly through the John Muir Wilderness, in which only 75 overnight parties may stay per day; in the South Fork Basin of California's San Gorgonio Wilderness only 26 day parties may enter and only 23 may stay overnight.

Regulation is coming to the wilderness, slowly but inexorably. Reservation systems, lotteries for entry tickets, first-come, first-served plans, and licensing based on wilderness skills are all being considered or are in actual Wilderness use by administering agencies. However, Wilderness remains an unpriced allocation of resources; lost employment and commodity opportunities due to Wilderness exclusions are not calculated in social or economic projections. Wilderness for the healthy, wealthy few is totally subsidized by all. Wilderness management costs are seldom mentioned by environmentalists. Contrary to assertions that Wilderness is an unmanaged, untouched, totally natural setting, every official Wilderness Area is constantly managed at considerable cost by highly trained professionals in the U.S. Department of

Agriculture and Interior. The Forest Service publication *Wilderness Management* points out, "In today's world, preservation of wilderness areas can be achieved *only* by deliberate management to minimize man's influence."

Among the many costly wilderness management tasks are the preparation of management plans, surveys, zoning, trail construction, campsite designation, protection of fragile sites and life forms, operational plans to cope with insect infestation, plant and animal diseases, and wildfire, visitor monitoring and policing, rescue facilities for sick and injured visitors, periodic closure of campsites and trails to allow natural regeneration, issuance of permits, protection of automobiles from vandalism at trailhead parking lots, and on and on. These costs are never mentioned in Wilderness preservation campaigns. Wilderness may be billed as paradise, but there's plenty of trouble in paradise.

The crowding of Wilderness Areas is constantly used as a campaign tool to justify more and more wilderness additions. Very practical alternatives to wilderness such as designated backcountry, and areas where facilities and comforts not permitted in Wilderness are desired, are viewed with suspicion by wildernists as somehow diluting the purity of their ideology. Surveys repeatedly show that many who enjoy wilderness experiences do not require official Wilderness Areas for their recreation satisfaction, but would be happy in more developed recreational areas. The fact is that Wilderness is a scarce resource, and we are running out of new candidate areas quite rapidly. Wilderness users must face up to regulating themselves and their recreational preferences just like all the rest of us who live in a world of ecology and economy—a world of resources including organisms and aesthetics allocated for the fulfillment of human wants.

CHAPTER 11
OUTREACH

The best way out is always through.
—Robert Frost

When James Watt was ready, he went to the public with his own story. The attacks did not stop; as soon as one wave of invective ebbed, another would crest. Environmentalist leaders had calculated that a continuous crescendo of protest would oust Watt during the summer of 1981, or fall at the latest. But they had misjudged Ronald Reagan. In early August the President sounded a theme for *Washington Star* reporters that would echo many months:

Jim Watt has my full support because I think that we have been victimized by some individuals that I refer to as environmental extremists. Now, I think I'm an environmentalist. But I do think there has been a lot of irrationality about Jim. And what Jim's trying to do is maybe a little like getting a mule's attention— you hit it in the forehead with a two-by-four first.

Watt definitely had the environmentalists' attention. His policy initiatives and blunt style saw to that. But soon after Under Secretary Don Hodel realized that Interior had been brought under control, it became evident that the attention of others was needed. Letting the critics run wild was taking its toll. Rumors in the press ran rampant. Unfavorable quotes were repeatedly attributed to White House aides: A July *Newsweek* article said, "privately, one senior aide worried about Watt's penchant for 'zinging out these things,' " and a *U.S. News & World Report* story claimed "a top presidential adviser" had told them, "he's not doing a very good job of public relations," while another had predicted, "he's probably got a short political life." The August 3 issue of *Time* flatly asserted, "Watt has been told to clear major policy announcements with the White House so that image-conscious aides can try to mute any potential public outcry."

No such thing ever happened, according to both Watt and the White

190

House. The rumors, though, were indicative of more basic problems. By staying at work inside the Department and speaking abruptly in his infrequent press appearances, Watt was no longer the newsmaker; the reporters were—more and more stories were being fabricated out of whole cloth by the media themselves. That left Watt's supporters in the public with no idea what was really going on and no way to defend their friend in Interior. By late July of 1981, it was becoming obvious that some sort of outreach was essential.

Nat. Enquirer Syndrome

The day after Under Secretary Hodel spent his sleepless night realizing that the Management By Objectives system was already basically in place, he took the time to grill the Department's top executives one by one, asking each what they thought about going to the public. Hodel says, "I heard a lot of good ideas, I synthesized many comments and began to see clearly the issues we needed to deal with. Once the outreach idea finally jelled, I spent about five minutes talking to Jim about it one day. He said 'I like that,' and we were off and running."

There was actually quite a bit more to it than that. The outreach concept was talked through by key staff people, particularly Public Affairs Director Doug Baldwin, and the central problems were sketched in. The first step was to identify the constituencies of Interior. Hodel says,

We have two basic publics in the Department. One I call the "Inside the Box" constituency, those people who are intimately tied in to Interior's basic role. The other is the "Outside the Box" constituency, those who look to Jim Watt for philosophical orientation in an informal way, Republicans and conservative Democrats, business and labor groups, and unaligned citizens who share Jim's belief in limited government and who realize that jobs require realistic resource policy.

The "Inside the Box" constituency was acknowledged as Interior's primary responsibility, and it was further refined into two categories. First was the "political" constituency, meaning the intergovernmental relationships such as with governors, attorneys general, state legislators, the National Governors Association, the Council of State Governments, county executive associations, and so forth. Second was the "Special Interest" constituency, meaning the array of organizations with interest in one or more issues under Interior jurisdiction. In passing, it is worth mention that when Jim Watt says "environmentalist special interest groups," it is not the insult environmentalists take it to be. "Special interests" is a technical term to Watt, including cattlemen and wildernists, miners and hikers, concessioners and birdwatchers. However, environmentalists use "special interests" as a swear word, and seem to take it in their own frame of reference.

Executive Assistant Steve Shipley and Director of Public Affairs Doug Baldwin worked closely with Hodel on the outreach idea, and Assistant to the

Secretary Emily DeRocco took responsibility for assembling the "Constituent Outreach Program" document. The document stated their problem thus:

We have identified approximately 225 special interest and political constituent groups, of which 7 have publicly denounced Administration policies and initiatives at Interior. The vast majority have either supported the new policies and programs or have reserved judgement but have the potential for supporting the new direction if properly "cultivated." We have not effectively marshalled these organizations to proclaim their interests.

The solution to this problem was:

We must address both the future and the past. That is, we must develop a systematic plan for future decision-making that "builds in" constituent outreach efforts and marshalls constituent support for Administration initiatives at Interior. At the same time, we must take steps to better explain past actions and put those actions in the context of the Administration's blueprint for change approved in November 1980.

The practical result of this planning was the creation of an "Outreach System." The system used two existing sources to identify upcoming issues that might be of interest to specific constituents: (1) the Management By Objectives (MBO) program, and (2) the SID, the "Secretarial Issues Document" program. A SID is prepared as part of the Environmental Impact Statement (EIS) process required by law, and contains every issue requiring Secretarial decisions, listing all the options and alternatives on primary decisions and their related sub-decisions. Once issues were identified by the MBO and SID, they were reviewed by the "Outreach Team," which was established from Interior's top executives and top staff officers. The team determines which issues will interest which constituent groups, and recommends action. In some cases groups are asked to comment on upcoming decisions; in others, they are notified in advance that a decision of interest will be made shortly; in yet others, no action is required. But once any decision is announced, the "Outreach Team" is obligated to make themselves "available as a 'bank' of responders to phone inquiries from constituent groups regarding the action." The "Outreach Team" encouraged constituents to make their views known to the press.

As Doug Baldwin, Watt's Director of Public Affairs, told me, "When Watt lifted his 'first six-months' travel ban, he instructed his executives to automatically make two tasks part of every out-of-town assignment; to make themselves available to the media, and to accept invitations to listen to constituents when invited." This order to listen to all constituents received no press coverage, but in contrast, a later Watt instruction about constituents made headlines. In late 1981, after numerous National Park Service officials had appeared as speakers at environmentalist conferences, it became evident that the only result was to give opponents an opportunity to boo government employees and to make headlines for the environmentalist group cause. Watt told his executives to stop accepting speaking engagements with environmentalist groups at government expense. However, the December 14, 1981, issue of *Time* wrote it up like this: "Watt decreed that members of the National Park Service and top Interior aides should refrain from 'wasting Government money by talking to national conservation leaders.' " Not noted was that routine Department meetings with environmentalist group representatives went on regularly with Watt's blessing.

But it was this kind of media treatment that the outreach program intended to correct. The staff worked on "Re-Directing the Past," searching out long-standing press errors. Doug Baldwin and others researched and assembled a "Fact And Fiction" package, culling 14 whoppers from among the worst misstatements, and laid out the facts of the case beneath each fabricated news claim. Subjects ranged from Watt's "intent to sabotage the Environmental Impact Statement process" to claims that Watt "plans to needlessly slaughter 5,000 wild horses and burros," and from the accusation that Watt was going to "drill, mine and log in National Parks, Wildlife Refuges and Wilderness Areas" to assertions that he planned "to overturn laws that protect the environment." Most of the answers to press fictions consisted of short quotations from applicable laws; in many cases Watt had been accused of doing exactly what Congress had mandated by law. For example, media charges that "Secretary Watt places a much higher priority on development and exploitation than on conservation and protection" were answered by citations of laws requiring the Secretary of the Interior to develop resources as well as preserve them, followed by a list of Watt's extensive environmental achievements, including the completion of ecological mapping of fish and wildlife resources on the Pacific Coast and the initiation of similar mapping of the Gulf of Mexico coast, and the approval of a land use plan for 12 million acres in the California Desert Conservation Area.

However, Watt was careful to clean up his own backyard first: he began a program of employee conferences to both talk and listen better with his own employees, and instituted an improved internal newsletter containing monthly messages from the Secretary, summaries of current issues and policy decisions, and a personality sketch of a Department executive to familiarize employees with Watt's leadership people.

Care was also taken to institutionalize certain routine consulations with constituents which had been held since Watt's first days in office. The Special-Interest Breakfasts were a weekly feature giving special-interest group representatives an hour of the Secretary's undivided attention. The first groups invited had been the large environmentalist organizations, whose leaders had used the breakfast as a springboard for a media event to denounce Watt and his policy. By the time Watt incorporated his breakfasts in the outreach program, the vociferous opponents had taken their turns. Watt didn't miss them; he was just as glad to meet with less extreme environmentalists, commodity groups, and multiple-use organizations.

Watt also made Conservation and Business Roundtable luncheons and "Action Seminars," or "skull sessions," a routine part of the outreach program, since they gave him a chance for regular updates on important events and the opportunity to fine-tune policy decisions accordingly. The "Resource Learning Sessions" that had informed Watt and his executives on whales, eagles, energy conservation, and other subjects were also formalized in the outreach system.

But the reality-testing of the outreach program would fall to Watt personally. He was the star, he was the lightning rod, he was the center-ring attraction, and he would have to make outreach work. A scheduled trip to Alaska would give him a trial run, but the upcoming September Western Governors Conference to be held at Jackson Hole, Wyoming, was a do-or-die proposition. As Watt's Executive Assistant Steve Shipley says,

The groups we were truly concerned with were the White House, the Hill, the constituent groups, Interior employees and the governors. The governors were critically important, and especially the 11 Western governors. If Watt was not to become a political liability to the President, it was vital to have a successful Governors Conference. If that went poorly, there would be little hope.

The Alaska tour was a smashing success. During eight days in August, Watt received one welcome after another. In Anchorage, a parade led by a horse-borne color guard escorted Watt to a speech at the Captain Cook Hotel where throngs of supporters carried signs saying "Watt Is Courage!" and "How much Power Does It Take to Enlighten an Environmentalist? One Watt!" In his speech to the Anchorage Chamber of Commerce, Watt told the audience, "Some of my detractors are trying to convince the American people that I am an enemy of conservation and environmental protection. Don't you believe it. We are enforcing the law and we will continue to enforce it. Those who feel that any land left open for development is too much will not like our programs. Neither will those who feel that any acre closed to them is the acre they most covet for exploration. I do not sympathize with either of these viewpoints." Network television reporters did not film any of this, but concentrated on six environmentalists who revved up chainsaws in the middle of the city to protest Watt's visit. Paula Easley, executive director of the Resource Development Council for Alaska, one of Watt's host organizations, took the media producers to task and obtained a more balanced coverage of Watt's visit.

Watt spent time in Alaska wading in trout streams, praising National Parks, and extended unprecedented protective measures to endangered humpback whales in their summering ground in Glacier Bay. I asked Watt why he did this, since no law required him to do so, and he said, "I became fascinated with this singing whale in an outreach session by Dr. Sylvia Earle, and on the basis of her scientific observations found that a small change in motorboat restrictions in the area would be beneficial to the whales. So I did it."

It was in Alaska that Watt-watchers began to notice his rhetoric toning down. Watt told reporters that "I had to come in and yell commands that would be heard and obeyed. So I yelled, and the change came faster than I thought it would. Now I can change my style, my rhetoric and my mode of operation. I'm mellower now." Watt was determined to change his abrasive image, and even said, "There's a real change in my style. I'm warm and cuddly and easy to get along with." This soft-pedaling was uncharacteristic and unnecessary. In the words of columnist James J. Kilpatrick, "Watt is as cuddly as a porcupine." Fortunately, Watt came to his senses within a few days and resumed the managerial stance demanded by his policy and position. The Western Governors Conference at Jackson Hole, Wyoming September 12 and 13 showed a different side of Watt the orator. There, in a setting of Grand Teton majesty, the lords of the Far Country, the 11 Western Governors, came to hold court around a horse-shoe shaped table in a barn-like building packed to the rafters with expectant throngs. As J. J. Casserly, editorial writer for the *Arizona Republic* reported it, "Jim Watt entered. Lanky, loose. Western boots. A country-boy smile as wide as this endless valley. An open-neck cowpuncher's shirt in vivid colors of the range."

The cowboy Cabinet officer held forth three-and-a-half hours, talking energy, water, land and environmental protection—but really saying, "If there are differences, let's work them out face to face." Casserly commented, "Watt was a man of courtesy, charm and conciliation." Republican Governor Jay Hammond of Alaska said, "Watt is not the same man portrayed in the media." Bill Prochnau of the *Washington Post* wrote, "Watt had the once-hostile governors eating out of his hand." When Watt told the conference that he was reversing the Carter Administration policy allowing federal pre-emption of state water rights and returning all control to the states, Republican Governor Robert List of Nevada said, "If I'd been on my horse, I'd have fallen off. In the past, we had to bleed on the floor to get any help from Interior."

Watt that day delivered on his good neighbor policy: he agreed with Alaska Governor Hammond to delay several offshore oil lease sales in Bristol Bay until the impact on fisheries resources could be thoroughly studied. He pledged to act on 384 requests for transfers of 700,000 acres of federal land to local governments. He said the Reagan Administration would fight any attempt to condemn Western lands for coal slurry pipelines. He announced his intent to expand the National Wilderness Preservation System by proposing to the President wilderness status for Arizona's Aravaipa Canyon. Democratic Governor Scott M. Matheson of Utah told Watt he was "close to driving the last nail in the coffin of the Sagebrush Rebellion." *Newsweek* clucked, "Even the most skeptical Westerners had to admit that Watt deserved much of the credit for dissipating their cause—by easing tensions between them and the federal government."

It was a triumph. Only 40 environmentalist protesters picketed with anti-Watt signs and these were outnumbered by a caravan of pickups loaded with cordwood symbolizing multiple-use of the forests. Watt shook hands with the pickup drivers but turned his back as the protesters closed in. His big cowboy hat hid his bald pate and gave Watt a photogenic appeal that shocked network cameramen. One was heard to say, "Boy, those environmentalists better start praying if Watt ever buys contacts and a wig." The news conference after Watt's three hour-plus session was a study in regionalism: Western reporters asked about specific issues while others doggedly focused on Watt's personality, asking, "Why did you call environmentalists monstrous?" and "Does your belief in the Second Coming of Christ interfere with your stewardship of federal lands?" and "Define environmental extremist." One Western governor muttered under his breath "Those network performers are ignorant savages."

The Governors Conference kicked off a three-week tour of Western States by Watt. He visited Yellowstone National Park, gave speeches, and generally made himself noticeable. But the mission of the outreach had been accomplished. As Steve Shipley tells it, "We poured a lot of effort into that Conference. Those Governors were very important to us, and we had an exceptionally fine meeting. After that, there was no question in our mind about our political viability. After that, it was just a matter of the media catching up with the reality." The outreach program then settled into place as a routine part of the Watt management style.

Watt said of his tour, "It seems as though when we crossed the Continental Divide on the first day of my western swing, we crossed an important watershed figuratively as well as literally. Press interest seemed to shift from pseudo-analysis of Jim Watt's character to concern over issues which affect natural resources, the land, and the people of the region."

Watt had over a dozen meetings during his trip with more than 5,000 Interior employees in 8 states. Watt told me, "I was impressed with the dedication of our employees. A lot of them were worried about criticism of the Department. I told them I wasn't worried about attacks on me as Secretary, but that I am concerned when critics begin smearing the integrity of dedicated, career Interior employees. This is where employees in the field must counterattack." Time and again, Watt stood up to the press for his employees. Everywhere he went, Watt also fostered personal communication with Interior workers in question-and-answer sessions. One GS-8 asked a question of Watt and evidently got the wrong answer. Watt said, "I can tell by your eyes that wasn't the answer you wanted. Well, let me ask you: What should I think about that issue?" In another session, a GS-10 asked, "I wonder how committed you are to conservation?" Watt responded:

Fair question, good question. I don't know how we present ourselves as being conservation-oriented, because there's no common definition when you deal with critics. I happen to be one who believes you can build a dam and be a conservationist. But some of my critics feel that if you go anywhere with anything other than a backpack, you're violating nature. I don't share those views.

The role of Leilani Watt in the Reagan Administration has been seriously slighted by the press. Mrs. Watt, as most Cabinet wives, has played the usual role of providing the "social glue" that holds together Administration solidarity in breakfasts and luncheons, receptions and galas. But Jim Watt's wife also played an important part in the outreach program as a traveling companion to the Secretary and as a foil to his tough managerial stance. Her charm and easy grace with people has been a tremendous asset to the Watt Secretariat. Watt says,

I won't travel on all this fund-raising circuit business unless the Party sends her along, too. We're frequently separated when I'm out on official business in the field, and she has social responsibilities as part of the Administration in Washington that keep us apart, too, so I enjoy the time with her on these political trips, and she can frequently get along with people in the Party that I don't see eye to eye with. I also take Lani along on official Department business in the field on occasion, where she has many times helped a situation for the Administration that would have been less fruitful if I had gone alone.

The Management By Objectives system had by now reached to the lower ranks of Interior management. On-the-ground results could be seen clearly, even in the field 3,000 miles from headquarters. Watt mused,

Skeptics had warned me that I would get little cooperation and that changing the direction of the Department would be slow, tedious and frustrating, and in the end, fruitless. Boy, were they wrong! Instead of opposition and resistance, most of these people agreed with the need for changes in programs and policies. With very few exceptions, the career workers pitched in with the new leadership and revamped programs, made constructive suggestions, trimmed budgets and implemented mandated changes. They were terrific!

Most of the dyed-in-the-wool preservationists had long since fled, and others were being terminated by reductions-in-force. The philosophy of conservation—wise use of resources, including wise preservation—gained a thorough foothold in Interior, sweeping away the philosophy of preservation purism that had dominated the Department for many years. Watt told his employees plainly: "There is a place in the world for 'preservationists,' but it is not in the Department of the Interior during my tenure." Conservation became the watchword. Preservation was relegated to its present position as one of many tools in the conservationist's kit to promote the wise use of resources.

By October 1981 Interior was operating at optimum efficiency under Watt's management. Under Secretary Hodel and Watt were working in near-perfect mesh. Hodel explains:

Virtually everything that went to the Secretary passed through my office. I made sure that every Department with an interest in an upcoming issue saw it and had the chance to review and comment on it before it went to the Secretary. Before, there was a tendency to take finished work right to the Secretary without paying attention to other Assistant Secretaries or the Solicitor or our Congressional Liaison.

Today our issues are networked together. That doesn't mean I handle everything—I don't. There are lots of quick turnaround, one-person issues. But wherever multi-department issues appear, and I can see them coming on the computer well in advance now, I make sure that everybody's looked at it. I make sure that every issue is ready for a decision before we go see Jim with it. Many managers allow everyone to go to the boss prematurely and ask him what he wants to do about something before there's enough information to make a rational decision. I don't let that happen. I have a flipchart and blackboard in my office, and I find they're helpful tools for our executives to sort out things like "What is the objective, what are the alternatives, is there a recommendation, and if not, why not, what are the Secretary's options, and what should he do?" and other questions.

On many issues the executives will come into my office and we'll hash things over for 2 or 3 hours so we can go in to the Secretary and present him with the real issue and options in 15 minutes. Sometimes, in fact, I think Jim gets a clearer picture in that 15 minutes than I got in the first 2 hours talking to the executives.

It is management skills such as Hodel's that allow Jim Watt's rapid-fire intuitive decision-making style to function realistically, a fact I am certain his critics are unaware of. A great deal of Watt's success must be chalked up to hiring well: his executives do all the work they are supposed to do so that Watt can do all the work he's supposed to do.

One day while I was talking to Hodel, I happened to see several personality charts and asked whose they were. Hodel said, "Oh, we were fooling around one day trying to see how our management skills would mesh best, and all of us filled out the questionnaire of this personality test. It was interesting, and confirmed what we already knew about ourselves." One seldom sees the personality of a Cabinet officer analyzed, but there lay that of James G. Watt, graphed out on paper, before me. Watt and Hodel are almost exact opposites. The graph of Watt's traits sweeps from upper left to lower right, while Hodel's runs from lower left to upper right. The meaning of these lines is spelled out in four vertical columns measuring four traits. The left-most column measures "dominance," described by the interpretation sheet as "emphasis is on shaping the environment by overcoming opposition to accomplish results." Watt was high above the mid-line, Hodel a little below (mid-lines presumably denote average behavior norms). The second column measured "influencing of others," or "emphasis is on shaping the environment by bringing others into alliance to accomplish results"; Watt and Hodel were both in the same place, just above the mid-line.

The third column measured "steadiness," or "emphasis is on cooperating with others to carry out the task." Watt was a little below the mid-line and Hodel a little above it. The fourth and last column described "compliance," or "emphasis is on working with existing circumstances to promote quality in products or service." Watt was well below the mid-point on this feature and Hodel well above. Hodel's chart was labeled "Practitioner Pattern," and the test manual explained that

Practitioners value proficiency in specialized areas. Spurred by the desire to be "good at something," they carefully monitor and critique their own work performance. Although their aim is to become "the" expert in an area, Practitioners frequently give the impression of knowing something about many things. They tend to concentrate on developing procedures and increasing their own skills, but Practitioners need to help others build skills.

And what about Jim Watt? His chart fell into the "Result-Oriented Pattern." The manual explained,

Result-oriented persons display a self-confidence some may interpret as arrogance. They actively seek opportunities which test and develop their abilities to accomplish results. Result-Oriented Persons like difficult tasks, competitive situations, unique assignments and "important" positions. They undertake responsibilities with an air of "I'll do it!" Result-Oriented Persons are quick in thought and action. They may lack empathy, appearing to others as cold and blunt.

The only things missing here are Watt's sense of humor and his warmth and loyalty to those close to him.

Watt lets his executives run their shops the way they want. Dick Harris, Director of the Office of Surface Mining told me,

It came as a surprise to many people, but Watt is letting me run this agency freely in my own style. He has only discussed one regulation change with me, and that was the "Two Acre Exemption." The only thing we discussed about the Exemption concerned that it was a loophole built into the law, and it was being abused, particularly in Virginia. Jim said he wanted it closed as soon as possible. In everything else, he has given me total autonomy. He does impose the MBO, but that's fair enough as far as I'm concerned. We set the objectives for our own agency, we set the target dates. Then if I don't produce, whose fault is it really? This is no longer the "Prevention Of Surface Mining Department" as it was in the previous administration; we're tough, but we're reasonable. I think we're doing what the nation needs.

November 18, 1981, Watt held a "Staff Round-Up" for his top people in Gettysburg, Pennsylvania. There, he finally sat down with his Assistant Secretaries and agreed upon the final Management By Objectives statement as their basic contract. Everyone signed the final document and realized, as Under Secretary Hodel said, "This is our system. We live by it, we created it. We'll never get 100 percent of our decisions in Interior on it, though: it's basically a working draft and will always be a draft as time changes our goals and objectives."

Jim Watt said about the system:

You Assistant Secretaries realize that I have placed young, aggressive, forceful guys in deputy positions beneath everyone of you, and I think you know why. Deputies really run the government, and I put these deputies where they are to force their bosses to do the things I need done. With this MBO system, your deputies can manage upward with it, they can force you to get your job done with your complete agreement.

At another session of that meeting, the role of the deputies was being discussed in a roundtable, and Derrell Thompson, Interior's Western Representative headquartered in Denver, told Watt after looking around the room,

Jim, what you've got is the strongest, most conservative deputy-level people that have ever existed in Interior, or probably in any Department—and may ever exist anywhere else in government, what with Perry Pendley in Energy and Minerals, Moody Tidwell in the Solicitor's Office, Dave Russell in Land and Water Resources, Bill Horn as Deputy Under Secretary, and all the others. You've not only got the most conservative true politicians in the Assistant Secretary rank, but you've got a bunch of people carrying the conservative banner solidly in the deputy levels. You've got management in depth.

Watt grinned, "We planned it that way, Derrell."

Mid-October, 1981, had been a good time for Anti-Watt forces: Watt became the first Reagan Administration official to claim executive privilege in refusing to turn over documents John Dingell's House Energy and Commerce

Committee had subpoenaed to see if the Administration was planning any retaliatory actions against Canada's restrictive investment policy initiatives. Watt had a well-publicized argument with House Interior and Insular Affairs Committee Chairman Morris Udall, threatening to withhold funds for a $2.1-billion central Arizona water project unless Udall moderated his pointed attacks on the Secretary. The third week of October was designated "Watt Petition Week" by the Sierra Club, and on Monday the 19th, 1.1 million names on "Dump Watt" petitions were ceremoniously delivered to certain Democratic members of Congress. The media circus was spectacular.

However, there was a little hitch: someone leaked the Sierra Club's secret memo that bluntly spelled out its methods in a letter prominently stamped "CONFIDENTIAL" from Club President Joe Fontaine and Club lawyer Doug Scott.

The memo's cover letter said,

It is vital that this plan remain absolutely confidential and that you [Club leaders] remain sensitive to that point as you pursue it with your Chapter leadership. For maximum impact, what we are planning must remain closely guarded until we are ready to launch it—and that means confidential from *everyone* outside your top leadership circle. If word of this plan and its timing gets out, it will be possible for Watt and his supporters to take counter-action which could seriously blunt the political and media impact we are seeking.

This attempt at secrecy is amusingly naïve, since the Club sent copies of the memo to dozens of Chapter Chairs, Conservation Committee Chairs, Board Members, Issue Committee Chairs, and Chapter staff people. The internal politics of the Sierra Club are fraught with jealousies and ambition that would make it a near dead certainty someone would leak such a memo out of spite or, in some cases, to protect personal economic interests—there are a number of these people who make a living clipping dividend coupons from Daddy's investments.

The memo also said: "This plan has been developed by Doug Scott and the Conservation staff, on the basis of careful political soundings and 'inside' advice from Capitol Hill." My Washington sources traced this "inside" advice to Senator Alan Cranston, and Representatives Phillip Burton, John Seiberling, James Weaver, and Toby Moffet.

The *Kansas City Star* editorialized that the petition was "the 1981 version of a lynch mob," referring to the Sierra Club and its memo, which said, "We foresee media opportunities on two levels. First, the local story ('Sierra Club leader Jane Doe presents a million anti-Watt signatures'); second, the national story ('Congress receives millions of anti-Watt signatures.')"

The Santa Rosa, California *Press Democrat* urged President Reagan to "ignore the media merchants of the Sierra Club," whose leaders were advised to review each Chapter's petitions to get names of local VIPs who had signed, and then have private meetings with state Republican and Democratic party chairmen. "This should be an off-the-record visit," warns the memo, "to convey the message that we are a bipartisan group, but that there is very strong grassroots sentiment against Mr. Watt and the policies of the Reagan Administration he symbolizes."

Texas' *Amarillo Daily News* accused the Sierra Club of striking at Watt because "it does not dare draw a figurative bead on Reagan himself," and blasted the secret memo's advice to hold meetings with political chiefs, including governors. "All of these meetings are proposed as a kind of 'courtesy call' in which the stack of petitions offers you a kind of 'crutch' as the excuse for meetings in which you can deliver the message of grassroots opposition to Watt-style policies," the memo said.

The *Albuquerque Journal* quoted Watt saying "The Sierra Club petition has really backfired on them." The secret memo had called for "meetings with the press, particularly editorial writers, local environmental writers, and local political columnists." The Club leadership had suggested off-the-record "deep background" meetings to be held "with these folks" to brief them in advance on what would be done with the petitions.

"We hope to provide glossy photos (and perhaps taped footage for TV) of what the whole million look like in a heap," crowed the secret memo. An airport rally was suggested to "send off" each Chapter's petitions. "In most states, this will play as a very BIG story. Your airport rally can comprise several actual events, but can be staged to assure maximum coverage—especially for television cameras!"

An editorial writer in a large Utah newspaper was stunned by the secret memo, saying: "The Sierra Club is exposed by the memo as a conniving, calculating and definitely not grassroots outfit. Despite its repeated emphasis on talking up the 'grassroots' nature of its action, it is obvious that the whole thing is being manipulated by national club officers." Of course, this editor is correct, but it is just as shocking to me to discover that a hardened news veteran had not already figured that one out from years of environmentalist media manipulation. He went on: "What is appalling about the affair is that the local Sierra Club officials were happy to go along with it. They should have resigned instead, and denounced the organization." Fat chance. The Sierra Club is not run by environmentalists, but by politicians, which should be obvious to anyone who has studied the record.

The Boise *Idaho Statesman* quoted Bruce Brocard of the Idaho Conservation League as saying that "Watt is a land-development advocate run amok. He's taken a mandate for economic recovery and is using it to carry out wholesale destruction. Watt's designs would ruin much Western rangeland because of overgrazing, kill forests by neglecting the sustained-yield concept, pollute rivers, lakes and streams with mining and water-project wastes and could wipe out various endangered species." Idaho Sierra Clubber Chris Yoder was quoted as saying, "In the end, workers will be out of jobs because the resource will be depleted." This horrifying image was not just the spontaneous outburst of a "concerned citizen," but the product of hours of careful deliberation by group committee people, many of them academics with doctoral degrees, calculating each word so it would be most terrifying yet still convincing.

But the "Dump Watt" petition drive didn't work, except to fill the coffers of environmentalist struggle groups. Watt stayed on. It is interesting that most American newspapers covering the "Dump Watt" petition drive made hay of the Sierra Club's secret memo, except for the *New York Times*, *Washington Post* and *Los Angeles Times*. The *Dallas Morning News* printed a capstone that neatly put the issue to bed:

1.1 million Americans want to dump James Watt as Interior Secretary, says the Sierra Club, which regards Watt as an environmental criminal, oil company tool, etc., etc. Fine. That leaves a mere 225,404,825 Americans who *didn't* sign the Club's petition and may think more kindly of Watt's efforts to conserve, as opposed to deep-freeze, our natural resources. Now that the vote's in, maybe he can get down to work.

As the outreach program blossomed, Watt's reputation gained another facet: he became the Republican Party's fund-raising star, cranking out bucks from the faithful at prodigious rates, second only to President Reagan himself. (Some observers have also pointed out that Watt was the environmentalists' best fund raiser, too. A *New York Times* article by Phillip Shabecoff headlined "Watt and Foes Are Best of Enemies" reported that "most of the major environmental groups" discovered "their fight with James Watt was an excellent base on which to build membership and fund-raising drives," as "money and membership applications began to pour into the groups' headquarters." Denver's *Rocky Mountain News* speculated that environmentalist groups "secretly hope he stays around for a while," since he "is the biggest promotional tool they have come across in a long time.")

The fund-raising Watt is always a shock to those who only know him from the media. I've seen Watt on the road, flying into a town at mid-morning, delivering a luncheon speech at noon, visiting projects with local dignitaries in the early afternoon, hosting a small intimate hour for big-money Party members at 4:00 P.M., a larger reception for the less affluent but diligent stalwarts at 5:00, and speaking at a huge rally for the general Republican rank and file at 6:00. When Watt gets on the podium among friends, where his remarks are "all in the lodge," he becomes a figure of power and grace. The professorial bald pate and academic coke-bottle glasses, with their air of brittle, dry and humorless frailty seem to change before your eyes. Watt's soft voice deepens and grows resonant. His gestures shape the air and the minds looking on.

As Len Edgerly wrote for *Western Energy Magazine,* "His speaking cadence is rhythmical, his timing often flawless, building up to a ringing phrase delivered to a hushed audience, expectant and believing. He sprinkles his serious statements with anecdotes from his boyhood ranch days—things his uncle Ralph said to his aunt Mabel while they were hitching up the horses. James Watt giving a political speech is a far cry from the image he has been given in political cartoons. . . . At the end of one speech, the veteran producer of a '60 Minutes' crew said, 'I've never seen him this effective.' "

I have never seen Watt give a political speech from a prepared text—all are off the cuff, eschewing polished diction and precise delivery. He will occasionally stumble on a word, or have to back up and start a sentence again. Sometimes he seems unable to recall the point he's leading up to. But then, while you are still off guard, he will gather his thoughts, build a verbal edifice, rising, growing, enchanting, only to leave a single word booming in the silence, and finish his phrase with a whisper. He speaks with disarming sincerity, personal, embarassing, painful sincerity. On the podium he is not spouting some political ideology, but revealing his most secret, private, intimate emotions. Seldom does Watt leave a political audience without many wiping away tears.

Watt uses several stock political speeches—not written, no notes— that he delivers differently to different audiences. One is what Doug Baldwin calls the "Two Streams of Life" speech, which provides an insight into who James Watt really is that is not available from official utterances as Secretary of the Interior. This is how he usually delivers it:

Through the pages of history, we can study that man has flowing from his heart a stream that cries out for political liberty. And it's a cry that you can read in the pages of centuries of mankind. And yet from the same heart, there's another stream that flows, and it's a stream that yearns for spiritual freedom. And these two streams flowing from the heart of man have been allowed in the plan of God to come together in a mighty river that's been called America.

The enemies of liberty and the enemies of freedom have fought us for years. And sometimes the ebb and flow of that battle becomes very discouraging, but, friends, there's a new power, there's a new determination that is saying—and I hear it calling—"America will be great again." America will be that land again where the river flows strong to assure our liberty and our spiritual freedom.

One does not have to share Watt's fundamentalist Christianity, or any religion at all, to feel his love of liberty and freedom in matters political and spiritual. But another of Watt's political speeches has made headlines, and it usually goes like this:

For all of my college years I took abuse from those liberals who challenged us because they said we didn't want to change. Now it is the conservatives that have the ideas, the depth of commitment. It is the liberals who want to hold onto the failure of the '60s and the '70s. We conservatives stand for change, and there couldn't be a more exciting time to serve in government than now.

After delivering this speech to farmers in California in 1981, Watt discussed water issues and in response to a question said, "These are not partisan issues. They're not Republican issues; they're not Democrat issues. In fact, I don't even use those terms any more. I just talk about liberals." Then he laughed and added, "And Americans." The political audience loved the joke, but Eastern papers later made it sound dark and sinister. The "liberals and Americans" remark became a cause celebre.

Lobbyist Timothy L. Donohoe was fired from his $30,000-a-year job with the Dallas-based natural gas company Ensearch after writing on company stationery to Watt questioning the "liberals and Americans" remark. Congressional and Legislative Affairs Director for Interior, Stanley W. Hulett, sent a copy of Donohoe's letter to Ensearch chief executive William C. McCord, who fired Donohoe because he had identified himself in the letter to Watt as an energy company lobbyist. The lobbyist's firing was played in several newspapers as a direct action of Watt, even though Watt found out about the incident by reading it in the newspaper himself.

Many are put off by Watt's political speeches, but Jennifer Hillings, press secretary for the Republican National Committee, noted that when Watt shows up as a speaker, attendance jumps anywhere from 10 percent to 20 percent on the average. State party leaders point out that Watt can draw 70 activists to a small town luncheon and Susan Cohen, assistant finance officer of the Colorado GOP, said Watt's appearance prompted five new State memberships for the Elephant Club—for contributors of $1,000 or more.

Among the many sidelights of the outreach program, one is fascinating for its complexity and perplexity: the rash of Watt bumper sticker slogans. The creative juices of friend and foe alike seemingly gush at Jim Watt's name. At first the slogan was simply "Dump Watt." Jim, in fact, complimented Des Moines on his outreach itinerary for varying the line to "Oust Watt"—he was bored with the old one. But in quick succession, dozens more appeared: "What's Wrong? Watt's Wrong!" with its counterpart "I Know Watt's Right!" Then came "Watt: One-Man Apocalypse!" and

"Keep Watt, Fire Sierra Club!" Then, "Short Out Watt," and "One Dim Watt is No Environmental Enlightenment," countered by "Out of Work and Hungry? Eat an Environmentalist" and on a logging truck, "Sierra Club, Kiss My Axe!" The anti-nuclear advocates got in their licks with "Save Our Land, Air and Water—Nuke Watt!" the water project opponents struck with "Dam Watt" and the birdwatchers got one off with "How is Watt Like an Eagle? They're both Bald and Endangered!" Then the pro-Watt crew came up with "Save the Environment from the Environmentalists—Support Jim Watt!" and "Where There's Watt There's Freedom!" and "I'm A Mega-Watt-er!" The frenzy evidently demented one sloganeer who lurched forth with this pot-pourri: "Watt: Nuke The Unborn Gay Whales."

During the autumn outreach, a serious problem erupted in Congress: Ranking Minority member Manuel Lujan, Jr., of the House Interior and Insular Affairs Committee learned from a newspaper report that three oil leases had been issued in the El Capitan Wilderness in his home State of New Mexico. Newspaper coverage of Lujan's reaction provides an object lesson in media distortion. Lujan, according to the *Washington Post,* "was so provoked that he introduced legislation that would have immediately barred all leasing in any wilderness area. That led to a confrontation with Watt, who agreed to a moratorium prohibiting any leasing until this June [1982]."

Technical and political facts were omitted from these reports that would have provided the public with much-needed insight. Technically, the disputed leases were for "No Surface Occupancy," that is, no drilling rigs could enter the Wilderness Area, but rather had to begin work outside a buffer zone and use *slant drilling* technology that would eventually reach oil beneath the Wilderness Area. No damage of any kind would be done to the Wilderness Area itself.

The disputed leases had not been issued by Watt himself, but by officials well down the command line without Watt's knowledge, which was perfectly within their power. However, Watt himself has issued five such No Surface Occupancy leases for slant drilling under Wilderness Areas. Cecil Andrus issued ten of them during his stint as Secretary of the Interior. None of this was mentioned in the press.

Politically, Lujan had not originated the idea to legislate against all Wilderness Area leasing; a new staff aide had done it, and Lujan introduced the bill upon the aide's advice. This staff aide, I later found, was so poorly informed on New Mexico politics that he also recommended that Lujan introduce gun control legislation, which in the American Southwest is tanta-mount to political suicide. What's more, when Lujan introduced his aide's anti-Watt bill, he was planning a joint fund-raiser with Senator Harrison (Jack) Schmitt, former NASA astronaut. When news of Lujan's legislation hit the streets, his fund-raising campaign collapsed. Jim Watt told me, "I had to get on the telephone and personally put his campaign back together because of his ill-advised move." Lyn Nofziger of the White House staff says, "If anybody [in Republican ranks] takes on Jim Watt, their funding dries up."

Later, Lujan lamely told the *Washington Post* that the anti-leasing bill was "merely his way of calling attention to how loose and easy the leasing policy is." The row about leasing, I think, was primarily anti-Watt sentiment rather than substantive concern. As evidence, 45 oil, gas and geothermal leases have been issued by previous administrations in Wilderness Areas with no fuss. Fourteen of them went to Dyco Petroleum Corporation of Minneapolis for Colorado's West Elk Wilderness. Diane O'Connor, press officer to the U.S. Forest Service, said four oil and gas leases had been granted in Montana's Absaroka-Beartooth Wilderness, three in Wyoming's Bridger Wilderness, three in New Mexico's El Capitan, and seven geothermal development leases in the Mount Hood Wilderness of Oregon. Environmentalists compared drilling in wilderness to "graffiti in the Sistine Chapel." In similarly colorful terms, one might consider environmentalism a loose cannon on the deck of our stormy economy.

While the key environmentalist group public relations people were denouncing Jim Watt, their executives were making important deals with him. This fact, while never admitted, is well-documented. Deputy Under Secretary William P. Horn describes two major agreements environmentalists made with Watt in 1981:

In June, the Sierra Club, the National Wildlife Federation, and the National Audubon Society dropped their opposition to a hydroelectric dam within the Kodiak Wildlife Refuge in Alaska after negotiations with Watt's management team. In August of 1981, the "Trustees for Alaska," an environmentalist umbrella group including the Sierra Club and many others, settled a complex lawsuit over Alaska lands by an out-of-court agreement after negotiations with Secretary Watt's representatives.

In the Kodiak case, a proposal had been made by the Kodiak Electric Association (KEA) during the Carter Administration to build a power dam on Terror Lake on Kodiak Island. The city of Kodiak is so remote its only electric power had been derived from generators run by diesel fuel flown in at exorbitant cost. However, the KEA proposal would inundate part of the Kodiak Wildlife Refuge, some of the best bear habitat in the world. The three environmentalist groups intervened during the Federal Energy Regulatory Commission's hearing process and stopped the project. When Watt took office, he instructed his managers to get the project going because of demonstrable benefits to the city of Kodiak. Watt got all the parties in a room and they hammered out a wildlife mitigation agreement. The State of Alaska committed some adjacent lands to cooperative management with the U.S. Fish and Wildlife Service for the benefit of the bears, the Kodiak Electric Association agreed to put up some money for a bear study project, and the environmentalists agreed to stop obstructing the dam project.

The lawsuit over Alaska lands was much more complex, but was settled by Watt's team using similar negotiating skills. The case of *Alaska* v. *Reagan* involved many legal issues concerning the right and ability of the federal government to withdraw lands under the Antiquities Act (President Carter had unilaterally declared 120 million acres of Alaska to be National Monuments and other preserves, and this lawsuit was originally filed against him), what obligations the Interior Department had to convey lands on a timely basis to Alaska under their Statehood Act, and some future studies on the disposition of contested land selections on the Alaska Peninsula. The environmentalists had intervened in the lawsuit and Watt gave a directive in March 1981 to settle the issue. After intensive negotiations, all parties to the suit, including the environmentalists, settled out of court. It is ironic that the environmentalist group leaders have kept these agreements secret, attacking Watt publicly while making deals with him in the back room.

By February 1982 the outreach program had worked. All except the large Eastern liberal newspapers and the television networks were saying favorable things about Watt and his policy. The "Dump Watt" campaign had fizzled. While Sierra Club executive director Michael McCloskey said, "This is the best year in Sierra Club history," National Wildlife Federation leader Clifford Young moaned, "What good does it do us to be strong when the rules Watt promulgates are against what we have in mind?" In part because of the sympathy generated by Watt's courage in standing up and taking the battering from environmentalists, Watt had become the Republican Party's surprise fund-raising star. Watt continued his policy direction with a growing base of support, but timing his policy announcements as if following the ancient Chinese motto, "Confusion to the enemy!" A page in history closed: never before had such raging abuse hit an Interior Secretary; many in the office had been destroyed by much smaller outcries. Watt had survived the unsurvivable.

CHAPTER 12
THE GOOD, THE TRUE, AND THE MEDIA

*All I know is just what I read in the papers,
and that's an alibi for my ignorance.*
—Will Rogers

William Ruckleshaus, former director of the Environmental Protection Agency, once told me a striking parable of the media. He was attending a party on the Washington cocktail circuit and chanced upon Ben Bradlee, editorial boss of the *Washington Post*. Bradlee was still reveling in the role of media monarch after helping to depose "King Richard" Nixon with his aggressive investigative reporting of the Watergate scandals. He told Ruckleshaus and all within earshot the policy of his great newspaper: "We don't print the truth. We don't pretend to print the truth. We print what people tell us. It's up to the public to decide what's true."

That rather cavalier attitude may express the operating philosophy of editors far beyond the *Washington Post*, but it is fair enough if everyone understands the rules. Distortion and yellow journalism were not invented for the Watt Secretariat. It goes with the territory of high office, even though Watt reporters at times seem to have stretched the limits of advocacy into prpopagandizing and beyond. English playwright Tom Stoppard once said, "The aspects of journalism that one might well disapprove of are the price we pay for the part that matters, and the part that matters is absolutely vital." But most Americans don't realize the extent to which truth is disregarded by the media; most have never been exposed to the computerized cynicism of a large daily newspaper or the electronic bowels of a network newsroom. Too often the primitive awe of print overwhelms our veneer of sophistication. Too often television's most trusted father-images mislead the global village. Too often we do not understand the rules.

Journalists themselves have been obliging enough to reveal some of the rules—the real rules, not the nuts and bolts of *The Washington Post Deskbook on Style.* Listen to *Washington Post* editor Charles Seib:

We of the media like conflict, tension, the suspense of contest. We like these things because they make good copy. Our banner might well carry the motto "Let's You And Him Fight." . . . We desperately need a contest.

Respected journalist Theodore White:

You don't make your reputation as a reporter, and I did not make my reputation as a reporter, by praising anybody. You make your reputation as a reporter by gouging a chunk of raw and bleeding flesh from this system. And I did that, all young reporters do that. You gotta be able to prove you can snap' your jaws for the kill. But maybe we've gone too far and maybe there should be someone to call us to account for this.

Newsweek columnist George Will:

Only man is perverse enough to feel most alive when the news is most lurid. . . . If some great catastrophe is not announced every morning, we feel a certain void. Nothing in the paper today, we sigh.

Statements such as these are the basis for the real rules of journalism *and audience participation.* We have become struggle junkies and disaster addicts; the media give us our daily fix. But it is good to be fully aware of our case. We should realize that the news story itself is actually a dramatic literary form, not a strictly informational form of writing such as the technical paper or business memo. Drama, the active pursuit of conflict, has become a basic convention of newswriting, and that is not likely to change. Every page of the newspaper is the drama page. Every newscast is a soap opera. News stories may refer to reality, but they are not real in the same sense: they have been carefully composed and edited into a dramatic framework by a writer and news team. And regardless of professional protestations to the contrary—my own included—every story is filtered through the biases of the writer.

Biases would be of no concern, and might be great good fun, if we looked to the media only for distraction. But we don't. We look to the media for information on vital matters. If "it's up to the public to decide what's true," then we need enough facts from which to form a reasonable conclusion. Media coverage of James Watt and his Department of the Interior has not provided the public with enough facts; from an analysis of more than 2,000 news clippings since Watt's confirmation, I have found an overwhelming tendency in the media to stress environmentalist commentary and to minimize coverage of Watt's actual policy and deeds. Some biases tend to misdirect attention away from one set of facts to another; time and again news coverage of Secretary Watt has shifted attention from his basic premise that we need to wisely develop our natural resources and focused on dramatic scenarios of what *might* happen in the worst possible case of overdevelopment. Other biases arouse our emotions to short-circuit rational thought; immense micro- and macro-economic investment decisions affecting the daily lives of millions of Americans rest on Interior policy, yet media stories continually reduce the Department's functions to a simplistic matter of recreation ethics and preservationist aesthetics. The least worthy biases found in the media are those directed to mere character assassination; Watt has received more than his share of these in the press.

Media biases serve to set the agenda of our entire society by publicizing issues and partisans of issues, thereby increasing the influence of particular viewpoints. When these viewpoints negate the importance of material values through Maslow's "postgratification forgetting and devaluation" and Kahn's "educated incapacity," as environmentalist viewpoints seem to do, media coverage can promote potentially dangerous mindsets affecting the economy and national security. Like it or not, industrial civilization still needs resource development in order to survive; man lives not by the Sierra Club alone.

Secretary Watt and other conservatives often blast the media for promoting only liberal viewpoints and for acting as willing advocates of organized environmentalism. Most journalists pooh-pooh this notion as being merely sour grapes, but scholarly studies indicate there may be some truth to it. A survey by S. Robert Lichter and Stanley Rothman for the Research Institute on International Change at Columbia University, "Media and Business Elites," found that 54 percent of their journalist respondents identified themselves to the left of center, while only 19 percent identified themselves as being on the right, and only 8 percent were described by their fellow workers as conservatives. Some journalism professors with whom I have discussed this study discount its findings, and note that even liberals are professionals striving for fairness in their news coverage and are people of personal integrity. I would not argue with that defense of liberals, but I would not accept the idea that their liberality has no impact on their reporting. There is too much evidence that it does.

Senator Alan Simpson (R-Wyo.) is convinced that liberal attitudes bias reporting of Jim Watt. In a discussion in the Capitol lobby one day in early 1982, Senator Simpson told me,

Jim paid a terrible price for staying in the Department those first six months getting the bureaucracy under control and refusing interviews. People came to me from the *Washington Post* and the *New York Times* and the *Los Angeles Times,* and they'd say, "We're doing a piece on Jim Watt and we can't see him, so we want to ask you because you've known him for 20 years. Of course, it will be a balanced piece."

Well, I smiled at that because they had almost a slavering kind of "flunk-the-saliva-test" mentality pursuing him like the hounds of hell. They'd start right off with a question about Jim's religion. And I'd say, "What the hell does that have to do with the price of prunes in Alaska? That's a nutty way to start an interview." They'd go to the business about stewardship and the Second Coming. And then we'd have drilling in Yellowstone National Park. And I'll be damned if this morning [Feb. 11, 1982] Mary McGrory's column in the *Washington Post* didn't say "Of course, Jim Watt favors drilling in Yellowstone National Park." I enjoy reading her, even though I don't always agree with her. But I'm going to drop Mary a line. Good Lord, talk about a total distortion, that business about sucking all the steam from Old Faithful and drilling in National Parks is a plain old phony lie.

I have researched a few outright distortions of Watt's actual policy and found most to originate in quotes from an environmental group leader. The process usually begins in an environmentalist's evaluation of Watt's policy which was reported with proper attribution. Then a later news story will pick up the environmentalist quote and accept it as *being* Watt's policy. Thus did the myth of drilling the Parks begin, which first appeared in a comment by William Turnage of the Wilderness Society during Watt's confirmation battle. Reporters must crib from each other more than I suspected, because many similar inventions made the media rounds for months before being corrected. And even though *Newsweek* set the drilling in National Parks story straight June 29, 1981—"Parks are inviolate, by decree of Congress, and Watt has no quarrel with that"—more than six months later it was still circulating in Mary McGrory's column.

An entire web of false claims about Watt's policy blossomed in news reports during late 1981. Forty-three of them were assembled by the Wilderness Society in a four-pound compendium bound in red and disarmingly titled, *The Watt Book*. This collection of "Watt's Wrongs" was described by columnist James Kilpatrick as "a labor of loathing." The Society listed 43 actions or proposed actions claiming to illustrate how "Watt has begun a campaign to systematically dismantle two decades of environmental progress" with initiatives "that run counter to federal law or clearly established public sentiment." The Wilderness Society's book did not document the federal laws that Watt allegedly violated, however, but rather reprinted *news articles* which largely quoted environmentalist leaders commenting on Watt's policy. As time has revealed, most of the actions listed were not Watt's policy to begin with, and none of the Watt policies listed correctly were illegal—if they had been, liberal Democrats in Congress would have wasted no time initiating impeachment proceedings. Yet the Wilderness Society's *Watt Book* was a highly successful media event, receiving coverage far and wide while spreading rumors, speculations and outright falsehoods as fact. Ben Bradlee's remarks are brought back to us.

The irony is that among themselves, environmentalists admitted their media lists of Watt misdeeds would be ineffective in Congress. Ron Wolf, writing in the May 1981 issue of *Audubon* magazine, said of his peers' searches, "They found much to fuel their anxiety, but no smoking pistol. That was because there was no smoking pistol to be found—only an opposite view of the world." The public would benefit if Audubon's leaders such as the vocal Russell Peterson admitted this to the media.

The media certainly have the right and obligation to cover the responses to national policy of interest groups such as organized environmentalists—and, like it or not, James Watt's resource policy is the resource policy of the United States. But it is a serious disservice to the public to spread opposition commentary as if it were an accurate description of national policy. As mentioned, the problem became so serious that during Watt's outreach program in the fall of 1981, a "Fact and Fiction" package had to be assembled for reporters in order to rectify what had become firm beliefs as a result of uncritical repetition of lies. The Interior Department news package consisted primarily of quotations from U.S. law, simply to remind reporters that Watt was acting not contrary to the letter or spirit of Congress, but contrary to the preferences of a powerful special interest.

Among the many assertions Watt took care to correct was the claim that his policies were opposed by a majority of American opinion. To the contrary, Watt's information package pointed out, the June 29, 1981, edition of *Newsweek* contained a Gallup Poll that showed more than 70 percent of the American people endorsed his basic policies and general philosophies:

More than 75 percent of the American people believe it is possible to maintain strong economic growth in the United States and still maintain high environmental standards.

More than 76 percent of those polled favor increasing oil exploration and other commercial uses of federal lands.

More than 76 percent of respondents favor spending money to improve the condition of the national parks rather than expanding the national park system.

And, more than 70 percent of the American people favor enlarging the area of offshore oil drilling on the East and West coasts.

Watt's blunt and abrupt personal style has certainly provoked many media attacks for which he has no one to blame but himself. Besides, guerilla warfare between Cabinet officers and the press has a long and honorable tradition. Nevertheless, media reporting of Watt seems to have taken on the characteristics of a vendetta, with even small details of his everyday administrative tasks cast in the most unfavorable light, to the point of fabricating events that never happened. In researching these distortions, I discovered that an issue of the normally reliable *Time* published a severely biased description of an actual event back-to-back with an utter fabrication. When Watt ordered his executives to stop accepting speaking engagements at government expense for environmentalist banquets and conferences, *Time* wrote it up in the Dec. 14, 1981, issue: "Watt decreed that members of the National Park Service and top Interior Department aides should refrain from "wasting Government money by talking to national conservation leaders." This clearly implies that Watt had forbidden all communication between his people and environmentalist group staffs. In fact, only government-paid speeches had been stopped. All normal ongoing person-to-person contacts continued uninterrupted.

Following on the heels of this slanted interpretation was the sentence: "He [Watt] also requested, in a move of dubious legality, a list of department employees who are members of environmental groups." I queried Interior personnel on this point from top to bottom, and no such thing ever happened. *Time* would not reveal their source for this assertion. But the report is most likely derived from Watt's order that the federal government stop paying for Interior employees' membership dues to environmentalist organizations. Not long before the *Time* article appeared, Watt discovered that the U.S. Treasury was paying groups such as the Sierra Club and Audubon Society about $85,000 a year in membership dues, and ordered the practice stopped. My guess is that some disgruntled environmentalist contacted *Time* with his own version of the story and speculated that if Watt had cut off funds for memberships, he must have first requested a list of Interior employees who were members. But Watt's management style is much more pointed: he never asked for a list; he chopped the funds wholesale in his budget office. Watt says, "I didn't need any list. I couldn't care less who joins these groups with their own money. I pulled the plug on the practice, not on my people." But the media report added to the image of Watt as an environmental ogre.

A year and a half of similar distortions in the media made Watt one of the best-known but least-liked members of President Reagan's Cabinet. The fact that he has survived such concerted and sustained media attacks is astonishing, reflecting the toughness of Reagan's commitment to the changes being brought to Interior by Watt. Presidential support has been unwavering, but appeared to flag briefly during the most remarkable media flap of Watt's first year and a half in office, the July 1982 furor over a letter to Israeli Ambassador Moshe Arens concerning Jewish support for the administration's Outer Continenral Shelf oil and gas leasing program.

Sunday, June 13, 1982, Watt attended a Bonds For Israel dinner in Washington. As the highest-ranking government officers present, Watt and Minnesota Senator Rudy Boschwitz were seated flanking Ambassador Arens. The Beirut war raged at the time, and there were none of the usual dinner festivities or theatrical acts. Ambassador Arens spoke and explained the status of the war. The tone of the gathering was subdued. But during dinner conversation, Watt explained to the Ambassador his OCS oil and gas-leasing program, noting the opposition that had surfaced and commenting on the U.S. intention to achieve energy self-sufficiency. Ambassador Arens asked Watt, "Don't all of our friends in America support you?" Watt replied, "No, even Rudy hasn't supported us." Senator Boschwitz smiled and said, "I support you, Jim. You've never asked me for help." Watt laughed, "Well, I'm asking now!"

The next day, Watt mulled over the dinner conversation and realized that he hadn't asked many friends for help, particularly his constituency in the American Jewish community. "It was time to correct that oversight," says Watt. Thus he came to write this public letter to Israel's Ambassador Arens:

It was a delight spending some time with you Sunday evening at dinner. Your remarks were extremely well delivered and interesting.

I appreciate the opportunity of discussing with you the need for a strong, energy self-sufficient America. If we do not reduce America's dependency upon foreign crude energy, there is great risk that in future years America will be prevented from being the strong protector and friend of Israel that we are and want to be.

If the friends of Israel here in the United States really are concerned about the future of Israel, I believe they will aggressively support the Reagan Administration's efforts to develop the abundant energy wealth of America in a planned, orderly and environmentally sound way. If the liberals of the Jewish community join with the other liberals of the Nation to oppose these efforts, they will weaken our ability to be a good friend of Israel. Your supporters in America need to know these facts.

I look forward to opportunities to speak to groups of your supporters in this Nation so that I might share with them the truth of what this Administration is trying to do for America and the free world.

Sincerely,
James G. Watt

The letter was sent on official Interior Department stationary, headed "A PERSONAL COMMUNICATION," with a copy directed to Senator Boschwitz. Watt says, "Personal does not mean private. Nothing we do in Interior is private. The letter was widely circulated." In fact the letter was so widely circulated that John Lofton, Jr., editor of the *Conservative Digest*, gave it to an editor of the *Washington Times*, the Capitol's second daily newspaper since the *Star's* demise, where it was printed with no adverse response. Watt followed up on his intent to spread the message about his OCS program to American Jews by arranging for late July meetings with the B'nai B'rith's Anti-Defamation League in New York and the American Jewish Committee in Washington. Watt openly mentioned his letter to Ambassador Arens in several speeches, with no adverse reaction.

However, on July 21, Watt wrote another letter, this one to Senator Edward Kennedy defending his OCS program from a scathing attack by Kennedy and 28 other liberal Democrats in Congress. Watt's letter took these Congressmen to task for writing a July 9 letter "harshly criticizing our five-year plan to reduce America's dependence on foreign, unstable and sometimes hostile suppliers of energy as if the consumers of America did not matter, as if the freedom of Israel were not important, and as if there were no concern about peace or war in the Middle East."

Three days later, the *Washington Post* splashed Watt's letter across the front page—not his letter to Kennedy, but the month-old letter to Ambassador Arens. *Post* staff writer Dale Russakoff noted that the letter had "triggered an angry reaction yesterday from American Jewish leaders who variously called it 'inappropriate' and said it was 'deeply offensive' to appeal for American Jewish support through a foreign Ambassador." Rabbi Alexander M. Schindler, president of the 1.5 million-member Union of American Hebrew Congregations said, "I don't like being appealed to as a Jew on issue that is essentially of concern to all Americans." David Saperstein, head of the Interfaith Coalition on Energy, said, "I hear a veiled threat that the administration might cut back its support for Israel if Jewish liberals do not remain quiet about energy policies, even if they think these policies are bad for America and bad for humankind."

The next day, Sunday, July 25, the *New York Times* printed a story by Phillip Shabecoff quoting New York Senator Daniel Moynihan saying "James Watt should resign immediately for this act of bare-knuckled bigotry. If he does not, President Reagan should fire him immediately." Two Democrats, Toby Moffett of Connecticut and Tom Lantos of California, wrote President Reagan saying, "Mr. Watt's remarks were highly inappropriate and inflammatory. The Secretary seems to have enunciated a new American foreign policy requiring supporters of Israel to back Mr. Watt's offshore drilling plan" in return for assurances of American support for Israel.

Watt says, "I intended to stir a fight with my letter to Senator Kennedy, but I was surprised and shocked by the belated response to my letter to Ambassador Arens. There was no threat implied or intended—I have the most profound respect for the Jewish people of America and admiration for the people of Israel—I only wanted to point out the plain truth about America's energy dependency."

Assistant White House Press Secretary C. Anson Franklin said: "Secretary Watt's unofficial letter to Ambassador Arens represents his own personal views. The White House regards his remarks as unfortunate." It was the first time the White House had distanced itself from anything Watt had done. Calls for Watt's resignation flooded Washington to such an extent that key Interior officials were deeply alarmed. One told me privately, "It looked like Jim had finally done it." Watt has always characterized himself as "running for the long ball" and "Reagan's high-risk player," giving no thought to his own permanence or survival but only to forwarding the Reagan program. The events of this weekend gave all indications that Watt would be cleaning out his desk the following Monday.

What actually happened was quite different. By coincidence, Watt's meetings with the Jewish organizations had been scheduled a day apart during the week of July 26. Watt visited the Anti-Defamation League and came away with praise that he was "sincere" and that the matter of the Ambassador Arens letter "was closed." Then Watt met with the American Jewish Committee and came away with their endorsement for his OCS leasing program. Jewish leaders across America said they had long shared Watt's view that the United States should speedily reduce its reliance on imported oil and that such an approach will benefit Israel as well as other American allies, according to a *Washington Post* article. The White House quickly stated that "President Reagan continues to have full confidence in James G. Watt" despite any letter repercussions. Headlines began to appear announcing "Jews Now Seek to Quiet Calls for Watt Dismissal." During a mid-week press conference, President Reagan personally defended Watt's intent in writing the Arens letter and the issue was finally laid to rest. Once more Watt had survived the unsurvivable to emerge politically stronger.

But the media flap appears suspiciously to be yet another example of liberal bias confirming Lichter and Rothman's findings. Consider these facts: Watt's letter to Ambassador Arens had been widely distributed, published, and commented upon with no adverse reaction from the Jewish community for more than a month. Only *after* Watt staunchly and successfully defended his OCS plans for energy self-sufficiency against liberal Democrats was the Arens letter resurrected. It is not known who revived the Arens letter. The Eastern press sought comments only from liberal-leaning Jewish spokespeople, some of whom, as I later discovered, had not even read Watt's letter. None of Watt's many defenders in Congress was interviewed or quoted—with the exception of Senator Boschwitz, who said, "What the hell? It's a free country. He can write a letter to anybody he wants." Every complaint and demand for Watt's resignation came from a liberal Democrat. The truth of Watt's comments on his OCS plan and the need for energy self-sufficiency was never addressed by the press. Outraged responses from partisan advocates who had opposed Watt from the day of his confirmation received more than 80 percent of all commentary devoted to the story by the *Washington Post* and *New York*

Times during the height of the weekend flap. Stories of the successful resolution of the issue between Watt and the Jewish community were short and tersely worded. The rules of journalism laid down by Bradlee, Seib, and White had been vindicated.

However, beyond the range of the large Eastern newspapers, media support for Watt and his programs is substantial. The *Chicago Sun-Times* wrote a straightforward piece on Watt's enthusiastic backing of a National Heritage Corridor recommended by the Open Lands Project, a Chicago environmentalist group. The proposal involved National Park Service technical assistance in setting up the park, and staffing for dozens of interpretive stations along the banks of the Illinois-Michigan Canal running from Chicago's Southwest Side to La Salle, Illinois. Park Service personnel were to explain industrial operations, local history, and canal folklore to visitors, and the project would take $16 million in federal funds. Reporters pointed out that the Open Lands Project wisely did not fight for National Park status for the project, and had carefully garnered corporate support before an important meeting with Watt and key business people in the office of Illinois Republican Senator Charles H. Percy. The story treated Watt as friendly and supportive to realistic environmentalists, reinforcing Watt's assertions that he opposed only extremist environmental groups.

The *New Orleans Times-Picayune/States-Item* gave Watt an editorial pat on the back for his unequivocal support of Congressional efforts to halt the use of federal money for private development on coastal barrier islands. They quoted Watt (correctly): "This is precisely the sort of imaginative environmental legislation we need—legislation which can solve real problems in the stewardship of our national resources while at the same time responsibly addressing America's equally serious economic problems." Federal construction subsidies and flood insurance had encouraged development of the fragile barrier islands off our Southern and Eastern coasts which are regularly battered by hurricanes and conspicuously unsuited for permanent human habitation. The editorial refuted environmentalist charges that "Watt gives higher priority to development than to preservation," pointing out that in this decision, Watt went against the lobbying of his supporters in the National Association of Home Builders. Evidently, Watt is not merely "the obsequious tool of big business interests" as portrayed by some environmentalists.

Flagstaff's *Arizona Daily Sun* applauded Watt's decision to stop the Bureau of Reclamation's plans to add two generating turbines to the Glen Canyon Dam on the Colorado River above Grand Canyon. The project would have added 250 megawatts to the dam's power production, but would have also increased the river's flow about 40 times during peak generating periods. The peak flow would have unpredicatable impacts on beach erosion and wildlife, as well as on the popular raft trips through Grand Canyon. Watt said of the project, "It was the wrong idea in the wrong place at the wrong time," and of the possible danger to river rafters, "we simply could not allow human lives to be put in such jeopardy." Other sites had been identified that Watt felt could produce more power than the Glen Canyon dam at much less risk and environmental impact.

When Watt made the August 23, 1982, cover of *Time*, the truth was evidently catching up with the media: the 7-page cover story on federal land sales was fair and accurate. Environmentalist comments were clearly labeled. Watt's policy was correctly identified and critiqued on its merits by well-informed writers. The factual tide was turning, but underlying prejudices remained.

Media coverage of James Watt appears to be only a special case of a broader problem. Columnist Ben Stein, in his insightful analysis of the television industry, *The View From Sunset Boulevard*, describes the stereotyping of businessmen in the entertainment field. "One of the clearest messages of television," Stein says, "is that businessmen are bad, evil people, and that big businessmen are the worst of all." Stein's impressions were verified by the Washington, D.C.-based Media Institute in a study of 200 episodes of 50 prime-time programs broadcast during the 1979–80 season. What they discovered is fascinating.

Two out of three businessmen (66 %) were portrayed as "criminal, evil, greedy or foolish." Nearly half the work-related actions of businesspeople on television involved the commission of a crime ranging from fraud to murder. Over half of the business leaders portrayed were cast as criminals. On comedy shows, businessmen were depicted as clowns, conmen or pompous buffoons; on adventure programs as thieves, cutthroats or murderers. No other career group, doctors, policemen, lawyers, politicians or scientists, are portrayed in such a distorted manner. The Media Institute's study confirms what defenders of private enterprise have known for some time: there is a hate-business campaign being promoted in at least one medium. Ben Stein's interviews with Hollywood writers and producers showed that media moguls feel fear and loathing of the business community. Jim Brooks, producer of the *Mary Tyler Moore Show*, said of businessmen, "They're all sons of bitches. They're all cannibals."

What effect does this have on the television-watching young, who spend more time in front of a TV than in the classroom? A 1980 poll by Educational Communications, Inc., surveyed 24,000 high school leaders, of whom 37 percent agreed that "The typical big company is above the law and can get away with anything," and 43 percent felt that "business profits are excessive and should be limited by law." Such attitudes bode no good for the future of corporate capitalism and encourage youngsters to lean toward socialistic or centralized systems of government. Columnist Don Feder wrote in the Bellevue, Washington *Journal-American*, "Any other group subjected to such slander would be up in arms, picketing television stations and filing civil rights actions. Businessmen not only placidly submit to this abuse, they actually subsidize its broadcast through commercial advertising."

Perhaps the most serious media distortions against business and industry are those which lead to political action banning important technological tools. Anti-pesticide activism in particular has narrowed the ability of American farmers to produce abundant food. The media tend to publicize environmental campaigns freely. While the heated contemporary battles over James Watt and his policy can seriously influence our economic future, the long-term impact on industrial civilization of uncritical television and press coverage of environmental issues could be devastating.

To the average reader or viewer, environmental horror stories, and particularly those about chemical poisoning such as the Love Canal incident, appear to be totally spontaneous events that arise because of quite legitimate concern for immediate health and safety issues. Many such stories are indeed spontaneous, but not all: a significant number are carefully crafted campaigns designed by a specific environmental group with a well-defined political goal. The story of the Carter administration's ban on the herbicide 2,4,5-T is a study in organization and media pressure on the part of an environmentalist coalition.

The herbicide 2,4,5-T has been used successfully for many years in controlling plant pests that affect rangelands, rice crops and young seedlings growing in commercial forests. Foresters in particular relied on 2,4,5-T to control competing brush species that threatened to crowd out valuable species such as Douglas fir in the Pacific Northwest. The chemical has been studied exhaustively for its efficacy and safety; the Council for Agricultural Science and Technology notes there have been "more than 35,000 scientific papers and technical reports over a 30-year period." The British Advisory Council on Pesticides found, "There is no valid medical or scientific evidence that 2,4,5-T harms humans, animals or environment" in approving it for use in the United Kingdom. In fact, a number of suicide attempts by drinking pure undiluted 2,4,5-T have failed to do the job, inducing only episodes of what Shakespeare would term "mewling and puking." However, this useful herbicide had been one of the ingredients of the notorious Agent Orange of Viet Nam war vintage, which aroused instant ideological prejudices among many people. And 2,4,5-T contains minute traces of the unavoidable manufacturing contaminant TCDD, one of the 75 kinds of dioxin, and one of the most toxic substances known to science.

April 11, 1978, a woman named Bonnie Hill and seven others from the tiny rural town of Alsea, Oregon, sent a letter to the Environmental Protection Agency complaining they had suffered an epidemic of miscarriages, and containing charts they had drawn up correlating the dates of their miscarriages with spraying of nearby forests with 2,4,5-T for brush-control purposes on Douglas fir plantations. The eight women asked EPA to investigate their concerns.

EPA agreed, and sent a team of scientists to Oregon. They gathered data and also had a technician administer a medical history questionnaire to the women (nine of them: one letter-writer refused to participate and two others volunteered). The questionnaire probed their miscarriages, diet, physical surroundings, lifestyle, medical and family histories and other factors of scientific interest. The completed questionnaires were sent to ten medical experts in toxicology and epidemiology for evaluation. All ten came to the independent conclusion that there had been no epidemic of miscarriages and that there was no causal link between the Alsea women's problems and spraying of 2,4,5-T.

The EPA issued these findings to the public, saying there was "no evidence of connection between 2,4,5-T spraying and the Alsea miscarriages." There was no mention in the EPA release of what the medical panel had found, or the reasons why its conclusion had been reached. Immediately, a well-coordinated media campaign was initiated by the Friends of the Earth and a Eugene, Oregon-based group called Northwest Coalition for Alternatives to Pesticides (NCAP), asserting to the EPA, President Carter and numerous Congressmen that the truth was being "whitewashed" and that EPA was covering up "the horrible truth that 2,4,5-T had killed the Alsea babies." It was later ascertained that Bonnie Hill was a member of NCAP.

NCAP has an interesting background: it has 32 member-groups in the Pacific Northwest and exists for the purpose of eliminating the use of agrichemicals in favor of organic farming techniques. One of its affiliate groups, Citizens Against Toxic Herbicides in Clarkston, Washington, published a handbook entitled *The Toolkit* containing 13 rules for "fighting toxic sprays." Rule No. 3 advises: "Raise enough hell politically and through the media to get the spray plan postponed 'for further study.' From the start, spend time consulting your elected officials. They may not agree, but they're wary of offending active voters. If your name is in the paper a lot that helps even more. In this way, you can at least neutralize some people who might be speaking out against you otherwise." Rule No. 9 states: "If your job [in the anti-pesticide group] is evaluating research, *never* trust the conclusions of the author." Rule No. 11 says, "Stay on the attack. You select the issues."

Toolkit author and NCAP spokesman Paul Merrell told an April 16,

1981, meeting of the Izaak Walton League in Waldport, Oregon, "It doesn't matter how many studies are done. It doesn't matter what the facts are. This is a political issue and the political realities are that these chemicals are going."

The political orientation of NCAP may be indicated by a public statement of founder Fred Miller in an *Oregon Times* magazine interview dated April 1977: "I'm for centralization. . . . I want to wipe out capitalism, eradicate it from the face of the earth."

After a flurry of letters, newspaper and magazine articles, EPA decided to re-study the issue and began the project known as "Alsea II," repudiating the initial study which was now known as "Alsea I." The new study did not seek hard facts, or laboratory examinations of miscarried fetuses or medical examinations of the parents, but instead searched for a *statistical* link between miscarriages and spray times. EPA's final report claimed to find such a correlation in one month of one year of six years under study. Within days, still under a media barrage, EPA used this statistical event as the rationale to place an emergency ban on forestry use of 2,4,5-T.

Scientists who were aware of 2,4,5-T's excellent safety record were baffled. The EPA "Alsea II" report was carefully scrutinized, and more than 25 institutions found it to be "politically motivated" and "unscientific." The Environmental Health Sciences Department of Oregon State University called "Alsea II" flatly "erroneous," which is strong language coming from reputable scientists.

But everyone was baffled by the ban itself: 2,4,5-T could not be used in forestry operations, but would still be permitted for rangeland use *and could still be sprayed directly on rice.* Significantly, no environmental protest erupted over these permitted uses.

I was curious about the peculiarities of this case and began researching it for a possible magazine article. The first thing on my agenda was to get those medical questionnaires to see why ten independent experts thought 2,4,5-T had nothing to do with the Alsea miscarriages. My telephone calls to EPA were stonewalled. My letters to EPA were not answered. Oh, well, I thought, I can always use the Freedom of Information Act, which I did. I duly received copies of the ten medical evaluations of the women's questionnaires, which had been heavily censored. Interesting passages describing important factors were interrupted by rubber-stamped notices of "CONFIDENTIAL MATERIAL." Some entire pages had been expunged.

I had expected the womens' names to be deleted, but much else had fallen to the cutting-room floor. The medical evaluators all listed many other possible causes for miscarriage among the Alsea women than 2,4,5-T exposure, but even tabulations telling *how many* women fell into each category of "other possible causes" had been censored. So an unknown number of the

women "drank raw unpasteurized milk from local cows," or "smoked ciga-
rettes during pregnancy," or "heavily used alcohol," among a dozen or so
other factors listed. The medical panel suspected the presence of diseases
ranging from brucellosis to toxoplasmosis that could arise from the womens'
living conditions and counterculture lifestyle. But the most puzzling deletions
were entire paragraphs scattered among the "other possible causes" listed by
the medical experts.

One thing was clear: there were at least a dozen other factors than
2,4,5-T that could have caused the Alsea miscarriages, and someone in the
EPA didn't want anyone to know what all of them might be. The other
factors that had been revealed drew a picturesque portrait of a counterculture
lifestyle—homes with no running water except from surface streams, homes
with no refrigeration, much drinking of raw milk, eating quantities of deer
meat—but so what? The early settlers lived much the same way. What were
all the mysterious deletions covering up?

I had reached a dead end. I could find no more. But a year later, Dow
Chemical and a number of 2,4,5-T users had taken the EPA to court to clear
their product of all charges and return it to the farm and forest. The record of
testimony before EPA's Administrative Law Judge was public information.
Perhaps some witness would discuss those medical questionnaires and solve
the mystery. I ordered copies of the entire proceedings and sifted through
more than 7,000 pages of testimony and over 1,500 exhibits. And sure
enough, in Exhibit No. 853, there was the testimony of Dr. Steven H.
Lamm, an epidemiologist on the clinical faculties of Georgetown University
and the University of Maryland medical schools. Dr. Lamm had tabulated the
data from the medical questionnaires without revealing names or in any other
way violating the privacy of the Alsea women. In scanning Dr. Lamm's
testimony, it quickly became obvious why EPA had stonewalled my requests
and deleted so much information: among the many lifestyle-related potential
causes of miscarriage the women had listed in their questionnaires, one word
stood out—marijuana. Dr. Lamm certified that this potential miscarriage-
causing drug had been used among the Alsea women, which had been
admitted by some in their medical questionnaires. Scientific studies have
confirmed that the psychoactive ingredient of marijuana, delta-9-tetrahydro-
cannabinol, has miscarriage-causing powers similar to the dioxin in 2,4,5-T.
Now all the pieces of the puzzle fit together.

One of the bigger flaps over the anti-pesticide movement has been
"The Marijuana Connection." It is essentially a statement that part of the real
reason anti-pesticide groups protest forest herbicide use (but not rice crop
use—marijuana won't grow in wet rice fields) is the fact that herbicides,
particularly 2,4,5-T, are potent marijuana-killers. In this view, environmen-

talists are seen as protecting their habit, their own crops in some cases, and even a source of some of their funding, by anti-pesticide activism. Any hint of the marijuana connection in EPA's banning of 2,4,5-T would be potentially explosive: Carter administration bureaucrats had read the questionnaires and obviously knew marijuana was involved in the Alsea incidents. That could have cast them as pawns of the marijuana industry, or possibly as conspirators in a marijuana-industry protection scheme. It is a fact that "guerrilla growers" with marijuana plantations on federal lands such as National Forests benefited greatly by the ban on 2,4,5-T. No wonder I had been stonewalled.

Anti-pesticide groups hotly deny that any marijuana connection exists. Arrest records indicate otherwise: The November/December issue of *Parity Foundation Newsmagazine* notes:

On a summer evening in June, 1978, Paula Downing was stopped by a Josephine County (Oregon) deputy sheriff following a highway chase after he suspected seeing marijuana plants in her car. He discovered 77 marijuana plants, which Mrs. Downing said she was going to bury because they had grown too big for transplanting.

That same winter Mrs. Downing could be seen demonstrating against the Bureau of Land Management spraying programs. She and her husband Art, who also owned the Southern Oregon Post and Pole Company, were founders and leaders of the Headwaters Association and were members of the Southern Oregon Citizens Against Toxic Sprays.

This group, Southern Oregon Citizens Against Toxic Sprays, is an acknowledged affiliate of NCAP. This link between an arrested marijuana cultivator and an anti-pesticide group is documented beyond dispute. Many other such links exist. A recent General Accounting Office report, *Illegal and Unauthorized Activities on Public Lands—A Problem With Serious Implications*, documents beyond reasonable doubt that "guerilla growers" are a major problem on the West Coast, where anti-pesticide activism is strongest. The marijuana connection has been repeatedly shown to be more than an anti-environmentalist pipe-dream; coverage of specific incidents has appeared in *Newsweek*, the *Wall Street Journal*, and many metropolitan daily newspapers. Yet our memory seems so short that we forget how the media make anti-pesticide advocates appear only to be earnest, appealing and dedicated to the truth.

To the best of my knowledge, the media have never revealed the fact that marijuana was involved in the Alsea miscarriages or the banning of 2,4,5-T. Consultant Rick Main did present a paper before an Accuracy In Media conference in Washington saying, "Many of the Oregon women reporting miscarriages have admitted to long-term use of marijuana," but his statement was not picked up by the press. Anti-environmentalism is not a popular subject. Perhaps we are still too close to the movement's ideology to realize that one can fight environmentalists without fighting the environment. Perhaps we have not sufficiently matured in our judgments of environmental ideology to realize that there may be more to the movement than what we are told by its advocates. Perhaps we should demand more of our media in critical examination of environmentalist methods and motives.

It is difficult to challenge the popular appeal of environmental activists. The world is in need of purification, most agree. We want to be able to take the purifiers at face value. The final irony of the good, the true, and the media lies in a statement given in testimony before a Congressional subcommittee by Mrs. Bonnie Hill, one of the Alsea women who had been lionized by the media into a folk heroine for winning her David-and-Goliath battle against the agrichemical industry—and who knew full well the truth of the marijuana connection that was later documented and admitted. Her words were broadcast, printed, and believed:

Lobbying groups and industry representatives have been making uninformed generalizations in Washington, D.C., as well as here in Oregon, about the Alsea women. . . . Most of these comments are focused on the "lifestyles" of the Alsea women, and include such suggestions as marijuana use. Such intimations, even if only implied, are slanderous and totally without substantiation. . . . We have not responded to these intimations because they are not true, and because they simply are not issues, but are rather attempts to distract people from the real issue.

Ultimately, we are forced to accept Ben Bradlee's four-line philosophy as being more profound than it appeared at first blush. Particularly when faced with the politics of environmentalism, whether centered about James Watt or not, it *is* up to the public to decide what's true.

CHAPTER 13
A YEAR OF CHANGE

> The history of liberty is the history of limiting
> government power, not of increasing it.
> —Woodrow Wilson

The title Secretary Watt gave his first annual report to the President was *A
Year of Change: To Restore America's Greatness.*[*] In 18 printed pages Watt
summarized his 1981 technical and policy changes, dividing them into 6
subject heads: Energy and Minerals; Parks, Wilderness and Wildlife; Water
Management; the "Good Neighbor" Policy; Indian Tribe and Island Territory
Development; and Good Management and Decisive Leadership.

Watt's concrete first-year achievements were substantial. In energy,
oil production amounted to 470 million barrels compared to 427 in 1980;
natural gas production exceeded 5.8 trillion cubic feet, .2 trillion more than in
1980; 94.6 million tons of coal, 31 percent ahead of 1980. In offshore oil and
gas, Watt leased 424 tracts on 2.23 million acres, 96 percent higher than
1980, and revenues were $9.6 billion compared to $6.3 billion in 1980. In
onshore oil and gas, Watt increased the number of leases 36 percent over
1980 and the number of acres leased 152 percent. He opened more than 100
million Alaska acres to geophysical exploration and offered for lease 1.5
million acres of the National Petroleum Reserve in Alaska. In coal, Watt
increased the acreage leased by 420 percent over 1980, increased tonnage sold
by 275 percent, and increased revenues from $22.3 million in 1980 to $40
million.

Although Watt mentioned it only in passing in his annual report, all
of this added development, which contributed substantially to President
Reagan's economic recovery program, did not give rise to a single incident of
environmental damage. There were no offshore wellhead blowouts or oil spills;
no detectable increases in air or water pollution on federal lands under

development, no wildlife kills, no impact on wilderness. Critics continued to warn of "possible" or "potential" damage, or things that "could" or "might" happen because of Watt's program. None of the dire consequences predicted by environmentalist groups actually occurred.

In the area of National Parks, Wilderness and Wildlife Refuges, Watt doubled the funding request for park restoration and facility improvements over what the Carter Administration had requested. Watt asked for a 90 percent reduction in funding for adding new units to the park system and Congress gave him a 70 percent cut. Watt required park concessioners to contribute a major share of their earnings to improve visitor facilities. He, formulated a new national land protection policy that encourages creative alternatives to onerous and unjust government condemnation methods, authorizing easements, leases, donations, bargain sales, and other protection methods in eight case studies.

Watt also finalized the purchase of 24,349 acres of wetland habitat for migratory birds, began acquisition of two new National Wildlife Refuges (Bon Secour in Alabama and Bogue Chitto along the Louisiana-Mississippi border), initiated recovery plans for 168 endangered species, 65 more than in 1980, conducted a successful "sting" operation uncovering a multimillion-dollar black market traffic in domestic and foreign endangered reptiles, arresting 27 people and seizing more than 1,000 live animals. He extended protection to the humpback whales in Glacier Bay, Alaska, and many more favorable wildlife actions.

In water management, Watt accelerated long-stalled progress on 70 water development projects; streamlined the federal water project planning process, thus reducing the 17 years formerly required to complete planning before construction to 7 or 8 years; chose an alternative to the Central Arizona Project's Orme Dam, thereby precluding flooding of Fort McDowell Indian Reservation; and he slashed the obstructionary principles and standards for review of federal water projects in favor of more flexible and less time-consuming guidelines.

Watt's "Good Neighbor" policy had several thrusts: first, to open the processes of government to commodity users as well as environmentalists, second, to promote states rights, and third, to defuse the "Sagebrush Rebellion." Watt opened his office to governors, state legislators, county commissioners, and officials from local water, public land and park agencies. He also met with hundreds of special-interest group representatives and private citizens including paid environmentalists, both in Washington and in their own states. Watt hosted breakfast meetings with 184 members of Congress, 63 Congressional staff members, and 160 individuals representing groups and agencies with interests in matters under Interior's jurisdiction.

Watt returned several important rights to the states: the primary authority to allocate water resources; the implementation of surface mining reclamation and environmental enforcement; transferred, exchanged, or sold 9,000 acres of federal land to state and local governments; and renewed efforts to honor states' rightful claims for federal lands they were granted upon entering the Union. For example, Watt gave Alaska 7 million acres of federal land in 1981 and 12 million more in 1982. He also gave the lower 48 states 58,825 acres as compared to the 168 acres meted out during the entire 4 years of the Carter Administration. Watt also made record payments of $539 million in revenue-sharing to state and local governments, 15 percent more than in 1980. In these and many other actions, Watt defused the potentially explosive "Sagebrush Rebellion."

The 1981 Indian and Island programs were directed to provide the people involved with adequate means to conduct their own affairs to *their* satisfaction rather than the government's. The Indians for the first time got a reservation Indian directing Interior's Indian Affairs program; there was no more rhetoric when Ken Smith took over. He dealt with the real problems. Smith stepped up efforts to protect Indian water rights, pursued key negotiations on behalf of Indian fishing rights, stopped the illegal sale of salmon on California's Klamath River, rehabilitated 24 Indian schools, created a reservation for Washington State's Skagit Indian Tribe, and stepped up the conveyance of land to native Alaskans, among many other positive activities.

Island territories received Watt's cooperation to help them toward full internal self-government, and Watt took a leading role in supporting their proposals to the Federal Communications Commission for satellite earth stations to provide a reliable communication network for the sparsely populated, widely distributed Pacific Islands.

Watt's Good Management and Decisive Leadership program had three major thrusts: to use the best available management techniques in running the Department; to aggressively impose internal controls on waste and improper use of government property; and to reduce the size and cost of government. Watt fostered good management by hiring only senior political appointees with previous federal, state, local, or tribal government experience. Professional career government leaders were chosen to direct the U.S. Geological Survey, the U.S. Fish and Wildlife Service and the National Park Service. The advice of career professional resource managers was sought and heeded in all major policy decisions. The Management By Objectives system was adopted to guide and monitor effectiveness in the Department from top to bottom. Watt conducted major investigations and audits into revenue losses and waste from oil and gas royalties and other federal property. Watt slashed 9 percent in 1981 and 17 percent in 1982 from the Interior budget request as compared to the previous administration. Watt simplified 22 sets of regulations, stream-lined Interior's energy and minerals leasing procedures and saved well over $10 million in the Bureau of Land Management alone by eliminating needless paperwork. Watt's legal expertise and his Solicitor's Office's tough stance on enforcing the law helped reduce the number of lawsuits in 1981 by 30 percent compared to 1980. Environmentalists found it unprofitable to fight lawyers as shrewd and dedicated as their own. The fact that Watt won more lawsuits than his predecessors severely damaged environmentalists' program to build an ironclad edifice of legal precedents in their own image.

All in all, this is not a bad record for a "hick from the sticks" of Wyoming during his first year in office. When Under Secretary Hodel saw the first copy of this annual report, he said to me:

If I had been Secretary, we'd still be holding meetings with the Sierra Club trying to figure out if we didn't have some common ground and none of this would have gotten done. I think the Watt approach is going to set a standard of diligence for all Secretaries of the Interior to come, regardless of their feelings about the environmental movement. Watt has done more in this single year than most Secretaries achieve in a whole Presidency, and he did it under the most appallingly stressful conditions imaginable.

The National Wildlife Federation, however, lashed out at Watt's first-year record. April 29, 1982, they issued a 54-page rebuttal of Watt's 18-page annual report in a paper called *Marching Backwards: The Department of the Interior Under James G. Watt*. The Federation study steps into exact opposition of every one of Watt's statements, regardless what that did to the rebuttal's consistency.

An amusing example was the accusation against Watt's accelerated oil leasing plan: "Accelerated Leasing May Not Increase Production." Inactive leases don't harm the environment. The point seems not to be promotion of the Federation's program, but mere blind opposition to anything Watt said.

Much of the rebuttal was not a critique of Watt,however, but text-book sermonettes like "Protection of fish and wildlife requires good planning, both to avoid habitat destruction whenever possible and to mitigate the effects of unavoidable use of habitat." Two paragraphs of such statements, which were never followed up, preceded every section in the rebuttal. Then came the real point: to challenge one of Watt's annual report statements. This is a typical approach:

Claim: U.S. Fish and Wildlife Service purchased 24,349 acres of wetland under the duck stamp program.
        Response: True, but inadequate.

This is a bit more to the point, yet simply reflects the Federation's insatiable appetite for the federal government to spend tons of money during recessionary times for endless land acquisitions from private owners. No amount would have been judged adequate.

Some of the Federation's charges came embarrassingly close to hysteria: "A strict, result-oriented 'management by objectives' management program has been implemented." The charge, of course, is quite true, but what would they prefer? No alternative was suggested.

Perhaps the most revealing aspect of the Federation's rebuttal can be found in its constant and deliberate use of the terms "preservation" and "conservation" interchangeably, as if they were synonyms. They are not, but it serves the struggle group purpose to leave these notions fuzzy in the public's mind. Yet the Federation complained, "Conservationists are frustrated by the fact that, although they use the same vocabulary as Secretary Watt, they speak a different language." The footnote explaining this charge quoted a statement by Secretary Watt at the 46th North American Wildlife and Natural Resources Conference in March, 1981:

At the conference he outlined the "four solid cornerstones" of his conservation policy, none of which has anything to do with conservation. They are:

1. America must have a sound economy if it is to be a good steward of its fish and wildlife, its parks, and all of its natural resources.

2. America must have orderly development of its vast energy resources to avert a crisis development which could be catastrophic to the environment.

3. America's resources were put here for the enjoyment and use of people, now and in the future, and should not be denied to the people by elitist groups.

4. America has the expertise to manage and use resources wisely, and much of that expertise is in State government and in the private sector.

The Federation's accusation that these things have nothing to do with conservation is enlightening. Conservation means wise use. Preservation means protecting from commodity use. Watt's four points may have nothing to do with *preservation*, but they have everything to do with *conservation*. The Federation's accusation could only have been made by a preservationist, not a conservationist. Only a preservationist would fail to admit that being a good steward of nature costs money, allocates resources, and requires a strong economy. Only a preservationist would object to orderly development of America's energy resources. Only a preservationist would deny that resources— the very word resource means "a source of supply or support"—are for the use and enjoyment of people.

All the changes that Watt brought in his first year can be understood in a single, simple concept: conservation. Watt dethroned preservationism as the ruling force of Interior and established conservation, wise use, as its ✱ guiding principle. Everything Watt has done can be seen in that basic framework: who he kept and who he fired, policies he repudiated and policies he installed, special interests he courted and those he merely listened to, and all his public statements. Watt makes sense as a conservationist rather than a preservationist.

Just as Watt's first six months had been dedicated to taming the bureaucracy and his second six months to outreach, so his third six months was devoted to completing the changes, implementing the Watt policy at the deepest level before the storms of the 1982 Congressional elections. As Executive Assistant Steve Shipley put it, "We actually had to get everything done in the first four or five months of 1982 because the election campaign was obviously going to heat up early." Watt told his crew, "Make sure you get everything done that will rock the boat before April first." It got done. In early June of 1982, Watt told me, "From now on, it's just maintaining and managing, no big changes." The range of things that got done between January first and April first of 1982 is astonishing.

One of the first orders of 1982 business was to attack royalty under-payments to the federal government for oil and gas production on public lands. January 22, 1982, Watt delivered the report of the Linowes Commission to President Reagan. David F. Linowes, chairman of the commission Watt named to study oil theft and underpayments, pointed out that "collection of these royalties is on the honor system," and that "only a handful of audits have been conducted and they have revealed significant underpayments.Site security is deficient. Theft of oil is common." Watt told the President he favored all 60 recommendations of the Linowes Commission, including doubling its inspector force and other measures to improve Interior Department checks on royalty payments. Watt acted immediately on the Commission's recommendation to establish a Minerals Management Service to monitor royalties, a job previously done by the science-oriented U.S. Geological Survey.

The Linowes Commission, formally the Commission on Fiscal Accountability of the Nation's Energy Resources, revealed in its 267-page report that many firms audited were found to owe additional royalties, including El Paso Natural Gas Company, Conoco, Texaco, Ocean, Mobil, Getty, Cabot, Sun, Amoco, and Chevron. Watt said changes in policy would add from $200 to $600 million in annual royalties. "Look-back" audits were being conducted at 25 oil companies which pay 85 percent of the royalties on the 17,600 federal or Indian leases in effect in 27 states.

President Reagan told reporters that it was "unconscionable" that previous administrations had relied on the outdated collection system for so long, and approved penalties for future violators. Secretary Watt asked Congress for authority to prosecute truck operators who remove oil from federal or Indian lands without proper sale documents, and for power to impose civil penalties of as much as $10,000 for each violation in cases where companies don't adequately protect oil fields or tank farms against theft. Democratic Representative from Illinois Sidney Yates told Linowes that previous Interior Secretaries "did not have the political courage to move forward" on oil theft and royalty protection. These moves revealed Watt as one of the toughest regulators ever to sit in the Interior Secretary's chair.

February 21, 1982, Secretary Watt took the wilderness bull by the horns on a *Meet the Press* broadcast. When asked about his feelings about opening up wilderness areas to oil exploration, Watt replied, "This week I will ask Congress to quickly adopt new legislation that would prohibit the drilling or mining in the wilderness to the end of the century." There would be only one exception: "If there is an urgent national need, the President should then with the concurrence of Congress, be allowed to withdraw those few acres that might be needed to meet the national need." February 24, Representative Manuel Lujan of New Mexico, ranking minority member of the House Interior and Insular Affairs Committee, introduced the Reagan Administration's Wilderness Protection Act, which was numbered House Resolution 5603.

Immediate reaction was delight: Wilderness Society head William A. Turnage said, "We congratulate the administration. It is a victory for the American people and for wilderness preservation. . . . It was Secretary Watt who first raised the threat to wilderness. This is a complete turnaround in administration policy." Marion Edey of the League of Conservation Voters said, "Watt's announcement is incredible. Even if there's some weird twist, even if he just wants that kind of camouflage, just being pro-wilderness, it is an important sign."

Watt's proposal was: Until the next century, no development requiring surface occupancy for mining, oil and gas, mineral and geothermal leasing could be done in (a) existing wilderness, (b) areas under study for possible wilderness designation, (c) lands recommended for wilderness under the Forest Service RARE II plan, and (d) Bureau of Land Management lands identified as wilderness study areas in the lower 48 United States. Slant drilling with no surface occupancy would still be allowed.

What was left of the 1964 Wilderness Act's 20-year exploration and development "window" ending December 31, 1983, would be eliminated immediately. Lands being studied as possible wilderness would become subject to deadlines: if Congress did not act by officially dedicating the study areas as wilderness, they would revert to multiple use, some in 1985, others in 1988. This would end the uncertainty for many industries about raw material supply and investment decisions.

The President could permit specific mineral development in specific wilderness areas in the event of an "urgent national need," with the consent of Congress. Buffer zones around wilderness would be forbidden to insure that non-wilderness use could continue on lands not officially designated wilderness by Congress, a move that would prevent the "endless Buffer Zone" syndrome and finally answer the question "How big is a wilderness?" Mineral inventories would be permitted in all wilderness areas, including seismic studies, core sampling and other operations not requiring the construction of roads, "if conducted in a manner compatible with preservation of the wilderness environment." National Park and National Wildlife Refuge areas would continue under existing laws, so that wilderness within their boundaries could not be considered for leasing, exploration, and development after the year 2000.

When these details were released, the usual environmentalist distortions began. Tim Mahoney, Washington Sierra Club lobbyist, called Watt's proposal "A Trojan Horse" that would preempt designation of future wilderness areas. Congressman John Seiberling, National Parks and Public Lands Subcommittee chairman, called the bill "the worst wilderness legislation I've ever seen. It would mean the wilderness system would continue only at the discretion of the President." Charles M. Clusen of the Wilderness Society called it "a wilderness destruction bill."

A fascinating aspect of the press coverage was its interpretation that Watt's Wilderness Protection Act was somehow a change of policy. The Associated Press, referring to Watt's *Meet The Press* statement, said, "Until Sunday's announcement Watt had favored just the opposite approach." One wonders what they had been reading to come to such a conclusion. Watt had never advocated surface occupancy leases, but the press said he did. Watt had issued no surface occupancy leases, but the press never mentioned a distinction between the types of leases. Watt had called for mineral inventories, but the press did not distinguish between inventories and drilling or mining. In fact, the Wilderness Protection Act was Watt's request that Congress give their stamp of approval to the policies he had from the day of his confirmation hearing. The *Anchorage Times* in Alaska jumped on the Associated Press for their failure to comprehend Watt's real policy: "It is dismaying that national press associations such as the Associated Press should ignore certain facts. It appears that the environmental groups have managed to brainwash some reporters."

A few days later, environmentalist money came to light: dozens of contracts for studies of wildlife, land management and other technical assessments had been shifted during the Carter Administration from Interior professionals and university scientists to environmentalist groups. Hundreds of thousands of dollars were flowing each year to private lobbying organizations such as the Sierra Club and the Audubon Society from the taxpayer's pocket. Watt ordered an independent survey of the situation, and when the findings were in, he cancelled every contract from the Department of the Interior to any environmentalist group.

By March, some Reagan Administration energy initiatives were showing results. Dr. Daniel Miller, Watt's Assistant Secretary for Energy and Minerals told me:

The national election of 1980 brought about changes that were needed just in time to prevent further severe deterioration of the nation's economic base. Before 1980, energy exploration efforts by industry were inhibited through massive land withdrawals that denied access to public lands.

Lease sales were cancelled, lease applications were never processed and a morass of rules and regulations made seismic and drilling operations almost impossible. Since President Reagan's decontrol of oil prices, the petroleum industry has accomplished some remarkable achievements: Seismic crew activity is up more than 30 percent; about 4,500 drilling rigs are operating; more than 78,000 test holes were drilled in 1981, a 26 percent increase over 1980; more than 39,000 wells were completed as oil and/or gas producers, an increase of 40 percent; some 9,331 wildcat wells were drilled, a 25 percent increase; new oil reserves discovered in the United States are up more than 100 percent over 1980; the federal government's total receipts from all mineral production rose from $4.8 billion in 1980 to nearly $11 billion in 1981; royalties on oil and gas alone rose from $637 million in 1980 to $823 million in 1981; and the federal government's policies toward energy management are clearly perceived to be more stable than in the past.

Secretary Watt's own comments on our energy problems: "We do not have a shortage in energy resources. We have had a shortage in the will to manage those resources for the benefit of America and Americans."

James G. Watt's Secretariat was the first to begin with an Assistant Secretary for Territorial and International Affairs. Formerly a Director-level job, the new Office of Assistant Secretary was established by Secretarial Order No. 3046 of February 14, 1980, during the last year of the Carter Administration. Created in recognition that much of the Pacific Ocean was an "American Lake" coveted by the Russians, the new office is responsible for promoting the economic, social, and political development of America's far-flung territories and trusts, and the Assistant Secretary serves as a focal point for analysis, development and review of Interior's international activities, supporting U.S. foreign policy with expertise in natural resources.

The man Watt picked for this sensitive position is Pedro A. Sanjuan. Sanjuan is a mustachioed James-Bond-handsome man of 52 with silvering temples and achievements worthy of a Renaissance man. His father was a composer and conductor, founded Cuba's Havana Philharmonic in the 1920s, and was music director of the Madrid Symphony Orchestra in Spain. Sanjuan lived through the Spanish Civil War's early days and fled with his family to refuges in Europe and the United States. He is fluent in nine languages, has taught Russian at university level and is widely read in the literature of five cultures. He was graduated Phi Beta Kappa from Wofford College in South Carolina, won a Master's degree from the Harvard University Russian Program, and took advanced studies at Columbia, Rutgers, and the Asia Institute. He has served on the faculty of Tufts University, has been a journalist, a newspaper editor, an educational television director, Deputy Chief of Protocol for the State Department, Deputy Director of the Law of the Sea Task Force and of Policy Plans in the International Security Affairs Bureau, and has served on detail to the Carter White House staff. Watt said of him, "His diplomatic experience and his extensive work with developing nations make him superbly qualified for this position"—during Africa's rush to independence in the 1960s, Sanjuan had helped their emerging nations set up embassies in the United States. There is hardly a place in the world he has not been.

Sanjuan describes his job:

Interior has two major types of territories to deal with. First are the Flag Territories, which are part of the United States, including Guam, American Samoa and the Virgin Islands, which are being joined by the Commonwealth of the Northern Mariana Islands. Second is the Trust Territory of the Pacific Islands, which prior to World War II was a Japanese Mandate, but after 1945 was assigned by the United Nations to the United States as a strategic Trust with the idea that they would one day become independent. A Compact is now being negotiated that would divide Micronesia into three new nations, The Marshall Islands, The Republic of Palau, and the Federated States of Micronesia which include Ponape, Truk, Yap, and several other islands. The entities would be fully self-governing in Free Associated Status, with the United States retaining defense responsibilities.

The Soviet Union is closely watching how the United States handles this time of change in the Pacific, eager to fill any power vacuum left by an American withdrawal. The Kremlin has already made numerous advances into the Pacific, but has been repeatedly snubbed by island governments that have refused all offers of aid and even closed their ports to Russian cruise ships in protest of the invasion of Afghanistan, despite their desperate need for tourist revenues. Sanjuan points out,

Most Pacific Island cultures share our Christian and Western values. Their native societies were and are innately conservative. These people are exceedingly distrustful of communists of any kind, but have tolerated new Chinese embassies while rejecting the Russians, whom they see as aggressive and expansionist. The Pacific Islands are unique in the Third World in that their Universities are not full of Marxists and other socialists—you can hardly find a Marxist in our Territories.

I am organizing to provide the technical assistance that will prepare these Island people as much as possible for the responsibilities of nationhood—and also to prepare Congress as well to realize what they're dealing with, because I don't think they yet know. We use Interior's Management By Objectives system, but we have totally adapted it to our needs; it's helpful to bring decisiveness to what was previously a rather tenuous idea of management in the Territories.

I was particularly interested in Pedro Sanjuan's opinion of Jim Watt. He is as unlike the cowboy Cabinet officer as one can be, a veritable study in contrasts—Watt's direct manner and Sanjuan's continental European sophistication of thought.

I am absolutely not a sycophant. I have told off Presidents. But you cannot relate to the Secretary exclusively on a bureaucratic level, although that was my first impulse. You have to deal with him on human terms as he is a preeminently human being. He is a breath of fresh air in this musty town. He radiates honesty and sincerity; there is nothing sham about him.

He cannot quote Milton or Cervantes, but there is something uplifting and contagious about Jim Watt. It is a tribute that even in our Monday morning eight o'clock meetings, which are difficult at best, people eagerly look forward to seeing him enter the room. The moment he gets there the cobwebs are removed from your eyes. Within a minute he always says something spectacular or fascinating or innovative or original.

The nation will come to realize that Watt is a man of tremendous optimism. He really thinks he can change government for the better. That's a totally absurd idea to anyone who has lived in Washington long; it's impossible. But Jim Watt has done it. And that's what so many of his critics hold against him. He has made a difference, and that's the ultimate insult to the power-hungry.

Among the power-hungry that Watt insulted were Congressional staffs who had been poking and pilfering through Interior at liberty for many years. Staff members of hostile Democratic Congressmen had made a practice of strolling through the halls of Interior, ransacking files—even private ones—stealing in-work memoranda, spreading rumors and creating misunderstandings. In early 1982, Watt got tired of the constant harrassment and threw them all out.

Immediate outraged responses came from Congressmen Udall and Seiberling, among others. The gist of their message was, "Direct staff-to-staff contact is essential to Congress's Constitutional duty to provide oversight to the Department of the Interior. You are in direct violation of the United States Constitution."

Watt politely replied, "The Department of the Interior will be happy to answer any question on any subject from any Congressman. Submit your questions in writing and you will receive a prompt and complete reply." This satisfied the Constitution, but it did not satisfy the Democrats.

At the February 8, 1982, Monday morning staff meeting, Watt told his political appointees how to enforce his order forbidding Congressional staffs from roaming the Interior building.

We have no secrets, first and foremost, so don't hold anything back that is requested.Anything specific that any committee member wishes to know, give them a speedy and complete answer. But make sure you have a written question first. Do not give answers over the telephone and do not accept invitations to special closed meetings. Closed government has been used to distort what we are doing so we want *everything* between us and Congress in the open. We want everything on the record; if it's written, it's on the record. If Congress asks a question, tell the whole nation; when you give the answer, tell the whole nation. We're not going to allow government in the dark of night anymore. We're not going to allow "fishing expeditions" by Congressional staffers anymore. We're not going to allow our opponents to cash in on public ignorance any more. We're going to have government in the sunshine. If Congress wants to fight against government in the sunshine, we'll fight them.

Watt told his people to handle any flak from Congressmen by insisting on full public hearings on the subject, with emphasis on the *public*. He knew that those of wrongful intent would not want their dirty linen aired in public, and that those wishing legitimate oversight information would not object to writing their questions for public scrutiny. It was a bold and ingenious solution to an age-old problem in the checks and balances of American government, and it utterly stopped a major source of upset and distortion.

Incidentally, it was during this Monday morning staff meeting that I heard Watt come closest to making an off-color remark that anyone can recall: Russ Dickenson, Director of the National Park Service, asked what to do in the event that hostile Congressmen hearing his testimony persisted in complaining about Watt's "government in the sunshine," arms-length policy toward oversight. Watt replied,

Russ, you and I know that because we made our changes administratively and sent no big legislative package to Congress that their staffs have nothing to do and just come up here to waste Interior's time and look for trouble. That's the real issue, and if they get tough with you, insist on *weekend* hearings with no breaks. We'll see then who has the biggest bladder—because that's about all of the value that comes out of debating this issue.

By April, 1982, the changes were complete. The Watt policy was infused into every last pore of the Department of the Interior. Watt had heeled the vast bureaucracy in less than 18 months to a new heading—marching forward once again toward conservation after years of preservationist regression.

Doug Baldwin, Watt's Director of Public Affairs, sent me a clipping from Nevada's *Reno Gazette Journal* indicative of the new direction. A Bureau of Land Management official in Battle Mountain, Nevada, had noted how the Management By Objectives system and the "good neighbor" policy was working in his area: Michael Mitchel told a reporter, "It's the best thing that's happened to us since I started with the Bureau. The higher-ups now teach us to go out and see the people instead of writing letters to them. They're telling us they want to delegate authority and it's making our job more fun and easier."

The first few months of 1982 also brought raging controversies over Watt: John Dingell's House Energy and Commerce Committee cited Watt for contempt of Congress, raising the remote possibility that the Secretary might actually go to jail. The contempt vote was split 23 to 19 along almost exclusively party lines. The Committee had demanded that Watt turn over to them more than 200 documents on Canadian energy policy and its impact on U.S. firms, but on President Reagan's orders and the Justice Department's advice, Watt refused to surrender a few documents, citing executive privilege. Dingell was enraged and pushed the contempt citation through the committee. Under an obscure rule Watt might be taken into custody by the sergeant-at-arms, tried on the House floor and imprisoned for the remainder of the Congressional session. In 1975 a similar vote was taken against Secretary of State Henry Kissinger for refusing to surrender information on U.S. covert operations abroad. Those charges were dropped before the full House voted and, likewise, Watt's contempt citation came to nothing and the issue was resolved without Watt going to jail.

Then the "Party Flap" arose over two events held in December 1981 at the former home of Robert E. Lee, which is now a national memorial known as Arlington House, an antebellum residence of the Custis and Lee families overlooking the Potomac River and Washington. One event was a $6,912 cocktail party for 200 government officials, the other was a $1,921 breakfast hosted by Watt's wife Leilani for 20 Cabinet wives and others. Watt used no taxpayers' money, but billed a special account made up of donated funds for both gatherings, and the General Accounting Office ruled that Watt could use the $4,500 remaining in Interior's appropriated entertainment budget for the cocktail party, but the other costs would have to be paid for by Watt himself. Congressman Edward Markey ordered Watt to show up at an inquiry "with checkbook in hand," but Watt declined the invitation. Watt reviewed the applicable laws, rules, and regulations concerning his actions and determined that he was perfectly within the spirit and letter of the Secretary's privileges in holding the events when and where he did. Previous administrations had used the facility for identical purposes with no furor, raising the likelihood that this flap was just another way for his opponents to harrass Jim Watt. Watt refused to budge from his assertion of propriety and billed the events as he originally planned. Opponents seem to have lost interest in the ruckus, as nothing further came of it.

Watt was tossed on the griddle again in March when he held up approval of the proposed Vietnam Veterans Memorial in Washington D.C. The winning design for the memorial was chosen from 1,420 entries by judges for the private Vietnam Veterans Memorial Fund, and was submitted by a 22-year-old Yale undergraduate named Maya Ying Lin. Her design consisted of two 200-foot-long slabs of black granite laid in the ground in the shape of a huge V, with the surrounding ground sloping down toward the point. One juror described it as, "In a city of white memorials rising, this will be a dark memorial receding." Critics called it a pit, a "hole in the ground," and James H. Webb, Jr., a decorated ex-Marine and author of the Vietnam War novel *Fields of Fire*, resigned from the sponsoring committee because the design excluded traditional memorial symbols like the flag, predicting that the monument would become "a wailing wall for future anti-draft protestors and demonstrations." A compromise emerged from a meeting on Capitol Hill allowing an American flag and statue of a serviceman to be added to the design. Watt still refused to allow ground-breaking to begin, insisting that local commissions on planning and the fine arts approve the design first. Finally in March, the fine arts commission approved the design and Watt gave his approval for construction to begin.

As April progressed and the changes finally came in place, less and less press notice centered around the anti-Watt campaign. A few loose ends of policy such as Watt's final Offshore Oil and Gas leasing proposal attracted media attention, but the heavy furor sank to a dull roar in the background. Trivia began to appear in the press: someone noticed that the name of the Water and Power Resources Service had been changed back to the original Bureau of Reclamation and the remark rated a paragraph in one Western newspaper. I asked Watt why he had made the change, and he joked, "I was never smart enough to learn the other name." Pressed for the real reason, he said,

The new title was created by the Carter Administration to emphasize that there would be no more reclamation of any new lands, that they would just be providing service for what had already been built and never reclaim anything more for agriculture and human use—just the old preservationist line about free-flowing rivers, nature first, and no growth. I decided to change the name back when I took office because we are going to reclaim lands, we are going to be conservationists like Teddy Roosevelt who created the Bureau in the first place.

In May, the management of the Department of the Interior shifted gears into operating mode. There were no more changes to be made prior to the election. Now routine items filled the agenda and among them was a meeting of the National Public Lands Advisory Council Watt had appointed in 1981. The makeup of this Council came under heavy attack from environmentalists, since Watt had filled most positions with a representative of one or another commodity producer and not a single person from a preservationist group had been invited to join. The 21 charter members of the Council came from the fields of real estate development and investment, mining, ranching, petroleum, logging, farming, woolgrowing, and other basic raw materials interests. A few seats were filled with service sector advisors: Ben Avery of Phoenix, Arizona, is a journalist. He received the Arizona Wildlife Federation's Conservationist of the Year Award in 1973 for his outdoor and political writing for the *Arizona Republic*, where he has worked 38 years. John E. Butcher of Logan, Utah, is a Professor of Animal Science at Utah State University and is a Fellow of the American Association for the Advancement of Science. Paula P. Easley of Anchorage, Alaska, is the Executive Director of the Alaska Resource Development Council, Inc., Alaska's largest citizens group devoted to balancing the interests of fishermen, foresters, miners, energy users, and conservationists. Raymond L. Friedlob of Denver, Colorado, is an attorney specializing in the practice of federal securities and taxation law. He is an Adjunct Professor of Tax and Securities Law at the University of Denver College of Law. Verna M. Green of Helena, Montana, is an investment broker and member of Business and Professional Women. David Little of Emmett, Idaho, is a State Senator, chairing the Senate Finance Committee, and is also a rancher, so he doesn't really count as a non-commodity producer. Guy T. McBride of Golden, Colorado, is the President and a Professor of Mineral Engineering of the Colorado School of Mines. B. Wells O'Brien of Reno, Nevada, is an attorney.

I asked Watt about the environmentalist attacks on his Public Lands selections, and he said:

They are absolutely right. I stacked the deck. When I go to give speeches to the producers and working people of America, I tell them, "You bet I filled every seat with someone who is responsible for the economic well-being of thousands of people. You bet I didn't ask a single preservationist to serve who has no obligation to meet a payroll, or put food on peoples' tables, or to support the nation's material well-being. Every individual I picked is an outstanding conservationist and not one of them is a preservationist." And you know, after listening to their advice and following it, the world hasn't come to an end, and we haven't had a single environmental catastrophe. In fact, our environmental record is one of the best there is for a single year. But the environmentalists don't want to talk about that, they just want to wring their hands and talk about "what if?"

More and more, Watt's duties turned to politics. The 1982 Congressional campaign was kicked off with the Oregon primary election in May. Watt's field visits on official business were soon nearly matched in number by trips at Republican Party expense for political rallies and fundraisers. The President expected every Cabinet member to devote 15 days to stumping for Republican candidates and causes. Jim and Leilani Watt became a traveling team again, just as during the outreach program.

Watt's Republican Party speech rhetoric was honed to a fine edge as Democratic opponents began to zero in on Watt's Interior policy as a campaign issue. "We will never compromise, we will never retreat," Watt told the GOP faithful in town after town. Some of the one-liners from these speeches would make up a reasonably accurate verbal sketch of the Watt philosophy. Here they are, gathered together in a small compendium:

I believe in proper management of natural resources so human resources will be given their proper place in creation.

Those of us in the conservative movement have a mission: our motto should be "Whatever It Takes.

We must, as conservatives, be willing to have confrontation to bring about the changes to restore America's greatness.

A conservative brings greatness by championing political liberty and the freedom to love God. A conservative is compassionate and strong, caring and willing to bring about change.

In making environmental decisions, I view every issue from the basis of America: will that decision create jobs in the private sector, will they enhance our environment, will they improve our national security so that we might have political liberty and spiritual freedom?

There will be no retreat, there will be no backing down, there will be no compromise. We will win.

Liberals don't know what stewardship really is. Liberals know how to take, but they don't know how to take care.

We have never had an energy crisis in America. Our soil contains energy reserves to last many centuries at a substantial rate of growth. We have had a crisis in government. There was no energy crisis, there was an energy production crisis.

The Reagan Administration has the finest environmental record ever put together—because we care.

As conservatives, we believe in people; liberals believe in institutions. Liberals believe in centralized socialistic planning to run your life, and I won't stand for that.

When I took office, I found too much air and water pollution and national parks deteriorated to a shameful state. The vast public lands were not managed for the benefit of us. They'd been set aside, stifling economic activity.

America can't afford the yo-yo economics we've had the last several years. When we came into power we faced interest rates of 20 percent and inflation in the double digits. We can't let liberals bring us back to that economic course.

A good conservationist knows how to use the lands wisely as well as preserve them.

Watt has earned a reputation for entering the lion's den without fear or trembling, having addressed numerous hostile environmentalist audiences, dishing out as good as he takes in the verbal slug-fests of question-and-answer sessions. In Yosemite once, a Sierra Clubber rose and shouted angrily in response to a Watt remark about improving access to the National Parks, "You are not speaking to the real problem. The real problem is people and the degradation they bring to the National Park resource. We have to *prevent* people from coming here, not make it easier for them" Without missing a beat, Watt shot back, "Fine, you be the first one to stay away."

In Arizona, Watt responded to other complaints. "I'm meeting with my state directors Friday morning," Watt told one utility official who had cited a problem in dealing with Interior underlings. "If that attitude prevails, as you say, I assure you it won't Friday afternoon."

Watt became an awesome figure in his own Department because of his management skills and his personal style. Stan Hulett, Watt's Director of Congressional and Legislative Affairs, says:

Watt began by using shock techniques to draw people out. He tends to ask questions and raise issues that people don't think should be raised. He tends to throw out an idea and see if anyone will bite on it. When we're in meetings, he'll get two people going at each other, to use management-by-conflict methods to make sure both sides of an issue are heard. And sometimes he'll come at you as if he disagrees with your idea just to see if you can defend it on its merits or how much you really believe in it. But there's nothing at all sly or devious about it. If you ask him if he's just testing you, and he is, he'll say yes. He's frank. He says what he thinks. If Jim Watt has a dagger for you, it's not up his sleeve, it's out on the desk.

Tom DeRocco, Doug Baldwin's Deputy Director of Public Affairs says:

Watt is a genuine environmentalist who looks beyond the horizon. He understands preserving resources for their natural values and he understands wisely using resources for human well being. He wants to inventory lands for resources so the country can chart a sensible course when shortages occur in the future, rather than suffering mass pillage in a panic.

Robin West, Assistant Secretary for Policy, Budget and Administration, says, "Watt is terribly candid. He's open to ideas. You can hit him cold with something he's never heard of before and he doesn't flinch or close his mind: he looks. This man is not administering the Department, he's governing it."

And through it all, Leilani Watt is probably the single person in the world who really knows who Jim Watt is. She has said of the controversy surrounding her husband:

It has taken its toll. It would be macho to say he has a tough hide and it doesn't bother him, but it does. The personal insults and the attacks on his religious beliefs are unfair, and it gets to him. He is a very human being and he has feelings the same as everyone. He has his down times. But he is basically a happy person and he doesn't stay down long. He loves life and he loves his work and he loves his country. Jim's closeness to God gives him great spiritual strength, so he is resilient, bouyant, the eternal optimist, and that enables him to take the punishment. Jim Watt is a very special man, and I love him deeply. I think that when America comes to know and understand what he is really doing for his country, they will love him too.

As the political season of 1982 wafted its first breezes over the Potomac, Jim and Leilani one evening began to feel cooped up with all their security, and decided to give their Secret Service people the slip. Jim says, "Every now and then we break out and do something without our security, just so we can feel like a free soul." They went to a Washington-area Sears Roebuck retail store to pick up some small household items, and were standing in line at the cash register waiting to be checked out. A man walked up to Watt and said, "Are you who I think you are?"

"Well, who do you think I am?" asked Watt.

"Well, are you the Secretary of the Interior?"

"Yeah," admitted Watt.

The passerby smiled and said, "Man, you're in a tough position."

"Yeah, it sure is tough," replied Watt, making polite chit-chat.

"You were obviously picked because you're tough enough to take the abuse," the stranger ventured.

"That's right."

"You're obviously the right man in the right place at the right time."

"I hope so," said Watt. "We're making a lot of changes and a lot of progress."

"So I've read," the man went on, "and I hate to tell you this, but it's going to get a lot worse."

"What do you mean by that?" asked Watt, startled.

"You've won just about all your issues from what I can tell, and the other side from now on is going to have to get an equalizer."

Leilani looked alarmed and Jim stiffened. His memory raced back to when he was a small boy walking with his father and first saw a billy club hanging from the service belt of the town policeman. He had asked, "What's that thing?" and the cop pulled it out and showed it to him, saying, "Son, when I meet a bad man who's bigger than me, I take this out and then we're equal, so I call it my equalizer." Another incident flashed: One of the adult Watt's security guards had told the newly confirmed Secretary of the Interior, "Wait a moment, Mr. Secretary, I have to get my equalizer," and strapped on his handgun.

The stranger stood still for a moment, looking puzzled at Watt's discomfort, then smiled and said, "I don't know what it will be, but I'm sure they're looking for one." He walked away, calling over his shoulder, "Good luck," and vanished among the evening shoppers.

The conversation still lingered the next morning at the eight o'clock Monday staff meeting. Watt told his political appointees the story of his meeting with this unknown man, and wove a parable around it.

We won everything we had to last year. This is going to be a political year, and we've got to be careful because the opposition will be looking for an equalizer. And we don't know what that equalizer might be. If they can't get me, maybe they'll try to get you. It could be something out of your private life, your financial affairs, double-dipping on a hotel bill, or messing around privately. So you folks have to be supercareful. They're looking for an equalizer to get me, and if they can't find it directly, they may use you as an equalizer to get me, and I wouldn't want you people to be hurt because of me. You're my friends, and I wanted to give you fair warning. All of you know politics: they don't fight somebody who's not powerful. Keep doing a good job and be careful.

In June 1982, the Watt Secretariat passed that magic number of 18 months, that magic number in Washington testing whether a new Administration can effectively put its programs in place. The Reagan Administration's Department of the Interior had passed the test. And the opposition was busy looking for an equalizer.

CHAPTER 14
THE NEW BEGINNING

> *Life is either a daring adventure or it is nothing at all!*
>
> ——Helen Keller

The most basic difference between James G. Watt and his environmentalist foes is their vision of the future. Watt is optimistic about the future and environmentalists tend to be pessimistic. This is the basic antagonism from which spring all their contrary goals, policies, preferred forms of government, and the other specific points of contention. Watt sees a future of human action, risk and danger, of the will to overcome and solve problems, of liberty and plenty derived from proper management of our natural and human resources. Environmentalists, as demonstrated by their literature, see a future of dwindling resources and growing scarcity, of withdrawal from resource management in favor of resource preservation, and of authoritarian government deciding how the scarcity will be shared. It is well known that visions of the future tend to become self-fulfilling prophecies. The question facing us is, which vision shall we, America, live by?

Environmentalist literature is the clearest, most convincing source by which to demonstrate their vision of the future. Probably the classic study from the ranks of environmentalism is *The Limits to Growth* by Donella and Dennis Meadows, Jørgen Randers, and William Behrens, sponsored by The Club of Rome, a group of industrialists, educators and bureaucrats interested in global systems of economics, politics, society, and resource use. The vision of the future that came out of this study is well summarized in this publisher's description: "A world where industrial production has sunk to zero. Where population has suffered a catastrophic decline. Where the air, sea and land are polluted beyond redemption. Where civilization is a distant memory." This is the acme of pessimism.

The book was essentially a study based on computer models of the world system that predicted total ruin for civilization as a result of pollution and depletion of resources within the next hundred years. This horrifying image has been used as a justification for various methods of controlling the American economy by numerous environmentalist groups, despite serious flaws discovered in the study's basic assumptions and methodology. A study by Herman Kahn and the Hudson Institute found that even assuming no advances in efficiency, our present growth rate would not deplete even basic resources for 300 to 1,000 years, and that foreseeable improvements in technology indicate a sustainable growth economy for long periods of time. This study, entitled *The Next 200 Years*, also found that affluence lowers population growth quite effectively with no regulation at all: wealthier nations all demonstrate declining birthrates.

Nonetheless, the vision of impending doom and inevitable scarcity riveted many environmentalists, and out of this basic assumption about the future certain unavoidable conclusions were drawn, one of them being that centralized government control was a logical outgrowth of austerity. The paradigm of this argument was stated by British historian Arnold Toynbee in the April 14, 1974, issue of the *London Observer*: "The future austerity will be perennial and it will become progressively more severe. What then? . . . Within each of the beleaguered 'developed' countries there will be a bitter struggle for the control of their diminished resources.This struggle will have to be stopped. A new way of life—a severely regimented way—will have to be imposed by a ruthless authoritarian government." In such a "siege economy," Toynbee predicted, most private property would have to be nationalized.

Economist Robert L. Heilbroner prefigured this opinion in his 1973 book *An Inquiry Into the Human Prospect*: He wonders whether the "exigencies of the future . . . point to the conclusion that only an authoritarian, or possibly only a revolutionary, regime will be capable of mounting the immense task of social reorganization needed to escape catastrophe." He also muses whether we may have to face the prospect that "values and beliefs precious to us may be assaulted by overriding claims of human survival," and warns of "intolerable strains on the representative democratic political apparatus."

A staff member of the Conservation Foundation applied these intellectual speculations to concrete policy in a January 1975 newsletter article citing expert opinion:

A healthful and attractive urban environment "might have to be sustained to a considerable degree by coercion," write Martin and Margy Meyerson, both experts on urban planning. Most qualitative improvements in the environment— including pollution control, better transportation, more open space and recreation, decent housing—depend on public, collective actions, including not only taxation and funding support, but "regulation of behavior," or "requiring individuals or firms or agencies to refrain from previous practices—practices they have come to regard from habitual usage as freedoms."

The idea of coercion seeped into environmentalist philosophy slowly at first, but was soon embraced aggressively. The Friends of the Earth stated in an early publication, "We will strike lightly along the soft energy path. We will be less populous and more decentralized, less industrial and more agrarian. Our acquisitive consumer society must give way to a severe conserver society." However, it was not long before this implied coercion was stated by the group in unmistakable police-state terms: "Some day childbearing will be deemed a punishable crime unless the parents hold a government license. Or perhaps all potential parents will be required to use contraceptive chemicals, the government issuing antidotes to citizens chosen for childbearing."

Coercion is the dominant social metaphor of environmentalism, infecting even Garrett Hardin's much-reprinted classic, *The Tragedy of the Commons*. Biologist Hardin first compares the earth to a "commons," or pasture:

The tragedy of the commons develops in this way. Picture a pasture open to all. It is to be expected that each herdsman will try to keep as many cattle as possible on the commons. Such an arrangement may work reasonably satisfactorily for centuries because tribal wars, poaching, and disease keep the numbers of both man and beast well below the carrying capacity of the land. Finally, however, comes the day of reckoning, that is, the day when the long-desired goal of social stability becomes a reality. At this point, the inherent logic of the commons remorselessly generates tragedy."

After numerous examples of how our air and water are commons and our National Parks are commons, Hardin comes to the point: "The social arrangements that produce responsibility are arrangements that create coercion, of some sort." The solution to the tragedy of the commons, he tells us, is "mutual coercion, mutually agreed upon." He admits that "To say that we mutually agree to coercion is not to say that we are required to enjoy it, or even to pretend we enjoy it."

In *Environmental Politics*, edited by Stuart S. Nagel, environmentalist William Ophuls defined the central philosophy of the environmental movement in clear, precise language of chilling honesty:

In a situation of ecological scarcity . . . the individualistic basis of society, the concept of inalienable rights, the purely self-defined pursuit of happiness, liberty as maximum freedom of action, and laissez-faire itself all require abandonment or major modification if we wish to avoid inexorable environmental degradation and perhaps extinction as a civilization. We must therefore question whether democracy as we know it can survive.

The problem that the tragedy of the commons forces us to confront is, in fact, the core issue of political philosophy: how to protect or advance the

interests of the collectivity as a whole when the individuals that make it up
. . . behave in a selfish, greedy and quarrelsome fashion. The only answer is
a sufficient measure of coercion.

Ophuls here set the tone for the entire intellectual structure of the
environmental movement. Future scarcity is the basic assumption. Coercion is
the logical solution. Everything we have discussed in this book falls into place
at the deepest level here in Ophuls' frank admission: fear of environmental
degradation, emotional outbursts against industry, preservationism, regulationism,
alarmism in the media, environmentalist group political activism, severe
restrictions on resource use, centralized federal control, recruitment of political supporters in a thrust for environmentalist power—it all makes sense in
terms of the two basic assumptions of future scarcity and government coercion.
It should be plain from Ophuls' language that among the casualties of an
environmentalist victory would be U.S. values and documents such as the
Declaration of Independence and the Constitution.

Competent and serious scientists such as Paul B. Sears continually
refer to ecology as "a subversive science." In fact, Sears published a paper in
BioScience, July 1964, entitled, "Ecology—A Subversive Subject," which
began: "My choice of title is not facetious. I wish to explore a question of
growing concern. Is ecology a phase of science of limited interest and utility?
Or, if taken seriously as an instrument for the long-run welfare of mankind,
would it endanger the assumptions and practices accepted by modern societies, whatever their doctrinal commitments?" Sears answered the question in
favor of the latter, that ecology is indeed a subject subversive of basic
American values if taken "seriously." Another scientist, Paul Shepard, asserted in his essay *Ecology and Man—A Viewpoint* that "The ideological status
of ecology is that of a resistance movement. Its Rachel Carsons and Aldo
Leopolds are subversive."

It is difficult to take Rachel Carson for a subversive in anything but a
mild ideological way. Her idea of abandoning all agrichemicals may have been
revolutionary, but her recommended political methods of lobbying were not.
Nevertheless, the implicit goals of environmentalism to drastically reduce or
dismantle industrial civilization and to impose a fundamentally coercive form
of government on America are real, even though they tend to be hidden in the
complex structure of the movement. It is all too easy for middle-range liberal
environmental groups to use radical group actions as a spearhead for their own
drives and to make their own actions and demands seem reasonable by
comparison, while relentlessly advancing the movement's overall goals. Time
and again, industrial firms have expressed intense frustration with this hydra-
headed nature of the environmental movement, spending weeks negotiating
with one faction only to wake up and find that another has bombed their

power stations. Industry often mistakenly assumes there is some underlying conspiracy being worked by an unseen central control source with strings leading back to Moscow or Peking. Nothing could be further from the truth. My years of experience in the movement lead me to believe it is entirely home-grown. There are, however, definite linkages between all environmental groups, but industry's conspiracy theory comes from a failure to grasp the true nature of movements.

Anthropologists Luther Gerlach and Virginia Hine have studied movements for nearly 20 years and in numerous scholarly journals have spelled out their actual workings. For one thing, movements do not work in the same way that ordinary business or bureaucratic organizations do, with their specialized departments and a hierarchy of leaders necessary to the functioning of the whole. Movements consist of many autonomous groups, some national, some local, many loose ad hoc groups (so many that Alvin Toffler called movements "adhocracies"), many egalitarian, face-to-face groups here today and gone or reorganized tomorrow, and even some organized according to the conventional bureaucratic hierarchy of command such as the National Wildlife Federation and the Sierra Club.

For another thing, movements do not have a single paramount leader; you can't suppress a movement by, for example, jailing or killing some top dog—there are always new talented leaders waiting to fill the gaps. There is no one person who can control a movement or even speak for it all. Each segment, each faction, has its own leader, its own preferred tactics, and its own followers. But all groups in a movement do have at least three things in common: one, an ideology which acts as the "glue" that binds the movement together; two, commitment to that ideology; and three, they all require opposition as a force against which to unite their disparate segments. Movements actively seek out opponents and provoke attacks, then use the attacks to gain greater commitment from members and sympathizers, as James Watt discovered the hard way. As Gerlach and Hine put it, "This fact, little understood a few years ago, is now sufficiently obvious to have crept into the headlines of newspaper stories. . . . This kind of mutual escalation of opposition and commitment is a hard fact of movement dynamics and a powerful weapon in the hands of those who understand it."

Movements also behave as *networks* of person-to-person linkages. Some of these linkages in the environmental movement can be found in overlapping memberships. Feuds and dissension in environmental ranks have produced a number of overlapping memberships, such as those that emerged from a heated election of Sierra Club officers in the spring of 1969 when David Brower's radical faction was ousted and quickly founded the Friends of the Earth. Many Sierra Club members happily joined Brower's new group *and* remained active in the Sierra Club. Splinter groups, far from being a weakness in the organization of the environmental movement, are one of its main strengths, widening the overall fabric of the network and creating whole new tactics and constituencies.

The central idea, the ideology of the environmental movement is based on these few key concepts: the notion of an ecosystem, spaceship earth, earth as a closed system, limited resources, inevitable future scarcity, anti-technology, anti-civilization, anti-humanity and the need for centralized political control. What many Americans fail to notice is the fact that any one of these ideas can be clothed in rhetoric of many colors: conservative, middle-range, liberal, radical, revolutionary. The boundary between liberal reform and revolutionary takeover can be easily blurred in the public's eye. How many ways could you look at carving new parklands from the private homes of unwilling sellers? "Bounty hunter" laws that pay environmentalists to take industry to court? The Carter Administration's lockup of nearly three-quarters of our public lands from resource development? Environmentalist disruption of opposing testimony in public hearings? Anti-pesticide activists blowing up herbicide spray helicopters? Anti-civilization advocates blowing up power stations to prevent industrial and residential growth? Any one of these actions could be justified and rationalized, but all contain the seeds of radical social change and a more coercive form of government. Moderate environmental groups may talk a good line of only protecting the environment, but the social change goals of the whole movement are clearly set forth by their philosophers like Ophuls, Hardin, and Sears. The movement does indeed spread across a spectrum, but it is obvious that the whole structure is moving in a discernible direction (see Fig. 5 in Appendix). It is not so important where they stand as in which direction they are moving.

I have routinely quoted from the movement's philosophers during speaking engagements, which got me in trouble with the Sierra Club in 1980. Michael McCloskey, the Club's Executive Director sent me an angry letter complaining about my quotations from Ophuls, Hardin, and the Friends of the Earth, during an Alaskan speaking tour, saying, "By implica-tion, one would also be led to believe that the Sierra Club was committed 'to the destruction of industrial civilization.'" I responded by suggesting that he should "Leave no question where you stand. People can't tell; they constantly ask me if the Club is out to destroy America. I tell them to ask you." I also advised that the Sierra Club should "publicly disavow environmental advo-cates who by word or deed act to destroy industrial civilization." I had a good idea that McCloskey could not do without these violent extremists, and his reply was not disappointing: "We no more have an obligation to run around denouncing extremists using the environmental movement than Republicans and Democrats have an obligation to go around spending most of their time condemning the views of left or right wing extremists."

McCloskey's assessment of politicians' obligations to check the faithful who stray to extremes was far off the mark: James Watt does not hesitate to take on his own conservative supporters when they get too extreme. A January 23, 1982, Newhouse News Service story headlined "Watt Spanks 'New Right' For Pouting" makes this point nicely: Watt checked criticisms of President Reagan from conservatives who thought his programs were "too weak and halting."

An amusing sidelight to this episode was McCloskey's final complaint about my point of view, saying, "you have cloaked it in terms which are so sweeping that they smack of demagoguery." This from the same man who wrote of James Watt and Ronald Reagan:

There is no hope that this administration will be true to its oath to execute the laws of the land. People with the attitude of vandals have been put in office. The full burden of stewardship falls on organizations like the Sierra Club. In this dark age, we must be the repository of conservation. We have the institutional memory and continuity to bridge bad moments. The Sierra Club has launched a nationwide drive to have Watt replaced. Don't Let Them Get Away With It! Please, make your check payable to the Sierra Club. . . .

The core of the environmental movement is its ideology, those ideas about ecosystems, limited resources, interdependence, future scarcity, spaceship earth and centralized government control that give the movement its shape. Although widely accepted today, the ideology of environmentalism is only one interpretation of the available facts. An alternative view is just as valid, one that does not demand necessity crying out for an authoritarian government to coerce us into sharing scarcity, one that remembers William Pitt's words, "Necessity is the plea for every infringement of human freedom." The environmental interpretation has made millions of Americans pinched and peevish victims of tomorrow, plagued with defeatist attitudes and squelched hopes, and all ultimately for no real reason.

"The future is made, not born," says Dr. J. Peter Vajk in his book *Doomsday Has Been Cancelled*. He is one of the few scientists to attack the gloom and doom writers of *Silent Spring, The Population Bomb, The Limits To Growth, The Coming Dark Age, Small Is Beautiful* and *Future Shock* without the traditional blind and naïve technological optimism of classical engineering. Vajk instead sees through to the underlying assumptions of the neo-Malthusians and destroys the fallacies in their unspoken beliefs, their fundamental misperceptions of reality, their values that unconsciously lead them to select which facts they will regard as being relevant to any given issue and thus distort their conclusions. He found that the doomsayers, for example, tend to accept all problems and reject all solutions without being aware that they are doing so.

Vajk became interested in the doomsday syndrome in late 1974 during the OPEC boycott on petroleum exports to the United States and Europe when the voices of despair sounded most convincing. In 1975, Dr. Vajk analyzed the "Limits To Growth" computer models of "world dynamics" and found that their scenarios of rapid resource depletion assumed artifically limited inputs and, most significantly, the absence of future innovation and creativity. He pointed out that dire predictions of a ruined future totally ignored such well-known existing technologies as *ephemeralization*, the trend toward ever-increasing efficiency in the utilization of matter, of getting more from less, as in the well-publicized case of computer evolution—a pocket calculator today can do more than a roomful of mechanical and vacuum-tube circuitry 40 years ago. This trend already encompasses virtually every product of industrial civilization—airplanes for example that would have weighed about 2,150 pounds and cruised at 100 miles per hour in Charles Lindbergh's day compare to a modern craft of only 1,900 pounds cruising at 160 miles an hour. The end of this trend is nowhere in sight, yet the doomsayers go to elaborate lengths to disqualify it from consideration in predicting future conditions.

In the field of wildlife management, quantum leaps in our knowledge of biology and wildlife population dynamics have made it possible to save and enhance genetic stocks that only a few years ago seemed headed for certain extinction. William Tucker in the January 1982 issue of *Life* offered some good news in his article "Apocalypse Deferred." Robert Jones, director of Connecticut's State Fisheries told Tucker, "Connecticut salmon have been extinct for almost two centuries. But we took salmon from some Maine Rivers," installed fish ladders on the dozens of dams on the River, and released "about a million juveniles into the river every year. They've gotten as far up as New Hampshire and Vermont now. I think we've got a foothold."

Energy use is another field burgeoning with hope. Since the Reagan Administration's decontrol of oil prices, people have had an incentive to conserve. All the exhortations and preachments about conserving fuel in the '70s were ignored as long as cheap energy was available. We will indulge ourselves as long as it doesn't cost too much. More realistic energy prices, however, have caused a huge wave of energy conservation. The market is a remarkably effective force for conservation as long as it is allowed to function realistically. As Jim Watt says, "There's so much room for improving production and use that the best thing government can do is just get out of the way and let competition and people deliver the results."

Like James Watt, many scientists have come to the paradoxical conclusion that our minerals supply is absolutely infinite. A little-known study, *Scarcity and Growth*, by Harold J. Barnett and Chandler Morse, pointed out that even though nature imposes particular scarcities of specific matierals, it does not impose a general scarcity because of two human alternatives: substitutability and technological improvement. Herman Kahn of the Hudson Institute explains that "As we use up one resource, we find something else to do its job." Kahn described the truth behind such headlines as "World Reserves of Copper Ore Will Be Exhausted in Twenty Years!" with its companion conclusion that soon afterward we will have to abandon electrical power and electrical appliances—just the sort of disaster environmentalist groups love to dwell upon. Kahn points out that most of the copper mined in human history has not been "consumed," but is "alive and well and living above ground" in refined form as jewelry, elemental copper artifacts, or in alloys of brass and bronze which are scattered widely throughout the world. If the ore supply began to run out, the price of copper would increase, and at some point, the price would lead utilities to replace the copper wire in their generators and transformers with aluminum wire. If the price rose, say from the $1.00 per pound level to $10.00, you can bet that old brass beds, cuspidors and doorknobs, along with all manner of copper-bearing artifacts, would be "mined" from cellars and attics to meet the demand. But as a matter of fact, even though we are constantly taking more and more copper out of the ground, the price of copper relative to other goods has not increased and may even fall from time to time.

A good part of the reason is technological progress: our improved methods of using materials get more service from smaller quantities for a particular application, which ultimately makes them more accessible to future generations. We can stretch minerals thinner and thinner and find ways to use them better and better, as in the case of computer microchips—a tiny amount of material does an incredibly huge amount of work. And the idea of "using up" minerals is in large part an illusion: they haven't vanished, they are hard at work in industrial civilization, feeding, clothing and sheltering us, transporting and entertaining us, grooming us and teaching us. The world supply of minerals has been recycled time and again throughout history and will continue so with minimal real losses.

Even though the non-renewable minerals include petroleum, which will eventually be depleted, we tend to continually underestimate our reserves. As David A. Witts put it somewhat caustically in his book *Theft*, "In 1977, Chicken Little and the White House Troubadors were chanting: 'There's no more oil, there's no more oil.'" And then the Overthrust Belt was discovered. (Imagine their disappointment that Apocalypse keeps failing to meet the date they set for it)." But there is substance behind Witts' sarcasm: In 1954, the U.S. Geological Survey announced flatly that the last American oil reserves had been defined, and that we were going to run out shortly after the year 2050. However, in 1960, North America's greatest oil field was discovered at Prudhoe Bay, Alaska. Qualified technicians as well as struggle group leaders have helped make doomsaying one of America's largest growth industries. We continually fret about shortages just over the horizon and have been doing so for centuries.

But what about petroleum for non-fuel use, for the synthesis of complex organic compounds such as plastics, lubricants, and pharmaceutical products? As Dr. Vajk comments: "For these purposes, the vast quantities of oil shale, in just the uppermost kilometer of the Earth's crust, are sufficient for at least 3.5 million years, at current worldwide consumption rates." And all manner of biomass sources of burnable oil are in the experimental stage. It has been noted that 1961 Chemistry Nobel laureate Melvin Calvin and his wife Genevieve have been cultivating a small species similar to rubber trees that requires scant water and can yield five to ten barrels per acre of useable fuel a year.

Julian Simon, professor of economics at the University of Illinois and author of *The Ultimate Resource* was one of the experts to speak before the Interior Department's "Resource Learning Session" audience. To Dr. Simon, the human mind is the ultimate resource, human ingenuity. He told the Interior executives, "The only limits that put restrictions on what we can do with what is available to us are the limits of our own imagination. That is why we have nothing to fear and everything to hope for from technological progress."

These ideas are drastically different from the environmentalist interpretation of modern events.They are new ways of looking at old facts. They are *paradigm shifts*. Paradigm shift is a term originated by science historian Thomas Kuhn in his 1962 classic *The Structure of Scientific Revolutions*. Paradigms are perspectives on reality. A paradigm (from the Greek word for "pattern") may be a way of looking at things that gives sense and coherence to existence, or a frame of reference by which things are understood or explained. For example, the idea that the earth is a planet is a paradigm, as is the notion that humans are natural organisms embedded in nature.

A paradigm shift is a sudden drastic change in outlook. It's something like looking at one of those geometric drawings of stairs: you may first see it as the top of the stairs, but suddenly it looks like the bottom. Paradigm shift, too, is an all-or-nothing sort of thing, and nobody can talk you into it. Either you see it or you don't.

Kuhn wrote his book because he discovered that new theories in science didn't evolve slowly as older theories were gradually corrected to greater and greater precision as many had thought, but rather appeared suddenly in great flashes of personal insight on the part of some talented individual scientist.

And so it is with the paradigm shifts that have come to scientists and thinkers within the last few years. Just as we were getting used to the earlier paradigm shifts from ecology and the environmental movement, their ideologies began to show tatters around the edges, their ideas seemed to be on shaky ground, and a new paradigm suddenly appeared.

The old ecological paradigm shifts had been dramatic enough. Suddenly in the 1960s we had seen that man was not the master of the world as he had thought, but was a natural organism irrevocably embedded in nature. Old ideas of infinite abundance and affluence seemed to be mirages, development suddenly looked evil, and we felt that a severe conserver society must be built rapidly to avoid ecocatastrophe. Our older hierarchical organization styles seemed to be inhumane and bad for people, so new coalitional-interrelated-network organizational styles ought to inform our society; the new idea of "ecosystem" appeared to rule everything, as expressed in John Muir's remark, "When we try to pick out anything by itself, we find it hitched to everything else in the universe," and Barry Commoner's corollary, "You can't do just one thing."

But the new ecological paradigms quickly fossilized into environmentalist dogma. The fact that human beings are embedded in nature was interpreted to mean "We must stop reworking the face of the earth like conquerors because everything we do has unpredictable bad consequences"—with accompanying paralysis. The ideas of spaceship earth and limited resources were interpreted as inevitable future scarcity and hardened into demands for coercive governmental programs to prevent the use of resources and to force people to share scarcity. By interpreting theories and facts from the science of ecology as social models of behavior, many environmental paradigms were turned into intellectual traps and imagination blinders. The thrust was redirected from learning to utilize resources efficiently and minimize pollution toward changing society into a mold that would not use resources and would not pollute—without too careful an examination of what that society might actually be like. No-growth economies and organic farming agriculture may be appealing to some, but there has been no great voluntary rush to them by those who support the rest of us. And most ironically, sociologists discovered that the gigantic multinational corporations so hated by environmentalists were perfect models of the new coalitional network style of organization, and had evolved into networks quite naturally as an adaptive mechanism to cope with many different nation states. Obviously, there were many unanswered questions and shaky assumptions in the old environmentalist paradigm, and new ideas began to emerge.

Some of the new paradigms were simply alternative interpretations of well known facts. Take the ideas of spaceship earth and limited resources, for example. The earth is a reasonably closed system, even though metals from other planets are now within our technical grasp, and colonies in space may be on the agenda of the day after tomorrow. But for all practical purposes, the earth is a limited sphere with a fixed amount of resources. That is the raw uninterpreted fact.

The old environmentalist paradigm interprets that fact with claustrophobic alarm: limited resources, unavoidable future scarcity, coercive government control to make us share scarcity. The new beginning's interpretation sees nearly infinite resources in that fact. Why? Because it knows there are many kinds of infinity. The old environmentalist paradigm only recognizes the kind of infinity of indefinitely large numbers, indefinitely large piles of oil and timber, minerals and energy and other resources, which obviously do not exist. But the new paradigm can see another kind of infinity: the one between the two ends of a yardstick. You can keep subdividing feet and inches into infinitely smaller slices. To the unfettered imagination, that means we can learn to utilize resources more and more efficiently, getting more from less, making smaller amounts of material do more work, and that is the assumption behind the idea of ephemeralization. It is a new way of creating abundance. But it is not a reversion to the pre-ecology paradigm of unawareness of limited resources and the "gobble-it-all-up" attitude that went along with it. It still understands care, efficiency, maximum utilization, minimum waste, conservation, preservation, and all the other eco-paradigms. It has not forgotten, it has merely taken the next step in the evolution of thought.

Other paradigms of the new beginning were not merely alternative interpretations of well known facts, but were rather totally new discoveries based on more recent scientific work. One of those is the idea of human ecology. Modern science has known of ecology since the word was coined by Ernst Haeckel in 1866 to mean the science which studies the interrelationships between organisms and their environments, dealing with such specifics as natural cycles and rhythms, ecological community development and structure, relationships between organisms, geographic distribution, and population alterations. The social interpretations were not added until ecology became a kitchen word in the 1960s and it was taken over by the environmental movement. It was also in the 1960s that scientists began to wonder about human ecology as a separate subject. As recently as 1964, the subject was still in a primitive formative stage. Paul Shepard's introductory essay for *The Subversive Science* maintained that human ecology wasn't even a science, "It is not a discipline: there is no body of thought and technique which frames an ecology of man. It must be therefore a scope or a way of seeing. Such a *perspective* of the human situation is very old and has been a part of philosophy and art for thousands of years." It is indicative of how poorly advanced human ecology stood at the time that Shepard's essay—intending to prove his area of study was not a science—was received politely.

However, by 1972, an entirely new approach to ecological studies was embodied in Dr. Walter Isard's work, *Ecologic-Economic Analysis for Regional Development*. Dr. Isard acknowledged that combining the two words "economic" and "ecologic" was unusual, but it was "set forth, nevertheless, as a true combination, in the sense of a synthesis of analyses of two systems within the world of actuality." Out of this study came a whole new paradigm of human ecology. Isard and his colleagues at Harvard did the study to evaluate the proper way to develop a marina in a Massachusetts estuary, and decided to get rid of the old unworkable method of trying to put a dollar value on ecological disruption. Instead they created a way to express both ecologic and economic costs and benefits in similar terms. They did it with a system called Input-Output charting.

Input-Output economics had been known for some time, and was an approach largely developed by Wassily Leontieff of Harvard University in the 1930s to analyze the national economy. Input-Output analysis divides an economy into meaningful sectors, arranges them graphically on a chart, and the matrix thus formed is then filled in to show how much money flows from one economic sector to another. A fine-mesh input-output chart containing 300 or so sectors of an economy reveals an astounding amount of information clearly and quickly. A trained analyst can grasp an entire economy in a few minutes using this method.

A very simplified Input-Output chart or flow table of the American economy could be symbolized using only 3 sectors (most use about 100 sectors, and the U.S. government uses charts with upwards of 400), and would look something like this:

INDUSTRY
PURCHASING

INDUSTRY PRODUCING	Agri-culture	Manu-facturing	Trade and Services	FINAL DEMAND	TOTAL GROSS OUTPUT
Agriculture	1	3	2	6	12
Manufacturing	4	6	4	10	24
Trade and Services	2	3	5	8	18
Total Intermediate Inputs	7	12	11	24	

Let's say the numbers represent billions of dollars. What it means is that Manufacturing sold $4 billion worth of goods to Agriculture (left-most column), or that Agriculture bought $4 billion worth of goods from Manufacturing, and so forth; every sale is also a purchase. But notice that the "Final Demand" column doesn't always add up to the numbers from the left side of the chart (add up the second row and see). The reason is simple: final demand takes into account external forces such as government and exports; it shows how we came out after taxes and export income, foreign payments, and government purchases. Then the "Total Gross Output" column neatly *does* add up to everything on its left. In this graphic way, an entire economy can be seen at a glance and previously hidden interrelationships can be more clearly understood.

But what is astonishing, and important to our story, is that professional ecologists have known for some time that ecosystems also behave in an Input-Output manner, with gases, minerals and organic nutrients cycling in and out of various organisms and physical objects. Thus it is possible to chart very complex ecological systems in this same Input-Output format, but instead of dollars the numbers would represent amounts of, say, gases like oxygen and nitrogen, minerals such as phosphorus or magnesium, or organic nutrients such as amino acids, proteins, and so forth. In this way, the real interrelatedness of an ecology can be revealed in numbers very appropriately just like an economy, without doing something absurd like trying to say that so much ecological value can be expressed by so many dollars.

When Dr. Isard and his colleagues gathered all their data and filled in all their economic and ecologic charts, something very interesting appeared. Everything is *not* hitched to everything else in the universe. Muir was a better poet than naturalist. The hitches are quite specific and only in certain definite places. There are as many disconnections as there are connections. In fact, all organisms must maintain *absolute separation* from certain environmental influences such as extremes of heat or cold, wet or dry, high or low atmospheric pressure, and so on. The actual interrelationships of an ecosystem are highly specific, and its isolations are highly specific, and they vary from one ecosystem to another in exact ways.

But that was not the most important conclusion. The true discovery to be derived from this work relates to human ecology. If ecology is the study of the interrelationships between organisms and their environments, then how, we may ask, do humans relate to their environments? In other words, what, really, is human ecology? Dr. Isard's work suggests a stunning answer: humans relate to their environments by creating an economy. An economy is human ecology. The Input-Output method makes it obvious: you can trace goods in an economy back to the raw materials in nature, and forward to the environment as pollution and waste materials with great ease using this system. You can graphically represent the workings of a natural system with great accuracy using the same method. An economy and an ecology work on virtually identical kinds of principles. Recent work in General Systems Theory found basic similarities between the dynamics of biological populations and quantitative economics and econometrics. Marston Bates said as much years ago in his book *The Forest and the Sea*: "Economics can be seen as the ecology of man; ecology as the study of the economy of nature."

Obviously, the academic subjects of ecology and economics are not the same things; they are severely cubbyholed from each other, taught on different parts of college campuses and populated by practitioners who generally do not hold each other in warm regard. But the real barriers to a functional integration of ecology and economics are more ideological than methodological. I once showed Dr. Isard's work to Michael McCloskey of the Sierra Club in his San Francisco office, and he dismissed it with a characteristically contemptuous gesture. I doubt that other environmentalist leaders would welcome it any more eagerly; it would tend to break down artificial barriers in our society and deflate environmental ideology as it now stands. But it is a new paradigm. An economy is human ecology. And once a new paradigm has been seen, it is difficult to go back to the old awareness.

When James Watt says, "We have potentially great abundance in the natural resources of America and we don't have to go on a system of sharing scarcity," he is not speaking from the old, pre-ecology paradigm of rape, ruin, and run. He's speaking from the paradigm of the new beginning.

But the general public is not yet well aware of the new beginning's scientific discoveries and interpretations, and those who have invested years of personal effort in the old eco-paradigms are not likely to eagerly embrace new understanding. Part of the reason is contained in the basic assumptions of the eco-paradigms themselves, in a philosophical-psychological mindset called by anthropologists "cultural primitivism." This trait was first described by Arthur O. Lovejoy and George Boas in their 1935 classic *Primitivism and Related Ideas in Antiquity*: "Cultural primitivism is the discontent of the civilized with civilization, or with some conspicuous and characteristic feature of it. It is the belief of men living in a relatively highly evolved and complex cultural condition that a life far simpler and less sophisticated in some or in all respects is a more desirable life."

The scholar Lewis S. Feuer applied this concept to modern environmental ideologists in *Ideology and the Ideologists*: "Cultural primitivism, an enduring theme of human nature ever since the civilizing process began, probably began . . . when early men sought out the refinements of cave-dwellings, and brought down upon themselves the first primitivist protest. . . .

Now it is a universal law that every ideology tends towards a revival of primitivism. . . . The current Leftist ideology is preeminently one of cultural primitivism. . . . Young ideologists emphasize the restoration of the tribal community and its drug rituals, and they aspire toward a restoration of magic, astrology and primitive dress."

Old-line preservation groups such as the Sierra Club embrace a highly refined version of cultural primitivism, as expressed in the Club's motto "not blindly opposed to progress but opposed to blind progress"—the operative word is still "opposed" and it is still "progress" that is being opposed. But the environmentalist element that has lived for years in West Coast communes, dubbed "The New Lawless" in a 1982 *Sacramento Bee* series of articles describing their vast guerilla marijuana plantations, fits Feuer's description quite well. Among such primitivists living in many Western states, vandalism against nearby encroachments of civilization has become a way of life. For example, hundreds of pieces of expensive logging equipment have been destroyed by these environmentalists since the mid-1960s. Many of the vandals leave behind eloquent expressions of their primitivist beliefs and nature mysticism on their wreckage.

Opposed to this, one positive indication that a new idea is awakening is the growth of pro-civilization, pro-industry citizen activist groups, grass-roots organizations much like the early environmentalist groups, all promoting the idea that human beings are as natural as anything else in creation, and that we have a right to be here.

There are still many questions to which we do not know the answers: Since man is obviously the dominant species on this planet, how do we deal with that uncomfortable fact? Deny it? Say it's immoral? Control our activities with authoritarian government? Educate ourselves about our real impacts? What should we do about endangered species? Stop all human activity? Try to find out how life on earth survived crises such as the disappearance of the dinosaurs? Adjust development methods in certain cases? How shall we handle resource extraction and conversion? Stop it all? Regulate but not obstruct? Laissez faire? Since the basic law of ecology is change—that is, dynamic adaptation—how reasonable are preservation efforts on a large scale? Can wilderness survive the onslaught of its friends who are loving it to death? Should the earth become a nature museum, a National Park? What should be done about the lobby for future generations, one of the largest in Washington according to "Father of Environmental Law" Joseph Sax, in trying to keep our present generation economically healthy? Should federal regulation be extended to Big Environmentalism? Should the large, wealthy environmentalist groups be held legally and financially liable for the increased costs of projects they delay, or responsible for replacing the economic loss from projects they stop? Asking such questions and more will become an increasingly important part of future U.S. life. The answers may not be easy, but the exasperating, exacting asking is essential.

The New Beginning is more than a political slogan of the Reagan Administration. It is a growing trend of solid scientific paradigm shifts that add up to a more hopeful, brighter, expansive view of tomorrow. As Dr. George T. L. Land put it in his work, *Grow or Die: The Unifying Principle of Transformation*, creativity, mental illness, urban decay, self-sacrifice, colonialism, revolution, sadism, beauty, and human love all obey nature's command to grow or perish. The fearful no-growth philosophy of environmentalism is as much a path to extinction as careless development. There are alternatives to environmentalism. Viable, happy, healthy alternatives. And James Watt is working on them.

Where to, What Next?

Arthur C. Clarke, scientist and author, once quipped, "The future ain't what it used to be." When it comes to James G. Watt, it also ain't what it seems now. Watt's career has been singularly unpredictable; who would have guessed he could survive the Siege of the Environmentalists or the flap over his letter to Israeli Ambassador Arens. Now the question is appropriate: What will become of him? Will he serve out the full term of President Reagan? The odds are much against it. Only three Secretaries of the Interior in American history have served the entire terms of their Presidents: Harold L. Ickes under Franklin D. Roosevelt, Stewart Udall under John F. Kennedy, and Cecil Andrus under Jimmy Carter. Twelve Presidents have appointed new Interior Secretaries upon reelection. Many Secretaries of the Interior have resigned or been fired in midterm. No previous Secretary of the Interior has survived even a fraction of the outcry against Watt.

Watt could be long gone before the next Presidential election. I have asked him what could put him out of office. "If we lost a lot of Republican seats in the West in the 1982 Congressional elections, I would be honor-bound to offer the President my resignation," Watt said. "But I've been working the West hard in my political travels, and I think we're okay there." But something new has been added. The large, wealthy environmentalist groups like the Sierra Club and Audubon Society with its oil millions are also working the West hard. They have for the first time in environmentalist history become partisan politicians, running dozens of state-level Political Action Committees. Observers cannot tell whether the Democrats have coopted the environmentalists or the other way around, but nothing like this has ever been done before. The "Green Vote" has never been tested. One way or another, 1982 will be an environmentalist watershed.

But if Watt is fired, or resigns, then what? Doug Baldwin, Watt's Director of Public Affairs and friend of 20 years says: "Then he'll just smile and say "I did the best I could," and he'll turn and walk away with dignity."

Sitting in a Governor's mansion today there may be just the person to undo Watt's Department of the Interior. Or perhaps some talented environmentalist manager is working in obscurity with the clock of destiny ticking away on his desk. I have seen Interior inside and out, however, and my guess is that the stamp of James G. Watt will remain on the Department of the Interior many, many years after his retirement, no matter who his successors may be.

If Interior held its farewell party for Jim Watt this very day, they, and all of us would owe him a vote of thanks. He has brought sound common sense management to all our public lands. He began the repair and restoration of our National Parks. He created, at long last, a National Strategic Minerals Policy. He brought the Indians a long step on their journey to self-determination. He presided over a new Territorial Policy that held the Soviet Union at bay in the Pacific while giving the Islands independence. He took us further toward U.S. energy self-sufficiency than any of his predecessors since the advent of environmentalism. He made intelligent and sensitive proposals to protect our wilderness heritage yet provide administrative flexibility to carefully obtain material values in time of emergency. He defused the Sagebrush Rebellion, which could flare up again under new "coercive utopians." But perhaps Watt's most socially significant contribution will be least recognized: Watt began the challenge of Big Environmentalism's power and self-righteousness.

Watt the man, the real man, has been obscured by partisan press flackery, as we have seen. Yet the off-duty Jim Watt is an interesting and interested person. In some regards he is common as an old shoe: he inspects his flower garden each morning before work and relaxes by wallpapering the house. Leilani says he doesn't know the names of his flowers, "but he loves the color." And at a buffet dinner Watt once chose peanut butter and jelly on Wonder Bread, and kidded his wife: "This stuff tastes better than the health food bread you've been feeding me."

But in other ways, Watt is highly uncommon. One of his unusual traits is his choice of vacation activities, as described by Ann Blackman in a June 1982 Associated Press article:

It was 1970; he was Deputy Assistant Secretary for Water and Power Resources. Leilani Watt recalls: "We took a trip once with the kids down South, and we stopped in every factory that there was along the way. We saw men's slacks being cut. We saw them making shoes. If they didn't have tours in their factories, they made up tours for us."

I thought I was the only one who did that: I've taken my kids through sawmills and the first thing we looked at in Death Valley was the old mines. But Watt is a spontaneous person who once took his family to Pennsylvania and asked an Amish man if he could ride in his horse-drawn carriage. According to Leilani, Jim "hates tourist kinds of things."

The Watts have not taken a real vacation since their two grown children were little, but now they will sometimes spend weekends visiting National Park facilities around Washington with one or two other couples, staying in rustic cabins and bringing their own food. Jim cooks breakfast. Leilani, according to Ann Blackman's article, says, " 'We spent an Easter weekend there and had great discussions, walked in the woods and walked the trails.' Among friends, Jim likes to get into discussions about politics or religion—he loves to argue both sides of an issue and pin a clever opponent to the wall. But Leilani says, 'He never does that with me.' "

The controversy and lightning strikes from wrathful environmentalists have taken a terrible personal toll of Jim and Leilani. Jim frankly admits, "Yes, it has hurt personally, but it has helped the White House." Leilani smiles through the pain in her eyes and softly says, "I've cried. I've laughed. I've prayed. Jim has been a great help even though he has been hurt himself. His perspective on things is tremendous. It helps me. He doesn't allow those arrows to stay in place for long. Being with Jim helps heal the wounds. With the political season upon us and all the travel, we spend more time together now than ever before." Referring to his speechmaking and political fund-raising trips, Jim says, "I won't travel unless the Republican Party pays for her to come with me."

And Watt's parents have entered the fray of environmentalist controversy: Jim got a call once from his mother admonishing him, "James, you should be nice to those critics." Watt replied, "But, Mom, you have to understand these people are out to kill me!" His Mother replied, "James, you just be nice and they'll understand what you're doing." Perhaps this was what prompted him to say "I'm warm and cuddly" once. But Watt's parents are resigned to their son's Cabinet role, and simply say in reference to all the comments on Jim's wide smile, "Are we ever glad we spent all that money on James' orthodontic work."

By the time Watt's Cabinet term is over, those who have worked with him will be able to look back on an authentic redirection of the future, will have lived one of Interior's "peak experiences," will have dwelt close to a mythic center of American history. Watt has shown how to bring fundamental change to Interior, he has truly made a New Beginning, and that lesson will not be lost on the leaders and the bureaucracy of the future. The "arrogant vandal" of the environmentalists' denunciations is a figure of strength, integrity, and honor to those who work with him in government and the private sector. He has shown that singleness of purpose and persistence in the face of overwhelming odds can survive even against the most scathing criticism. James G. Watt will not be soon forgotten—by his enemies or his friends. As Watt is a formidable enemy, so he is a firm friend.

Robin West, Assistant Secretary for Policy, Budget and Administration, testifies to Watt's friendship: "Jim is devoted to his people. It's profoundly moving. He is not the usual bureaucrat who takes a somewhat casual and expedient view of such relationships." Moody Tidwell, Deputy Solicitor, says, "I have never seen Jim run out on a colleague in trouble, or fail to back an associate when the going gets rough." Executive Assistant Steve Shipley: "Jim is loyal to a fault. No matter what his people need, on the job or in their personal lives, Jim is there." Under Secretary Hodel: "I've warned Jim about that loyalty of his. Someday, someone from outside will see it and use it against him. Jim's greatest strength is his loyalty to his people, but it's also his greatest weakness."

If Watt's enemies ever find that "equalizer" they're looking for, it most likely will have nothing to do with his policy or his management skills, but will probably involve his loyalty to his people. Watt constantly tells his people to take care of themselves and assures them of his personal backing.

This kind of treatment gives a "family" feel to the bureaucracy that works directly with Watt. The bonds of loyalty stand out in sharp profile in an incident from early 1982: Perry Pendley, Watt's friend and Deputy Assistant Secretary for Energy and Minerals, came up to Watt and out of the clear blue sky one day told him: "Jim, you remind me of Bonnie and Clyde."

Watt laughed and said, "I don't rob banks!"

Pendley said, "I mean you remind me of a scene from the movie about Bonnie and Clyde, the one with Faye Dunaway and Warren Beatty. Just after they robbed their first bank, Clyde tells Bonnie: 'Now it's gonna get rough. They know who I am, and they're gonna be runnin' after me and anybody who's runnin' with me. Right now I can't get out, but you still can. You mean a lot to me, honey, and I just ain't gonna make you run with me. If you stay with me, you ain't never gonna have a moment of peace.' Now that's what you keep telling us, Jim, and my answer to you is the same as Bonnie gave to Clyde. When he said 'If you stay with me you ain't never gonna have a moment of peace," she answered, 'You promise?' "

Jim Watt was moved. He said only, "Thank you, Perry."

The next Monday morning, Watt came into the eight o'clock Political Appointee's meeting as usual, and as usual, things were rough. A Contempt of Congress citation hung over Watt's head. His wilderness plan was taking a beating in the press. Liberal Congressional Committee members were threatening to impeach him for demanding that oversight questions be delivered in writing. But Watt dealt with the problems in his normal cheery manner, and gave the team instructions with his usual upbeat smile. He fired up his people with a final rah-rah talk about how "we're going to fight this thing through," and "there's no substitute for victory."

Then he remembered Pendley's story. With Perry in the room, Watt retold the Bonnie and Clyde episode for his 35 political appointees. He closed the meeting with: "Keep that story in mind. If you stick with me, I guarantee you'll never have a moment's peace."

Silence. Then applause thundered and the executives stood in ovation, as if to give James Watt the storybook response, "You promise?" Watt sat bemused for a second. He quietly left his chair and walked past his applauding friends, joining Steve Shipley and Doug Baldwin at the door on their way to the next appointment.

A few executives picked up their notebooks and strode down the hallway to their obligations while others gathered in knots within the large austere conference room, drifting slowly toward the doorway. Someone opened the west window's heavy drapery and let in the morning scene. Sounds of traffic on wet pavement filtered in.

At the other end of the building, James Watt entered another conference room crowded with waiting executives, laid his briefcase on a table, and, as usual, said: "Let's get to work."

A new day had begun.

APPENDIX

Fig. 1. 101 "Political Ecology" Laws on Energy, Land, Food, Technology, Health and Social Change as Passed or Amended by Congress Since 1960

1. Motor Vehicle Exhaust Study Act of 1960
2. Multiple Use, Sustained Yield Act of 1960 (forests)
3. Organic Act of the National Parks Service of 1960
4. Sikes Act of 1960 (wildlife management on military reserves)
5. Wetlands Loan Act of 1961 (wildlife fund)
6. Tariff Classification Act of 1962 (regulates imports of feathers, fur, etc.)
7. Federal-Aid Highway Act of 1962 (mass transit)
8. Trade Expansion Act of 1962 (centralized government control)
9. Forest Service Omnibus Act of 1962
10. McIntire-Stennis Act of 1962 (forestry research)
11. Admiralty Extension Act (relating to oil spills)
12. Urban Mass Transportation Act of 1964
13. National Forest Roads and Trails Act of 1964
14. Land and Water Conservation Fund Act of 1964
15. Public Land Law Review Act of 1964
16. Administrative Procedures Act (relates to who can sue in courts)
17. Wilderness Act of 1964
18. Classification and Multiple Use Act of 1964 (forests)
19. Motor Vehicle Air Pollution Control Act of 1965
20. Water Resources Planning Act of 1965
21. Highway Beautification Act of 1965
22. Solid Waste Disposal Act of 1965
23. Motor Vehicles Information and Cost Savings Act
24. Anadromous Fish Conservation Act of 1965
25. Department of Transportation Act of 1966
26. National Historic Preservation Act of 1966
27. Endangered Species Act of 1966
28. National Wildlife Refuge System Administration Act of 1966
29. Clear Water Restoration Act of 1966
30. Demonstration Cities and Metropolitan Development Act of 1966 (mass transit)
31. Fishermen's Protective Act of 1967
32. Air Quality Act of 1967
33. Federal Aviation Act of 1968 (aircraft noise control)
34. Radiation Control for Health and Safety Act of 1968
35. Federal-Aid Highway Act of 1968 (mass transit)
36. Estuarine Areas Act of 1968
37. Wild and Scenic Rivers Act of 1968
38. National Trails System Act of 1968
39. Redwood National Park Establishment Act of 1968 (seize private land)
40. Intergovernmental Cooperation Act of 1968 (centralized government control)
41. Safe Streets Act of 1969 (cultural environment)
42. Endangered Species Conservation Act of 1969
43. Coal Mine Health and Safety Act of 1969
44. National Environmental Policy Act of 1969
45. Lacey Act of 1900 as amended in 1969 (wildlife conservation)
46. Black Bass Act of 1926 as amended in 1969
47. Federal-Aid Highway Act of 1970 (mass transit)
48. Clean Air Act of 1970
49. Clean Air Act Amendments of 1970
50. Family Planning Services and Population Research Act of 1970 (population control)
51. Airport and Airway Development Act of 1970 (noise pollution control)
52. Federal Aid in Wildlife Restoration Act of 1937 as amended in 1970
53. Merchant Marine Act of 1970 (relating to oil spill control)
54. Occupational Safety and Health Act of 1970

55. Resource Recovery Act of 1970 (recycling)
56. National Historic Preservation Act Amendments of 1970
57. Water Bank Act of 1970
58. Environmental Quality Improvement Act of 1970
59. Youth Conservation Corps Act of 1970
60. Mining and Minerals Policy Act of 1970
61. Economic Stabilization Act of 1970 (centralized federal control)
62. Urban Mass Transportation Assistance Act of 1970
63. Mineral Leasing act of 1970
64. Fish and Wildlife Coordination Act of 1970
65. Rivers and Harbors Authorization Act of 1971
66. Wild Horses and Burros Protection Act of 1971
67. Bald Eagle Protection Act of 1940 as amended in 1962 and 1972
68. Federal Environmental Pesticide Control Act of 1972
69. Water Pollution Control Act Amendments of 1972
70. Advisory Committee Act of 1972 (multiplied red tape)
71. Noise Control Act of 1972
72. Marine Protection, Research and Sanctuaries Act of 1972 (Ocean Dumping Act)
73. Coastal Zone Management Act of 1972
74. Ports and Waterways Safety Act of 1972
75. Volunteers in the National Forests Act of 1972
76. Rural Development Act of 1972 (forest-service related)
77. Marine Mammal Protection Act of 1972
78. Federal-Aid Highway Act of 1973 (mass transit)
79. Emergency Petroleum Allocation Act of 1973
80. Mineral Leasing Act Amendments of 1973
81. Agriculture and Consumer Protection Act of 1973
82. Emergency Daylight Saving Time Energy Conservation Act of 1973
83. Endangered Species Act of 1973
84. Federal Nonnuclear Energy Research and Development Act of 1974
85. Safe Drinking Water Act of 1974
86. Energy Supply and Environmental Coordination Act of 1974
87. Freedom of Information Act Amendments of 1974 (helped environmentalist lawsuits)
88. Forest and Rangeland Renewable Resources Planning Act of 1974
89. National Independent Refinery Development Act of 1974
90. Federal Energy Administration Act of 1974
91. Energy Reorganization Act of 1974
92. Deep Water Port Act of 1974 (oil spills)
93. Trade Act of 1974 (centralized federal control)
94. Eastern Wilderness Act of 1975
95. Energy Policy and Conservation Act of 1975
96. Federal Insecticide, Fungicide, and Rodenticide Act Amendments of 1975
97. Energy Conservation and Production Action of 1975
98. Solid Waste Disposal Act of 1976
99. National Forest Management Act of 1976
100. Toxic Substances Control Act of 1976
101. Fishery Conservation and Management Act of 1976

Fig. 2. Eight Key Cases out of More than 500 Brought by Environmentalists Since 1960

1. Scenic Hudson Preservation Conference v. Federal Power Commission (December 1965). A complex case in which a group of wealthy estate owners fought power lines across their Hudson River view. The 2nd Circuit Court held that factors other than economic interest could be the basis for being an "aggrieved" person, which with other rulings gave environmental groups legal standing to sue in defense of scenic, historical, and recreational values which might be affected by power development. Opened the gates to a flood of environmental litigation.

2. Zabel v. Tabb (July 1970). The 5th Circuit Court held that the Army Corps of Engineers had authority to deny dredge-and-fill permits not only on the basis of traditional considerations of navigation, flood control, and hydroelectric potential, but also on environmental and ecological grounds.

3. Sierra Club v. Morton (April 1972). The watershed case of Mineral King Valley in which legal rights for natural objects became an explicit theory of jurisprudence. The U.S. Supreme Court held that once a citizen or group established its direct stake in an environmental decision, the plaintiff could assert the interest of the general public as well. This case reaffirmed that being "aggrieved" is not limited to economic values, but extends to aesthetic and recreational values as well.

4. Sierra Club v. Ruckelshaus (November 1972). The Circuit Court in Washington, D.C. held that the EPA had acted in violation of the Clean Air Act in approving state plans that permitted certain relaxations in standards for existing air quality.

5. The United States v. SCRAP (June 1973). The U.S. Supreme Court held that in class action suits, if the alleged harm will affect a small group of people, the plaintiff must be able to prove that he will be one of those affected; but, if the harm affects all citizens, then any citizen may bring suit. Spread standing to sue in environmental matters to more and more groups and individuals.

6. Scientists' Institute for Public Information v. Atomic Energy Commission (June 1973). The circuit court in Washington, D.C. held that the National Environmental Policy Act of 1969 required the preparation of an environmental impact statement, even at the research stage of any federally-funded project.

7. Kleppe v. Sierra Club (July 1976). The U.S. Supreme Court held that no immediate preparation of a regional environmental impact statement was required from the Dept. of Interior concerning regional coal development in the northern Great Plains area, since there was no federal plan or program involved. Environmentalists viewed this case as a defeat in their drive to push environmental impact statement requirements into private commercial developments.

8. E.I. duPont de Nemours and Co. v. Train (February 1977). The U.S. Supreme Court held that EPA has authority to establish uniform 1977 and 1983 effluent limits for categories of existing point sources of water pollution, provided that allowances are made for variations in industrial plants. This decision affected pulp and paper mills.

Fig. 3. The Top 10 out of 3,000 U.S. Environmental Groups in 1980

Rank	Group Name	Members	Annual Income
1	National Wildlife Federation	4,000,000	$24,000,000
2	National Audubon Society	350,000	8,000,000
3	Sierra Club	167,000	8,500,000
4	The Wilderness Society	75,000	1,700,000
5	Izaak Walton League	53,000	400,000
6	National Parks and Conservation Association	45,000	950,000
7	Environmental Defense Fund	44,000	1,600,000
8	Natural Resources Defense Council	35,000	1,900,000
9	The Nature Conservancy	28,000	8,500,000
10	Friends of the Earth	22,000	670,000

Massachusetts Audubon Society, although only statewide, has 25,000 members, annual budget of $2.4 million, operates network of natural areas.

Professional organizations: The Conservation Foundation, Environmental Policy Center, Scientists Institute for Public Information, National Council for Environmental Balance.

Source: Groups shown and *The Unfinished Agenda*. G. O. Barney

Fig. 4. Personnel of the U.S. Department of the Interior During the Period Covered in *At the Eye of the Storm*

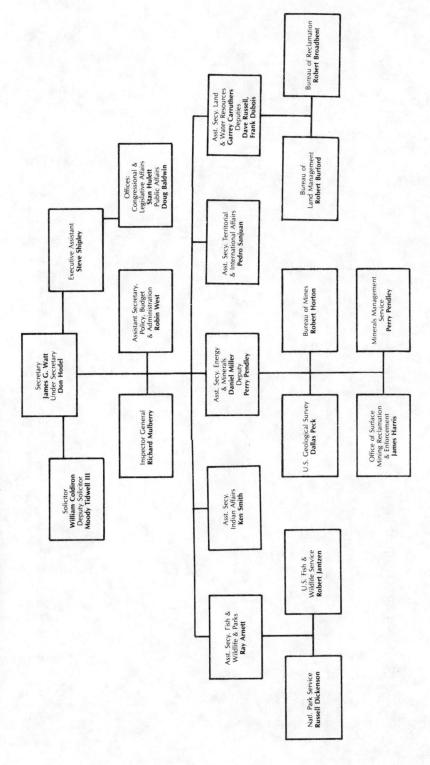

Fig. 5. Proposed Spectrum of Environmental Organizations

The social impact of this structure tends toward the right-hand side of the chart; groups placed farther to the right-hand side provide those on the left-hand side with the appearance of moderation while furthering the movement's goals.

Preferred Tactics (cumulative from left to right; each set of tactics may include those listed to its left on this chart)

Cooperation Education Research	Lobbying Litigation Pressure	Strategems Confrontations Demonstrations	Civil Disobedience	Direct Action Ecotage Violence
American Forestry Association	National Wildlife Federation	Environmental Action		Greenpeace — Edward Abbey Disciples
	Environmental Defense Fund	Friends of the Earth		
National Audubon Society	Sierra Club			
Izaak Walton League			Clamshell Alliance	
	Wilderness Society	Union of Concerned Scientists		Earth First
Conservation Foundation	National Parks & Conservation Association	Northwest Coalition for Alternatives to Pesticides		
Save-the-Redwoods League	Natural Resources Defense Council		Association of Community Organizations for Reform Now (ACORN)	Anonymous Ecotage Saboteurs
Nature Conservancy		Zero Population Growth		
Resources for the Future	Trust For Public Land	League of Conservation Voters		
		Friends of Animals Rural America		

| Political Orientation: Conservative | Liberal | Radical | | Revolutionary |

A proposed spectrum of selected environmental organizations, located according to their major actions as reported in newspaper articles since 1965, and according to their own descriptions from brochures and newsletters. Each group may perform single actions in other areas of the spectrum. Relative placements judged by the author upon the evidence described.

BIBLIOGRAPHY

Books

Abbey, Edward. *The Monkey Wrench Gang*. New York: J.B. Lippincott, 1972.

Ashby, Eric. *Reconciling Man with the Environment*. Stanford: Stanford University Press, 1978.

Barbour, Ian, ed. *Western Man and Environmental Ethics*. Reading: Addison-Wesley, 1973.

Barnett, Harold J. and Morse, Chandler. *Scarcity and Growth*. Baltimore: Johns Hopkins Press, 1963.

Bates, Marston, *The Forest and the Sea: A Look at the Economy of Nature and the Ecology of Man*. New York: Random House, 1960.

Callenbach, Ernest, *Ecotopia*. Berkeley: Banyan Tree Books, 1975.

Carson, Rachel. *Silent Spring*. Boston: Houghton Mifflin, 1962.

Claus, George, and Bolander, Karen. *Ecological Sanity*. New York: David McKay, 1977.

Cohen, Abner. *Two-Dimensional Man: An Essay on the Anthropology of Power and Symbolism in Complex Society*. Berkeley: University of California Press, 1974.

Coser, Lewis, *The Functions of Social Conflict*. New York: The Free Press, 1956.

DeBell, Garrett, ed. *The Environmental Handbook, Prepared for the First National Environmental Teach-In*. New York: Ballantine Books, 1970.

Ehrlich, Paul R. *The Population Bomb*. New York: Ballantine Books, 1968.

Feuer, Lewis S. *Ideology and the Ideologists*. New York: Harper & Row, 1975.

Florman, Samuel C. *The Existential Pleasures of Engineering*. New York: St. Martin's Press, 1976.

Friedman, Lawrence M. *A History of American Law*. New York: Simon & Schuster, 1973.

Giedion, Sigfried. *Mechanization Takes Command*. New York: W.W. Norton, 1948.

Gughemetti, Joseph, and Wheeler, Eugene D. *The Taking*. Palo Alto: Hidden House Publications, 1981.

Hays, Samuel P. *Conservation and the Gospel of Efficiency: The Progressive Conservation Movement 1890-1920*. Cambridge: Harvard University Press, 1959.

Heilbroner, Robert L. *An Inquiry into the Human Prospect, Updated and Reconsidered for the 1980s*. New York: W.W. Norton, 1980.

Inglehart, Ronald. *The Silent Revolution: Changing Values and Political Styles Among Western Publics*. Princeton: Princeton University Press, 1977.

Isard, Walter. *Ecologic-Economic Analysis for Regional Development: Some Initial Explorations with Particular Reference to Recreational Resource Use and Environmental Planning*. New York: The Free Press, 1972.

Kahn, Herman; Brown, William; and Martel, Leon. *The Next 200 Years: A Scenario for America and for the World*. New York: William Morrow, 1976.

Kristol, Irving. *Two Cheers for Capitalism*. New York: Basic Books, 1978.

Kuhn, Thomas S. *The Structure of Scientific Revolutions*. Chicago: The University of Chicago Press, 1962.

Leopold, Aldo. *A Sand County Almanac*. Oxford: Oxford University Press, 1949.

Maddox, John. *The Doomsday Syndrome*. New York: McGrow-Hill, 1972.

Marsh, George Perkins. *Man and Nature, Or, Physical Geography as Modified by Human Action* (1864). Cambridge: The Belknap Press of Harvard University Press, 1965.

Maslow, Abraham H. *Motivation and Personality*, 2nd ed. New York: Harper & Row, 1954, 1970.

May, Allan. *A Voice in the Wilderness*. Chicago: Nelson-Hall, 1978.

Meadows, Donella H.; Meadows, Dennis L.; Randers, Jørgen; and Behrens, William W. III. *The Limits to Growth*. New York: Universe Books, 1972.

Nash, Roderick. *Wilderness and the American Mind*. New Haven: Yale University Press, 1967, 1973 rev. ed.

Neuhaus, Richard. *In Defense of People: Ecology and the Seduction of Radicalism.* New York: Macmillan, 1971.

Ophuls, William. *Ecology and the Politics of Scarcity: Prologue to a Political Theory of the Steady State.* San Francisco: W. H. Freeman, 1977.

Roszak, Theodore. *The Making of a Counter Culture: Reflections on the Technocratic Society and Its Youthful Opposition.* New York: Doubleday, 1969.

Shepard, Paul, and McKinley, Daniel. *The Subversive Science: Essays Toward an Ecology of Man.* Boston: Houghton Mifflin, 1969.

Simon, Julian. *The Ultimate Resource.* Princeton: Princeton University Press, 1981.

Steen, Harold K. *The U.S. Forest Service: A History.* Seattle: University of Washington Press, 1976.

Tucker, William. *Progress and Privilege: America in the Age of Environmentalism.* New York: Doubleday, 1982.

Vajk, J. Peter. *Doomsday Has Been Cancelled.* Culver City: Peace Press, 1978.

Wessel, Milton R. *The Rule of Reason: A New Approach to Corporate Litigation.* Reading: Addison-Wesley, 1976.

Witts, David A. *Theft.* La Verne, California: University of La Verne Press, 1981.

Articles, Technical and Scholarly Papers

Adler, Jerry: Cook, William J.; Hager, Mary; and Fuller, Tony. "James Watt's Land Rush." *Newsweek,* June 29, 1981.

Baden, John; Stroup, Richard; and Cox, Patrick. "A Radical Proposal: Saving the Wilderness." *Reason,* July 1981.

Casserly, Jack. "Mr. Watt of the West." *Petroleum Independent,* December 1981.

Chrisman, Robert. "Ecology, A Racist Shuck." *Scanlan's,* August, 1970.

Cowen, Robert C. "Minerals: Breaking the Import Habit," 3-part series. *Christian Science Monitor,* January 13, 1982.

Current Biography. "James Watt." January, 1982, vol. 43, no. 1.

Drew, Elizabeth, "A Reporter At Large—Secretary Watt." *New Yorker,* May 4, 1981.

Edwards, Lee. "Secretary Jim Watt: He's Bringing Much-Needed Balance to The Department of the Interior." *Conservative Digest,* October 1981.

Enzenzberger, Hans Magnus. "A Critique of Political Ecology." Translated by Stuart Hood. *The New Left Review,* London 1974.

Fairfax, Sally K. "Watt May *Not* Be an Enemy of the Parks." *Los Angeles Times.* February 4, 1982.

Hardin, Garrett. "The Tragedy of the Commons." *Science,* December 13, 1968.

Heritage Foundation. "Mandate for Leadership." Washington, 1980.

Isaacson, Walter. "A Watt That Produces Steam." *Time,* August 3, 1981.

Kellert, Stephen R. "Public Attitudes Toward Critical Wildlife and Natural Habitat Issues." Yale University, October 15, 1979. U.S. Fish & Wildlife Service Phase I.

Kilpatrick, James. "Why Don't They Like James Watt?" *Washington Post,* August 10, 1981.

Kohn, Howard. "After James Watt, What?" *Rolling Stone,* October 15, 1981.

Lichter, S. Robert, and Rothman, Stanley. "Media and Business Elites." *Public Opinion,* American Enterprise Institute, October/November, 1981.

McGrory, Mary. "Bread and Water for Watt in Confrontation With Congress?" *Washington Post,* February 11, 1982.

McKinley, Donald, M.D. "Why Wilderness?" *Forest Industries,* February 1963.

Metzger, H. Peter, Ph.D. "The Coercive Utopians: Their Hidden Agenda." Paper presented at the National Meeting of the American College of Nuclear Medicine, Colorado Springs, Colorado, April 28, 1978.

———. "Government-Funded Activism: Hiding Behind the Public Interest." Paper presented at the 47th Annual Conference, Southeastern Electric Exchange, Boca Raton, Florida, March 26, 1980. Both printed by Public Service Company of Colorado, Denver, Colorado, April 28, 1978.

Missett, Kate. "James Watt: Threat or Promise?" *Wyoming Issues,* Spring 1981.

National Wildlife Federation. "Marching Backwards: The Department of Interior Under James G. Watt." NWF Staff Analysis of Secretarial Actions, April 29, 1982, Washington, D.C.

O'Leary, Jeremiah. "Reagan Says He Supports Watt Fully." *Washington Star,* August 5, 1981.

Puleston, Denis. "Protecting the Environment." *New Scientist,* September 28, 1972.

Reed, Nathaniel Pryor. "In the Matter of Mr. Watt." *Sierra,* July-August 1981.

Reese, Michael; Lubenow, Gerald C.; and Cook, William J. "Watt Defuses a Rebellion." *Newsweek,* September 21, 1981.

Schrepfer, Susan R. "Conflict In Preservation: The Sierra Club, Save-the-Redwoods League, and Redwood National Park." *Journal of Forest History,* April 1980.

Sears, Paul B. "Ecology—A Subversive Subject." *BioScience,* 14(7):11-13, 1964.

Shabecoff, Phillip. "Watt and Foes Are Best of Enemies." *New York Times,* November 11, 1981.

Train, Russell E. "The Beginning of Wisdom." *The Wilson Quarterly,* Summer 1977.

Tucker, William. "Apocalypse Deferred." *Life,* January, 1982.

Turner, Frederick Jackson. "The Significance of the Frontier in American History" presented at Columbian Exposition, Chicago, July 12, 1893.

Walsh, Kenneth T. "James Watt, Reagan's Lightning Rod, Won't Be Leaving Soon." *Denver Post,* August 23, 1981.

Watson, Clark. "Denver Black Raps Hart for Racism Challenge of James Watt." *Denver Post,* January 12, 1981.

Wilson, James B. "When You Hear Him Out, Secretary Watt Makes Sense." *Asheville Citizen-Times,* August 2, 1981.

Government Documents and Reports

Forest Service, Department of Agriculture—

Wilderness Management. John C. Hendee, George H. Stankey, Robert C. Lucas. Forest Service Miscellaneous Publication no. 1365.

Wilderness Users in the Pacific Northwest—Their Characteristics, Values, and Management Preferences. John C. Hendee, William R. Catton, Jr., Larry D. Marlow, and C. Frank Brockman. U.S.D.A. Forest Service Research Paper PNW-61.

General Accounting Office—

The Federal Drive To Acquire Private Lands Should Be Reassessed. CED-80-14, December 14, 1979.

Lands In The Lake Chelan National Recreation Area Should Be Returned To Private Ownership. CED-81-54, May 14, 1980.

The National Park Service Should Improve Its Land Acquisition And Management At The Fire Island National Seashore. CED-81-78, May 8, 1981.

Federal Land Acquisition And Management Practices. CED-81-135, September 11, 1981.

Illegal and Unauthorized Activities On Public Lands—A Problem With Serious Implications. CED-82-48, March 10, 1982.

House of Representatives of the United States—

Part VII, Hearing Record, House Appropriations Subcommittee on Labor-HEW-1979, 96th Congress, 1st Session. On ACTION Abuses and funding of environmental groups. U.S. Rep. Robert H. Michel (R, Ill.) 2112 Rayburn House Office Bldg.

Orientation Briefing By The Secretary of the Interior, House Interior and Insular Affairs Committee, Thursday, February 5, 1981 Room 1324 Longworth House Office Building, Hon. Morris Udall, presiding. Document name: HII036000. Reporter: Dinkle.

Interior Department—

A Year of Change: To Restore America's Greatness. Department of the Interior, January 20, 1981–January 20, 1982.

National Materials and Minerals Program Plan and Report to Congress. The White House, April 5, 1982.

Outdoor Recreation—A Legacy for America. Bureau of Outdoor Recreation, 1973.

Senate of the United States—

James G. Watt Nomination Hearings before the Committee on Energy and Natural Resources, 97th Congress, 1st Session, on the Proposed Nomination of James G. Watt to be Secretary of the Interior, January 7 and 8, 1981. Publication No. 97-1 Parts 1 and 2. Printed for the use of the Committee on Energy and Natural Resources. U.S. Government Printing Office.

Workshop on Public Land Acquisition and Alternatives. Committee on Energy and Natural Resources, Publication no. 97-34. 97th Congress, 1st Session. October 1981 Committee Print. U.S. Government Printing Office.

ACKNOWLEDGMENTS

Writing a book is like making a film only more so. In a film, hundreds of hands craft the final product and the names of a few appear in lights; in writing a book, hundreds of hands shape the final product and the names of the author and publisher appear on the cover. In writing this book I was aided by many people who gave generously of their time, their knowledge, and their support. Paul M. Weyrich of the Free Congress Research and Education Foundation conceived the project and nursed it through many travails to completion. To him and the Foundation I am profoundly indebted, first for Weyrich's telephone call that began "How would you like to write a book about Secretary Watt?" and for the Foundation's contnuing support through a writing grant, editorial assistance, and advice. Eric Licht of the Foundation has been a faithful editor and friend, along with Sue Arico, who provided many helpful comments and suggestions.

My greatest debt is to Interior Secretary James G. Watt, who has devoted many hours of his personal time to me and who opened his Department to my questions and requests. I am especially grateful to Secretary Watt for personally reading and correcting the first draft of the odd-numbered chapters that trace the history of his Secretariat's first 18 months; I am equally grateful that he refrained from expressing his views about the even-numbered analytical chapters other than playfully calling them "the smart chapters." To Leilani Watt must go a special thank you for her patience with the project, and for her warmth and graciousness in sharing personal incidents and feelings about her husband. I am also grateful to Secretary Watt's father and mother, William G. and Lois M. Watt, for accounts of the circumstances surrounding their son's birth, infancy, childhood, and family history.

I particularly appreciate the contributions of those who submitted to the lengthy interviews on which this book is based. All of Interior's Assistant Secretaries and their Deputies were most generous to me, but I would particularly like to thank Ray Arnett, Ken Smith, Pedro Sanjuan, and Garrey Carruthers for volunteering personal experiences of their tenure in office. Likewise, all of Interior's Bureau Heads provided vital background for the text, yet I want to single out Bob Burford, Dick Harris, Russ Dickenson, and Bob Broadbent for the depth of their discussion of events and issues. Among the Deputies, Perry Pendley, Moody Tidwell III, and Bill Horn were particularly helpful, and Steve Shipley, Emily DeRocco, Tom DeRocco, and Stan Hulett provided priceless personal insights into Jim Watt the man. Under Secretary Don Hodel added a personal and professional dimension to this book with candid discussions of his own and Watt's personalities and the intricacies of the Management By Objectives system. If it had not been for Bob Walker of Interior Public

277

Affairs, who scheduled my appointments and guided me through miles of Interior's halls, I would never have found all these people. Jim Watt's friend of 20 years and Public Affairs Director Doug Baldwin has offered encouragement and advice as well as ferreting out information and acting as my contact point in the Department. And a rose to his helpful secretary Ruth Edmondson. Ric Davidge opened his personal files to me for certain items and helped verify certain environmentalist group abuses that I had traced but could not previously prove.

Senators Alan K. Simpson and Paul Laxalt generously provided personal views on Jim Watt, and their staffs were most helpful in finding legislative details. Michael Horowitz of the Office of Management and Budget provided a critique on conservative public-interest law firms, and Renee M. Jaussaud of the National Archives made available to me the newly discovered papers of Interior Secretary Ethan Allen Hitchcock from 1906 who faced opposition similar to Watt's. The White House staff helped confirm a number of facts and refuted certain media reports.

Charles S. Cushman of the National Inholders Association checked my draft chapters on federal land acquisition abuses, and Harold K. Steen, Ph.D., of the Forest History Society provided scholarly insight on the Redwood National Park controversy and gave permission to quote extensively from the *Journal of Forest History* in Chapter 4. Various sections of the manuscript were read by scholars, experts in various fields of study, and by officers of the Reagan Administration. Their knowledge and understanding has helped me to see many problems and avoid many errors of fact and judgment; nonetheless, every judgment in the text is ultimately my own, and any errors must be attributed solely to me.

Among others who helped me were Willis Kriz, Paula Easley, Joseph Gughemetti, Joseph McCracken, Gene Ellsbree, Jim and Betty Denison, Bill Farrell, Dan Goldy, Rich Berner, Ralph Hodges, Buck Erickson, Elmo Richardson, Farrell Higbee, John E. Benneth, Dr. Jack D. Early. Dr. Irwin Tucker, Lowell Jones, Frank Schnidman, Dr. Michael Newton, and the Republican Study Committee.

The members of my family—my wife Janet, especially—not only bore with good grace the isolation of an author chained to the typewriter, but also helped make my time in the fresh air of family conducive to good spirits and creativity.

To all those who over the years have assisted my understanding and appreciation of basic industries and the U.S. economic system, who are too numerous to mention, you know who you are, and you have my sincere thanks.

INDEX